HANZI FREINACHT

D1240612

NORDIC
IDEOLOGY

A Metamodern Guide to Politics
Book Two

METAMODERNA

First Edition, 2019

ISBN 978-87-999739-2-7

Metamoderna ApS | www.metamoderna.org

Here's one for Jonas,

> And one for Jimmy
> And for all the kind, intelligent
> And sensitive people
> Who bow down
> And break down
> Under the existential pressures
> Of modern life

And one for Tom,

> This mischievous man
> Who was the first reader of this book
> And passed away shortly after

Contents

Part One, The Map: How Society Develops

Introduction

BLAZING NEW PATHS

L et it first of all be said that the previous book, *The Listening Society*, wasn't all that good or important.

The previous book basically hammers home one point: that development is real and that it matters. It stays mostly within the realm of psychology. There are a few innovations, true, but they aren't that big.

The present volume is different. Fewer people will like it, no doubt, as it's not as light-weight. This is a much heavier, more original and, in my opinion, a more significant piece of work. Essentially, the first book was only the introduction to this one, which contains about three times more in terms of theoretical content and innovation. It presents you with an actual to-do plan to save the world. Without this plan, we're still just playing around.

This is where it gets real. Welcome.

—

Ah, back in the Alps. It's a sunny winter's day. Clear skies. Open horizons. Majestic mountains. Swathes of pine trees burdened with a thick layer of slowly melting snow, naked cliffs in glistening black and white, rising above misty valleys. It's quiet here.

Only the buzzing flies keep me company in this *chalet* of sixteen beds, five bathrooms, and one jacuzzi. I've just spent half an hour chasing a veritable army of them out the windows. Many more remain. They want to see the sun, but the moment they make their way out, they freeze to death. I watched a few of them land in the soft snow; it takes about ten seconds before their last spasm.

I don't know if it's preferable to a forty-eight-hour life of beating against a window until you dry up and roll over—and eventually have your body swallowed by the vacuum cleaner. I just sentenced a good fifty of them to death. I can't say I regret it.

Still, I wonder what it would be like to be one of them. They have about 10,000 neurons each. Apparently, this wooden house has parts where maggots thrive and eggs can be safely laid. But once the flies have won their wings and confidently lift off to explore the world, they find a barren landscape of wood and glass, with no scrap to eat, no water to quench their thirst, no cow dung to relish in. During the summer, there are cows grazing about, their bells chiming and echoing until sunset, fields of dung aplenty. But now there is only a hopeless struggle against the window, an invisible barrier granting no solace.

From a human perspective, the relentless efforts of these creatures appear futile. Their way of understanding the world—"just go for the light"—seems much too simpleminded. Quite clearly, their intuition betrays them.

But are we so different from our distant house fly kin? Evolutionarily, we parted ways about half a billion years ago. For certain, we have taken divergent paths. Vertebrates like ourselves develop a "second mouth" during early embryonic stages, whereas the "first mouth" becomes our anus. These little bastards, banging their heads against the window, still eat through their anuses. They live short lives and multiply quickly, dying *en masse* to let some lucky few pass on their genes—*lots* of genes. We, on the contrary, live long lives and invest huge energy into our rather few offspring for many years. Some of us even love them.

But like the flies, we are born into a world of greater circumstances beyond our control. Some of us are born on hot, humid summer days, with plenty of space to buzz around and cows to bother; to live the lives we were, in some sense, meant to live. Others are born to a merciless struggle spent beating our heads against invisible barriers.

Had I been born elsewhere, I could have been a drug-addicted child soldier in Sierra Leone, a sweatshop worker in Bangladesh, or brainwashed in a North Korean labor camp on the Russian taiga. Talk about barren landscapes for human growth and flourishing.

BREAKING THE LIMITS

Nature is a cruel mistress. On one hand she graciously endows us all—mice and men, and yes, even flies—with unlimited potential to flourish; on the other, she sooner or later throws us against an impenetrable glass barrier. We always hit limits such as lacking resources, harsh climatic conditions, hostile life forms, or diseases, to either stump our growth or kill us off.

No one ever reaches their full potential. But nature isn't being unfair; on the contrary, it's life that is utterly unreasonable in its aspirations. To life, to the primordial impulse of the will, the world is simply not enough; the moment it wins the world, it seeks to conquer another.

Take a pair of flies, for instance; without any natural barriers, one mating couple could grow into a swarm exceeding the mass of the Earth in less than a year.[1] A simple house fly may appear a humble creature; but don't be fooled: If given the chance, it'll consume the world and everyone in it. Lord of the flies.

Humans are no less unreasonable; just closer to conquering the world. Human crops now account for more than a third of the Earth's non-marine biomass, 83% of the terrestrial biosphere is under direct human control, and we and our domesticated animals now make up 97% of all land mammals. Insects may be more numerous, but the biomass of all humans has been estimated to be slightly larger than the combined biomass of all 12,649 species of ants. Quite impressive when you think about it. I couldn't find any estimates for how we compare to flies, but a recent investigation has shown that in certain parts of the world we have killed off around 75% of all winged insects in the last 30 years.[2] At this rate we'll beat the flies pretty soon.

Victory at last. If perhaps a lonely one.

However, the explosive growth from a few million to soon-to-be eight billion humans in the course of a mere 10,000 years is not the most extraordinary fact about our species. What's even more extraordinary is that we're not about to reach 80 billion.

We're often led to believe that the Earth is severely overpopulated, but *overconsumed* is a more accurate description. Theoretically, we could easily sustain a much larger number of human bodies with the currently available resources and technologies. We have plenty of possibilities to go forth and be fruitful and populate the Earth as God told us in the Bible. But somehow this godly command wasn't enough for the human race. We wanted something more. We wanted to become gods ourselves. Gods of electricity and economic growth. Gods of information.[3]

Evolution truly is a strange beast. The moment natural selection finally had produced a species capable of overcoming most of the natural barriers inhibiting its biological expansion from subsuming the entire biosphere, a new evolutionary principle enters the stage and takes the lead role: symbolic evolution.

Unlike the flies I callously froze to death, our ape bodies appear to be infected by a strange ghost that strives to expand its single *self* rather than the number of bodies carrying its genome. Our minds have been infected with an intricate and mysterious symbolic world that somehow convinced us that spreading our genes isn't ultimately what life is about.

Instead, human life has come to revolve around the expansion of our *inner* world; a world that is both personal and intimate, and inescapably connected to the wider field of symbols shared with others. In short, all of us have values, ideals and ideas that we seek to imprint upon the world. That's our way of expanding.

This has turned humanity into a restless creature, unceasingly on a quest to expand our consciousness: ever higher states of joy and pleasure, even at the price of great torment; new knowledge to satisfy our never-ending curiosity; deeper spiritual insights to relate to the unanswerable question of why we are here; and increasingly complex ways of thinking in order to make sense of it all.

Just like flies cannot stop multiplying until the entire world is consumed by their offspring, we can't stop ourselves from expanding the scope of our inner world until we reach the impossible ideal of a god— even if it kills us. We just can't help it; we reach higher and higher, deeper and deeper, in a futile attempt to transcend the many limits that insult our divine pretensions.

However, we cannot (foreseeably[4]) escape the natural barrier that is the frailty of our biological bodies. No matter how far our mind develops beyond its primal instincts and impulses, no matter how abundantly our spiritual depth and intellectual complexity allow us to manipulate the world beyond our bodies, we still remain biological creatures with all the limitations that entails.

Of course, bodies are beautiful. There is, as many have observed, an intelligence in the body—if we only listen to its signals, if we come "out of our heads". But bodies are also messy, gory and vulnerable. The same principle that gives us life and mind also leaves us raw and utterly exposed.

Ernest Becker famously argued, in his psychoanalytical account of the denial of death in modern society, that we are "gods with anuses".[5] This was meant to underscore the strange duality of the human condition: that we are conscious and intelligent beings who can strive for beauty, love and truth—but we can never escape the frailty of our bodies. Even the exalted Dalai Lama will solemnly shit his robes during a sacred ritual if his bowels betray him. Gods with anuses; the primordial mouths we share with the flies.

Yet nature is not the *only* barrier to stand between our god-like aspirations and all too human predicaments. Societal barriers, such as institutions, laws, common understandings, language structures, technology, markets and social norms are *both* scaffolds for our growth and expression, *and* prisons for our bodies and souls. The instances I mentioned above—the child soldier, the sweatshop worker and the brainwashed forced laborer—are all clear examples of how societal factors can limit our lives, our wellbeing and our psychological development.

Yet, even in more favorable environments, there will always be societal barriers limiting us: social conventions restraining us from becoming who we really want to be, economic circumstances preventing us from using our greatest talents, lacking support structures and so forth.

But thanks to our oversized brains and the wonders of symbolic language, we can conceptualize the barriers ahead and take measures to change the circumstances within which we live our lives and to which future humans and other sentient beings will be born. Or at least we can die trying.

As I write this, we are, as a global society, still waking up to the fact that there are significant natural barriers ahead of us: the multidimensional ecological crises, the most well-known of which is human-caused climate change. Science is part by part revealing the grim rules we have to play by. If we play our cards right, we can avert some or even most of these barriers, at least for a significant period of time.

What we *haven't* woken up to, however, is the fact that we can change the societal barriers and social-psychological landscapes of everyday life. And indeed, because the different kinds of barriers interact with each other, we must change some of the struts and beams of society if we are also to overcome the natural barriers. But to do so, we need to know what it means for humans to grow and flourish, and we need to know the logic of how societies develop.

This book raises a bid for that last part, the logic of the development of societies. It is Book Two of Hanzi's "metamodern guide to politics". We will examine how the state develops, how freedom develops, how equality develops—and suggest a narrow but workable path for the next step in society's evolution.

That the very social fabric of everyday life can and *must* be intelligently developed is the essence of political metamodernism. We take a creative and playfully developmental stance towards society and existence as a whole. Wider and more abstract perspectives on society's evolution can allow us the luxury—or at least the possibility—of forging the path that society takes. In other words: We can affect *how* society develops, what everyday life becomes. This is made possible by us understanding the directionalities and potentials inherent to how societies function.

To blaze new paths. To write new values on new tablets. The goal is to steer clear of the barren landscapes and breach the invisible barriers—so that the shackled members of humanity can wake up on a lush summer day, grow their wings, buzz around in freedom, and relish in cow dung.

Captain! Set the controls for the heart of the sun.

THE LAST BOOK AND THIS ONE

If you haven't read the first book, don't let it haunt you at night; you'll still get plenty of bang for the buck in this one, even if some of the wider context may be lost on you.

So let's begin where we left off in Book One, *The Listening Society*. The final words were:

> "We can go ahead to create a Green Social Liberalism 2.0, working non-linearly, co-developing ourselves towards a listening society. We go ahead with pragmatic idealism, with magical realism and informed naivety. At the crossroads of fact and fiction, we work and play with religious fervor, keeping an ironic smile at our own self-importance."

A lot to unpack in a few sentences. Here's what it means:

"Green Social Liberalism" is the dominant "meta-ideology" in the Nordic countries today. Here, environmental and social-liberal values have become so widespread in the general population that more or less all the major political parties compete to be the most trustworthy advocate of this ideology. Since there is a wide consensus that the best model for society is a competitive market economy with a universal welfare system, the traditional ideological struggle between Left and Right has waned in favor of a rhetorical spectacle that conceals just how similar the political parties have actually become.

This is not a uniquely Nordic phenomenon. If things run smoothly long enough, Green Social Liberalism is where every liberal democracy with an industrial capitalist economy and publicly financed welfare is heading. It's just because Scandinavia has been exceptionally stable and prosperous for such a long time that we see the tendency most clearly here.

For the same reason it's also here we find some vague but substantial bids for what lies beyond this "modern" equilibrium; the 2.0 version of Green Social Liberalism. This new updated meta-ideology is a synthesis that, by today's standards, would be perceived as far Left, far (libertarian) Right and very Green. And if you look closely, it is taking shape in the Nordic countries as we speak, hence the name "Nordic ideology".

"The listening society" is the name for a vision of the future welfare system which expands and deepens the current universal welfare programs by addressing the higher psychological needs of human beings such as belonging, esteem and self-actualization—a welfare system determined to ensure that as many as possible don't feel lonely, socially inferior or trapped in meaningless lives.

The listening society is a welfare society that considers the emotional wellbeing of people just as important as their economic welfare; a society that takes into account the more intimate psychological needs of human beings: good relationships, inner security, meaning, self-knowledge. This would be a society where depression, stress and alienation have become political issues in the same vein as security, jobs and housing are today.

Metamodern activists are unafraid of putting forward such visions; of exposing our necks—although we hold these with a "sincere irony", always admitting that we are probably, after all, mistaken.

We think that society needs to move in some kind of direction; and if we play with fictions, make experiments, and combine these with sound factual analyses of our time, there is a likelihood that something good will come out of it. Hence such "both-and" concepts as "pragmatic idealism", "magical realism", "informed naivety", and working at "the crossroads of fact and fiction". These concepts are central to metamodernism. They put us in the space where we can play and be creative around large and serious issues.

In the last book we offered a view of developmental *psychology*, which explains how people grow "more conscious"—i.e. how we become more complex thinkers, become "happier" (long story, that one), come to adopt more universalistic or progressive values, and relate to more profound aspects of life and reality. A large part of this has been firmly established through psychological research.

This developmental perspective was linked to the vision of the aforementioned "listening society". **The central idea is that by cultivating a listening society, we can not only create much happier human lives, but also dramatically spur the psychological development of larger parts of the population into the higher stages.** Such development is necessary for people to create, participate in, and uphold functional societies in this increasingly complex world—an endeavor that has both incredible potentials and great risks.

Now is the time to make it happen. It is time to achieve this goal.

THE MAP, THE PLAN AND THE PROOF

If the last book gave you an introduction to developmental psychology, this book presents you with a **developmental *sociology***, and then links it to a concrete political plan of how you change society.

The book has three parts:

1. **The Map**

2. **The Plan**

3. **The Proof**

- The first part of this book is **The Map.** First I guide you through an understanding of what it means to be a *realistic* utopian, one who seeks to change and evolve the everyday games of life. Then I go on to argue that there is a certain kind of evolution of society going on—that we can see where things are going; again, a *developmental sociology*, i.e. a view of how *society itself* develops. So I present you with a number of "attractor points", or "attractors". These constitute evolutionary steps: How do state and governance evolve, what's the next step? What is freedom, and what is a higher freedom than the one we experience in the "free world" of today? What is equality, and how can it become deeper? Most people, still today, living in societies committed to freedom and equality, cannot answer these questions.

- Armed with this map, you may then reap the rewards: The second part of this book is a large-scale strategy being rolled out before you—**The Plan** for how to fundamentally transform modern society into a metamodern (relative) utopia. I'd like to underscore that **this plan fills a void**: I can't think of anyone else who has a plan like it—a plan for the design of global politics, for a new political system, and how to enact it. If you understand the plan, I hold, you are morally obliged to act upon it, to make it happen. If you see where this is going, you're either obliged to act, or to come up with something better. It's a bit vulgar, I suppose, to straightforwardly put a plan out there, not a very scholarly or respectable thing to do. But on the other hand, people reading the first book all wondered: What's the plan? What do we do? I'll tell you what I think. We need a political program. This is a political program that *constitutes*, all said and done, the Nordic ideology. It includes six new forms of politics, all explained in detail: **Democratization Politics, *Gemeinschaft* Politics, Existential Politics, Emancipation Politics, Empirical Politics—and Politics of Theory**. It ends with zooming out and viewing **the Master Pattern** that connects all six forms of politics, including some tactical observations for how to make it happen.

• Does this plan make sense? Does the Nordic Ideology work? Shouldn't we subscribe to one of the existing political ideologies instead? This is where **The Proof** comes in. This third part of the book is, admittedly, perhaps a bit self-celebratory: It shows you how the Nordic ideology—or political metamodernism—eats all of the existing ideologies alive. It beats them on their own terms. Part Three presents you with the proof for why you can't just skip metamodernism and stay with one of the old ideologies. Having this understanding helps you organize a transnational metamodernist movement and to outmaneuver all the modern political forces: socialists, libertarians, conservatives, anarchists and ecologists alike—while still helping each of them achieve their respective goals. So you get armed with some well-needed *tactics* to go along with your *strategy*. At the very end, we discuss our three evil cousins, the totalitarian specters of the 20th century: communism, fascism and the New Age. All of these dangerous dreams have uncanny but important lessons to teach us. So let us listen.

These are going to be crazy days. We're going to have to invoke a few forbidden phantoms™.

But then again, that's how the world is. To make sense of it, we sometimes need to take wild trips to the outskirts of sanity and deep into the underworld. If you ever get a bit lost during this journey, simply remember whether you're reading Part One, Two, or Three and you will know what it's really about: either I am drawing The Map of historical development, or I am presenting you with The Plan to take over the world (apply sincere irony), or I am trying to provide The Proof that this is a sound plan. Map, Plan, Proof—it's not so hard, is it?

But still, we're going on this trip together. Remember to work hard—and try not to have too much fun. It's all quite serious, after all. And I bet you don't have a better plan. If you do, please tell me.[6]

HANZI: YOUR SUSPICIOUS FRIEND

Before we go on, let's discuss our relationship, me the writer to you the reader.

If you've read Book One, you might wonder why I've become so nice all of a sudden. Where is Hanzi, the arrogant and obnoxious prick that guided us through the last book? Why am I not bragging, or finding ways to bust the reader's self-deceit, or just hitting soft-spots in my trademarked calculative, manipulative manner?

Don't worry; I'm still here. Still a prick. I haven't become any humbler, not at all. Nor has my heart softened and, no, life has certainly not "taught me a lesson or two".

Au contraire. If anything, I hold my own entitlement with greater self-evidence than ever. Because I honestly believe I have something interesting and important to say, I feel entitled—intellectually *and* morally, mind you.

I do recognize that many readers enjoy a good spanking from time to time, to be challenged and dominated, to have their weak-spots revealed by psychoactive literature.

Others, the ones with big egos, get really mad when challenged and start blaming the author (which, by the way, is the same as having an argument with a dead piece of text). But those people aren't going to play any major parts in creating the new developmental stage of society. They lack the emotional self-knowledge required for handling this level of depth and complexity.

So if we alienate a few of them, good riddance.

There is a masochistic side to most of us. We all love displays of power. Power feels real and substantial, somehow. People with poor self-knowledge tend to deny this drive in themselves; but if you watch their actual behaviors, their self-deceit becomes apparent. In fact, the deniers of power tend to be the most hysterically power hungry. Anarchists and moralistic far lefties come to mind. Power is very erotic, and in our fantasies, erotic or not, we display it in different forms: unhindered, determined agency, being in the right, showing great conviction, putting up heroic resistance, sporting impressive self-control, the earning of respect, the eliciting of admiration, displays of towering wisdom and equanimity, the inspiring of awe and perhaps even envy or fear. All of this stuff is ultimately about power, and the possession and expression of power.

Democracy, deliberation and good citizenship, alas, are just not as exciting as power and hierarchy. And our erotic minds exercise great influence upon what we find worthwhile in terms of time, energy and attention. This is a paradox not only in writing, but as many psychologists have observed, in society and human relationships at large: especially in gender relations, love and sex.

But still, let's go for good citizenship in this book, shall we not? We're dealing with serious matters, after all. We can be grown-ups about this, can't we? Let us calmly, rationally and *maturely* consider the future of humanity.

Because, after all, *you* are far above those other readers. You are mature, aren't you? You are not impressed with unstoppable, throbbing, sexual power—not at all. You just want to discuss important ideas. And we already did most of that delicious power mongering and emotional button pushing in Book One. The reason we did it (apart from me being a bad person; rotten to my core; bad to the bone, baby), is that we needed to get beyond the defenses most people have against metamodern thinking. In particular, we had to break through the mental barriers that protect people from understanding the issues of developmental psychology—the stages of adult development—and go through the painful process of throwing the ridiculous modernist political identities (Left, Right, Libertarian, Green, etc.) in the garbage. Then kick the garbage can.

But in this book we're doing something a bit less touchy: looking at wide, abstract patterns of political development. And most readers will already be acquainted with the work in Book One. So, we're starting from a different place.

You see, in the last book I had to write with the assumption that I was working in an extremely hostile environment. Almost nobody has the same worldview as Hanzi, so most people start off at an adverse angle. And it paid off. But in this book, I write with the starting point that we are roughly on the same page. The last book was written for enemies; this one is for friends.

Hence, I use a little less of the psychoactive judo, even if it might make the text a little less juicy.

But one thing remains the same: the **transpersonal stance**. I am not an individual. I am much larger than that. I am a thousand voices crisscrossing and whispering within, from my earliest biological impulses to my some 10,000 year history of civilization, to my unconscious drives and weaknesses, to my spiritual capacities which link me to the skies and the unyielding mysteries of the cosmos itself. And so are you.

As such, I don't think of myself as an individual author, reaching out to you, a separate entity—a single atom of a rational reader. Rather, we are both part of the same process of knowledge creation, and I sometimes need to speak past you, to other readers, and sometimes I need to push a few of your buttons. Likewise, you need to cut and paste me, and animate me, in creative and novel manners. You can cut me up and put pieces of me into places I couldn't dream of. The reader, not the writer, has the power.

I don't expect you to leave me be, but to recreate me. And when you gaze into the transpersonal mystery that I am, I also gaze into you.

—

Why Hanzi Freinacht? Wherefore art thou Hanzi? It's a fair question. Why not a humbler and more conventional persona, one who speaks mildly and invitingly? Most authors manage to do that. Hey, even people like Hitler can sound kind of nice in writing. There are a couple of reasons for this knowingly insolent diversion from the norm.

The first one is just to shake you up and get your attention.

But there is another, much more important reason: **I want you to be suspicious of me.** I am, after all, making very large claims. If I turn out to be wrong, and people follow these ideas with the righteous fanaticism that has shown its face time and again, terrible things can happen. And on a more mundane level, you can screw up your own life too, for that matter.

But just including a "humble clause" against fanaticism here and there —and adhering to a general openness towards new information and perspectives is not nearly vigilant enough. That opens up another kind of trap: "Oh, of course I am not fanatical. I bloody well *live* for good criticism! I have more clauses against fanaticism than anyone else. I labor by far the hardest to take in others' perspectives... I know words, lots of words, all the best words!"[7] And *voilà*, another avenue of insulation against being wrong.

No, for our relationship to make any sense at all you have to be able to be reached by my ideas; but in the end, you need to really not like me. That's the deal here. Hanzi isn't nice. You're not supposed to have too much fun or enjoy my company too much. On the other hand, this allows me the luxury of not concealing any of my thoughts or emotions, to write with pristine sincerity. Because I am not working to win your trust.

Brutality is honesty's flipside. All those humble and kind authors out there are not brutal because they are, frankly speaking, not very frank. Whereas politeness certainly is a virtue, it's often a good idea to master both virtues: the polite and the frank. And we need to know *when* each of these should apply. In a book like this, frankness must trump politeness. So, put up with a little writer brutality, and at least you'll get to hear what I really think and feel. We can be polite later, like when we meet at a mingle party. Deal?

If not, just stop reading and you'll be fine. Or if you have objections, leave a message at the beep.

All the major bad guys in the world were thoroughly convinced they were the good guys. George W. Bush went to free the Iraqi people and fight terrorism, (even God approved), and then boom, hundreds of thousands dead, war crimes, torture, instability in the region, ISIS, refugees, corporate power abuses and exploitations, more terrorism. We don't know what would have happened without the invasion, but this one wasn't nice. Marx, Lenin, Hitler, Mao, the colonialists, the missionaries, the Ayatollah, spiritually enlightened cult leaders, Milton Friedman, Pinochet, Colonel Gaddafi (who by the way, like me, also wrote green books about something beyond socialism and capitalism)—you know the drill. They're all "good guys".

I really don't know if I'm a good guy or a crook. So, if even *I* don't trust me, why should *you*? Again, this is not an excuse for being able to say that I'm humbler and thus the good guy after all. I *really* don't know. "Liberal innocence lost", as we said in Book One.

But as far as my mind and heart can see—with whatever obfuscation and self-deceit the many layers of my limited mind may be pulling on me—I do see that political metamodernism, the Nordic ideology, can save and dramatically improve millions of lives. **So listen, friend, and distrust me.**

Make an Effort

Productively relating to this book requires at least a somewhat *correct* understanding of what I'm saying. If you're responding or reacting without having properly understood and seen the greater context, you're just wasting your time, and everybody else's.

A good test for this is if you can summarize the main point of each chapter to a friend. If you can't, you probably don't get it. And only when you understand *all* of the chapters can you see how they make sense *together*. From there on you can go back to nitpicking—just don't let details get in the way of the overall picture. Don't protect yourself from actually understanding. That's not being critically minded, it's cowardly. Most people of course do chicken out with some excuse. Don't be most people.

If I can kindly ask something of you as a reader, it would be this: Please try to connect the dots of *the whole book*, and preferably Book One as well, before you form an opinion. That's where the action is; in the **pattern that connects**. That's where you see it—the attractors ahead, the potentials of future society, how the method of political metamodernism can help us manifest "the Nordic ideology", and why it truly matters.

Sometimes, changing the world takes an effort.

PART ONE

The Map: How Society
Develops

Fanfare to Part One:

ATTRACTORS

W elcome, dear reader, to the first part of the book. What you get here is the backdrop for the political to-do list of the second part: we're going to see the *direction* of society's development, where we're going, and why.

It's **The Map**.

This part requires a bit of weight-lifting; it's the most difficult part, eleven chapters packed with theory. But I guarantee it will be worth your while and that rewards shall be reaped. Can you stomach it, or will you bow under its weight? It's a bit of a marathon; you'll find most other readers in the ditch.

The chapters that follow will explain how society evolves and point out the direction of its further evolution. First, we see how society *has* evolved, how the logic or pattern of its evolution has unfolded, then we examine how such a developmental pattern still applies today.

In many ways, it does:

- The state has evolved in recognizable ways—and a new stage of its development is underway. Another way of saying this is that "order" develops.

- Freedom in society has evolved, and a new stage of political freedom is underway.

- Equality in society has evolved, and a deeper form of equality is becoming possible.

- Norms and values have evolved, and new values are being written on new tablets for new times.

Order, freedom, equality and norms—all of these evolve and stabilize around certain **attractor points**. Let's start this fanfare, then, by understanding what attractors are. Then we will explore Utopia in a full chapter. What does utopian thinking mean today? And how can it be used responsibly? Then we turn to what it means to change the games of everyday life—the principle of Game Change.

Two chapters and one subsection I have omitted from this first part of the book and placed, at thy service, as Appendices A, B and C: The first one is about why communism failed. A lot of people think the Nordic ideology is a repackaged far-left project. It is not, at least not in any conventional sense. If you want to see my thrashing of communism, go read Appendix A. This discussion is further deepened in Appendix B. There you find a theory chapter that is more over-arching, discussing "the four fields of development"—i.e. how psychology, behavior, culture and economy develop *together*. These two appendices go together: the "four fields" solve the murder mystery of why communism killed a hundred million people.

There is also an Appendix C, "Effecting Game Change", which takes a closer look at ways to develop society across the boundaries of state, market and the civil sphere.

Go read these if you get the red scare or if you hunger for more theory.

In this first part of the book you will also find long endnotes that score extra points, expand discussions and explain details. Some readers are curious.

But now—sound the trumpets! Blow the horns!

Modernity's own horns of Jericho.

A Winner's History

Let me start you off with a simple question: What is the main difference between the winners and losers of history?

Answer: Getting the **attractors** right.[8]

Whereas the amateur studies how the present has been shaped by the past to foresee the future, the pro studies how the future is *already* shaping the present. Many of the great change-makers in history, whether we're talking about political figures such as Mahatma Gandhi or entrepreneurs like Steve Jobs, seem to have had an intuitive understanding of the way the future exerts a kind of gravitational effect upon the present; that developments in the present in certain ways are pulled towards the unrealized potentials of the future. What happens in the present is namely just as much a result of what *has* been as what *can* become. Without knowing the attractors, you are destined to miss the starting gun.

Gandhi saw the world was headed towards universal principles like democracy, human rights, racial equality and rule of law, which inevitably would render colonial rule ethically indefensible, even to the colonizers themselves. This enabled him to understand how India could be freed in a peaceful and democratic manner; he knew that history—the long-term attractors—was on his side. Similarly, because Jobs saw that digitization was the future, he realized before most others that everyone would want a personal computer.

To those who couldn't see these attractors, home computers or the end of colonial rule appeared as distant dreams or science fiction. Moreover, blindness to attractors makes it exceedingly difficult to know what exactly to do if you actually do indulge in such dreams. With a well-developed sense of the attractors you get a much clearer picture of what is possible in the near future and what remains a more distant prospect.

If you are able to discern different attractors from one another, understanding their gravitational pull and intricate dynamics, you will be much more capable of successfully navigating the tides of historical change. The most astonishing and admirable achievements have rarely been made by those who set about to wrestle history and singlehandedly initiate a great change, and more often by those who knew the direction of the winds and adjusted their sails accordingly.

If you still don't get it: **Attractors make you smarter.** Gandhi's understanding of the attractor of a democratic society and national sovereignty enabled him to "push the right buttons" at the right time so that colonial rule could be ended without firing a shot. He knew he did not have to force change to happen, but that it was more effective to gently steer the forces already in motion in a more preferable direction. By getting the attractor right, Gandhi grasped the golden opportunity that had dawned in his time: that freedom could be obtained, not by threat of physical force, but simply by holding his colonial overlords to the same principles they themselves had sworn allegiance to. Brilliant. One person getting the attractor right may just have saved a million lives.

Jobs' understanding of the attractor of a digitized society enabled him to see the computer as more than just a fast calculator to aid governments and businesses, as most of his contemporaries did, but instead as a universal tool to enable common people be more creative and empowered. He knew he didn't have to know all the things people would use them for, just that he should make them more user-friendly—and a revolution would follow. Getting it right made him filthy rich *and* turned him into one of the most beloved public figures of our time.[9] Quite extraordinary really.

The Spirit of the Laws Evolving

In this first part of the book, we familiarize ourselves with some important attractors: the future state, higher freedom, deeper equality. It will make us smarter, together.

In the second part, we'll engage in the risky, exciting business of "state crafting", or, indeed, "society crafting". We are going to look at how six new forms of politics together form a *greater whole*; how they can and must balance each other out.

Each of these six forms of politics comes with major potential risks, so you can't just do one or two of them without major negative consequences. Indeed, by their very logical structure, they must go together, or not at all. That's why they form an attractor point. Like Alexandre Dumas' three musketeers: one for all, and all for one.

Speaking of pre-revolutionary France; these six forms of politics are not so unlike Montesquieu's "separation of powers", presented in his 1748 treatise *The Spirit of Laws*. Of course, earlier versions of this idea can be traced back to Athenian democracy, but Montesquieu gave it a more philosophically and logically coherent theory: that the legislative, executive and judiciary powers (parliament, government and courts) must be separated from each other if we are to avoid tyranny and corruption. This tripartite separation of powers still informs all democratic constitutions in the world today. Well done, my good Baron. You hit upon an attractor.

But today we are dealing with a more abstract form of governance that concerns wider as well as more intimate spheres of human life. So the issue naturally becomes more complex: Instead of a three-part division of powers, we need *six* dimensions; each new power being balanced by no less than five others.

Fiction—written words, sheets of paper—was all that Montesquieu's idea of the separation of powers was to begin with; nothing really "real". But his words came alive because, in some abstract sense, the Baron was *right*. His prevailing intuition was that power, whenever unchecked and unbalanced by other powers, is detrimental to freedom. He had no studies to show it, no empirical evidence by today's standards. No "proof" he was correct. And yet many of us now live in societies governed, at least partly, by Montesquieu's principles. To this day his ideas draw the fine line between democracy and dictatorship—but we would probably have never known the former if we had demanded proof he was right before making his fiction reality.[10]

Consequently, if you sense an attractor and seek to act upon it, but people around you demand proof whether it's going to work, don't mind these people, carry on; they won't be the winners of history, whereas you might end up as the new Gandhi or Steve Jobs.

AN ATTRACTOR IS…

So what is an attractor precisely? And how is it their knowabouts can make you so smart? Let's get more precise.

Technically speaking, **an "attractor" is a pattern or equilibrium that under certain conditions is very likely to emerge and stabilize within a dynamical system, such as a society**. We went from hunter-gatherer societies to agriculture—in Eurasia and the pre-Columbian Americas separately—because agriculture was an attractor. We electrified the world, because electricity was an attractor. We all started using interconnected computers, because digitization was an attractor. These things did not happen randomly.

The world is a chaotic place and the future is never predetermined; but on the general level, some things are just more likely to happen than others, and some are *very* likely to happen. How likely one development or another is to occur is determined by the "gravitational strength" of the attractors. Yes, they even talk about "great attractors" also in cosmology, hence the analogy of gravity or pull.[11]

The advantages of a digitized society, for instance, are simply so great that the gravitational pull of this attractor makes it very, very likely that we would all own a computer one day once it was invented. Today we see that solar and wind power, self-driving electric cars, crypto currencies and nano-technologies act as strong attractors in a similar vein as digitization. These are all (potential) attractor points. Getting it right can make you a bitcoin billionaire or turn you into a star entrepreneur like Elon Musk.

It's hard to reject the idea of how technological attractors play a role in shaping historical developments. Few would claim the personal computer was a fluke or that it is just as likely we today would still light candles rather than light bulbs.

However, when it comes to how we think and how we organize society, people tend to be more dismissive of the notion that such delicate matters are under the influence of attractors. We like to think it's all a big coincidence that things turned out the way they did, that the future has never been set in stone; that we can decide in which direction history should unfold. "We do have a choice, don't we?"

Yes we do. But some choices are just much more likely to be made than others. We all make choices, and we take great pains to ensure we make the right ones in order to avoid our actions being completely haphazard. As such (given that certain choices have proven so abundantly preferable to others), wouldn't it be fair to claim that our choices, on a collective level, tend to form certain patterns that are more likely to emerge than others; that we are destined to decide between a limited range of societal models whenever they become possible?

After all, there are a million ways to organize society. Yet human societies tend to be remarkably similar at any stage of historical development. We could organize society in accordance with the teachings of the Jonestown suicide cult, or Robert Nozick's minimal state, or set out to make reality of Orwell's big brother society, or make children the only electable candidates for government, or have all decisions made by rolling dice— the possibilities are endless. But for some reason most of today's countries have chosen and tried to organize themselves along the lines of a modern state or polity[12] with a tripartite structure of governance.

Even if the courts in some cases aren't really free and independent from those who govern, and the actions of those who govern aren't always held accountable by the governed, most such despotic regimes still pretend to abide to the principles of the rule of law and the notion that the "people" is the sovereign. Coincidence? Or just a way to avoid pissing off the democratic West? Probably not. Even the communist regimes of the past claimed to uphold the principle of rule of law and to represent the "people"— hence the frequent use of "the people's republic" in the name of many of the most brutal dictatorships. Even Nazi Germany claimed the German people to be the highest sovereign. And the brutal dictator Gaddafi also put great efforts into explaining how he had made a special deal with the Libyan people. So even if the *de facto* circumstances remain a far cry from the modern template of governance, rulers still try to make it appear *as though* the system works in accordance with democratic ideals.

The fact that Montesquieu's system, in one form or another, spread to most of the world can hardly be coincidental. And the fact that the evolution of democracy, at least in terms of its constitutional structure, more or less makes a *full stop* at this point—can hardly be a coincidence either. You reach a plateau; everyone reaches some version of the same system, and then we all stay there for decades, even centuries.

Beyond all the thousands of unique historical events, personalities, tenfold increases of GDP output, and conflicts and cultures and markets and random plot twists (like tsunamis and whatnot), the same system emerges with a regularity revealing itself with crushing clarity.

Coincidence? No. The correct answer is: attractor. The modern democratic state is not the only attractor, but it is certainly one of the most competitive ones.

SOCIETY AND EVOLUTION

So is there an attractor for the kind of polity that comes after, and goes beyond, modern market-liberal democracy? Of course there is. But what, then, would be the proper method for discovering it so that we may better navigate the tides of change?

This is where a little Darwin comes in handy. We must answer the question: **What structures are *most likely* to survive and outcompete other structures under the currently emerging historical circumstances?**

So we're not just fancifully making up what "would be nice"; we are looking for "what is likely to beat the living crap out of all the others under the current and emerging circumstances". For the rest of this book, I argue that the Nordic ideology is aligned with such an attractor—one that has extensive competitive advantages.

Such a system of thought must be inherently logical, like the tripartite division of powers—or else it can hardly be sustainable as a new equilibrium. What you need to do is to learn to see this attractor, how it is inherently logical, how and why it gets its competitive edge. **This attractor is the lodestone of the navigator, allowing us to blaze new paths for society, because we can see—not quite *where* we are going—but which directions do exist: where is north and where is Mecca?**

If we can see the directionality of how our societies evolve, and where we are on this map, the point isn't necessarily that we should always go "forward". The point is rather that we should navigate more proficiently, adjusting to every wind and current, because we know our position and our direction. This can include waiting for the right moment and taking some strategic retreats. But instead of "north" and "Mecca", we are dealing with another dimension by which we can navigate: **the stages of development; each stage being an attractor for society to stabilize around.**

Understanding where you are in a sequence of attractors doesn't necessarily mean you can go to the next stage, or indeed, that you should always try to do so. But it means you can *tilt* the likelihood of going in a direction that is more sustainable and is likely to have positive effects in the lives of people.

Imagine you have two governments in similar countries: one sees the attractor points ahead and the other doesn't. As they each make a thousand policy and implementation decisions for their administrations over a period of time, the "attractor-aware" government will gain an advantage over the "attractor-blind" one. The difference might not be visible from the outside unless you study their many policies in great detail. In practical reality, however, one country is likely to thrive while the other is not. As the differences stack up over the years, one society will be happier, healthier, more resilient and gain a more central position in the global system—economically and culturally.

The people who recognize the attractors of course don't have all the answers to the questions of life and society; they just have an extra hint on how to navigate in each unique situation that surfaces. So that's how you use this text: You learn the attractors, and then you navigate to affect any number of situations in which you play a part. Because you can see through the goggles of political metamodernism, you can implant a little of the metamodern DNA here and there: in a political debate, in a media production, in your company's values and culture, in the way you pose your research questions in social science—or just by hinting at something in an art project.

It's like spreading a virus (if you will allow me a switch of metaphors), except this one improves society instead of making it sick. Hence the political method is—again—of a more non-linear kind than the political revolutions that grew from the Enlightenment. These revolutions required constitutional reform, and to achieve that, you had to scrap the old society, *l'ancien régime*, which was only possible by toppling the sovereign or at least ending the monarchic form of governance (or the colonial one, if you are the often-overlooked Haitian revolution).

The "virus strategy" proposed here works differently. **We are not really targeting the constitution and designing "a system" you can "establish" by promulgating certain laws.** We are talking about cultivating new *processes* that target culture itself and the developmental psychology of everyone; about creating a more existentially apt and emotionally sensitive civilization—a listening society. And we are exploring why contemporary society is driving us in this direction, and why the ones who fail to recognize this, and to act accordingly, will be severely punished and outcompeted in the many games of life.

Or actually, this virus *can* be harmful if it turns out we're wrong about the attractors; if we make the wrong assumptions. There is nothing more beneficial than a good theory. Correspondingly, there is nothing more dangerous than a bad one. Getting it right is just as important as *not* getting it wrong. The wrong theory can and will land us in a sea of troubles.

Marxism comes to mind. Of course, Marxism has been an incredibly productive intellectual field for the last century and a half, but Marx's attempt to identify the attractors of historical development was simply not satisfactory. Society did not follow the fundamental dynamics he proposed, nor did it develop through the stages he and his followers imagined. The mistakes of this theory killed about a hundred million people during the 20th century—however indirectly.

And of course, all things are both good and bad. If communism has left us with no substantial positive legacy in terms of socialist societies or historical developments, it still played a major and positive role in many people's lives, and it has taught our global consciousness some hard-earned lessons about political and economic development.

Then again, it's not like there is a default "no-theory" place from which we can develop society; we are always within the framework of a theory of some kind. So just "not being a Marxist" is hardly a mark of intelligence and critical thinking. We have to make assumptions, explicit or otherwise. (More on Marxism and communism in Appendix A.)

False assumptions mass murder people (like climate change denial) and correct ones save millions (like correct preemptive action against climate change). Montesquieu was successful in identifying the tripartite division of powers. If Marxism ended up killing people, how many lives has Montesquieu's theory *saved*—if we understand the question in an indirect, non-linear sense? How about liberal democracy, human rights, market economy, free enterprise, the welfare state; how many lives have these saved, how many have they improved? What would have happened if these ideas had not taken hold? What about feminism and environmentalism? What about animal rights? You do the math.

SET THE LODESTONE RIGHT

I hold that our current society is based on a number of false assumptions; a number of sacred cows must be brought to the slaughter house and shown little mercy (said by a vegan, mind you). I hold that these false assumptions can and will kill or otherwise harm millions—in indirect, non-linear ways—because they do not match the new dynamics of a global, digitized, postindustrial society. The chief such false assumption is that we can and should continue the current social-liberal "business as usual" politics within the framework of left-right party politics.

The failure to spread more accurate ideas about society can cause, or fail to prevent, unimaginable quantities of suffering. So we must put forward the best ideas and try to spread them—to the right people, at the right moments, from the right angles.

But how can we make sure this is Montesquieu and not another Marx? A common reflex, championed perhaps most clearly by the "father of libertarianism" Friedrich von Hayek, is to denounce all greater plans and plots for society. In this regard libertarianism and conservatism tend to agree: Top-down social engineering and utopian ideas enforced upon society according to the blueprints conceived of by our limited minds can hardly do justice to the complexity of society. Edmund Burke, "the father of modern conservatism", underscored in his dismissal of the French Revolution that customs and mores are based upon a long-tried and arduously evolved sum of human experience, whereas intellectual ideas can hardly take into account all the subtle contexts of these collective wisdoms. Radicalism tends to build fortresses in the skies that collapse and backfire when imposed upon the complexities of real life.

This is also largely the line of argument in Hayek's 1943 book *The Road to Serfdom*, in which he basically tells us that the road to hell is paved with good intentions of social and political reformers and revolutionaries. The tendency of humans to think we can understand the complexity of our own societies and "plan them" has led to huge mistakes, the communist experiments being only the clearest example. Instead, society should self-organize through the interactions of many independent players who engage on a free, unobstructed marketplace (as well as in other arenas).

In some ways, this is an appealing idea. It lets us off the hook, intellectually speaking, when it comes to imagining future society, and lets each of us focus on whatever we can do ourselves, as agents on the market and in the civil sphere. It is a humbler stance, its adherents argue, because it's difficult to know what is good even for oneself—let alone all other people, or society as a whole!

But it is, ultimately, a lazy stance and it quickly leads to dead ends. It begs the question about the libertarian stance itself: If humans cannot understand the complexity of society, or if you are too "intellectually humble" to try, how come you can still diagnose which thoughts about society lead to oppression and which ones lead to freedom? Such humility quickly reveals itself as hollow. How come you are allowed to argue that the market is the most free and rational form of self-organization? How come you are allowed to determine that individuals are more real and important than collectives, that a minimal "night watchman" state is best, or that corporate structures are less oppressive than political ones? Or that "freedom" should be defined in this particular manner?

This "libertarian reflex" also avoids answering another question: What about all the social engineering and utopianism that *did* work? What about Montesquieu's tripartite division of powers; would we have been better off without it if it had never guided the formulations of the constitutions of countries? And how come some of the most successful countries in the world, by most measures the Nordic ones, have also been subject to extensive social engineering and the perhaps most thorough penetration of the state into the everyday lives of the citizens?

Scandinavian libertarians and conservatives like to point out that Sweden was in fact a very liberal economy up until the 1970s, and that its main spur of economic growth occurred in the period *preceding* the social democratic expansion.[13] While this point is correct, it does not take into account that Sweden's population became the most progressive in the world during the Social Democratic period and that other measures of human development did very well. It appears as though good societies can be built by a dynamic balance between free markets and democratically governed bureaucracies.

The libertarian reflexes warn us of important risks, but as a general dismissal of social engineering they don't compute. They offer no defense against the Nordic ideology, which seeks to create a deeper and more psychological form of welfare. Lene Andersen and Tomas Björkman show in their book, *The Nordic Secret*, how Scandinavian reformers explicitly sought to support widespread psychological development in the population.

There is only one proper reply to all of this: **studying major societal attractors is a good thing when your analysis is correct, and it's a bad thing when you're wrong.** Once in a blue moon, a good analysis can grow from a bad one and *vice versa*, but there it is.

So the question is not: "Is it okay to try to see how society overall develops and to try to act accordingly?" Yes, it's okay. We just need to make damn sure we set our lodestone right before we sail the seas of history, lest we be left paddling in the cold.

NAVIGATORS OF HISTORY

Back in the days, until the 18th century, European ships had to navigate the seas with latitude but no longitude. You wouldn't know how far east or west you were. There simply were no clocks available that could keep the time on board a ship as it kept waving back and forth. That Britannia so easily ruled the waves in the 19th century had a lot to do with the British inventing a "marine chronometer" before anyone else. In 1714, the British parliament offered a huge prize sum to whoever could solve the problem of longitude. This led to any number of experiments, including the stabbing of rabbits, in the faint hope that onboard rabbits would suffer some measurable consequences of their siblings on land being tormented at a set point in time. But no luck. Decades went by.

In 1773—more than fifty years later—the carpenter and self-taught clockmaker John Harris finally collected the prize, after a lifetime of incremental improvements to his invention: an advanced mechanical clock which included a contraption that countered the rocking of the boat. The prize was £20,000, about 3.5 million US dollars in today's currency (which was, by the way, more than a thousand times the average yearly income at the time. Ka-ching.)

The marine clock was expensive, so they couldn't make too many. Still, the British fleet could now navigate the world in a manner unparalleled by all other powers. And it saved quite a few sailors from scurvy and other maritime miseries as well. The British government saw an attractor point —the measurement of longitude—and with its help the British navy could eventually navigate the world with much greater ease. The competitive advantages were immense. The same holds, I believe, for the map I wish to present you with: the Nordic ideology.

It would be foolish to claim that the Nordic ideology as proposed in these pages is free of error or makes up a complete blueprint for how to renew society. You, the reader, need to help out by critically evaluating this theory as we go along—it might need tweaks, serious revision, or downright rejection.[14]

In this book, you need to evaluate which parts of my theory should be kept or scrapped. But, again, to do that you need to *successfully* understand the theory first. You can only be a navigator of history to the extent that historical circumstances place you in a position to think and act. You are always part of a greater, self-organizing system of society. The study of self-organizing systems has been called many things—and it stretches across many sciences. One of its early names, the one used at the influential Macy Conferences back in the 1950s, was *cybernetics*; the word's root comes from Greek for "navigator". **You *navigate* history, just as history navigates you.** This makes you a part of the self-organization of global society. This book helps you to become a part of the self-organization of the "metamodern" layer of societal development.

On a last note on historical attractors, I'd like to underscore that these exist in the logical structure of things, much like mathematical theorems.

They are "out there", available to be discovered and made visible—perhaps not as "natural laws", but certainly as discernable dynamics under certain given circumstances. Attractors aren't "inscribed into a pregiven universe", but they can still guide us, just as any other discovery.

Once discovered, mathematical truths can be put to use as we navigate the world. For instance, the Indian mathematician prodigy Srinivasa Ramanujan who went to Cambridge in the 1910s, left behind a notebook with some ideas he never published. These proofs were jotted down in his idiosyncratic and intuitive manner, self-taught as he was. The notes were rediscovered in the 1960s, and they were still original at that time. These ideas have since been used in research about black holes. The logical structure was there to be uncovered all along.

But even if the attractors follow from what is logically coherent, they do not represent a "manifest destiny". After all, even if it is logical for a system to evolve in a certain direction, any number of things can happen to disrupt it. You can get hit by a comet (outside shock to a system), or you can run into an ecological limit that was not accounted for (inside breakdown of a system)—or there may be other, stronger attractors that you failed to spot, pulling you in another direction altogether.

So even if there are some arrows that point history in certain general directions, this is not the same as saying this and that *will* happen. There are no guarantees here. But that only serves to make our own conscious participation in the self-organization of society all the more necessary. This is the paradoxical relationship at hand: Potentials become realities in part *because* we recognize them and act upon them.

But please note that history doesn't allow for an "individual" to see it "from the outside"; we can only ever see history from a vantage point within it. History can only be seen from the inside, and that is in itself a part of its evolution and path. Again, history navigates us and we it. This is the cybernetic view, the perspectival view.

In other words, we can be diligent students of the attractors of history and faithful navigators of its winds and currents—while still remaining agnostic as to what actually will happen. The point is that the ones who are best at recognizing what *can* happen, also have the greatest chances of affecting what *will*.

Do you now believe attractors exist and that they can be studied, and to some extent can be known in advance?

What we are trying to do in this book is to take the vague currents currently forming in the Nordic countries and flesh out a more coherent and clear Nordic ideology, to be manifested in a few progressive societies and eventually spread to other parts of the world. There are paths society can take, and some of these are more logical, coherent, viable and conducive to human flourishing than others. We should find these paths and travel them together. Dreamers must learn to steer by the stars.

Easier said than done. But let's say it first, then do it.

Chapter 1

RELATIVE UTOPIA

> "Here's the deal. The human soul doesn't want to be advised or fixed or saved. It simply wants to be witnessed—to be seen, heard and companioned exactly as it is. When we make that kind of deep bow to the soul of a suffering person, our respect reinforces the soul's healing resources, the only resources that can help the sufferer make it through."
>
> —Parker Palmer

In a way, we're living in our ancestors' utopia. If they could have witnessed our lives today, they probably wouldn't have believed their eyes: all the food you can eat, a minimum of hard manual labor, the expectation to see *all* your children reach adult age, and no drunken lords to abuse you—truly a paradise compared to what most of them had to put up with.

We have access to a large number of conveniences that in the past would have been the envy of even kings and nobles: modern healthcare, comfortable and speedy transportation, and safe, fresh food from all around the world, even during winter.

Few of us would want to switch our pleasant modern lifestyle with that of Louis XIV 300 years ago. After all, not even the extravagant Sun King himself ever flew to the Canary Islands during his winter holiday and sat on a beach without catching malaria while enjoying his favorite show on Netflix. And we would presumably soon tire of court jesters and pheasant dinners in leaky castles anyway.

We have become accustomed to a standard of living so high not even Moses parting the Red Sea would impress us. Why wander to the land of milk and honey when we can cross the seas in comfortable jets to places with much more interesting cuisine? Jesus too would probably have needed to up his game if he were to make disciples out of us modern people. Turning water into wine hardly competes with the marvel of a good 3D-printer.

Even in the social realm we have opportunities and privileges unimaginable in the past. A medieval farmer would not have believed it if he was told that his descendants would have voting rights, freedom of expression, property rights, police protection and the freedom to choose their religion. And a 19th century factory worker would have been dumbstruck by the life-conditions of common folks today: considerably shorter work hours, vacations, pensions, unemployment benefits and an abundance of cheap consumer goods that used to be considered luxuries. Lenin's grandiose promise of peace, bread and land that made a generation of workers start a revolution is so modest and unambitious in comparison to all the things we take for granted today.

There are of course still people who struggle to make ends meet: single unemployed parents, paperless immigrants, people with mental illnesses, substance addicts, and so on. But overall, we must admit we have come very far. We may not live in a true utopia, but in comparison to the past, modern society is at least a **relative utopia**; truly utopian relative to what used to be.

But the word "utopia" actually means "nowhere". It goes back to the proto-modern thinker Thomas More's book *Utopia* from 1516. In this meaning of the word, we do actually live in yesterday's Nowhereland, in a fairytale, a technological Shangri-La that in the past only could have existed as fiction. Yet, as things went on, the fictional became all the more factual.

As such, there is little reason to believe the metamodern society we are headed towards won't be a relative utopia; that what is currently only conceivable as a fictional account one day will materialize and acquire ostensibly utopian properties—relative to what we're putting up with today and take for self-evident conditions of life.

THE "BOTH-AND" OF DEVELOPMENT

Even if the argument *can* be made that traditional society was "better" than the modern one (as so-called "integral traditionalists" like Frithjof Schuon and Réné Guénon have argued: less pollution, more spirituality, a more enchanted sense of the world, less destructive weapons, less mindless consumerism and alienation, more independence in having the skills to produce what you need, more humility, etc.); this should not blind us to the circumstance that modernity largely solved all of the major problems of pre-modern society. Yup, pretty much all of them.

For most of recorded history, child mortality was high, starvation commonplace, slavery institutionalized, serfdom ubiquitous, wars frequent, violence a part of everyday life, monarchical oppression unquestioned, disease rampant, poverty the rule, literacy low, cruel norms limiting individual freedom prevailing—and so forth.

Yes, all of these miseries exist in the modern world too. In absolute numbers, some of them are perhaps worse than ever as the world population is so much larger. On the other hand—and this is the point here—all of these problems have decreased dramatically in *relative* terms. Indeed, if you look at the highly modernized, democratic parts of the world, there is an apparent decrease in all of these problems at least by a power of ten. Look at Sweden today: How many people are starving for each one hundred who starved in the 1700s? One? Probably not even that. When people are poor in the US today, they get food stamps and have to stand in line. In pre-modern times, they simply starved to death.

So modernity, with all its technological and social advances, has practically solved all of the problems of all earlier societies: famine, disease, oppression, war, poverty, lack of education, slow and dangerous transportation, superstition. Yes, even war; even if we count the world wars, the risk of being killed by another human being was statistically smaller during the 20th century than at any time before. Steven Pinker wrote an often-cited book about it in 2011, *The Better Angels of Our Nature*, and then another one in 2018, *Enlightenment Now*. Since the millennium, the number of people killed globally in violent conflicts has been extremely low compared to any previous period (in *per capita* terms).

Yet, of course, modern life is no walk in the park; it is still incredibly cruel and full of suffering—something that granny's granny probably would have had a hard time imagining if we went on for hours about all the awesome sauce (I imagine I'd pause for a long time to describe what I get to eat, where I have traveled and so forth).

Hence, it's a *relative* utopia: It really *is* super-duper mega awesome not to starve, to have modern medicine, to be able to speak and think freely, to have dominant sex with hot young men if you're an old guy (I suppose granny might have had a problem with that part), to choose how to live your life and what to do for a living, to have internet and all kinds of abundance (even when unemployed, you can eat well and have shelter and use many of the technologies). It really is nice.

At the same time that doesn't mean life has become "perfect". So today's developed societies really *are* utopian, but only in a *relative* sense. This is the **both-and** of development. They are utopian as *compared to* what came before. But that doesn't mean today's society has no problems. In fact, it has two very distinct kinds of problems:

- **Residual problems**
- **New emergent properties problems**

The **residual problems** are the percentages left here and there of the pre-modern stage of development: not all people are protected from curable diseases, some live in areas controlled by mobsters and are thereby still oppressed, some slavery still goes on (30 million *de facto* slaves is a figure people often bring up), and some people still starve or otherwise suffer from poverty.

It's true that the UN Development Goals were met in advance[15] and abject poverty is withering away as economic growth and ambitious, far-reaching aid programs take effect. But still, there are some residuals here and there, and they should certainly be accounted for; they still define hundreds of millions of lives. They are, however, not quite the *products* of modern society, as historical developments clearly indicate: Why else would they all be falling so sharply across the globe as the modern world-system progresses? Nay, amigo, they are *residuals*, leftovers. The most modern countries have the least of these issues.

The other category, which concerns us more in this context, are the problems showing up as a direct *result of* modern society: **the new emergent properties problems**. At a bare minimum, there are three such problems:

1. **ecological unsustainability,**

2. **excess inequality, and**

3. **alienation and stress.**

Notwithstanding that these are, on an individual scale, preferable to the wars, droughts and pestilences of yore, they are still quite serious. Sustainability issues like climate change, ecological collapse, mass extinction— not to mention the looming threat of nuclear holocaust and other increasingly tangible doomsday scenarios (haywire AI or nanotech, biological warfare)—can potentially cause miseries worse and more irreparable than even the black plague.

The inequalities of the world may seem bearable compared to the poverty of pre-modern subsistence farming, but nowadays we all live in the proximity of wealth and abundance, knowing for instance the diseases that kill our kids in fact are curable. Such knowledge can make our relative poverty even more bitter and insufferable than the harshness of premodern life. Indeed, it is one of the most robust findings of social science that income inequality correlates with violent crime, within countries and even more so between countries.[16]

And alienation—a pervading sense of estrangement and existential angst—causes young people to suffer depression and commit suicide to an unprecedented degree. It causes people to live meaningless and empty lives amidst what superficially looks like freedom and abundance; lives in which we become increasingly stressed out and often experience burnout.

I remember spending seven years fending off suicidal thoughts, as a pervasive but unspecific anxiety haunted my young adulthood. This is not uncommon in developed, modern countries where the trends generally point towards rising mental health problems in adolescents and young adults. These are perhaps not as acute or severe as the challenges that people faced before modernity, but they still remain quite serious issues.

All three of these problems are caused, in one way or another, by the dramatic expansion of our industrial productivity: sustainability because we produce and consume more than our ecosystems can endure, inequality because this wealth is distributed in a series of "scale free networks", where the most central positions gain a larger proportion of the wealth, and alienation because of the abstractness and distance that shows up between our everyday activities and their benefits for ourselves and others: Many of us lose a sense of meaning, purpose and direction. (Of course, there's a lot more to the story on each one of these, but we're just sketching here to get on to the point).

We have finally created a land that flows with milk and honey; literally, vast amounts of highly nutritional substances flow from the taps of industry—yet it's making us and the planet sick. The paradise of yesterday is great, but it carries with it a number of unexpected pathologies that need to be dealt with in tomorrow's relative utopia.

BEAUTIES LOST AND NEW HEIGHTS REACHED

Beyond the two categories—residual and new emergent properties problems—we can add two more to the list of troubles of today's society. The third category I've called "**beauties lost**". It entails all the good things that were prevalent in pre-modern societies, but for different reasons diminished as societies became modern.

A good example is "community", or what the classical 19th century sociologist Ferdinand Tönnies called *Gemeinschaft* (modern life, at least in its later urbanized stages, generally offers little cozy, genuine community in which you continuously relate to a wider group of family and neighbors).

As an example of *Gemeinschaft* lost, compare the expansion of electronically available music—millions of bands, artists and orchestras available online to be played with marvelous sound systems—to the fact that most of us have stopped singing. In all pre-modern societies, people got together and sang, pretty often too. The individualism and performance oriented attitudes of modern life somehow nudge us to shut up, unless we're alone in the shower or partake in a formally organized choir. Music gained, but singing lost.[17]

Another example of a beauty lost is "simplicity"; that life had a kind of directness and straightforwardness which allowed a certain modest satisfaction. Other such beauties lost are the "connection to the soil", appreciation of the small things—perhaps a well-crafted tool—or the *via contemplativa* of monastic life; the calm, ascetic life in service of spiritual goals. You get the picture.

These "beauties lost" have been brought up by many reactionary movements and romantics of all kinds (I mentioned the integral traditionalists, for instance). With each beauty lost, a part of us is left empty and aching. But the romantic and nostalgic longing lends itself to exaggeration—to overvaluing an imagined past, a yesteryear that never quite happened. What we should do instead is simply to acknowledge that all societal progression into later and "more advanced" stages entails some beauties lost, and that there may be good reasons to figure out how some of these can be regained and reincorporated without trying to turn the clock back.[18]

The fourth category of problems is more important. We can call it **"new heights reached"**. There are problems that are perhaps not directly *caused* by modern life, but whose solutions only now come within reach. Only when we acquire greater capabilities can we begin to see them and direct our attention towards them. In the old days, we simply didn't have the luxury to worry about these problems; now we can. We have reached new heights and hence we can begin to tackle *higher* issues. The soul always wants more; it is never contented. You never get to the end; there is always a new horizon after this one, and another.

What are these new issues then, these "new heights"? I would like to mention four of them.

The *first* "new-heights issue" is tied to alienation, but still distinct from it: the lack of meaning and fulfillment. What happens in a society where you already have food, shelter and abundance? People begin to worry that they might be squandering their lives; that they may not be making the best of it; that something is still lacking; that life has become boring and too predictable.

The *second* new-heights issue has to do with struggle and heroism; how can we align our own petty lives with the overarching story about humanity, the world and even the cosmos? How can we be something else, something *more*, than just an average Jane or Joe consumer? Now that we have relative safety and autonomy, how can we make it worthwhile? Once we have achieved a comfortable villa life, there is still, lingering in our hearts, a visceral longing for greatness within us. How can we transcend ourselves; how can we serve something greater so that our lives become imbued with crisp, clear moments of intense aliveness?

The *third* higher issue pertains to gender equality and freedom of identity: Can we be sexually emancipated, not only in the sense that we can be women with equal rights as men, but that we can be truly sexually and emotionally fulfilled? Can we experience erotic fulfillment and intimacy both at once? Can we be gay, transgender, or otherwise experiment with and create our sexual and gender identities? Women's liberation and the other gender/sexuality issues have come within our grasp in modern societies, but they are not conclusively solved by it.

The *fourth* and last higher issue is animal rights. Of course, a big part of the problem with the abuse of animals has to do with modern phenomena such as industrial farming. Animal suffering is exacerbated by modernity, even with the increased legislations for "animal welfare". There have been some pre-modern examples of principled concern for animals in the Eastern traditions (Buddhism and Jainism), but even these have not quite resembled the modern-day animal rights movement. In Jainism, for instance, concern with animals grew from a general non-violence principle, which is not quite the same as a modern philosophy of "rights". In modern life, we can now create an abundance of vegan and synthetic solutions that allow us to live without animal slavery and exploitation. Hence, veganism becomes a new issue within our reach.

So, sorry for tricking you into thinking we had only two categories of problems under modernity. We have four, these being:

* **Residual problems** (left-overs from before modernity).

* **New emergent properties problems** (caused by modernity).

* **Beauties lost** (qualities from earlier societies lost under modernity).

* **New heights reached** (problems that simply weren't viable to try to solve before, but now have come within our reach).

Yep, that's it. Modern society is truly utopian, truly glorious. Except it has these four categories of problems.[19]

Now to the point we've been working our way towards. We live today in what to most earlier generations could only be described as sheer utopia. Yet, we hardly wake up every morning to what we feel is a utopian society. It is a utopia only in a *relative* sense: The problems of old have all but vanished, just as new ones have appeared—as dark clouds on the horizon, growing cracks in the walls, and new subtle knots within our hearts and minds.

What about metamodern society; is it a utopian project? Yes. It is unapologetically utopian. **A society can be described as metamodern if, and only if, all of the problems of modernity have been more or less resolved, meaning that they have been reduced by at least a power of ten.**

In other words, metamodern society is defined as one in which the problems that emerged in modernity—lack of sustainability, excess inequality, alienation and stress—have been resolved. So that's what we're going for. Fucking utopia.

Fucking *relative* utopia, that is.

NEW MISERIES WORTH FIGHTING FOR

Metamodern society can and will follow the same pattern of relative utopia as modern society has. There will be:

1. **residuals** of the modern problems: still *some* inequality, environmental issues and alienation (whereas the pre-modern residuals are reduced by yet another order of magnitude);
2. and yes, there will be **new, emergent problems** *caused* by metamodern society itself (some of which we will discuss in this book in an attempt to preempt them);
3. and yes, some **beauties of modern life will be lost** along the way;
4. and yes, new dark clouds will form on the horizon, new bold challenges to civilization that **come within our grasp**.

And yes, in some sense, these new problems will be preferable to what we have today; but strangely, they are likely to somehow be **even *more* serious** than the challenges of modern society.

So that's the notion of "relative utopia" for you. We are trying to achieve a self-organization of society that is happier, in a profound sense of the word, than anything that has gone before it. But we're not saying it's going to be a perfect world. In fact, we're saying it's going to be as messy and risky as ever. More complex. Why should we expect anything else, when history—cultural, geological and astronomical—has thus far meant explosive increases of complexity?

It shouldn't surprise us that future society will manage issues that today may seem insoluble, out of reach, or downright impossible. That's what modern society did. It let steel float and fly, it saved us from disease, it conquered the moon, it brought peace—and so forth. Is it really wrong to think that future society, the one that comes after the modern, industrial one, could do what seems unimaginable today?

Somehow, modern life—and its relative utopia—*was* possible. Perhaps metamodern life can be too. A simple reason to assume this is the fact that so many intelligent people are working so hard, in so many different ways, to solve the problems of modernity: sustainability, inequality, alienation. Pretty much every smart and idealistic person is grappling with at least some aspect of one of these issues. It's all over the sciences, all over policy making, in the arts, even on the market—whoever can solve these problems is most cherished, most appreciated, even well-paid. Are we being pulled in some direction, towards a new great attractor point, upon which a series of attractors converge?

So I'll say it again. We go ahead with sincere irony, pragmatic idealism, informed naivety and magical realism—to entertain the *potential* of a relative utopia.

In the end, we still live in a tragic universe; as we noted in Book One, existence has us "eternally by the balls". But there are new miseries on the horizon, miseries worth fighting for. And there is fun to be had along the way.

Relishing in cow dung really is a hundred times better than banging one's head against the invisible barrier of the window. It really is. But it's still cow dung, and we're still flies, with our controls set for the heart of the sun.

Chapter 2

GAME CHANGE

W hat, exactly, does it mean when we talk about "societal progress"? What is it that makes a country like Sweden more "progressive" than, say, Saudi Arabia? In both countries people have access to an abundance of modern conveniences, so the deciding difference doesn't have much to do with wealth and high-tech gadgets. After all, when so called "progressives" talk about "change", they usually don't refer to technological progress. So what can it be? What does it mean to "make progress" on a societal level?

Here's my suggestion: At its fundamental core, societal progress is about "**game change**"; it's when the background rules of life's interactions—everyday, normal interactions—change and evolve. Progress is when the game of life becomes fairer, kinder, more transparent, more inclusive, more forgiving, more sustainable, more rational, more fulfilling.

Game change is a good thing. But it is, paradoxically enough, the bastard child of two evils: **game denial** and **game acceptance**. Ever knew anyone like that, a kind person with two horrible parents? Me neither. But unlikely as it seems, here is an example.

I will begin by introducing the two evil parents in this family.

GAME DENIAL

Life is a game. Always will be.

Since we inhabit a world of limited resources, our daily lives are full of zero-sum interactions where one party walks away with a prize while another leaves the table empty-handed; games with winners and losers. If you and I want the same spouse, the game is on. If you and I want the same job, the game is on. If you want to argue against this way of seeing the world, the game is on. There is no denying it, even when you do.

Yet, many of us frequently fall victim to what I call "**game denial**": the inability to perceive, or a negligence of, the logical and behavioral rules that regulate human relations. Game denial is when you ignore or "wish away" certain uncomfortable truths regarding human relations and how reality works. Or simply when you deny the realities of life and forcefully impose your own "ought" upon what "is".

In a subtle sense, your crime is against truth itself. And when the truth has been sacrificed for a few candy bars worth of emotional reward—people start dying as the consequences of your false assumptions begin to manifest. And from there on you are stuck with defending your lala-land from actuality, making things even worse.

Game denial is, to this day, rampant. And its victims are not necessarily dead; it has victims in all walks of life, all scarred by unsustainable and un-realistic social relations, expectations and moralistic impositions of "what ought to be" upon what "actually is". **Crimes against actuality are crimes against humanity, against all life on our planet.**

Since game denial often "sounds nice", it may be more convenient to defend in a public debate (because you can easily take the moral high ground), but in actual reality, in a given context, it tends to have negative or otherwise unsustainable consequences. You *pretend* that the world works by rules which it does not.

Game denial can show up in so many ways because life is always open to interpretation and reinterpretation. And of course, there is not one "set" game in life in which "God" crowns the winners. But the fact that life has ambiguity is a mixed blessing: It means we can make more favorable interpretations and save our positive self-images, but it also means the leeway to deny obvious competitions and conflicting interests is huge. And because there are such strong psychological forces driving us towards game denial, we all partake in it.[20]

It is difficult to overestimate just how powerful these inner pressures are. For instance, if we all of our life have felt oppressed and hurt in soft and sensitive places by norms that dictate how a "beautiful and feminine" woman should be, how compelling and satisfying does it not seem to make up a way to disqualify that game altogether, branding it as false, im-moral and ultimately unreal? If we are bad at sports, how good does it not feel to be rid of all anxieties about our physical inferiority by denying *that* game?

Game denial means to hate the game and try to eradicate it. It can take the form of liberal political correctness or, in its extreme form, crude communism. But the game won't go away. You can't eradicate it with a "let's all be friends". What about me and that other person who wants the same spouse, but only one can get her by winning her heart? Whether or not we have friendly relations with one another, there is a game with a winner and a loser—this is true even in polyamorous relations. It is bound to happen everywhere in *samsara* (as Eastern traditions have named the worldly realm of suffering), all the time.

Recent research has revealed an evolutionary struggle even between the pregnant mother and her fetus—the growing child's evolutionary interests are somewhat different from those of the mother (who may increase the chances of spreading her genes by having more children, and hence not be too drained by this particular fetus). No matter how profoundly symbiotic and loving a relationship, there is always an inescapable element of struggle. A game.

To try to eradicate the game is only a form of individual or collective repression, and it will always produce pathological results—namely oppression. **Whatever game you want to repress—like capitalism—this can only be done by activating a grosser level of game—like the game for political totalitarian power**. Communist states repressed the mechanisms of "games for profit" by playing a much crueler game for political power.

But oppression is not the worst part of game denial. Oppression can be toppled; evil reigns can end. No, the worst part is that **denying the existence of the game means that the game cannot be described, taught and learned.** The game is hidden away, made taboo. Hence, game denial is in the service of the privileged elite, making the game less fair by serving those who already know the rules and deceiving those who do not. They'll never know what hit them.

Let's take some examples of prevalent game denial. This list may insult a lot of readers and offend moral convictions. Brace yourself.

- Free immigration for all! All immigration is always good for everyone involved: the immigrants, the receivers, the left-behind!

  - Game denial: All societies have limits to how much immigration they can manage, and which kinds of immigration; and higher immigration rates often create fiercer competition at the bottom of society, hence harming its most precariously situated citizens.

- A Universal Basic Income that would cover a lower middle-class wage, the sooner the better! It would free all, and a creative explosion of solidarity would occur, and we would usher in a golden age of love and innovation!

  - Game denial: The labor market is a complex game of power relations and for people to sustainably perform less-than-rewarding but crucial tasks (e.g. cleaning blood off hospital floors), there must be a complex system in place of penalties, hierarchies and rewards. If you wreck this system, welcome to the Soviet Union. Stalinism next. Or worse. (Not saying that all such initiatives are game denial, but many are.)

- The LEFT is good, always and forever! If only the evil powers of greed were stopped, we would have high wages, safe employments, no unemployment, free immigration, high social benefits!

  - Game denial: Does not compute. If you have high wages, safe employments and high taxes, then business becomes extremely inefficient, so people can't really buy anything with their money (hello Soviet). If you have free immigration *and* social benefits, the system gets bogged down with costs and fosters resentments in the working locals, and you get ethnic violence and the rise of populist anti-immigration parties. And if wages are high, the immigrants won't be able to compete to enter the market. The bogged-down economy fosters clientelism. Greek economy next. Or worse.

- Feminism! If only men were kind and polite and respected women and stopped using "master suppression techniques" (as described by the social psychologist Berit Ås) and didn't greedily enjoy the oppression of women by means of patriarchy, this would make society fair, women unafraid of sexual assault, work-life satisfying and intimate relations much more functional.

  - Game denial, again: For this line of reasoning to compute, displays of male prestige, status and power must stop being sexually and emotionally alluring to women and hence desirable to men. As long as these traits *are* found desirable (as plenty of experimental research suggests is the case: women genuinely prefer high-status, in some sense "dominant", males), men can only stop using at least *some* strategies for social self-advancement at their own expense. The games of everyday life are denied.

- A wave of spirituality and "higher consciousness" will transform the world! In one way, this is very advanced and complex, in another way, very simple: a kind of perennial wisdom, that people wake up to a simple but profound message of love and acceptance!

  - Game denial: This one (or any version of "millenarianism") is quite common in more spiritually inclined people, but also, by analogy, in socialists and environmentalists. Here and there, many interesting and intense spiritual movements, waves and rebirths have waxed and waned throughout history. Most of them have been fool's gold, ending up in grievous mistakes and betrayed hopes. Some, such as Christianity and the other world religions, have caught on long-term and led to some lasting moral transformations. But none of them have been unambiguously good, and none have led to anything as fantastic as was imagined. This is because the games of life, with winners and losers, are still there to be played, even if people become a little nicer.

- If people turned away from the materialist competitive worldview of our age, there would be enough for everybody and people would be happy!

    - Game denial.

- A playful, creative schooling system which emphasizes growth and joy rather than the dull reciting of facts! No discipline needed! Ever!

    - Game denial.

- If the US just stops being imperialist/interventionist, there will be a peaceful and solidary international order instead!

    - Game denial.

- Everyone has something unique to contribute in this new economy! There is room for everyone!

    - Game denial.

- If only people learned about animal suffering, they would support the end of animal slavery!

    - Game denial.

- Interfaith dialogue will bring an end to religious conflicts!

    - Game denial.

- No military intervention is ever needed or justified!

    - Game denial.

- All animals (humans) are created equal!

    - Game denial.

- The meek shall inherit the earth!

    - If you mean cockroaches, you might be correct. Otherwise, go to "game denial".

You get the picture. I suppose a lot of this sounds familiar?

It's not always easy to tell game denial apart from more legitimate forms of idealism. A rule of thumb, however, is that game denial very often arrives in the company of her twisted little sister: *moralism*—being subtly (or not so subtly) judgmental and self-righteous.

The alliance between game denial and moralism works in cunning ways. They help each other staying in the background, so that neither has to come out in the light and get busted in all their obviousness. For inst-ance, in academia and critical social science, there is a presupposition of a pro-immigration, leftist economics, radical feminism, anti-militarism, anti-disciplinary view of education and a few other taken-for-granted opinions.

When you go to the liberal sociological seminars, listening for instance to Judith Butler's advanced, learned and very initiated talks about femin-ism, all focus is on the specifics of the argument, on the masterfully craf-ted critical social theory and research. All of this creates a thick smoke-screen concealing any number of game denials. All the left-wing game denial stays in the background and limits the discussion.

There is no focus on, and no leeway to discuss, all this game denial baggage (because it would be seen as morally wrong, and whoever brings it up is seen as impure). The underlying moralism covers up the game denial. And the game denial covers up the moralism because the fact that the games of life are hidden away makes the moralism appear as common sense and decency.

I'm not saying that Judith Butler's feminism will kill a hundred million people. I'm just saying that other kinds of game denial, like communism, *did* and that game denial is always a harmful or at least dangerous busi-ness.

Not believing in game denial and its ubiquitous presence is in itself a form of game denial. The reason people do all the game denial is often that it is a useful tool for them to win the small struggles in everyday life: for moral worth, for admiration, for power, money, sex and status—or just to avoid shaming and judgment, or to have the solemn pleasure of shaming and judging others.

Ironically, it is *because* people are always in a game that they can win by denying its existence. Of course, there are other reasons, such as lack-ing intelligence or relevant perspectives. But the social rewards of game denial are part of it—and they should not be denied. It is as if many of the progressive intellectuals are "bribed" by the social rewards they can attain by taking part in game denial. These are emotional and cognitive bribes that distort thinking processes, discourses and truth seeking.

Real kindness needs to make sense; it needs to compute. If the numbers don't add up, they simply don't. Hence, any kindness that does not com-pute is a disguised form of evil.

But it should also be noted that game denial is not only an intellectual form of self-deceit; there is also such a thing as **embodied** game denial. For those of us who have suffered from low social status during our upbringing and may be lacking in the psychological trait assertiveness (being able to stand up for oneself, etc.), we may unconsciously be preparing our bodies and minds for the impact of a social defeat. This sets our minds and bodies up for trying to win over reality by being kind or nice, a part deep inside of us keeps folding over and submitting, trying to deny that a competition or confrontation takes place.

The first victim of game denial is the truth. Its next victim is the innocent child who has to suffer the consequences of your lies. Crimes against actuality are crimes against humanity and all life on our planet.

CONSERVATIVE SATISFACTION

Thus far, readers of a conservative bent have probably felt a streak of satisfaction, while the radicals and liberals have cringed and condemned me.

So be it.

If game denial was the *only* part of the story, conservatives would simply be right. Deep down they've always known, or so they think, that dreamy idealism isn't quite "real"; that all those liberals are, in a subtle but pervasive sense, brimming with mendacities, filled with pompous self-deceit. There's a *real* world out there, a practical world of *real* people, and *real* limitations.

Ahh. "Like 'me', the no-bullshit conservative. The good person is not whoever can dream up the nicest fantasy and have us drive off a cliff in search of it, but rather those who can look at the *real world*, be strong enough to face it—and from there on, try to do what's best and most realistic given the circumstances."

The conservative mind seeks a darker, but soberer, point of departure: What to do with violent criminals? How should free-riding, cheating and loafing be discouraged? How do we get people to come out of their comfort zones and make sincere efforts for the good of themselves and others?

And what are the "hard truths" that we must all relate to? Here's a perspective from a "pickup artist", i.e. a man who has become a professional at seducing women:

> "There is a pride in being a pickup artist. It is a challenge. I have performer friends who can explode on stage like samurai and kill five hundred people, but they are afraid to approach a girl in a bar. I don't blame them. Most audiences are horny to be fucked. They want it hard and deep. But the girl sitting on the bar stool is more difficult. She is scarier. She is the five hundred pound gorilla in a little black dress. And she can bust you up, if you let her. But she is also horny to be fucked. We are all horny to be fucked."[21]

"Juggler", as is the *nom de guerre* of this fellow, tries to "tell it like it is". He tries to face up to the inherent challenges of life, ones that cannot be brushed aside with idealistic visions and wishful thinking. In short: he *accepts* the game of life (in this case seduction) and tries to take its consequences.

But it doesn't sound very nice, which is probably why Juggler is part of a secret society in the first place, where knowledge about the games of seduction is spread and refined. Speaking one's perceived hard truths often makes you sound like a douchebag.

This puts the conservative at a constant rhetorical disadvantage; you generally tend to sound less nice. Which is quite annoying—a tired and irritated look on the conservative's face unmistakably presents itself when liberals and radicals go on, performing their moral braggadocio and "virtue signaling" in the media or at any given dinner party.

Conservatives generally talk less. They tell themselves they are practical, down-to-earth, realistic—*doers* rather than talkers. And in more or less refined manners, they resent the game deniers, these cheap fakes who take every opportunity to shout out their opinions and to shine their own politically correct medals; liberals, loud as a motorbike, who choose moral bombasticity over sober analysis.

This "conservative silence" is supported by research, which clearly shows that the farther left you are, the more you tend to voice your opinions in everyday life. If you're rooting for the nationalist party, you talk the least about it. One such study was undertaken in Sweden by the polling company Demoskop: When asking over 4000 people, 56% of self-reported socialists were comfortable with voicing their opinions to strangers, while the same figure for nationalists was 27%—the other ideologies neatly arranged in order of left-wingness.[22] Similar figures have been found in the US, as shown by a recent Cato Institute report.[23] Ours is a world of liberal loudmouths and tight conservative lips (and quiet support of populist and conservative leaders).

And since nationalism and Trumpism are the least kosher and most difficult to publicly defend, people even hide supporting them when asked in polls (which, by the way, is likely a major reason that polling has begun to be less accurate lately). When they do support the Trumps of the world, they often add in small excuses, justifications, hedgings, accounts and disclaimers: "Well, I don't *like* Trump, I just thought we should shake things up a bit" and so forth.[24]

When rhetorical talents who understand the metamodern games of the media landscape—like the young, posh Brit Milo Yiannopoulos and perhaps, to some extent, Donald Trump himself—finally manage to break through and say the things that conservatives wish they could express, the response is huge. A sigh of relief echoes through many as what might loosely be termed the "Alt-Right" gains momentum. Even if Yiannopoulos and Trump may embody exaggerations of conservative sentiments, at least they rain some sweet vengeance upon the often so suffocating politically correct establishment, the smothering welfare state and perceived *status quo*. A mellow sense of satisfaction arises in the conservative tummy.

GAME ACCEPTANCE

But I have argued elsewhere that reality consists of *more* than "actuality"; that a deeper and fuller reality lies in the realm of what is possible. And the conservatives have a strong tendency towards accepting the games of life in their current, *actual* form in a way that disregards the very real *potentials* for alternatives and change.

I have said that crimes against reality are crimes against humanity. **But crimes against potentiality are *also* crimes against humanity, and against all life on our planet—against all beautiful futures.** Game acceptance also kills. In fact, these killing grounds are far greater and more brutal than the ones of game denial.

Game acceptance means to prostrate before the game and take it as a law of nature in its *current* form, denying that the game can and *must* evolve. Or, more often, the game accepter holds that real and substantial changes are only ever possible in a distant and irrelevant future.

This makes us justify illegitimate force and injustice. It makes us think the unfair sides of the game are somehow indeed fair, because someone, somewhere "deserved it". And that injustice is all for the best in the long run because it serves the game. Game acceptance is the tune of political realism, "political theology" (Jean Bodin, Thomas Hobbes, Vilfredo Pareto, Niccolò Machiavelli...), neo-liberalism, conservatism. The game accepter quietly mumbles:

> "It *has* to be this way! It's how the world works. Some were born to sing the blues. We have to let them starve, get screwed over, get stuck and crushed in systems that are not for them. If we only let the system play out and the game be played the way it is, it will turn out for the best for everyone. Besides, I can't help I won. Don't hate the player, hate the game!"

But game acceptance really loves the game and hates the player—correction—hates the player who happens to get the short end of the stick.

The billions of enslaved, tortured and murdered animals under global industrial farming find no heroic defenders among the game accepters. The unjust international order which keeps the global South exploited and subjugated is defended under the auspices of "free markets". The losers of everyday life—the unintelligent, the ugly, the sickly—they all deserve what they get.

The central principle of game acceptance is hence: That which *could* be *is* not, and hence it *should* not be. As David Hume warned us already in the 18th century, this is a fallacy—deriving an "ought" from an "is". That something *is* the case doesn't mean is *should* be the case.

At its most extreme, game acceptance goes beyond the existing games of life to invent fictitious ones so that we may revel in what "necessary evils" these games demand of us: "Western culture is trying to destroy the Arab world and undermine all of Islam. Ergo we *must* stop them by ramming airplanes into buildings full of innocent folks!"—or "The Jews are plotting to destroy Germany! I don't like it any more than you, but we *must* kill them! It's either them or us. Race against race!"—or "Species against species! Humans *must* kill and torture billions of piglets, lest we all starve! It's the terrible game of life. Alas!"—or "Men must be superior to women and make more money and be more respected in public life, or else—the impending collapse of civilization!"—or "We must have a schooling system which more or less systematically permanently breaks the souls of the less gifted and less privileged and lets them know their lowly place in society! And we need to beat the kids! I wish it weren't so."

But now that it *is* so, mumbles a voice at the outer fringe of your conscious mind, you might as well *enjoy* subjugating the weak and feel exalted with every proof of your own power.

And just as there is an embodied form of game denial, so there is an **embodied form of game acceptance**. Especially those of us who have had high social status during our upbringing and reflexively assume we can win out in any confrontation that shows up can be tempted to think all such confrontations are necessarily good and just. Losers get what they deserve; that's not just an idea, but a felt bodily experience that sets our mind up for game acceptance.

Exaggerated forms of game acceptance lead to the most brutal forms of social organization. If you look at Nazi Germany, it killed less people than the communist experiment, numerically speaking. But if you look at the relatively small spread of fascism and its shorter period of existence, you notice the killing *rate* was much higher and the brutality much more an end in itself. Game acceptance, at its most extreme, murders a lot more people than does game denial.

But it doesn't stop there. The worst crime of game acceptance is that it blocks legitimate, necessary and very possible change. The game accepter remains serial killer calm in the face of glaring injustice. If you look at the thousands of very preventable maladies that have been perpetuated by game acceptance throughout history, you see a silent, invisible death toll looming larger than any other crime in world history.

Should we be complacent towards obviously avoidable suffering? What the barreling fuck! Of course we could end slavery. Of course we can end animal slavery. Of course the rich world can and should support sustainable global growth with a significant percentage of its GDP. Of course the trade system should be fairer. Of course most wars were avoidable. Of course everyone can have free basic health care. Of course we can live less wastefully and still be healthier, happier and have meaningful lives.

Crimes against potentiality are crimes against humanity.

DON'T HATE THE GAME

Before we go on, I should note that **neither game denial nor game acceptance is a consciously held perspective**. They are, of course, *mistakes* we make because of unconscious biases and emotional investments in ideas and identities ("I am a radical anarchist!" invites game denial, etc.). They constitute subtle forms of self-deceit.

The moment game denial and game acceptance are recognized for what they are it becomes apparent that they cannot be sustained. Every one will vehemently deny their own game denial or game acceptance and claim to be a responsible "game changer" if confronted.

What then, is **game change**? It is the productive synthesis of game denial and game acceptance: **you accept that life is a game *and* you resolve to work to change it.** It's quite obvious when you think about it. Let's take a closer look.

Life is unfair because relations between sentient beings are layered in games for scarce resources. Through resources (of whatever form) we can reach for the sublime and approach our fundamental, unknowable God-nature: Through gaining access to food and favorable mates we escape the ever-present clutches of death and reach for immortality through reproduction. In human beings socialized within complex tribes or societies, death is defied by the extension of the idea of ego—my name, my recognition, my ideas, my deeds, my sacrifice, my devotion, my children, my ancestors, my style, my monument, my love, my passion. These are all, in their own ways, scarce resources, that are distributed, accessed and enjoyed through the playing of games.

The students of the psychology of death—a fascinating and promising field of empirical research that builds upon the heritage of Ernest Becker's *Denial of Death*—have produced plenty of experimental evidence to show we become more eager players of games when confronted with our own mortality. Humans have a strong unconscious drive to cheat death. When reminded of death, even in a subtle manner, we latch on to our identities, our wealth and our worldviews more eagerly—and we judge one another more harshly. True story.[25] The intrinsic and inescapable fear of the great gig in the sky distorts our cognition and turns us into game deniers or game accepters.

The bad news is that life is unfair. The good news is that life is a game and that its rules can change. These are two sides of the same coin. **The question is not "game, or no game", but the nature of our relationship to the game and the evolution of its rules.**

Games produce dynamics of interaction. They give life in *samsara* a temporal, fleeting meaning: maybe we can be winners, or at least avoid being losers, or at least hide we "really are" losers. They give an experience of *substance* to the fundamental, pristine, empty meaninglessness of phenomenal reality. They produce a story, a drama, where stakes exist, moves are made, victories won, losses cut and bitterly remembered. Games produce results. They produce losers and winners. Just like you and me. We all know both sides, in different contexts, to different extents.

The major objective of the metamodern political project is to **change the rules of the game**. Our simple message is that everyday life as we know it can and *must* evolve. The game change position holds:

- Life is a plus-sum game with possible win-wins.

- Life is *also* often a zero-sum game with lose-win.

- Life is sometimes even a tragic dilemma of lose-lose.

- But the rules of the game can change, evolving into *more* win-win, *less* lose-win and *less* lose-lose.

- Nobody actually ever "deserves" to lose games and suffer defeat or humiliation. Seriously—would you tell a kid that she "deserves" to be crappy at school? To be ugly and lonely or poor? To starve? To have low self-esteem? To have a fragmented, anxious mind? To be part of the losing side of globalization? That baby turkeys in industrial butcheries get what they deserve?

* All injustices in the world are caused by the playing of games.

* Humans and other beings have no choice but to partake in games.

* In the last instance, no injustice or suffering is ever excusable or tolerable.

* It is our ethical imperative, without compromise, to change the rules of the game.

* Successful changing of the game is that which:

  * produces more winners in life,

  * produces fewer losers,

  * softens the fall of the losers,

  * increases the rewards of the winners, and

  * makes people act kindlier and more fairly while playing the game.

The point is that **winning in life is never enough**. What if you become *that* successful? What if you get *those* hot young men? What if you save *that* many lives? What if you *really* save the world from climate crisis?

Then you'll still have a kid, or somebody else you care about, who is crushed and humiliated by the same game you played and happened to win. The game is still on. Still grinding. For every winner, there is a loser. You were that awesome idealistic writer who pointed out injustice? You were a hero? The very fact of your moral victory means that you just trashed, humiliated and outcompeted somebody else. That somebody else could have been you. It could have been your own child.

And more fundamentally—it *is* you. Winning in life is fun. But it's just not enough. Classical liberalism, neo-liberalism, conservatism, capitalism and fascism are all based upon accepting the game and an attitude of "may the best player win". They are all defenders and upholders of injustice, cruelty and suffering that just cannot be ethically justified.

So what if I win? In a deeper sense, you have still lost. You *must* change the games of life. That is the only result that counts. That is the only victory worth keeping, because it includes everybody.

The game of life will still produce losers and winners, but the results will be determined through much less bloodshed and losing will come at a much lower cost. This will be a society in which people get more than one shot at glory.

Don't hate the player, and don't hate the game either. We need to love the game, learn to play it—and change it, because we love the players.

Multi-Dimensional Game Change

Game change means to admit the game, even to play it lovingly, but seeking to change the way it works. Games have dynamics and these dynamics can work in directions towards grosser or more refined games.

All games have evolved from something else. When modern Western people compete for spouses we usually don't even reach the point of verbal confrontation. Lions fight and kill each other's cubs.

Our game is more refined, and its rules harder to learn. But obviously, games for sex, identity and partners have evolved. Just a few hundred years ago, intrigue in Europe would habitually involve physical violence and duels to the death. Nowadays it rarely does.

As we shall see in the coming chapters, game change is a *developmental* affair. It has to do with making advances into higher stages of societal development.

So, to sum this up, on the next page is a simple model of a holistic game change—presented as five-step process:

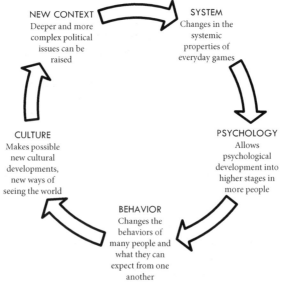

Figure: Game change. *See Appendix B for more on these different fields of development: system, psychology, behavior, culture.*

Can you see how the inner development of people is interlinked with the development of society as a whole? That society's function fundamentally relies upon the personal development of its citizens?

You can't just develop society by means of "imposing" a certain political system or changing people's values. Game change occurs by means of systemic change, psychological development of the populations, changes in habits and behaviors, and through cultural development. These fields— system, psychology, behavior and culture—develop together, as described in Appendix B.

Of course, many other interactions than the ones presented in this feedback loop are possible, but it gives us an idea of what it really means for society and humanity to develop.

Don't you ever dare tell me that dramatic and positive change is not possible. If you can't change people's behaviors, you might change something in the systemic incentives. If that isn't possible, you can always bring up new issues and find ways to change the cultural discourse. If that fails, you can always find a few people and help them develop their values so that they can form a new competitive social structure.

There is *always* a "chink in the armor". Somewhere there is always at least *some* leeway in any apparent grid-lock of society, which in turn opens up new possible developments somewhere else. There is always a promise of further development.

We are looking to create new contexts, new historical situations where what was impossible before now becomes possible. This is, needless to say, a dynamic process in which we need to let the different forms of development support each other.

The rest of this book is devoted to finding such promises. We'll squeeze in developmental leaps where people didn't think they were possible—so that we can make possible the transition to a metamodern society; one that is fit for the global, digital age.

For ardent readers: If you want to see how game change relates to some classical political philosophers, consult this footnote. [26] And, if you wish to examine some of the many levers you can pull to effect game change, read Appendix C, "Effecting Game Change".

Thus: Let go of game denial and game acceptance—and go for game change. The idea is not to eradicate competition from life, but to transform and refine the nature of competition in all aspects of life: on the labor market, in work culture, in the political deliberations and elections, in the games of love, sex and family, in peer groups and in research and education.

So again—don't hate the player.

And don't hate the game, either.

We need to love the game, learn to play it.

And change its rules.

Because we love the players.

Chapter 3

HISTORY'S DIRECTION

"Without order, nothing exists,
Without chaos, nothing evolves."

—From the rap text to *Heavy Metal Kings,*
  by Jedi Mind Tricks.

In this chapter we're going to catch the big drift of how human societies develop—more specifically, how the state develops: how order emerges. Obviously, this can hardly be done in any extensive manner in just a single chapter. Instead, what we're getting at here is a certain pattern relevant to the ensuing argument of this book: the **increasing intimacy of control**.

The reason we need to understand this development is that the metamodern politics I propose is a step in a historical evolution which has been unfolding for centuries. And, again, there is a logic to it. Counterintuitive as it may sound to many, **more complex societies need more intimate mechanisms of control.** This is because greater volumes of more complex human agencies and interactions are coordinated as society progresses to more advanced stages. You cannot reverse this trend without paying a very high price; namely, disorder and disintegration. Rather, the increasing intimacy of control must be made fair, balanced and transparent—as you will see.

It might be a bit heavier for readers not accustomed to studying history. But it's no less important. Take a breath of fresh air and get yourself a drink of fresh water (or something a tad stronger if that's your preference).

A DEVELOPMENTAL VIEW OF ORDER

For a more overarching view of historical development, you can consult my other book *The 6 Hidden Patterns of History*. Or, if you want a more comparative view of how polity has developed in China, India and Europe, you can take a look at Francis Fukuyama's masterly two-volume work *The Origins of Political Order* (vol.1) and *Political Order and Political Decay* (vol.2).[27]

Fukuyama argues there are three major ingredients of a modern liberal democracy:

1. **A meritocratic state bureaucracy** (where people are loyal to society as a whole, not only to their family or clan)

2. **Accountability of the government** (with a strong civil society capable of self-organizing and sometimes resisting the power of the state)

3. **Rule of law** (i.e. that laws are upheld and the government is restrained by the same laws as everyone else)

As we see today, some countries display all three characteristics (Western democracies), some display two (Latin American countries have states and accountability but generally a weak rule of law) and some display only one (like China, which has only a strong state bureaucracy and a limited form of rule of law). And they can be developed in different sequences. In this chapter, I focus more generally on the evolution of the state and its penetration into the everyday lives of the citizenry.

The developmental view of society has gone in and out of fashion a few times over the last few centuries as political and scientific winds and currents have changed. From relatively crude and moralistic ideas of the 19th century, according to which societies evolved from "savagery" to "barbarism" to "civilization", to the classical developmental modes of early sociology (including Marx, Comte and Weber), to the relativistic and nonjudgmental anthropology of Franz Boas, Margaret Mead and Clifford Geertz, to new generations of developmentalists who have chosen more careful wordings for the developmental stages—like the anthropologist Marshall Sahlins.

Even if the study of societal development is an issue ridden with landmines and potential misunderstandings, it is hard to deny the obvious fact that societies somehow develop—if not to "higher" forms, if not "forward", at least to *later* stages that are more complex, richer and form parts of larger systems of exchange.

The anthropologist Elman Service famously proposed four major stages: bands, tribes, chiefdoms and states. There is another model which I believe is far better at explaining the developmental aspects of historical change (the metamemes, as discussed in *The 6 Hidden Patterns of History*). But still, Service's model will do as a starting point for this chapter.

We are now to zoom in on the fourth and last of Service's stages: the state (or polity), in order to make an argument that is very relevant for understanding political metamodernism, the listening society and the Nordic ideology. Specifically, I wish to introduce a simple but exceedingly pervasive rule in the development of the state: **the rule of increasing intimacy of control**.

This rule holds that the polity, viewed as an emergent pattern of governance among humans, keeps evolving in ways that increase the monitoring and control of human behaviors by reaching into deeper layers of the human soul and putting it under deliberate, collective control. We are looking at the development of social order. It is furthermore, I argue, **this increased control that makes possible the civil liberties, human rights and liberal culture we currently enjoy. Order, freedom and equality go hand-in-hand. As with all three-part marriages, it's not always simple; but the three need each other.** I will qualify this controversial claim as we go along.

So, we will consider how the modern state has emerged in three subsequent stages: 1) the early modern state, 2) the nation state, and 3) the welfare state—and how we are now approaching the metamodern state, 4) the "listening society". This progression can be described in many different ways, but it quite certainly follows the rule of increasing intimacy of control.

1. THE EARLY MODERN STATE

Depending on how we delineate and define the issue, we can trace the beginnings of "the early modern state" to different times and places. Some kind of proto-modern state has existed for at least two millennia—Qin China, in the 200s BCE, was the first fully developed example. Qin China was more similar to modern bureaucracies than its ancient Egyptian, Mesopotamian, Greek and Roman counterparts.

Still, something quite distinctive happened around the 17th century in some European countries. With the risk of being simplistic and Eurocentric, we can focus on the year 1648.

The Peace of Westphalia in 1648 ended the grim Thirty Years' War. The war, which had raged across Europe and caused millions of deaths, triggered famines and elicited atrocities, was of course a complex and multifaceted affair. But roughly speaking, it was the result of a new order of political formations—early modern, Protestant, states—that ganged up on the old political order: the Holy Roman Empire, the papacy and the Spanish monarchy.

The Swedes, under Gustavus Adolphus, intervened in 1630, turning the tide of the war in favor of the Protestants—and according to some sources, in the subsequent five years they destroyed up to 2,000 castles, 18,000 villages and 1,500 towns all across Germany. That's some carnage; about a third of all Germany leveled to the ground.[28]

The Peace of Westphalia established the geopolitical influence of a number of states, notably the upstart Sweden. Most importantly, a new power balance emerged, guaranteed by the peace treaty, which replaced the old order based upon the idea of a universal, Catholic empire that knew no clear national boundaries, with that of a system of sovereign and mutually recognized nation states. No longer could one overarching power freely interfere in the domestic affairs of a foreign state. Each state now had the "right" to determine its own official religion, and religious differences were no longer considered a *casus bello* (an acceptable reason to declare war). The early modern state had come online.

At this point, in the 1600s, people's everyday lives were still at a considerable distance from the kings, queens, viceroys, stadtholders and councils who ruled them, and they rarely identified with their given "nationalities". People still spoke dialects, rather than standardized national languages, and they had relatively little to do with the state formation in their everyday lives, most still living off subsistence farming. People were yet to be *enfranchised* in the nation-building project to any greater degree. There were printed books, mostly Bibles, but no newspapers or any other press for the masses. Even if firearms had made knighthood less relevant, the landed elite and nobility still held distinct privileges by birthright, intriguing away around the royal courts.

Gradually, however, the state built up a stronger bureaucracy and aligned it with the social mechanisms of early capitalism and the growing merchant class. By instituting a higher degree of legal protection, granting the bourgeoisie political representation and adopting more rational fiscal policies, along with an uncompromising pursuit of mercantilist trading strategies (the practice of maximizing your own state's share of the international market), a number of smaller and more flexible states managed to garner increasingly rapid economic growth.

This early capitalism was of course geared towards a society in which, by our present-day measures, only slow economic growth was possible, so military, colonial and mercantilist expansion remained important throughout the period. But still, some powers successfully spurred growing economies. Hence, the Netherlands, England, Denmark and Sweden became strong European powers alongside France and Spain. In the Protestant countries, literacy rose as people were expected to read bibles, which complemented the needs of the growing merchant class and the expanding bureaucracy.

Even if France took measures to embrace the new economic and bureaucratic system, its problematic power balance between the crown and the nobility proved disastrous to its economy in the long term: As the aristocracy was favored at the expense of bankers and merchants, it lead to long-term fiscal crises and eventually to the French Revolution. Even in France's strong, absolutist bureaucracy, the attractors determined history's course: that its *ancien régime* of absolutist feudal monarchy was doomed. To this day, the glory of the baroque period and the reign of Louis XIV smack of excess and vanity.

In the 1700s, Russian ruler Peter the Great, and his spiritual heir, German-born Catherine the Great, struggled to reshape Russia in the image of the Western powers. They recognized that the structure of the early modern state was distinct from, and competitively superior to, the medieval estate system. What was initially an attractor in the sense that a certain inherent logic made it likely to occur, became an *explicitly recognized* attractor—it caught the attention of central actors and was deliberately strived towards by forward-thinking rulers.

So in the early modern state you see a first phase of modern governance: steps are taken to increase the rule of law, optimize taxation, support and stimulate businesses, increase manufacture, ally the state to the merchant class and hence create a simple form of polity enfranchisement in broader layers of the population, establish a class of bureaucrats and simple forms of accountants who made possible a kind of "national economy". And I have only briefly mentioned the military, which at this point played an important role by being the nexus around which e.g. Prussia and Sweden were built.

What you see, in other words, is an expansion of the level of control the state holds on people's everyday lives. The states that manage to increase this control the most are also the ones that became dominant during the period since this penetration of everyday life increased the ability of larger groups to cooperate in more complex ways.

This does *not* mean that whatever king is most despotic has the greatest advantage. On the contrary, the *less* monolithic states and rulers become more powerful because that's how the polity successfully manages the most information, coordinates the greatest quantity of behaviors, and enfranchises the highest number of agents. The issue at hand is to build the strongest institutions to manage such flows and to let people be productive within more complex divisions of labor. In this vein, in England, you even see the birth of modern institutions such as the Royal Society (1660), to actively and deliberately promote science, and the Bank of England (1694) to coordinate the monetary flows.

The libertarian view, and perhaps the common sense of our time, is that freedom grows as these developments unfold. But that's really only half the picture. It is no coincidence that this period, early modernity, is where the French philosopher Michel Foucault takes off in his studies of power and control in modern society. Writing primarily in the 1960s and 70s, his important insight was to point out that control *also* grows as modern society progresses: that everything—from trade flows, to births and deaths, to bodies, to inner organs, to sex and sexuality, to gender, to time management, to city landscapes—becomes increasingly subjected to minute control, monitoring and standardization.

Even if Foucault is sometimes accused of being overly paranoid in his depiction of these developments, he wasn't really talking about some deliberate conspiracy. Rather, Foucault simply showed that our common sense of increasing freedom and individuality must be seen as illusory in the grander scheme of things. Today, more than ever, we are being controlled by a multitude of sources that lie beyond our conscious consent—at a greater distance from us. These sources of control are much less tangible than our former feudal bonds.

It is not, then, the power of the king that grows, but the volume and density of *power itself* that increase. Not the visible authority of one person over another, but the raw capacity to shape and coordinate human bodies, actions and souls. Although Foucault never spoke in these terms, he was describing **power as an emergent property of the self-organizing system that makes governance of a more complex society possible**. And in that sense, power increases as the system becomes more differentiated and develops more intricate social technologies of control. The early modern state encroached upon the lives of peasants and merchants, beginning to shape them as cultural and psychological beings.

A new stage of order emerges.

2. The Nation State

The next stage of this development emerged during the 19th century in a dynamic interaction with the processes of industrial modernity: industrialization, urbanization, conscription, bureaucratization—and the growth of industrial capitalism.

Sometimes people like to focus on 1776 as a watershed: a nexus that unites The American Declaration of Independence, Adam Smith's *Wealth of Nations* and James Watt's steam engine. But the nation state grew in full only during the 1800s, beginning from the most industrialized countries, notably Great Britain.

The industrialization processes unfolded in what has roughly been described as "Kondratiev waves" (after the early Soviet economist Nikolai Kondratiev)—waves of new technologies that were introduced, expanded for a period of time and eventually came to form the basis of the economy. The details need not concern us here, beyond the fact that the nation state emerged in ebbs and flows during the first three of these waves of industrialization:

- The industrial revolution—1771 and onwards.
- The age of steam and railways—1829 and onwards.
- The age of steel and heavy engineering—1875 (until the wave of oil, electricity, the automobile and mass production, which is said to begin in 1908).

The point is that the transition into an industrial society makes state building possible on a whole new scale. As people move from farming to factory work and wage labor, many more people gather in small urban areas and develop new and similar economic interests. Because there are now quite effective firearms and printed papers or pamphlets that can easily be distributed to large groups, a new family of threats emerge to the order of society: riots, strike and revolution.

The birth of the nation state stems from the taming and harnessing of the forces of the growing urban masses: of the active and deliberate effort to coordinate people's everyday activities and lives at a massive scale. As industrial (and colonial) capitalism increasingly coordinates people's time and attention across time and space through the emergent patterns we call the firm, the company, the corporation, or just "business"—so does a corresponding coordination occur at the level of the state's monopoly of violence.

The increasing complexity and size of the market make it possible for states to garner the spoils of economic growth, in turn increasing how effectively their violence can be projected—internally, against the citizens, and externally, across the globe.

In this period you have processes such as the creation of a national narrative, a heroic story (often involving, among other things, gathering around a charismatic leader, inventing a semi-mythic past, and sometimes killing off some poor minority that happens to stand in the way and offer a convenient common enemy and/or scapegoat for mounting social and economic problems), spreading literacy, homogenizing language and scrapping local identities, instituting market laws and standardized court systems, getting rid of large parts of corporal punishment, gradually increasing the emotional and economic enfranchisement of larger groups into the state (vote for bourgeois men as well as conscription into the armies), i.e. turning people into "citizens". And, of course, there is schooling: turning kids into pupils and pupils into citizens. "Everyone" learns to read and write.

Classical social anthropologists of nationalism, such as Ernest Gellner and Benedict Anderson, have noted there was an inherent link between the growth of 19th century nationalism and the requirements of the capitalist-industrialist economy, and they are probably right.

From these nation-building efforts, another great modern sociological force is awakened. When citizens begin to read, gather in smaller spaces, communicate more easily, and have more in common in terms of interests and sorrows, a "civil sphere" is born.

People download a whole mental world of "ongoing events" fitting within a greater story, shared largely by any random person you meet on the street. Memes (ideas and cultural patterns) spread more easily. Strangers become oddly acquainted by means of a new world of abstractions: What is the time, what is this address, what is your nationality?—and later: What is your passport, your personal identity number? The French Marxist theorist Althusser has argued that an "ideological state apparatus" comes online, one that appeals to each person *as* a citizen, which thereby "creates" the citizen, the subject of a state.

And with the nation state and the civil sphere, "the individual" can be born since our "selves" no longer remain as intimately tied up with our clan, our family, our land. People start identifying with their nationalities, their class, their ideas, their professions and intimate relationships—a betrayal of all identities of old, but an expansion of our overall freedom to find our own paths, and, in some ways, an expansion of our circle of solidarity. We now care about people we've never met, given we share the same nationality.

But the birth of a nation is a dangerous affair. You grab thousands—no, millions—of people's attention for years; mold and discipline their minds: they become school teachers, doctors, professors, engineers, lawyers, administrators, accountants, scientists, military officers. Then you direct the awesome power that emerges as all of these specialists collaborate. Before you know it, you are capable of sending manned expeditions to the moon and taking pictures from within the rings of Saturn.

It's true, the Chinese had been educating mandarins—the culturally refined and meritocratically organized administrative class of the empire —for millennia. Medieval Europe had monasteries with monks, nuns and scribes, and some corresponding structures had appeared in the Arab empires and India. But this was different. The extent of differentiation and specificity of the modern professions were staggering. And then all of these people, competencies, forms of knowledge, forms of control, were unleashed—upon nature, yes, but even more so, upon the human soul: working, molding, transforming, transmuting, controlling, steering; all stimulating new shared patterns of thinking, sensing, feeling and behaving.

The birth of a nation is dangerous business *because* of the great powers unleashed when an emergent pattern coordinates millions of people's time and attention. What will this power do? In what image will it shape humanity? What will it do to nature and the environment? What ethics will restrain it? Who will control the controller? Wonders arise and abound: the Statue of Liberty, the Eiffel Tower, the World Fair. And when this power turns to murder and oppression, there is horror unbound: colonial oppression, the Belgian Congo, mechanized warfare, eventually Gulag. And because there is a civil sphere, it can be manipulated by relatively small groups or even a single person—for noble purposes or wicked ones.

There are any number of candidates for the lead roles in this story of the nation state, but I would like to specifically mention two. The first is Napoleon Bonaparte. It is true, of course, that Napoleon became the dictator of France and was crowned emperor, even marrying a Habsburg princess, in effect betraying the ideals of the French Revolution he claimed to serve. But if you look at his political regime: citizen enfranchisement, nationalism, standardization, rationalization, homogenization, the modern legal system (called *Code Napoleon*)—this is certainly a herald of, and model for, the modern nation state. The philosopher Hegel noted that Germany should follow suit. And Germany did.

The second protagonist is the public school. That many, then most, then all people go to public schools, is a development so radical and pervasive that it really has no counterpart in history. Not only is basic literacy spread to everyone—from the piano playing mansion girl to the drunk, train hopping hobo looking for work—but the nation state begins to mold the breed, in the role of pupils, into its mental framework. Millions of people taught and taught, and disciplined and manipulated for years on end. This even includes physical education for military purposes and public health. The democratic states legitimize their control over years of children's lives in terms of civic virtues the children are thought to acquire: reasoning, independence, a sense of equality, responsibility, self-discipline. All of this works in tandem with the stimulation of science and engineering. Armies of school teachers are raised and in turn taught to respect the authorities of universities within natural sciences and humanities. The public school transformed humanity in the image of the nation state.

But of course, there are other contenders for the protagonist role of the nation state. The police is one. Police forces emerged in France and England—first in 1667 in Paris, when law enforcement was centralized under Louis XIV's absolute monarchy.

But criminological historians generally draw a line at the so-called Metropolitan Police Act of 1829 in London. At this moment the police was given a lot of its present shape. The originator of the reform, Sir Robert Peel, explicitly relied upon the utilitarian philosopher Jeremy Bentham, who also suggested the *panopticon* model of criminal justice: a prison where all cells are open to surveillance from a central tower with shaded windows.

The army redcoats were redressed in blue and armed with batons rather than rifles so as not to cause confusion among the unruly workers. With this kind of organized, centralized monopoly of violence, targeting not foreign powers, but the delinquents and rioters of the population itself, you have a new kind of state formation. This model is then exported across the world until more or less all countries have police forces—today sometimes larger than the regular army.

But who were the police officers expected to discipline? The workers, of course—another contending protagonist in the history of the nation state. Workers. There were so many of them, crammed into such narrow spaces, under such strong pressures and strains, during such chaotic and dramatic upheavals, with such high-stake games and so many temptations.

The police show up in tandem with the industrial proletariat. To this day, all over the world, our criminal justice systems and policing target the lower classes of society. It is also the children of this segment who were first given basic education on a mass scale, before the peasants, which turned urbanized workers into citizens before the rural peasantry.

The bourgeois class existed already in the early modern period. But it was only with industrial capitalism that the proletariat emerged in full. Historians have perhaps insufficiently emphasized the intimate connection between the industrial worker and the nation state.

Napoleon and schools—or perhaps the police and the proletariat, played the major roles. The nation state is an emergent pattern of governance, of human self-organization, of the management of complexity.

The central insight here is that the sheer volume of political power increases. People begin to be freed from their immediate social surroundings (your extended family and vocation) and to be integrated instead in a more abstract common social reality: the nation state. Your *individuation* as a unique person is married, as it were, to your *integration* into a nation. (I will return to the issue of (in-)dividuation and integration towards the end of this chapter.)

When the individual "becomes" something more than her social role in the family or the village, she gains a kind of individual identity. And thus her "soul" can be conquered, tamed, seduced, manipulated in new and more profound ways. Napoleon's words echo through this period:

> "A man does not have himself killed for a half-pence a day or for a petty distinction. You must speak to the soul in order to electrify him."

In other words: You no longer buy power with mercenaries, because power lies in the minute control of the soul. The greatest power—the greatest force of birth, creation and destruction—lies beyond the early capitalist structures, beyond the human agency coordinated by money.

The individual's innermost thoughts and dreams can be aligned with a more abstracted social order of things, her longing and lust and search for immortality can be tied to the nation, its victories, tragedies and progress. Again, there it is: the increasing intimacy of control.

Who, then, will control the mechanisms and institutions that awaken and shape these powers, and for what purposes? The history of the 20th century, and its great wars, seem to revolve around this very question.

3. THE WELFARE STATE

In the 20th century this tendency towards greater intimacy of control takes on yet another level of magnitude. With the emergence of the welfare state, built "on top of" the nation state, forms of coordination and control that hitherto had been unimaginable become reality.

The strangest part is perhaps that the dramatic expansion of the state's control mechanisms happens so effortlessly, so inconspicuously. Nobody notices, really; it just sneaks up in the most self-evident manner. And it changes everything.

Early signs of a welfare state show up already in Bismarck's Germany, beginning in the 1880s. Even if some sprouts are visible already in the 1840s in Prussia, it is only with Bismarck's united Germany that redistribution of wealth is quite deliberately used as a means to increase the enfranchisement of citizens into the state project (and, as many have noted, to curb socialist movements and reduce the threat of revolution).[29]

The manner in which I here consider the welfare state is not only a matter of redistribution of wealth. It is rather, and primarily, a whole world of interrelated mechanisms of controlling and coordinating people's bodies, minds, personalities and behaviors.

At a very basic level, we see how the social expenditures of states went up, especially after the Second World War. In the US, for instance, income taxes went up dramatically from 1935 (14.6%) to 1940 (40.7%), due to the war effort. After the war taxes stayed at that level, even slowly increasing (by 2015 it was 46.5%).[30]

What you see here is a vast expansion of the capacity of the state to collect taxes in an orderly fashion over longer periods of time—earlier forms of states had simply not permeated the economic life of society to any comparable extent. Also, the economies were much larger, so the *de facto* revenues were increased by powers of ten. What, then, is this increased revenue used for?

Enter the minions of the welfare state: social workers, psychologists, sociologists, statisticians, public health officials, urban planners, more doctors and nurses and assistant nurses, dentists, accountants, economists, political scientists, public relations experts, employment counselors, more teachers, liberal professors—and, of course, administrators, administrators, administrators. An endless onslaught of highly educated people —professionals—monitoring and controlling increasingly complex and intimate parts of human interactions.

It is difficult to overestimate the scope and force of this transformation. These highly specialized people develop innumerable competencies in everyday life: how to measure us, how to avoid conflict, how to nudge us in different directions, how to steer conversations, how to elicit replies from us.

The sociologists Peter Miller and Nikolas Rose made a name for themselves by studying these many minute and subtle techniques social workers, counselors and accountants use to govern society. Without these many micro-techniques of control, the state we know today could hardly exist.

Miller and Rose noted, quite clearly, that the modern state apparatus relies entirely upon this massive, ongoing everyday activity. They also note these activities often underpin the existing economic and social power structures in society, in everything from social work to accounting.[31] Being leftwing sociologists, Miller and Rose naturally worry this intricate web of control may have become too influenced by "neoliberal" market logics of present-day capitalism. This political stance aside, Miller and Rose still touch upon something crucial: the enormous amount of coordinating and controlling "micro actions" people perform every minute of the hour, every day.

This is, unsurprisingly, also what I have found in my earlier ethnographic studies of the police. Sitting in the backseat while the police patrolled the inner city, I noticed any number of subtle strategies of control. Similar findings are present in other police ethnographers like Loïc Wacquant, Abby Peterson and William Ker Muir. The security and social services serve us, but they also control us. Serving one person often means controlling another's behavior.

Welfare and control, to a large extent, go hand-in-hand. They are two sides of the same coin. Think about it. In Sweden today, this "free" society, the state keeps almost everyone in school for twelve years, gets involved with broken families, brokers toxic marital relations, teaches us about safe sex, sexuality and gender equality, peers into the very cavities of our bodies: the mouth, the vagina, feeling through our breasts for cancerous lumps, recommends us what to eat, funds our smaller newspapers, supports us in getting our lazy buts to the gym, treats our madness—if necessary, force-feeding the non-compliant patient with drugs and liquid nourishment. Is this level of control not approaching what George Orwell imagined in his novel, *1984*?

And yet—strangely—the people of Sweden (and other welfare states) hardly seem to mind. Sure, there are a few frustrations and scoffs at exaggerations here and there, but by and large, people appear to feel relatively free, not oppressed nor violated.

Even if the Nordic countries offer a prime example, the growth of the welfare state is not isolated to these. The Danish sociologist Gøsta Esping-Andersen famously described the "three worlds of welfare capitalism" in his 1990 book with the same title, noting there are different systems: the social democratic (Nordic countries), the conservative (Germany, Japan) and the liberal (the US). Other taxonomies have been proposed, but they tend to largely overlap with Esping-Andersen's. Even if the welfare systems are different and their levels of pervasiveness vary, the overall pattern holds across the developed world: the rise of the welfare state, and with it, a great leap in the level of intimacy of control.

Never before have societies controlled the bodies and souls of their populations to a comparable degree. Never before have abstract patterns of power encroached this much on everyday life: minds molded with cognitive behavioral therapy and drugs, bodies shaped with health campaigns and changed with surgery, relations affected with counseling, brokering and advice. What a strange matter of affairs!

I am presenting this development of control as if it were an oppressive monstrosity. And it *can* be. In totalitarian societies it certainly is. As this power and control grows—which seems to be the case even today, given all the new research about behavior and all the available information and all the learning and acquired silent knowledge of the professionals—then so do the risks of people feeling violated, subtly manipulated. Or disappointed, because the expectations and general sense of entitlement also grow with higher welfare.

But it doesn't *have to* be oppressive. For the most part it isn't. Rather, what we see is a steady expansion of **social rights** or **positive freedoms**. Social rights are, in opposition to negative freedoms, the services people can expect from society. Negative freedoms have to do with what you can expect people *not* to do: imprison you, stop you from going about your business, stop you from expressing an opinion, harm your body. These are human rights or civil liberties expressed negatively, by what people must *not* do. Positive freedoms deal with the things people are legally bound to give you, if you ask: basic education, healthcare, a subsistence minimum. **Not then the "freedom *from*", but rather, the "freedom *to*"** (as many theorists of social rights, e.g. Erich Fromm, Sir Isaiah Berlin have noted).

There will always be a tension between the positive freedoms and the negative ones. If you, for instance, use the forced labor of one person to give someone else a basic subsistence, it would obviously mean you have sold out basic human rights. Hence, many libertarians and conservatives have argued, we would do best to scrap the idea of social rights altogether. Furthermore—so the argument goes—too many social rights can lead to unrealistic expectations and foster a population of spoiled brats, unwilling to and incapable of taking responsibility, lacking any industriousness and resourcefulness.

These arguments need to be taken seriously. If we have to choose between negative freedoms and positive ones, we should opt for the former. But the reality of the welfare state speaks its clear language: welfare systems exist in all advanced societies and they seem to increase, rather than decrease, the freedom of people. If carefully and skillfully implemented, they seem to subtly change the games of everyday life, leading to more progressive values, to higher effective value memes.

All of this leads us back to Michel Foucault and his observation that modern society has gradually expanded the system's control over every aspect of everyday life. His answer to this dilemma was to muster a staunch, intellectual resistance: to criticize and unmask power wherever possible. This, of course, only offers us an anti-thesis, and no clear pathway ahead, no visions for society.[32] I have a different take on it, as you will see in the next section.

Basically, again, we see that the increasing intimacy of control works in tandem with the evolution of a more complex society. We see that this increasing intimacy of control is, in fact, that which *allows* highly complex and free societies to function. What would happen if it—the massive control apparatus of the welfare state—was entirely removed, by a magic spell, next Monday morning? Would people be more free, or less?

Less.

4. THE LISTENING SOCIETY

Okay, this chapter has thus far been working its way towards a conclusion directly relevant for the future of free and democratic societies. Let's bring it home.

Can we really expect the next stage of society, following the modern industrial one, to have an equal pervasiveness and intimacy of control as compared to the current one? To have less? I'd be hard pressed to draw the latter conclusion. **The pattern over history is clear: more complex societies have more intimate mechanisms of control.** It is a development which has been ongoing for at least the last 500 years, and it is unlikely to be reversed for more than short periods.

Rather than dismantling or shunning this pervasive control we must make it publicly owned, talked about, transparent—full of checks and balances. **The issue is not to avoid *any* control, but to avoid bad, unscientific, corrupt or despotic control.** We need intelligent information systems—in an abstract sense of the term: not computers, even if they do play a part, but good ways of handling the huge amounts of information about which services work to emancipate us, and which ones oppress us, and who this applies to and why and under which circumstances.

After all, we *do* want someone to look into our mouths and vaginas to find out if we're healthy; this lends us more freedom rather than less. The question is just if it will be Kim Jong Un peering into our bodily cavities or an emissary of our own enlightened self-interest. The historical attractor is there, working with tremendous force, and we are left with the question: Who will gain this control and how will it play out?

With all the new science and technologies cropping up—neuroscience, psycho-physiology, collective intelligence, complexity science, bio-engineering, epigenetics, technological body enhancements, digitally supported education, virtual reality, AI—this power will increase by yet another magnitude.

A bold suggestion presents itself: We should embrace it. Carefully, kindly, openly.

That is what the vision of **the listening society** promises: creating an even *more* sensitive welfare system on top of the existing one. The welfare state is insufficient when it comes to match the sheer complexity of the period we are now entering (transnational, global, postindustrial, digitized, etc.). We can and must make certain we use these new powers to develop society. We should monitor and aid the growth of deep existential relationships to reality, of our growth as citizens, of pro-social and sustainable behaviors, of empathy, caring and norms, of complex thinking, of which meta-narratives we organize ourselves by.

Such development doesn't necessarily have to be organized around "the state". We can imagine other solutions in which civil society and markets play a larger part. But we cannot avoid the question altogether: Given these greater powers of intimate control, what should we do? Most likely, this greater control will need to be developed in a meshwork of state, markets and civil society.

Depending on how far Left, Right or anti-establishment you are, you are likely to want to see different balances between these elements. But let us leave that discussion to the side for now and focus on the main point: that the listening society can be built. And that it should.

No doubt, once political metamodernism grows, it will split into a right wing and a left wing—but these factions will still be *relative* allies when compared to the modern ideologies of socialism and libertarianism. The most important issue at hand, however, is to recognize this pattern in the first place and to raise it as a political, social and economic issue of primary importance and urgency: the cultivation of a higher form of welfare, of a listening society.

We have the possibility of creating a society in which we are happier, healthier and more of us have more universalistic values and strivings in our everyday lives. Such a society would be more stable and less prone to crisis—economic, political, social or ecological. It would be more resilient.

So after the welfare state, the next attractor ahead is yet another major increase in the intimacy of control: a listening society where the inner lives of all citizens are supported, where many more of us reach the later stages of personal development, and where there is much less alienation, loneliness and misery.

Utopian? Yes, in a relative sense.

THE PATTERN: (IN)DIVIDUATION AND DIFFERENTIATION

How do humans change as the intimacy of control increases?

A strange matter of affairs under this increasing intimacy of control is that populations don't really seem to become more complacent and homogenous as it unfolds. Quite the opposite seems to be the case, at least in the countries that maintain a solid rule of law and a strong civil society besides an efficient bureaucracy.

In larger and more complex societies, people seem to develop *more* individualized personalities, values and worldviews, not less. Or to be more specific and analytically correct, we could say that people in more complex societies develop more **dividualized** selves (borrowing the term "dividual" from Gilles Deleuze, which replaces the "individual").

An important aspect of this is that people develop into higher value memes and, despite their apparent individualism, also seem to develop more universalistic, inclusive and non-sectarian values. As we have noted, the people of welfare-jacked Sweden display much higher average value memes than their Afghani fellow world citizens. You will, for instance, find more environmentalists and animal rights activists in Sweden than in Afghanistan.

This is due to the dynamic, dialectical and painful dance between two poles: (**in)dividuation** and **integration**, an idea that has been proposed—albeit in simpler forms—by many theorists. The classical sociologist Émile Durkheim famously observed that modern society progresses by increasing the differentiation of the division of labor, which in turn makes each person work with more and more individualized tasks, hence developing more unique skills and experiences. These unique contributions are then integrated with each other in a more refined economy. Accordingly, this was an analysis of what Durkheim called "differentiation" and integration.

Erich Fromm, the 20th century social psychologist, argued that the development of human personalities evolve as each person finds an individual path and relationship to life, which in turn always reasserts more universalistic values and strivings. Fromm used the word "individuation"—but since I believe in the "dividual" rather than the "individual" I'll stick with "dividuation".

You can find a corresponding idea in classical American theorists of social psychology and education, such as George Herbert Mead and John Dewey. And, of course, you find similar theories in contemporary social philosophers like Jürgen Habermas and Axel Honneth. And all over philosophy, really. And there are even versions of it in complexity and systems' science.

I would like to offer a similar but distinct bid for this theory, one that relates more closely to the present theory of the increasing intimacy of control and history's developmental direction—a theory of "dividuation" and integration.

The idea here is, again, that richer, larger and more complex societies offer much greater opportunities for people to develop unique experiences, skills, ideas, relationships and perspectives. Societies that integrate larger quantities of human activities, natural resources and flows of information create fertile soil for the growth of a myriad of human perspectives and experiences. Greater economic and social integration spur higher dividuation: People are finding and recasting their "selves" and their relation to life on new, higher and more subtle levels.

The tragedy of the matter is that **this increasing dividuation *also* entails a corresponding difficulty for each of these unique souls to find ways to really match their inner drives, hopes, motives, ethics, skills and distinctive gifts with the world around them.** If you identify as a farmer, a family member and a good Christian, these identities are relatively simple to act upon and it is rather easy to have them accommodated by your social surroundings. If you instead become a vegan whose greatest talent is to write poetry and criticize society, your family members and colleagues are less likely to be as accommodating.

It is often our highest hopes and dreams, the parts of ourselves that are most universal and most intimately held and cherished, that are not seen, heard, given recognition and successfully integrated into society. Hence, more and more people simply feel *alienated*. It is not really that the world has become a colder, lonelier place. It's just that the integration of these many unique souls is a more complicated and difficult matter. *Because* people have come farther in their dividuation, more people also feel estranged, lonely and subtly dissatisfied.

As alienated and highly dividuated people we naturally struggle to find new social settings and environments in which we can truly "be ourselves"—hence the obsession with this imperative in today's culture. Sometimes we are at least partly successful in these strivings and feel we have "finally found a home": in a particular social network of likeminded activists, in the expressions of certain forms of music, anti-establishment sub-cultures, more personally sensitive forms of business management and so on. We find ways to *reintegrate* our new selves into correspondingly new social settings. But by doing so, we have again increased the integration of society. We end up creating new and even subtler forms of oppression. From there on, we can dividuate even further, starting the painful cycle again: Our new homes help us grow, but eventually we may outgrow them and end up demanding even more delicate forms of integration.

Modern society, for all its mechanisms of intimate control, has produced more highly dividuated people than any former society. And, as a result, you have a whole army of sensitive souls who feel unseen and misunderstood. Society as a whole becomes increasingly emotionally sensitive and in greater need of more subtle, profound and complex forms of social integration. When such integration fails, life feels empty and meaningless. The road to greater freedom and higher development of the self is a beautiful—but also tragic and ultimately very lonely—journey.

As such, modern society suffers from a chronic lack of deeper and more complex forms of integration. Societal development spurs the growth into higher stages of personal development, but higher stages of development create an increasing pressure upon society to break the prevailing alienation.

But—and this is a big but—**every attempt to create more intimate integration risks becoming a new source of oppression**. Whenever people try to relate to one another at a deeper and more intimate level, including larger parts of our authentic emotions and inner selves, to some it may become suffocating and pressuring.

New oppression—albeit on a higher, subtler level. When we, for instance, create new playful ways of organizing our corporations, in which everyone is invited to partake more authentically, we also share larger parts of our inner selves and are expected to show up more "fully" and to be more emotionally involved. But some are bound to not quite "feel it" and will necessarily feel pressured and subtly manipulated. When we create greater social engagement and caring, those who are unable to experience the same emotions feel suffocated and that unrealistic expectations are being shoved down their throats.

New oppression. When we democratize governance and more people get involved in decision-making, many of us feel stuck in endless discussions. When we introduce mindfulness and yoga at work, some will feel they are expected to waste their precious time with meaningless woo-woo. When we make our organizations more personal, some of us feel stuck in more personal issues and conflicts in which our vulnerabilities become all too apparent. When we create greater transparency, some feel more surveilled.

New oppression. When we use "nudging" to promote sustainable and prosocial behavior, some will feel that others are pulling their strings. When society becomes more tolerant and multicultural, some of us feel confusion and estrangement as we are expected to successfully interact with people from more varying cultural backgrounds—and may be shamed as racist if we fail to comply. When social movements adopt more profound communication techniques (such as *Art of Hosting* and *Theory U*), people can easily feel drawn in farther than they had expected or wanted. When spiritual and "self-development" communities create more intimate ways for people to share their inner lives, some feel pressured to overshare and end up having their intimate secrets used against them.

When we feel alienated, we seek reintegration. Metamodern politics, and the listening society, must empower people to reintegrate the parts of life that have been spliced into shards: the personal, the civic and the professional. We must be allowed to live as whole human beings. We need to live fuller lives. We need to be able to show up as a vulnerable, real person at work, and do work that is meaningful to us in terms of our values and views of society.

But the dark side of deeper reintegration of the spheres of life—the personal, the civic and the professional—is the emergence of new and more subtle forms of oppression. **Integration is necessary for more complex societies to function, but it can always, sooner or later, become controlling or even icky and creepy.**

This is the tragedy at hand: a painful wheel turning from integration, to oppression, to resistance and emancipation, to greater dividuation and alienation, back to new integration.[33]

The different political strands of mainstream Western politics relate to different parts of this wheel of dividuation and integration. None of them have successfully identified the whole process.

Socialism is largely an *integrative* movement, seeking to create greater integration by means of democratically governed bureaucratic measures, working against alienation—beginning already with the pre-Marxist socialists. Libertarianism and neoliberalism defend the rights of the individual against oppression, but they largely lack an understanding to balance out the alienating effects of modern society and its way of turning everything into a matter of money, material gain and calculated exchange.

Fascism and populist nationalism can be viewed as integrative over-reactions to the alienation of modern society, seeking to revive obsolete forms of community and belonging (corresponding to earlier value memes). And ecologism is largely an integrative movement, seeking to reintegrate human life into the biosphere and often into local communitarian initiatives.

The metamodern view is to support the necessary reintegration of highly dividuated modern people into deeper community—or *Gemeinschaft*—but to do so with great sensitivity towards the inescapable risks of new, subtler forms of oppression.

Hence, the task is to balance out and support the forces of integration *and* dividuation. This is what the listening society must be able to do.[34] Nobody said it was going to be easy. But there it is: The increasing intimacy of control is linked to higher personal freedom, though in a difficult and painful manner that easily spirals off into oppression. We must relate productively to this dynamic.

See the model below for a graphic summary:

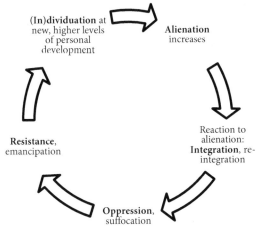

Figure: (In)dividuation and integration. The necessarily tragic and painful wheel of societal progress.

If things go well, the turning of this wheel—for all the pain and com-plication it involves—leads to higher freedom, to a profound kind of soc-ietal progress. We dividuate as people and integrate in more complex ways, and this changes the nature of society, which in turn affects who we are as human beings. If it goes poorly, it leads to oppression and/or alien-ation—and sometimes fierce overreactions against these.

This development of higher freedom is the topic of the following two chapters.

Chapter 4

ANOTHER KIND OF

FREEDOM

Are we free? Are you, me and everyone else in the democratic West, the supposedly "free world", as free as anyone is ever going to be? And how do we even measure how free a society is in the first place?

The mainstream way of measuring freedom in a country these days is championed by Freedom House.[35] This institute monitors the rights in each country, if there is free press, if there are free and fair elections, freedom of association, human rights violations and so forth. Each country is graded from a score of 7 (least free) to 1 (most free). Countries like Sweden and the US get a rating of 1, whereas countries like North Korea and Saudi Arabia are rated "not free" with a bottom score of 7. Russia is also, notably, "not free" with a score of 6.5.

The last decade or so, as I write this in 2019, freedom around the world has slowly been on the decline, reversing a long trend in the opposite direction. In the latest Freedom House report, 44% of countries were described as "free", 26% as "not free" and 30% as "partly free" (including countries such as Ukraine, Turkey and Mexico).

There can be no doubt that these are important statistics and that they offer an important tool for debate, research and political movements around the world. There are, however, also severe limitations to this measure. The greatest limitation is that it makes it appear as though there can be no higher conceivable freedom than what has already been materialized in e.g. Sweden or the US. I am not questioning the methodology of Freedom House—it serves its purpose and fulfills an exceedingly important function. Rather, I would like to suggest the possibility of yet higher forms of freedom being achievable through the transition from a modern society to a metamodern one.

My basic argument is this: **People are only as free as they really *feel* in their everyday lives**. If you look at the population in a country like Sweden, you notice that some citizens are in fact much *more* free than others. How can that be? I thought that, in Sweden, "all animals are equal"? After all, they all live in a country with the best Freedom House rating possible. Yet some people wake up in the morning feeling they have control over their lives, while others are driven by fear and shame, constricted in so many subtle or complicated ways. Consider these examples:

- Is a person freer if she gets to follow her dreams and work towards goals and ends that are genuinely inspiring, rather than having to work only to pay the bills?

- Is a person freer if she dares to speak her mind in every situation, rather than feeling she has to hold back in order to avoid the judgment and disdain of others?

- Is a person freer if she feels that she is a responsible participant of her community and society, rather than a passive spectator?

- Is a person freer if she can make life choices without fearing for her financial security?

- Is a person freer if she can walk down the street and meet no beggars, see less social misery and not have her mind filled with commercials vying for her time, attention and money?

- Is a person freer if she consumes goods and services in order to do something she believes in rather than acting out of inner insecurities?

- Is a person freer if her mind is affected by less cognitive biases and prejudices?

- Is a person freer if she makes most of her choices in a calm, harmonious state of mind rather than a stressed, anxious one?

- Is a person freer if she has many different positive identities to choose from, so that if she fails in one regard, she may still flourish in another?

We can safely answer each of these questions with an emphatic "Yes!" It should not surprise us, then, that from this perspective most people are not quite free in a deeper sense of the term—not even in the Nordic societies. From this viewpoint, the Nordic countries are not conclusively "free". Rather, these societies have the *prerequisites* for higher freedom.

Freedom House rating 1 is where the path to true human emancipation begins—not where it ends.[36]

As such, I would like to suggest **another kind of freedom**. Not a vague one that would offer excuses for (and obfuscations of) the oppression that goes on in China or Russia—but one that builds upon what has already been accomplished in the freest societies; a definition of freedom that points skyward, towards a more deeply felt and pervasive freedom encompassing all aspects of everyday life.

The basis for this theory is the idea that **freedom must be *felt* and *embodied* by the citizen in order to be real**. Hence, we look for support in the sociology of everyday life and, more specifically, in the sociology of *emotions*.

None of this is to downplay the significance of legal structures and the constitutional rights of citizens as measured by Freedom House. However, for the word "freedom" to have any value, to be truly meaningful, we need to include the emotional aspect. After all, if we don't *feel* free, what does it then matter to live in a country rated "1"? Emotions are just as important a part of freedom as our institutions and legal rights, and in order to reach higher levels of freedom, people must be *emotionally* emancipated.

To strive for less, to call it the day when we've established rule of law, independent courts, freedom of expression and universal suffrage, is not only unambitious, it is even unethical given the suffering caused by feeling unfree.

Let us speak about another kind of freedom; one that begins in chains, slavery and fear, in the wailing tears of a billion years' history of life—and ends as a democratic, inclusive dance of spontaneous becoming.

FREEDOM AS EMOTIONS

In Book One we discussed the "inner states" of people—and I claimed that these are more fundamental than emotions. The inner states relate to the totality of what your living experience *is like* at any given moment; every moment can be more or less clear, crisp, enchanted and alive—and this includes spiritual experiences. The inner states are very important since they make up the totality of how we experience the world: light or dark, high or low, harmonious or utterly confusing.

But even if subjective inner states are more fundamental, this does not mean emotions are unimportant. Emotions are different because they have a certain direction; we generally feel something *about* something, we are angry *at* this person, ashamed *because* of this or that misstep, proud *of* our this or that achievement. In grammar, prepositions specify relations between things—and emotions often come with prepositions. If we are in higher states, we generally react with different sets of emotions, but the states and emotions definitely do interact. And emotions still play a very crucial part in (almost) all social life for (almost) all people.

Another important topic in Book One was the study of human flourishing and happiness. Some readers, no doubt, felt the focus on happiness seemed a bit naive. But, of course, *negative* emotions also play a major part in everyday life and societal development. And if we are to expand human freedom and development, we are obliged to offer them their due concern, touchy and difficult as it may be.

If you accept this argument, it makes much more sense to believe that the collective good of freedom is always intermeshed with a wide array of basic and complex emotions, and that **the anatomy of freedom must always follow the anatomy of human emotions**.

The most solid way of introducing emotions into the study of freedom is to start from a negative: **Can we imagine a concept of freedom that would completely *exclude* all emotions?** Can we be free while being controlled by a paralyzing terror or shame? Not really.

So, if emotions should not be excluded from the study of freedom, what would be a productive way of introducing them? A simple but powerful way to do this is to study **how different negative emotions can and do constrain people's freedom.**

For that, we need to get some help from the sociology of emotions. As it turns out, when we point skywards, we also point inwards.

SOCIOLOGY OF EMOTIONS TO THE RESCUE

The great sociologist of everyday life interactions, Erving Goffman, wrote his most important works in the 1940s, 50s and 60s. He had a way of cynically describing and commenting upon how we adjust to, and are steered by, the situations in which we take part. This was the study of, in his own words, "Not, then, men and their moments. Rather moments and their men."[37]

Moments and their men. Situations. In psychology, a corresponding development occurred in the 1970s with the emergence of "situationist psychology". It argued, and showed experimentally, that people's actions and choices were more affected by the situations we are in and less by our personalities than previously assumed.

A key idea in Goffman's work was that people collaborate in each everyday situation to keep it going, to define what is going on, to keep up appearances. We "save each other's faces" by avoiding topics or withholding comments, we ignore small mishaps even if everyone noticed them, we stretch our backs and put on a face before we enter a friend's house, we conceal our nose picking and stained underwear, we find ways to subtly neutralize and diminish painfully obvious differences of class and status. When any of this fails we feel embarrassment or even intense unease and shame.

Ah, shame. That's the point here. We have all been implicitly trained, since early childhood, to try to avoid it. The reason everyday life functions so smoothly after all, despite us all being rather neurotic and unreliable, is that we all play a part in avoiding to be the "social marauder" who wrecks the flow of everyday situations. Small children will sometimes sabotage situations by pointing at someone and asking why they smell, or ask auntie why she never cleans her house. But the rest of us generally stay in line. With astonishing obedience.

Everyday life, in which we go about our business and seek to attain our goals, is only made possible because there is a huge underlying machinery that checks any attempt to break out of it. And we all keep the machinery running with exquisite skill, quite automatically. We don't stop and think about it; we simply adjust by not even considering the other options available for actions that could in theory be taken but just seem too weird. This is perhaps true of large, urbanized modern societies in particular, but it seems to have cross-cultural bearing. You can go to the shanty towns or slums in India or the favelas in Brazil, and most people will act in a recognizable manner: avoiding to shame themselves, avoiding to be of hassle (unless it's a desperate salesperson or a robber), saying hello before they speak, taking turns in conversations, displaying some dignified demeanor and signs of cleanliness. Sure, the norms vary, but some of the mechanisms are undeniably the same.

Yet shame is not the only emotion humans habitually and unreflectively avoid. There are, of course, a host of other negative emotions that steer our everyday choices and interactions: fear, guilt and the envy of others. We are all programmed with a huge battery of behaviors that masterfully avoid all such negative emotions. We are all obliged to wear that ball and chain. Only once the negative emotions are out of the way, once we are out of harm's way as it were, we can go about our day.

Indeed, the process of "socialization"—when we grow up and become members of society by internalizing how to talk, behave and so forth—can be described as the learning of a host of behaviors that serve to avoid negative consequences; from the most concrete habits of not walking on red and safely navigating the melee of cars and pedestrians on the streets, to the subtlest ones like knowing when not to speak our minds and pretending not to notice when someone spits when they talk.

This underlying machinery can look quite differently depending on which society you are part of. And different emotions will steer your behavior depending on the situation. Are you avoiding being slut-shamed by your family, or just avoiding the ridicule of your peers? Shame is steering your actions. Are you avoiding a death penalty for speaking up against the Great Dictator? Fear is steering your actions—even what thoughts you may allow yourself. Are you avoiding God's judgment of your inner desires and heretical thoughts? Guilt is steering you. Are you not following your dreams because people around you would disdain your attempts and subtly withdraw their support? The envy of others is controlling you.

The classical psychologist of emotions Paul Ekman noticed that there appears to be six basic emotions: anger, disgust, fear, sadness, happiness and surprise. There are of course more emotions than that, but these six come with their own more or less clearly recognizable facial expressions, which Ekman believed proves that they must be biologically rooted. Interestingly, four of them are *negative* emotions (anger, disgust, fear and sadness) while only one is directly positive (happiness), and one being more or less neutral (surprise).

A major challenge to Ekman's theory has recently come from the constructivist psychology of Lisa Feldman Barrett and her team. When they tried to reproduce Ekman's experiments by traveling to different foreign cultures to see if they could recognize the same facial expressions as specific emotions, they did not offer a set of pre-given alternatives as Ekman and his associates had. It turned out that people in foreign cultures indeed had different ways of understanding and describing emotions.

Emotions turned out to be less universal and more socially and culturally constructed than previously assumed. And not only that. There appears to be no specific "neurological fingerprint" in the brain as different emotions arise, or even a specific physiological pattern. You get angry, and it can mean anything from tension to release to calm seething. In other words, emotions are much more complex than our everyday language can grasp; a language we use to try to catch the essence of elusive chimera that are always momentary, specific, context dependent, observer dependent and where the description of the "thing" (the emotion) cannot be separated from the emotion itself. If "God" could see the truth of your emotions, "He" would not be limited by the confines of any specific language.[38]

Point being: Even if I go on talking about a set of "negative emotions", we should recognize that these can be delineated, described and known in any number of ways, with different results. As I go along to present the negative emotions and their interrelations, we must not make the mistake of thinking of these suggested terms as "inherent essences". The same, by the way, has been shown in the cognitive/cross-cultural study of colors— did you know that "blue" didn't really exist until the Egyptians came up with a word for it? That the older parts of the Bible are devoid of blue seas and skies, and that rural cultures in Angola still to this day lack a word for blue and that members of these can't even recognize the color, taking it for green? Likewise, emotions in general are delineated and described diff- erently across cultures—they aren't God-given essences.[39]

EMOTIONAL REGIMES: HIDDEN IN PLAIN SIGHT

It's not that negative emotions are all bad, or that they have no important role to play. We cannot just remove them and "be free".[40] In fact, society wouldn't be possible without negative emotions. If we all were to be enti- rely liberated from shame and guilt when behaving inconsiderately or harmfully towards others, society would soon plunge into a brutish and nasty state. Life would probably be considerably shorter too.

As such, it's not as simple as to merely liberate people from negative emotions altogether and then expect we'll all be freer as a collective whole. We must acknowledge that we as a society need negative emotions to reg- ulate our behavior.

But at the same time we need to remember that negative emotions aren't predefined by nature; that it is we, as a collective, who make others experience shame and guilt, and that these **emotional regimes** can be more or less justified, be more or less in tune with the current societal conditions. Negative emotions like shame, guilt and envy are socially dependent; they don't emerge autonomously in a given person, but are always derived from society's norms, values, routines—and most of all, the games of everyday life. But as we saw earlier, these games can be evol- ved, they can be changed. And the result can be more or less oppressive, more or less free.

For instance, a society where gays feel ashamed about their sexuality, women feel guilty about their perceived shortcomings as mothers, their lacking beauty and their inadequate careers, and men feel envious about the supposedly higher social status of others, is a *more oppressive* society than—all other things equal—one in which these emotions are less prevalent. People who have their lives controlled by such emotions are simply less free than those who do not. **There are different emotional regimes in different societies**.

Still don't see the connection between emotions and freedom? Well, try this sentence out for a moment and see how it fits: "All of my life, I have been controlled by shame, never daring to express myself because I felt so ridiculous, and I wanted to live as a homosexual but a sense of shame stopped me, and I wanted to move to another city but I stayed here because I feared to lose the support of my family which would have left me begging for food." Or how about: "I am profoundly unhappy in my marriage but I have no choice but to stay because my husband would guilt-trip me and I would have nowhere to go." Freedom blowing through your hair? Nah.

Then stop for a moment to consider: Are any of these examples covered by the definition of freedom as "political rights" or "civil liberties"? Certainly, legal rights and liberties may contribute to letting us break out of these little prisons, but they hardly exhaust the picture. You will find plenty of people in the free Kingdom of Sweden to whom the suffocating sentences above apply.

If you buy the hypothesis of **ever-present negative emotions being avoided through our choices and interactions**, you can see that these emotions, and the reasons we may have for feeling them, set the limit for our **degrees of freedom**. We act, think and even feel within certain constraints derived from the emotional dynamics of the society we live in.

And in a way, this is often *more* important to our sense of freedom than the legal rights we enjoy. After all, are we free to practice our sexuality if people spit on us on the streets for being gay or call us sluts? Do we have relational freedom if people tell us it's our own fault we got raped or beaten up by our spouse? How freely can we express ourselves in the face of the scorn of people we care about?

Emotions are *social* by nature, especially in humans. I feel something, pleasant or unpleasant, because of how you treat me or interact with me. If I'm turned down, I feel shame; if I'm scolded, I feel guilt; if I'm threatened, I feel fear. Other humans have the ability to produce intense emotions in me: you can mesmerize me with your sexy body, disgust me with your odors and unwanted sexual advances, comfort me with your touch, exalt me with your words of appreciation, frustrate me and depress me with your lack of response.

If freedom is emotional, and emotions are social, it must thus be apparent that **freedom is a "collective good"** in the sense that economists use the term. *Because* emotions are social, and freedom depends upon emotions, freedom is social, and thus <u>collective</u>. The degree to which I can enjoy freedom largely depends on a long chain of interactions in everyday life, on how you and everyone else act, think and feel. If you feel judgmental, disdainful, hateful or envious towards me, and I am not in a position to ignore your reactions, it limits my freedom. It curtails my very thoughts and motivations in a thousand ways. It stunts me in my becoming of myself.

If most people around me feel negative emotions towards me, I lose almost all freedom and I am reduced to an impoverished existence where all my choices are about avoiding these negative emotions targeting me.

There is, in this sense, an **economy of emotions**, where my feelings are profoundly interconnected with yours. Such an economy can be rich or poor; it can generate many lifetimes' worth of shame and fear or relative comfort and joy. This economy can be productive, or corrupted, have great ecological fallout (the joy of one being the misery of another); it can be lean or heavy-going, fair or unequal, effective or ineffective—just like the conventional economy of goods and services.

In this sense, our emotions have an inescapably transactional side. Negative emotions targeting me often cost me something. And *which* negative emotions you have towards me also make a great difference: If you disdain and shame me, it's after all more manageable than if you're in a hateful frenzy against me and threaten my physical safety. Hence the collective emotional reactions of my surroundings largely determine the severity of my shackles—or conversely, the heights of my freedom.

Since we avoid the negative emotions, since we avoid different forms of judgment by self and others, we are always being steered by an emotional regime, a regime present in every interaction—hidden in plain sight.

THE SPECTRUM OF JUDGMENT

So we have mentioned a few different emotions that control and limit our everyday lives with different avoiding-mechanisms—a somewhat different set than Ekman's basic emotions, these being:

1. Fear
2. Guilt
3. Shame
    and...

Sklavenmoral; the "internalized envy of others" (which relates closely to what Nietzsche called "slave morality" in German; with the risk of bending the Nietzschean term, I will use this word).

These four emotions target our *self*, or "ego": "I could die!" or "I am a loser!" Each of the four has a corresponding emotion when they target someone else, the *other*, when they target "you" or "alter"—as you will soon see. In any society you are likely to have these emotions lying dorment as control mechanisms of different sorts—whether it is Mamluk Egypt in the 13th century or present day Denmark.

At the basic level, then, beyond all measures and constitutional differences and changes of social norms, the reason we can say contemporary Denmark is "more free", is that people are avoiding different sets of emotions in their everyday lives than in 13th century Mamluk Egypt. If you screw up in today's Denmark, you get shamed on an internet meme and people call you names. It's nasty, yes, but you don't get tortured and stoned to death. If you have strange opinions and habits in Denmark today, people think you're a weirdo and you might have trouble getting a job. In 13th century Egypt, however, you may have to deal with the prospect of going to hell—before being ostracized and/or stoned at the town square.

Emotions are *always* there, and they always play a part in every political and social reality. After all: it's one thing women get stoned in Saudi Arabia because of sharia laws—but who exactly does the stoning? People with strong emotions of anger and judgment cast the stones, not holy scriptures. If people didn't have these feelings, would they remain just as eager about physically punishing women for violating dated chastity codices? Probably not.

Is it a coincidence that homosexuals enjoy greater freedom *to* express themselves and on average have more freedom *from* verbal and physical abuse in the "happier" Nordic countries than in the troubled, post-communist societies of Eastern Europe? No it's not.

The relatively higher freedom in the Nordic countries is closely related to a more tolerant and acceptant emotional regime than e.g. Russia or Pakistan. For instance, beating up gay people or throwing acid in the face of young sexually active women is as illegal in the former countries as in the latter, but somehow the emotional regime in the latter is more prone to generate negative emotions leading to such actions. Our personal freedom even often depends more on the prevailing emotional regime than on our legal rights. And the two develop together, or not at all. The freedom *to* be gay, but without the freedom *from* shame, fear and physical abuse, is, after all, no freedom at all.

Luckily, history has taught us that we can develop and change the emotional regimes that govern our lives, and that there is a progression in which we have managed to liberate ourselves from the extent to which negative emotions control us.

As seen in the following table, there are four different sets of negative social emotions, each being some form of "judgment" of the self or other:

"THE SPECTRUM OF JUDGMENT" Or: The Progression of Emotional Regimes	
EGO (self) aspect	ALTER (other) aspect
4. *Sklavenmoral*, internalized envy	4. Envy, jealousy, schadenfreude
3. Shame, embarrassment	3. Disdain, contempt, ridicule
2. Guilt, feeling impure	2. Judgment, moral outrage
1. Fear, terror	1. Hatred, rage, aggression

Hence, you can think of these emotions as **the spectrum of judgment**. It should be clear that the emotional development of a population plays a major part in determining how free life *de facto* is: We can, collectively and (in)dividually, climb or descend this spectrum of judgment.

These emotional regimes regulate our behavior by making us avoid repercussions from others: 1) fear impels us to avoid hatred and violent aggression, 2) guilt to avoid moral judgment, 3) shame to avoid contempt, and 4) *Sklavenmoral* impels us to avoid that *others feel envious* of us.

We normally don't walk around actually *feeling* these emotions; yet we are, to differing degrees, controlled by them: *Because* we avoid them, we don't usually feel them, but because we do avoid them, we remain in their grip.

They constitute the invisible machinery that lets everyday life in any society run smoothly; indeed, that makes any society functional at all. **Again: The avoided negative emotions are, as it were, *hidden in plain sight*.**

Subtler and less grossly oppressive emotions are of course the most difficult to detect and to understand. In the field of emotional psychology, there is relatively little work on envy, an emotion which is almost always hidden away, even to the person who feels it. *Sklavenmoral* (literally "slave morality") is the internalized envy of others; when we feel subtle shame, not for our shortcomings, but for our strengths, talents and aspirations. *Sklavenmoral* has, to my knowledge, only been theorized in Jungian terms —often in "integral" and New Age circles—as the "golden shadow". The golden shadow is an expression of disowned greater potentials within ourselves which can lead us to idealize others, or to envy their talents.

Scholars in this field sometimes make the distinction between "feelings" and "emotions". Feelings are more a day-to-day business; they fluctuate throughout the day, as we feel happy or sad, frustrated or calm and so on. The "emotions" I'm talking about here are more deeply layered processes within ourselves: we love our families, are ashamed of our positions in society, are embittered by perceived injustices or disappointments and so forth. When we talk of emotional regimes, we mainly mean these more durable "emotions", even if "feelings" may also play a part.

An important side to this is that the ego-emotions (fear, guilt, shame and *Sklavenmoral*) all partly depend on their "alter" counterparts (hatred, judgment, contempt and envy). If my mind is full of contempt towards fat and poor people, then I'm more likely to target myself with these emotions, feeling shame if I should become fat and poor myself. If I am judgmental towards the perceived moral flaws of others (justifiably or not), then I'm also likely to judge myself more harshly, feeling like an unworthy piece of dirt. And the reason I feel such contempt and judgment is that I have internalized a shame- and guilt-regime and begun to avoid certain behaviors. As you can see, the "ego" and "alter" versions of the emotions are intimately connected.[41]

All of this lands us in what might look like a paradox: On the one hand, all societies rely upon these negative emotions—and our elaborate, learned, often subtle behaviors to avoid them—on the other hand, they limit the freedom of each and every person and the expressions of our relationships in all aspects of life.

Yet everyday life doesn't work without sanctions. Sometimes we *do* need to condemn people for their actions. The question, then, is not how to get rid of these negative emotions altogether, but how to *develop* them. The answer to the dilemma is, again, a developmental-sociological perspective; **the insight that freedom is a collective good—that we are freed together, or not at all, and that this is a matter of collective, or rather "transpersonal", development.**

So once the highest Freedom House rating has been achieved, we are left with the momentous task of increasing freedom by developing how people truly feel, and specifically how we feel about and relate to one another.

Look again at the many citizens frolicking about in Stockholm. Each of them goes about their business, saying hello to friends, getting a coffee on the go, hurrying to their next appointment. On the surface they look as if they are making autonomous, individual choices. But then look at the streets of Pyongyang in North Korea—can you really tell the difference? Here people are also, by the look of it, moving around freely doing their thing. And still, we know that the people in downtown Stockholm enjoy much greater freedoms than citizens of Pyongyang. The invisible shackles are heavier in Pyongyang than in Stockholm, but they are present in both places, just to different degrees.

Look at it this way: What about all the things these people *aren't* doing or expressing, all the hopes and inclinations that are suppressed and never talked about? How many are driven to work to make money to buy expensive clothes in order to feel more adequate and less ashamed of themselves? How many are stuck in peer groups in which they are not respected? How many are pressured to do things at work that don't rhyme with their values and convictions? How many simply feel they aren't good enough? If all of these people were free in a deeper sense of the word, wouldn't they use this freedom to address these issues?

The lack of freedom is, in this sense, largely invisible. And yet it is there. Our shackles insert themselves even prior to our conscious thoughts, prior to our choices made, our values formed, prior to the formation of our personality and sense of self.

Freedom is a collective concern, yes, but it is also intimate and relational. Hence: transpersonal.

Yet this is no reason to despair; rather, it impels us to ask for higher freedom, for *another kind of freedom*. It's good news, in a way, because it means that the great game for human emancipation is still on.

The Hierarchy of Negative Social Emotions

Before we go on to analyze the emotional constraints to freedom, we must recognize the *hierarchy* of negative social emotions of control. The spectrum of judgment follows a certain logic or order.

- fear trumps guilt,
- guilt trumps shame, and
- shame trumps *Sklavenmoral* (the internalized envy of others).

This hierarchy is far from obvious; many of us have known severe feelings of shame and know how exceedingly painful and paralyzing they can be. But stop for a moment to think about it. If you had the choice of being shamed by everyone as an ugly, bizarre, stupid and smelly loser, *or*, living with the guilt of having pushed a toddler out the window from the tenth floor, which would you choose? Despite the intense pain of strong shame, most normally functional people would prefer shame over guilt.

But can fear really trump guilt? I offer you another gruesome example: the civil war in Yugoslavia of the 1990s. You had people torturing one another, slaughtering innocent civilians with knives and degrading them in death camps. When lives and physical safety were at stake, people circumvented their feelings of guilt and apparently acted without conscience— not to mention that any trace of a sense of shame and propriety was suddenly gone with the wind. Fear and hatred could easily overturn any moral order and turn society into a nightmarish slugfest of abuses. When intense fear was activated under an intermittent reign of terror, notions of guilt went out the window.

These grim realities speak volumes about the dark side of the human soul: that our notions of guilt can be expelled if we are put under sufficient pressure of fear and if the normal order of everyday life breaks down. To this day, people in Bosnia, Serbia and Kosovo are still grappling with the trauma that people they knew and cared about could commit such atrocities, inform on each other, refuse to help, or simply become passive onlookers to murders and crimes.

And shame certainly trumps *Sklavenmoral*; shame relates to feeling bad because of your perceived negative sides, lacks and weaknesses—*Sklavenmoral* relates to a subtler form of shame, one that targets your strengths, hopes and aspirations. *Sklavenmoral* is when you are ashamed of your own strengths and positive traits. Even if *Sklavenmoral* (and its corresponding "alter"-emotion, envy) can be incredibly corrosive, it is hardly as painful as feeling inferior or unworthy.

Another way of recognizing the hierarchy between the four families of negative emotions is by comparing it to Abraham Maslow's classical hierarchy of needs. As you may know, Maslow argued there is a complex (not entirely straightforward) hierarchy in which people first seek out physical safety and survival, then seek to establish membership and inclusion into a community, then to gain esteem, recognition and self-confidence within that community, and then move on to higher needs such as self-actualization, self-expression and even self-transcendence.[42]

If you compare this to the four families of negative emotions, a clear pattern presents itself:

- **Fear** relates to maintaining physical safety by avoiding rage, hatred and aggression, i.e. to the first, **basic** needs according to Maslow's hierarchy of needs.

- **Guilt** relates to being a worthy member of a community, to showing one's moral worth and value, that one is qualified to participate in society in the first place—so it has to do with **belonging.**

- **Shame** relates to being an esteemed and recognized member of our in-group; we feel ashamed when we do not consider ourselves worthy of respect, the opposite of which is pride and **self-esteem.**

- And *Sklavenmoral* relates to our higher aspirations and longings, holding us back from **self-actualization**, productive self-expression and ultimately from self-transcendence.

This is the hierarchy of negative emotions: fear, then guilt, then shame, then *Sklavenmoral*. By collectively climbing this hierarchy, we reach higher freedom.

FREEDOM AS SOCIETAL DEVELOPMENT

I have suggested that the different emotional regimes correspond to different stages of societal development, and that they follow the hierarchical logic described by Maslow: During early civilization, security remained the main concern in most people's everyday lives; hence the fear-regime was the most dominant. Then, as states grew stronger and increasingly managed to protect the life and property of citizens, the need for belonging became a more prominent issue, in turn making the guilt-regime the dominant one. And in modern societies, where the majority enjoy the privilege of being considered good citizens and no longer worry whether they're seen as sinners or heathens, self-esteem has become a greater concern in many people's lives, which has opened the door for the shame-regime to take over.

And today, in the most developed parts of the world, a new trend towards greater acceptance of people's differences and perceived flaws is increasingly making the shame-regime less prominent. As a result, a growing number of people tend to be more concerned with the higher emotional need for self-actualization.

This is a development of increased freedom: first we liberate ourselves from fear of violence, then we liberate ourselves from the guilt of not being deserving members of society, and finally, as we're seeing today, we're liberating ourselves from the shame of not being perceived as good enough.

This doesn't mean everyone in modern societies today never worry about violence or becoming moral outcasts. But most of us, most of the time, do enjoy the freedom to do and say what we damn please without risking physical abuse or social ostracism. And in a future, more listening society, most people will be free to be who they are without being ridiculed or looked down upon.

However, at each stage, as we liberate ourselves from the constraints of the previous emotional regime, there will always be another kind of "unfreedom" as well.

Allow me to put this into a historical context.

It is commonplace within social science to see early state structures as local warlord entities who uphold the social order by threats of violence and physical dominance. The main emotional regime is hence based on fear. If you remove the fear of the warlord, or the fear of outside threats the warlord is protecting you from, society falls apart—as has happened many times throughout history. The earliest state structures can therefore be said to be governed by the **fear-regime**. If you consider the gruesome dictates of early codes of laws, such as Hammurabi's code (dating back to about 1754 BCE, in Babylonia), you find all sorts of grim corporal punishment and death penalty for relatively small transgressions—the fear-regime in action. Grim as it is.

At the time of Hammurabi, fear simply remained the most efficient means available to governments to regulate people's behavior. But as societies grew larger and more complex, new social technologies came online—such as honor codes, ethics and organized religion. Fear and violence as regulatory means thus got supplemented by abstract ideas of right and wrong, pure and impure. Beginning in the 1st millennium BCE, in both the Abrahamic religions in the West and the Buddhist[43] and Confucian traditions in the East, we see an increased emphasis on moral purity and hence upon *guilt*. Then, the heroes were no longer proud warriors and conquerors, but saints and sages: those who are free from sin and who serve higher, often divine, purposes.

Supplementing a fear-regime with a **guilt-regime** offers notable competitive advantages to the governments who master it competently. Guilt is, first of all, more "cost-efficient" than fear. Coercing people into follow-

ing the law and paying their taxes requires expensive weapons and soldiers. Paying a priest to tell folks they'll accumulate bad karma and go to
hell if they don't behave nicely can be done rather cheaply. In addition,
since people generally do what they please if they believe they can get
away with it, fear of physical punishment will only be efficient as long as
the risk of being caught is sufficiently high. No spear, no fear. And since
it's impossible to survey and patrol all of society all of the time, there will
always be areas and situations where fear is less efficient. A guilt-regime,
however, doesn't require the continuous presence of soldiers to be efficient. If the socialization process of a person has been successful, emotions
of guilt arise automatically from the judgments of others whenever they
do something prohibited—all without any direct interference by rulers.
All that's needed is our own guilt-stricken soul.

The guilt-regime also has another perk up its sleeve: It can increase the
likelihood of people treating each other better. Fear is a rather rudimentary means of regulating behavior: "do this, don't do that, or else!" Given
the high costs of maintaining the trustworthiness of the "or else", it's only
economically viable to limit its use to things such as ensuring that people
don't kill each other or steal each other's property. Threatening people
with force if they won't treat one another kindly or help each other in
times of need just isn't very likely to work.

Religious leaders like Jesus and the Buddha argued against the rule of
sheer force and recast the theologies of their times in more egalitarian and
forgiving terms: The God of the New Testament is less fear mongering
and more forgiving than the one in the Old Testament—Yahweh was
originally the deity of war in the pre-Judaic Hebrew pantheon. But the
God of the New Testament is still more demanding when it comes to honest devotion and purity of intentions. And the Buddha places greater emphasis on personal responsibility for one's own enlightenment. The fear-
regime is thus supplemented by a guilt-regime, which partly diminishes
the logic of fear in everyday life.

The guilt-regime can even be militarily advantageous. The traditional
Japanese warrior code, the Bushido, let the minds and bodies of the Sam-
urai be trained to let honor and loyalty trump the fear of pain and death.
Such codes of honor and valor work by disciplining the mind and letting
guilt (and shame) defeat the more basic emotion of fear. This leads to
military strength and social cohesion, which makes for collective competitive advantages.

The transition to the third stage, the **shame-regime**, which is tied to
the emergence of modern society, has been extensively described by the

social theorist Norbert Elias (who never employed this terminology, but whose sociology certainly feeds into this model). When Elias lived in London as an exile (a German Jew who fled the Nazis), he sat down to work in the British Museum. There he came across a wide array of etiquette guides from different epochs and noticed a striking pattern: The etiquette became increasingly refined as Western Europe modernized. Whereas the early guides contained rather crude suggestions, such as not wiping one's nose in the table cloth and not burping in public, the later ones revolved around more subtle things such as the correct use of cutlery and how to entertain exquisite conversations.

From these observations, linked to an analysis of the political developments at the courts, Elias formulated his theory of *the civilizing process* (presented in a 1939 masterpiece with the same title).[44] What you see here is that modern life entails a transition into a behavioral self-regulation at the royal courts, into sophisticated "manners" instead of knightly "valor". These ideals later spread to the bourgeoisie (as these sought to emulate the nobility), and then to society as a whole as the middle class grew, emphasizing qualities of personal propriety and a "dignified" or "cultured" or "civilized" demeanor of ordinary citizens in urban life.

Elias shows us how the strong norms of cleanliness (showering, showing up at work in a ironed shirt every day, eating carefully, avoiding to let out bodily sounds or odors, keeping our homes neat and tidy) make an entrance and take root as modern society emerges. The fact that these norms hold people so firmly in their grip today can be seen as a result of this civilizing process. And the way we keep a polite distance, respect the privacy of strangers and generally keep our neurotic thoughts to ourselves can also be seen as outflows of this emotional regime.

If anyone breaches any of these codes without a good excuse (I'm a comedian; this is a bachelor party; this was a social media experiment or flashmob; you're on Candid Camera!; this is a therapy session, etc.), they do so at the risk of being viewed as weird, creepy or at least very unreliable. Instead of fearing the warlord, or feeling guilty before God or the community, modern people self-regulate according to a large host of mechanisms of shame and embarrassment. The obsession we have with embarrassment, in everything from movie comedies to reality shows to radio talks where people call in to share their embarrassing stories, serves to underline just how pervasive the shame-regime is in modern society.

Of course, shame exists in pre-modern societies as well, but it does not have the same degree of pervasiveness and importance as a regulator of everyday life interactions. For this reason, it is hardly surprising that the great sociologist of modern everyday life, Erving Goffman, focused so much on the role of shame and embarrassment in our interactions—as have many of the contemporary students of the sociology of emotions, notably Thomas Scheff.[45]

Again, it's not that fear and guilt entirely disappeared; it's just that they have been pushed further into the background. Fear and guilt are still the means used by the justice system to prevent people from breaking the law, but this plays a minimal role in most people's lives. In functional modern societies, violence and public condemnation are simply minor concerns to the majority compared to that of being seen as a loser, a slob, a hypocrite, being fat and ugly, not being sufficiently refined and cultivated, etc.

That modern people spend so much time and energy on such concerns may appear petty and unnecessary, and to a large extent it is. However, the shame-regime does regulate a multitude of subtle behaviors that are needed for society to run smoothly.

Modern society depends on a much greater amount of daily interactions among a higher number of people than in any earlier society. For this high level of social complexity to be possible, it is required that people interact with each other as little friction as possible, with little external regulation. In such a setting it is crucial to have a shame-regime that impels people to be more considerate: to treat one another with a minimum of respect and politeness, respect other's personal space, not saying offensive things, not to smell, not making a lot of noise, not showing anger, not throw garbage around, and so on.

This is quite important when millions of strangers with different beliefs, values, social status and interests must go about their daily business with one another in a hectic and stressful urban environment without ending up in quarrels and fights all the time. And it is something the fear and guilt-regimes just aren't suitable for. After all, sending in the cavalry or issuing a fatwa every time someone burps or says something offensive simply isn't feasible.

So once again we see a clear progression: *fear* is capable at regulating the most fundamental behaviors needed for society to function (preventing murder, theft, etc. make people pay taxes), *guilt* can make people treat each other in more benign way, and finally we have *shame* which can make people more considerate towards each other. Again, we also see how the later emotional regime is more cost-efficient than its predecessor: from the very expensive monopoly of violence of the fear-regime, over the less costly religious institutions of the guilt-regime, to the almost free-of-charge social norms of the shame-regime.

The transition to the shame-regime became much more pronounced in the general population during the 20th century. Shame and embarrassment may ultimately be less powerful than guilt and fear, but they are certainly easier to elicit in people in a world of mass media and an ongoing debate in a public sphere. During World War One, for instance, there was a clear difference between the propaganda posters of the Germans (emphasizing loyalty, honor and sacrifice) and those of the slightly more modern British and Americans (emphasizing the shame of being the only man not at the front, being a girlish coward "Gee, I wish I were a man, I'd join the navy!" or asking "Are you a man or are you a mouse?" or showing a picture of people contributing to the war effort, asking the viewer "What are *you* doing?"). These examples all speak to the esteem of the self, to shame. The British propaganda proved especially efficient, and there was even a problem with young boys pretending to be older than they actually were so that they too could go to war. As a result, whole cities and villages all over Britain were emptied of young men at the beginning of the war even though conscription had not been introduced yet.

The way the British government used the shame-regime to bolster its military capabilities during the First World War is actually similar to how modern companies make us buy their products. Commercials often rely upon an elaborate balance between eliciting desire and shame. Because self-esteem is such a prevailing concern in the lives of most modern people, we're flooded with commercials targeting our insecurities and emotional need for social recognition by tuning into the prevailing shame-regime. We're thus taught to feel ashamed about a bit of dandruff, being a little fat, having unfashionable clothes, even our hairy armpits (if you're a woman).

And with that, we enter the new battlefields of modern society: the many struggles to reconstitute the shame-regime; to change which behaviors and identities can and should be shamed, and which to be liberated from it.

You see, the struggles for "freedom" change at each stage. Initially, the fear-regime was contested by various monopolies on violence that challenged each other in mortal combat to determine who should be feared, who's freedom should prevail: the independent Greek city-state or the Persian Empire, Roman law or Attila the Hun, the Islamic caliphate or Genghis Khan—at stake is the kind of "freedom" that Mel Gibson yelled about at the top of his lungs in the movie Braveheart (disregarding the fact that Braveheart is notorious for being one the most historically incorrect movies of all time).

Then, as the fear-regime waned in favor of the guilt-regime with the great world religions and wisdom traditions, the struggle began to define and redefine what kind of guilt-regime should prevail: who does God condemn, what should be seen as sin, whose moral teachings should we follow, and so on. This is where we find the great schisms between Sunni and Shia Islam and the Roman Catholic Church and its Greek Orthodox counterpart, the many conflicts between Christians and Muslims, the brutal crackdown on heretics during the Middle Ages, and the religious wars between Protestants and Catholics.

Today, as we've killed God and freed ourselves from sin, the great struggles for freedom revolve around the issue of defining the mechanisms of shame and stigma: enter the queer movements, feminism, the recent #metoo phenomenon, in which women cast off the shame of revealing sexual abuse, campaigns against slut-shaming, fat-shaming, stigmatization of people with disabilities, you name it. They all seek to alter the everyday games of shame and acceptance.

The struggle for freedom has thus shifted from what society ought to consider crimes, to more subtle and intimate aspects: not being shamed as a slut, being fat, having hairy armpits. That the gay parades gather under the banner of "pride"—the opposite of shame—is a telling sign of it being an attempt to redefine and overthrow the shame-regime.

And when modern societies hold their leaders responsible for scandals and misuses of power, it is the role of the media to publicly *shame* them. This form of behavioral sanction is more common than outright legal prosecution. Officials avoid social and political *faux pas* and getting "involved" with the wrong people, as these things can end promising careers overnight. Shame controls our leaders, even the rich and powerful.

Hence, there is a progression from fear-regimes, to guilt-regimes, to shame-regimes. At each stage it can be argued that the degrees of personal freedom grow. But at each stage you also get another struggle, another playing field—another kind of freedom.

Chapter 5

FREEDOM'S BEYOND

F reedom, as we have now established, is not a question of either or. We will never reach the point of absolute freedom, and never will the quest for higher freedom come to an end.

Whenever we obtain one form of freedom, another kind appears at the horizon. So when it today seems as if our journey towards freedom has come to its final conclusion, "the end of history", it is simply because we have reached a temporary plateau from where we are yet to see what lies beyond—a new and higher plateau we may fail to understand because it is another and unfamiliar kind of freedom.

Freedom is inherently a highly developmental matter. It follows, as we have seen, a pattern of subsequently obsoleted forms of emotional control we humans exercise upon one another as we interact in society.

In this chapter we will thus investigate what lies beyond the emotional regimes that prevail today; an inquiry into how the current shame-regime is gradually waning in favor of an emerging *Sklavenmoral*-**regime.**

In-formalization and Nordic Envy

Modern society entails a kind of "civilizing process", as Norbert Elias observed, by which new forms of behavioral regulation come online. What Elias did not see coming, however, was the wave of *in*-formalization (i.e. customs and relations getting less formal) that takes place in late modern societies. Following the 1950s, social life has taken a distinct turn towards the "casual" and informal, but this was not apparent back in 1939 when Elias wrote *The Civilizing Process*.

We can all bring to mind the relaxed clothing and style of Steve Jobs and the employees at the Apple headquarters or at Google for that matter. Since the social revolutions of the 1960s, life has become increasingly informal: people addressing one another more causally, youth culture taking a more distinct and central position in society and the economy, people being more open about their personal issues, bosses becoming friendlier and recasting themselves as "leaders" who work with "support and empowerment" rather than direct supervision, humanities professors dressing "cool", children being given more liberal upbringings and education.

The social and sexual revolutions of the 1960s and 70s can be viewed as a direct challenge to parts of the shame-regime. Most telling is perhaps, again, the gay movement, which named itself "Pride"—the direct opposite of shame.

In the advanced stages of modern society, people have been working to emancipate themselves from some parts of the shame-regime. This development has perhaps gone the farthest in the Nordic countries, where sexual education is relatively developed, attitudes towards sex relaxed, displays of vulnerability seen as strengths and the relationship to authorities rather casual. It should not surprise us, then, that these societies have begun to display emotional regimes at the next stage: *Sklavenmoral.*

A well-known feature of Scandinavian culture is the Law of Jante, first proposed by the Danish-Norwegian author Aksel Sandemose in 1933. The Law of Jante is a set of attitudes that subtly devalue and ignore people who aspire towards greater achievement, fame and excellence. It is usually taken to be a distinctive cultural trait of Scandinavians, often contrasted with the more self-expressive American culture. But I would suggest that it in fact is the beginnings of a new emotional regime, the *Sklavenmoral*-regime, in which people are less shamed for their weaknesses, and more for their strengths and ambitions.

The Law of Jante states as follows:

1. You're not to think you are anything special.
2. You're not to think you are as good as we are.
3. You're not to think you are smarter than we are.
4. You're not to imagine yourself better than we are.
5. You're not to think you know more than we do.
6. You're not to think you are more important than we are.
7. You're not to think you are good at anything.
8. You're not to laugh at us.
9. You're not to think anyone cares about you.
10. You're not to think you can teach us anything.

Sandemose got the inspiration for the Law of Jante from growing up in a remote rural community in Denmark at the beginning of the 20th century. The Law of Jante has, as mentioned, been considered more of a cultural trait than a sign of a new stage of societal development. After all, since pounding one's chest and proclaiming to be the greatest is considered acceptable in a developed country like the US as well as in the less developed Arab world, whereas progressive Swedes and conservative Chinese alike frown upon this behavior, it doesn't seem to have much to do with the level of societal progress.

I'm not denying that non-developmental cultural factors may play a part, but I don't think it's the whole story. I believe there is something going on developmentally speaking, and I think it's linked to the emotional regimes.

What's interesting about the Law of Jante is how frequently it has been used to describe *contemporary* Scandinavian culture. In fact, what makes Jante relevant today is not how accurately it describes the norms of a remote Danish fishing village in the early 20th century, but how well it has come to correspond with a new emotional regime in the Nordic countries today.

Scandinavia wasn't that different from the rest of the world 100 years ago. Kings and nobles would unabashedly display all the grandeur and splendor as their peers anywhere else, and the well-to-do would certainly make sure no one failed to notice how successful they were. The Law of Jante may have characterized some rural communities, but it certainly didn't apply to bourgeois society in general.

This, however, has changed considerably the last 50 years or so. Today it's considered bad taste to display one's social status by driving flashy cars or wearing expensive jewelry, it's an absolute no-go for successful persons to talk about how much smarter and hardworking they are than common people, and even prime ministers, pop stars and royalty are expected to display humility and self-depreciation and constantly need to avoid giving the impression they believe they are "better" than others.

This kind of *Sklavenmoral*, which corresponds so well with the Law of Jante, is indeed more widespread in Scandinavia than in most other places. However, I hold it is less of a cultural quirk of the Nordics and more of a premonition for what may lie in wait for global society at large. In fact, if we look at some of the most progressive pockets elsewhere in the world, we'll notice that pride and self-glorification seem to have gone terribly out of fashion in recent years—Trump's unabashed boasting just isn't as cool in New York and Silicon Valley as it is in Alabama.

But if the Law of Jante is so prevalent in the Nordic societies, it may seem strange these societies, according the World Value Survey's measure of cultural values (as we discussed in Book One) score the highest in terms of valuing self-expression. How can the countries who value self-expression higher than anyone else be the same who simultaneously emphasize self-depreciation the most?

These circumstances (advanced modernity and the Law of Jante) are in fact two sides of the same coin. When a society advances to the later stages of modernity and people become less controlled by shame, more people also begin to strive for "self-actualization" to a greater extent (as we've see in Maslow's hierarchy of needs). The question then presents itself within society: Who will get to be truly unique and expressive, and who will be left with a bland, "mainstream" existence within the frames of the conventional economy?

In other words, *because* life in these societies is "all about" self-actualization, this—rather than wealth and status—becomes a touchy subject. It is increasingly on everyone's mind: How can *I* be special, rise above the herd? Why does *that person* get to be special? What exactly determines who is special and who is a boring mainstream person?

According to this hypothesis, we are seeing a logical outflow of the advancement of the degrees of freedom in society. Because people generally compete less to become "respectable" and more to be "special", the emotional regime of *Sklavenmoral* enters the stage. Consequently, people start to adapt by finding subtle ways of avoiding the envy of others, or else others will be unwilling to cooperate with them and may withhold social recognition.

And, of course, without the cooperation and recognition of others, you can hardly hope to be successful—and you are relegated back to the ranks of mainstream people. Dreams and aspirations are fed to the *Sklavenmoral*-regime and its feast of losses.

NARCISSISM DECODED

The rise of the *Sklavenmoral*-regime may very well be an underlying factor which explains the increased level of *narcissism* in the general population during the last decades, as first famously observed in Christopher Lasch's 1979 book *The Culture of Narcissism*.

Not only has research since that time shown that narcissism is on the increase, but the general discourse has likewise become filled with accusations of narcissism and lacking humility. Today it's one of the most common ways to chastise someone: you're arrogant, you should learn humility, you're a narcissist. Many have observed that narcissism indeed has become more widespread, but most fail to see that society at large has become increasingly obsessed with the imagined (correctly or not) self-image of other people; that we've collectively become obsessed with the perceived narcissism of others.

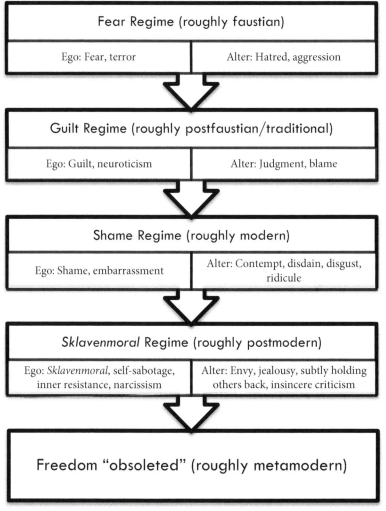

Figure: The emotional regimes that govern behavior and self-organization in society. The emotional regimes roughly correspond to the value memes and/or metamemes I describe in other works. For description of the last box, read to the end of this chapter.

In the same way 14-year-olds often talk about "being yourself" and others being "fake", because they obviously struggle with issues of identity, such obsessions often reveal the prevailing inner struggles of people: the scheming Italian families of the Renaissance were all about honor and loyalty as trust was in short supply in those days, the German Nazis were obsessed with national pride out of shame over losing the First World War, and the more it became obvious that the economies of the communist countries were lagging behind, the longer were the speeches about the decadence of the West. And today we are witnessing the rise of a global culture seemingly obsessed with narcissism and humility because we're afraid we ourselves aren't that special.

A core reason for why narcissism is on the rise, both psychologically and culturally, is that we are entering a *Sklavenmoral*-regime. Narcissism is simply the flipside of this emotion.

If we are controlled by internalized envy, or relate to one another through envy, is it then so strange we develop a toxic and charged relationship to our own higher potentials (or lack thereof) and the higher potentials of others? Narcissism—the obsession with our own image and the idea of our self—is born from the need to convince ourselves we really *are* special after all, from an inner drive to extinguish the painful doubts *Sklavenmoral* has sown in us. It is an unproductive defense against the subtly experienced envy of others.

In summary, then, societies advance through four emotional regimes: from fear, to guilt, to shame, to *Sklavenmoral* (which, if the pattern holds, is only truly becoming dominant in the most advanced modern societies, a sign of which is increasing narcissism as well as an obsession with the perceived narcissism of others).

Again, all of these emotions exist in all societies and all people, but the social logic governing everyday life still varies substantially: What hidden negative emotions are guiding your life choices and everyday interactions? What emotions are you avoiding as you calmly go about your day?

ENVY AND JEALOUSY

Understanding the role of envy—and its sister emotions of jealousy (envy in the realm of love) and schadenfreude (the subtle satisfaction procured from another's defeat or misery)—is paramount for navigating the coming period and to serve real emancipation at a societal level.

A number of mechanisms may in effect *increase* the prevalence and intensity of envy in present-day society: an over-exposure to highly successful and beautiful people in magazines and TV, a constant bombardment of all the carefully curated "perfect" moments of our friends on social media, all the new amazing gadgets and lifestyles we'll never afford or have time for. Simply, the overwhelming opportunities the global markets can offer—and the fact that a lucky few can rise to yet greater heights of fame, significance and prominence in such a larger system. The recent appearance of godlike public figures like the super-entrepreneur Elon Musk, the sales of so many Harry Potter books, the vast followership of the Kardashian reality shows, the sheer awesomeness of the discoveries in AI, nanotechnology, genetic engineering and so forth—all of it serves as further sources of comparison, and thus of envy. Most of us will know at least someone who is ridiculously successful in one or more areas of life. The lives, adventures and exploits of these so painfully visible chosen few make many of us feel yet more stagnated, dissatisfied, envious. Kierkegaard famously called envy an "unhappy admiration".

But envy very seldom announces its presence to us. As I mentioned, there is little research on the topic—but there is certainly much classical literature. There are few major philosophers, great artists or statesmen who haven't experienced it and written about it. Such writings show up in the myths particularly of societies which have at least some social mobility, dynamic markets and democratic structures, such as ancient Greece and republican Rome.

What the classics tell us, and modern psychology's sparse findings seem to suggest, is that **we mostly experience our own envy as *righteous anger***. We feel a: "Why ya little…!"

We quite easily become **symbolically invested in the failure of others'** dreams and aspirations. Whenever another person tells us about a dream or a great project we don't quite buy or agree with, a part of us almost automatically becomes invested in their failure. Think about it: If someone told us about a plan that can "save a million lives", and we don't play along, what does their relative success imply about *us*? If they then *do* begin to succeed in their plans, this suggests something quite unflattering about ourselves—namely, that we missed a great opportunity or that we failed to recognize a powerful vision when it was right before our nose. Their displayed greatness implies our own mediocrity and smallness. For this reason, we subtly but eagerly begin to look for signs of failure, and we often take on the role of unsolicited advisors. Whenever they do fail, we can then tell ourselves that it was because they didn't listen to our advice; and if they do act according to our advice, we can tell ourselves they only succeeded because of our own wise words (which cost us nothing). We may even find ourselves giving poor advice of insidious intent.

Symbolic investment in the failure of others can emerge either because their aspirations collide with some of our own ideological convictions, or because it conflicts with our view of how reality works, or simply because it disturbs our ideas about social hierarchies and who's the wiser and more competent person. Whatever the source of this inner resistance, the result is the same: It somehow feels good and reassuring to see them fail. This is **symbolic investment in another's failure**—we wish for their failure not because of the *results* of another's struggle for a better world, but because of what their success would *symbolize* and imply about ourselves. It is a rather frightening dynamic; suddenly, we may start preferring that someone fails to save a million lives, just to save our own sense of chosenness and immortality. That's how trivial and automatic envy can be.

We don't see it coming. We don't admit to feeling it—mostly, not even to ourselves. We just feel a silent resistance towards the envied, and we act upon it only behind a thick smokescreen, most often fooling not only others, but also (and often only) ourselves, with hollow justifications.

So basically, envy is sneaky. It is insidious, conniving. It sneaks up on us, seeps into our relationships, even among family and trusted friends—and it is rampant among professional peers. From there on, it is not surprising that our freedom is curtailed as we internalize the envy of others; an invisible force which sets up inner barriers and subtly pressures us to conform to mediocrity and never again seek to excel or to transcend our position in life or to try to change the world. Again, this is the *Sklavenmoral*-regime we can expect to be entering next. Slave morality.

I am suggesting, then, that society is breaking through the chains of shaming and contempt, but that we are hitting a great glass ceiling of *Sklavenmoral* and envy. This envy will likely target not primarily the power, wealth and attention of the fortunate. No. It will go after a much subtler and more sensitive aim: the highest inner potentials of our fellow human beings. Little pins in that voodoo doll.

Nothing hurts our sense of "chosenness" and immortality more than the manifest sublimity of another's soul. Not only that they are successful, but that they are idealistic, good-hearted, high-minded and fruitfully engaged in deeply significant pursuits—when we are not. That they are *powerful* in the deep Nietzschean sense of the word. That they are living their lives to the fullest—when we are not.

All of us long for power in some sense; all of us are born creators. To deny this is game denial. To defend suffocating inequalities is game acceptance. To accept this game of life and to evolve it—is game change.

This, I believe, is one of the greatest challenges of the times ahead: So many beautiful minds and hearts will emerge to rise to the challenges of the coming period, and so many will work—unconsciously but connivingly—to stop them.

And most of the time, the mediocre enviers will succeed in installing "humility" (veiled *Sklavenmoral*) into the birthing heroes and heroines, suffocating them in their sleep. The enviers won't know why they're doing it; they'll just act with a strange perceived "moral outrage" that eats at their hearts.

If I am roughly correct about this future diagnosis, it means that we're in for a lot of subtle, icky, sly conspiring. Glass doors quietly shut, dreams subtly dissipated, life projects discretely smothered.

And this in turn will unleash narcissism: both an obsession with exposing narcissism in others, and a corresponding increase of actual narcissism as we try to convince ourselves and our surroundings of our worth.

Where does it leave us then? We need to develop a corresponding level of introspective skills in as many members of society as possible. We need to be able to really look inwards. To bust our own bullshit. We must develop greater interpersonal trust, but we must also, on a profound level, become more trustworthy. We must develop self-knowledge; higher stages of inner development.

It is relatively easy to wish one another well, that no harm should befall our fellow citizens and peers. We don't wish for one another to fall off a cliff—that would be terrible! But rarely do we sincerely wish for our lowly buddy to become the next Barack Obama. We prefer it if he gets about the same amount of happiness and success as ourselves; preferably slightly less.

And if we have to choose between the unlikely exaltation of our lowly buddy to world-savior glory and him falling off a cliff—we may sometimes find ourselves quietly preferring the latter.

How, then, do we beat envy and emancipate ourselves from the *Sklavenmoral*-regime? I suggest three angles of attack: *First*, to improve our shared general skills of introspection, so that we can "bust our own bullshit"; *second*, to make it visible and to name it, so that more people can see it coming and not so easily be taken by surprise; *third*, to help each of us integrate and own our deeply held will to power—more on this towards the end of this book.

Thus, the prophet said:

"Brothers and sisters. The great religions have taught us to love one another. To wish one another well. To be able to say, from our truthful hearts, 'I wish you health, peace and happiness'.

But alas, this wish is insufficient for the journey we must now embark upon together. Kindness is too weak a word, too feeble a force.

We must purify our souls and intentions so as not to hate or envy the *greatness* of one another. To be able to share in the glory and mystery of life. And this is a much harder task than wishing health, peace and happiness upon our fellow human beings.

We must defeat the veiled demons of envy. Our very survival depends upon it—as we have never needed the audacity and creative intellect of others more than we do today.

Humanity will know no higher freedom until we are able to turn to our brothers and sisters in earnest to say: 'May your heart birth a visionary, a Plato or Marx, a great leader, a Napoleon or Mandela or Catherine the Great or Martin Luther King, an unparalleled creator, a Frida Kahlo or a Bob Dylan.' [46]

May the message ring:

'I wish you *power*.

I wish you *greatness* and superiority.

I wish you *transcendence*.'"

ESCAPE FROM FREEDOM

And yet, I must confess the naivety of the theory of freedom I have thus far proposed. Because even freedom does not set us free.

Once we manage to cast off the fear, shame, guilt and *Sklavenmoral* of society's conditioning, we are left with no forces pressuring us to do anything; no pre-given maps of meaning and no extrinsic motivations.

Where there's a whip, there's a way, they say—playing of course on the saying "where there's a will, there's a way". But without the whip, we may well *lose* our way—perhaps forever.

What if no profound and more spiritually satisfying carrot of "intrinsic motivation" presents itself to match all the carrots of immediate gratification? We may unexpectedly find ourselves choosing the Pleasure Palace and its Dark Playgrounds of infomercials and virtual reality over truth and meaning; endless distractions, spectatorship, consumption, perpetually unfinished wound-licking, ever refined excuses, and procrastination,

procrastination, procrastination. Endless fast carbs, endless gratification at the expense of meaning and dignity. Oh, the digital vanilla prison—oh, the candy cotton hell!

For all its terrible and visceral materiality, our slavery to negative social emotions at least protects us from the responsibility of being creators of our own lives or co-creators of the world. In actual slavery under penalty of death, at least we need not take any real responsibility for our own selves, beyond obedience. In slavery to guilt, we need not construct our own morality. In slavery to shame, we need not find our own path in life; only comply with what the neighbors might think.

And in slavery to *Sklavenmoral*, we need not take responsibility for our own highest dreams and aspirations, for our will to power, for our longing for creation and transcendence; for our greatest potentials and our sorrows for all sentient beings and our identification with society-as-a-whole, in its entirety and dialectical multiplicity of perspectives. We can leave that to someone else; "I'm just a usual person, I have no such pretensions, I am humble" we tell ourselves. But it is a deceptive humility, hollow and life-less as a plastic baby doll.

The truth is that once we have traveled the long road to freedom, we are back at the very point where we started: at fear, at sheer terror. It's just us and the blank page of our life that we must fill—the blank canvas of the artist staring right back at us, screaming, roaring: CREATE ME! It's just you, all alone, defining and recreating reality itself. You turn away from the canvas, trying to do something else, but you find that society itself is a canvas, begging for co-creation. You hurry outside, restlessly pacing in the pouring rain, staring up at the grey skies, tears running from your eyes, washed from your face by the cold rain, but no mercy is found: reality itself is a canvas. Blank.

Blank.

Blank.

Bam, motherfucker.

Go create. No excuses. Ever. Because you're free.

Suddenly, like on a bad psychedelic trip, you find yourself lost in the hall of mirrors, with no beginning and no end of "the self" *vis-à-vis* "the world". Just pure creation and full, unyielding responsibility for the universe. This whole "crossroads of fact and fiction" business just got eerily real.

Is it so strange that we usually turn at the doorstep and escape back into the relative safety of whatever slavery we just struggled to shake off? Man, have I felt this before I began writing these books. Man, do I feel it every bloody morning. The terrible truth is this: freedom is struggle; freedom is terror; it is the terror of facing pure chaos, the pristine meaninglessness of reality, the vastness of potential, and the weight of the responsibility that follows.

THREE VOICES WHISPER

I'd like to mention three authors, each of whom have described an important aspect of the fear of freedom.

A keen observer of this predicament was Erich Fromm, the Freudo-Marxist social psychologist who wrote *Escape from Freedom* back in 1941 as a commentary upon the rise of nazism and other authoritarian movements. To embrace freedom, Fromm argued, human beings must have the proper spiritual support—we need to *practice* to be able to recreate ourselves at higher levels of individuation. We must grow as human beings in order to manifest *positive* freedoms ("freedom to"), lest we retreat in fear and try to recreate the imagined safe havens of the past. That's what totalitarianism and reactionary movements promise—an escape from freedom itself.

But the totalitarian and fundamentalist movements betray us; they are entirely devoid of art and creativity, and if we subscribe to them we subtly feel that our souls have been oppressed and violated. They offer only perverted paths to submission and destruction, satisfying only these wishes and never reaching fulfillment.

This actually links rather elegantly to the work of Robert Kegan. I usually have little good to say about his developmental theory of "the self". You may remember I took some swings at him in Book One. But in this instance, we may well listen to him and learn. Kegan argues that the "self" progresses from a stage of a norm-conforming "Socialized" mind to a "Self-Authoring" mind, which in turn—in a small minority of adults—can make way for a yet higher "Self-Transforming" mind.

- Stage 1 — Impulsive mind (early childhood)
- Stage 2 — Imperial mind (adolescence, 6% of adult population)
- Stage 3 — Socialized mind (58% of the adult population)
- Stage 4 — Self-Authoring mind (35% of the adult population)
- Stage 5 — Self-Transforming mind (1% of the adult population)

Even if I don't subscribe to this theory at the level of individual analysis, I do think it has something to say at an aggregated, societal level. It does make sense that modern life requires many more of us to advance to a Self-Authoring kind of mind—and if this transition fails, but our life circumstances still demand a strong inner compass of self-organization, we can regress to the Socialized mind, or the Imperial mind, and subconsciously even to the Impulsive, i.e. to childish tantrums and wanton aggression (like nazism, etc.).

If our societal freedom is *not* matched by a corresponding level of personal development, we are terrified by the freedom gained. We don't experience it as wind blowing through our hair on an American highway, but as utter confusion and a horrifying abyss. Wild, staring eyes—and a mad urge to fly. The Chevy is driving off a cliff. We want out. We want to escape from freedom.[47]

One important aspect of this training for higher freedom that is not fully caught by either Fromm or Kegan is described instead by the novelist Steven Pressfield. In his book *The War of Art*, he vividly and intimately outlines the enemy of all artists: what he calls "resistance". How many of us can truly overcome the resistance to create? Can we tolerate the empty canvas staring back at us? How many of us keep stalling our innermost dreams indefinitely? How many of us can bear the terror of freedom and muster the discipline and die-hard motivation to defeat the inner demons of distraction and excuse? Simple procrastination can also be an escape from freedom.

Pressfield points out it is this denied and undealt-with inner resistance that shows up as an urge, not only to deny our *own* higher potentials, but to unproductively criticize and try to smother it in *others*—what I have called *Sklavenmoral* (and its two cronies, envy and narcissism).

So it's not just a matter of individual inner struggle. Even at a civilizational level, we are facing the onslaught of the inability to overcome inner resistance, which translates to envy, which translates to *Sklavenmoral*, and this translates to narcissism—all of which are corrosive, if not antithetical, to the collective good of higher freedom.[48]

Fromm's words are prophetic. Kegan's theory offers some useful hints to the structure of this challenge. But to get at the heart of the matter we must recognize that a profoundly free society would be one where all of us become artists in the most general sense. We would all have to bear the terrible burden of creation that Pressfield describes.

And by yet another tragic and ironic twist of fate, it just so happens that we live in a digital capitalist society in which every corner and every moment and every shelf is overflowing with excuses, distractions, quick rewards and new promises. How many ways are there not to lose our focus and sense of direction?

It's even worse than that; it is the case that the relative success of one person's manifested deeper potential and creative outlet easily becomes the source of distraction for others—if I am to be a successful writer, I must distract at least *some* of my fellow co-creators from *their* higher callings. The same goes for so many other creators. So much "amusement" and "support" around, so many workshops to take and genuinely breathtaking talents caught on YouTube-clips to be shared on Facebook. Millions of views. Billions of clicks. Digital weapons of mass distraction.

Higher freedom from extrinsic emotional pressures must grow in pace with higher stages of *inner* development, lest we be doomed to deceive ourselves into new sugarcoated escapes from freedom. We must learn to discipline ourselves—to crack the code of how inner self-discipline is taught and acquired.

Max Weber famously described modern life and its rational, disenchanted bureaucracy as an "iron cage". As we approach a postindustrial society of abundance, more and more of us suddenly find that we are caught in a gilded one. **The gilded cage, if you will, of metamodern society.** [49]

Not only must negative freedoms be matched by positive opportunities; both of these must be matched by a corresponding degree of inner growth.

When the intergalactic gods look upon human civilization on Cosmic Judgment Day, what will be their verdict? Will they see that we grew up and became artists, co-creators of the universe? Or will they see that we have escaped from freedom, into new Pleasure Palaces? Will they scoff:

"This species has amused itself to death".

A SIMPLE SCALE OF (IN-)DIVIDUAL FREEDOM

Thus far we have discussed and described freedom as a collective good in which your freedom is largely co-dependent upon mine and vice versa. This is probably the best way to understand freedom as a societal phenomenon because it treats freedom as something that can be approached through political and cultural development.

But there is still room for describing the different levels of freedom enjoyed by citizens as (in)dividual people. There are bound to be minorities within each country who have significantly lower degrees of freedom than others, just as there are elites whose freedom is significantly higher. Let me suggest this simple scale without lingering much upon it:

1. **Slavery**—your rights and freedoms are at the whim of another and you do not own even your own body.

2. **Serfdom**—you formally own your body but your lowly social position is predefined and you are not allowed to travel freely and others can take a significant portion of the fruits of your labor.

3. **Subjected citizenship**—you can travel around freely and do what you want but have no say in public matters.

4. **Impoverished citizenship**—you have a basic enfranchisement and entitlement in public matters but no real say in them without taking significant risks, such as in socialist republics.

5. **Basic citizenship**—as above, but you can try to have a say without significant risks.

6. **Socially active citizenship**—you have a meaningful and substantial relationship to public affairs that affect your life.

7. **Integrated citizenship**—you have real and effective ways of affecting things happening around you.

8. **Norm-defining citizenship**—you also have real and effective ways of affecting the political discourses and arenas around you.

9. **Co-creative citizenship**—society at large, its arenas, institutions and functions feel and effectively are as your own home and you feel comfortable and entitled to participate in any part of it.

Viewed from this perspective, it is clear that the majority of citizens even in the "most free" countries of today are quite far from the highest reaches of freedom. If you consider countries such as Sweden, Germany or the US, most people have a freedom level of "5" according to this scale, while significant minorities have freedom levels of 1-4: trafficking victims, illegal immigrants, kids stuck with tyrannical parents and so forth. If you look at countries like China, most people are in the ballpark of freedom 3-4.

The point here is that there are real demographics out there with different distributions of these levels of freedom. Even in theory it is impossible to imagine a society in which "everybody" has the highest level of freedom, freedom level 9. But it certainly *is* conceivable that we could create societies in which much larger portions of the population climb the ladder by one or two steps, and where there are smaller pockets of oppression.

Roughly speaking, however, it is clear that these different levels of freedom must be tied to the overall cultural and institutional development of freedom in society. It is difficult to imagine a society run by fear and guilt in which a significant part of the population would feel as deeply enmeshed cozy co-creators of the whole of culture (levels 7-9)—or even as dignified and protected citizens (level 5).

THE HIGHEST REACHES OF FREEDOM

Let us return to freedom viewed through a more transpersonal lens, with the emotional regimes. A part of us wants to escape from freedom. And yet, the future of society depends precisely upon our ability to cultivate such a higher freedom and embrace it.

What, then, happens after the emotional regime of *Sklavenmoral*? What lies beyond the chains of fear, guilt, shame and *Sklavenmoral*; beyond hatred, judgment, contempt and envy?

If a person is no longer constrained by such negative emotions, but still remains socially and ethically functional, I would argue that she is approaching a more profound existential freedom, one that Nietzsche personified in the concept of the *Übermensch*.

As we noted, this *Übermensch* can only come into being if there is sufficient inner personal development: self-discipline, intrinsic motivations, a strong compass, self-knowledge—and the four dimensions of psychological development: cognitive complexity, access to the right symbolic maps of the world, higher inner states and greater inner depths (intimate knowing of both the light and darkness of existence).

Übermensch is usually translated as "superman", but this translation is somewhat misleading. There is a distinction in the German language between different uses of the word *über*—it can mean "over" or "above", but it can also mean "through" or "across".

A better translation may thus be "the trans-human", a category that reaches *through* and goes *beyond* what we normally think of as human existence. In this interpretation, the *Übermensch* is not a superhuman comic hero, but rather a person who lives relatively unrestrained by the normal dynamics of everyday life as we commonly experience them.

And, in this view, the *Übermensch* is not really a description of a certain kind of person, but more of a *social* category. We have seen that my freedom depends on you. The *Übermensch* state in a particular person is only possible to the extent that the larger patterns of our social interactions and emotional exchanges can bring it into being.

So at the end of the painful and winding road towards freedom, a wheel turned through endless painful variations of dividuation and integration,

waits that crazy Nietzschean moustache: **the *Übermensch*, which renders** ○
the very concept of freedom obsolete. Human beings long to be eman-
cipated—the *Übermensch* wants to be unleashed.

What then, would a human being—her relational body and mind—be,
if she were entirely unrestrained by fear, guilt, shame and *Sklavenmoral*;
freed from the shackles of others' hatred, judgment, contempt and envy?

This is not a question of fantasy or theoretical speculation, but indeed a
real and empirical one, even if the answer at this point remains hypothetical. If these regimes that control us weren't there, but we were still highly
functional members of a global society, what would we do? What would
we be?

I'll tell you what I think. A life form unrestrained would begin to consciously self-organize in ways that create higher subjective states, greater
existential depth, grasping for greater complexity. It would gaze deeper
into the universe and recreate it, while recreating herself in the image of
the order of the cosmos.

In sheer terror before the empty meaninglessness of the universe that
reveals itself at the end of all external and societal oppression, we must
garner superhuman courage to resist folding over and escaping from the
formlessness of pure freedom.

I believe that we would—we must—plunge head-on into the mysteries
of existence, not as individuals, but as an evolving global network of posthuman transindividuals, living in volitionally organized virtual tribes. Un-
hinged, uninhibited, we would explore with rapacious curiosity, play with
religious fervor, worship with trembling devotion, fuck like beasts—dissolving our very sense of self into the crystal-clear night.

Serving beauty and mending tragedy, we would dance, fight and laugh
our way towards more terrifying heights and depths of consciousness,
manifesting pristine universal, impersonal love—a love that fathoms and
embraces reality, and all sentient beings, with mathematical precision. We
would co-create worlds and we would co-destroy them. And we would
bear the heavy burden of such responsibility.

At the top of this edifice we call civilization, when this tower of Babel
touches the skies, a profoundly familiar call echoes through all of us: the
call of the wild. This is the alpha and omega point. Before civilization,
there is the wild, the untamed, the naked. After civilization, there is the
wild, the untamed, the naked. But this time the call echoes into higher
complexity and into the terrifying emptiness of outer space. Freedom
must be hard and it must be wild.

At the highest reaches of what we think of as "freedom", we can explode beyond what has hitherto been thought of as human. Art conquers everyday life and subdues its tamed structures to a radical creativity. The wild. We become poets. And the poet *acts*; to create relative utopias, to pursue dangerous dreams.

To the sound of roaring electric guitars we recognize that we are indeed gods with anuses; and as the flies buzzing through the enchanted meaninglessness of the cosmos, in an act of necessary vanity, we set our controls for the heart of the sun.

Chapter 6

DIMENSIONS OF EQUALITY

Alright, let's sober up for a bit. Enough word candy. We still have another fundamental concept to explore in this first part of the book: **the evolution of equality**.

Unfortunately we live in a universe where equality is an even trickier and more complex goal than freedom. By its very nature, equality is ridden with yet greater inherent contradictions, with yet more intricate paradoxes.

We have already noted that negative rights ("freedom from") are less complicated than positive rights and entitlements ("freedom to"). It is easier to draw consistent lines for what people may not do *to* one another (physical abuse, theft, imprisonment, enslavement, and so forth) than for what we are obliged to do *for* one another (help in times of need, secure basic subsistence, provide education, healthcare, and so forth). But we have also noted that any real measure of freedom must be seen in light of the lived experience of humans and non-human animals, and as such it cannot be reduced to a libertarian defense of negative freedoms. *My* freedom depends on the inner workings of *your* thoughts and emotions, and vice versa.

Furthermore, we have noted a second paradox of freedom: while freedom is cast in terms of our emancipation from commonly held negative emotions which we all avoid during our everyday lives, it is also apparent that said negative emotions regulate our behaviors in ways making society possible in the first place. Without emotions of guilt and shame, it is difficult to see how we could make societal life function at all. And only highly functional societies can be expected to develop greater freedom. So freedom within a society always has to build upon *un-freedom*, upon an increasingly intimate form of self-organizing control. It is as though we were climbing a ladder with the goal of reaching above the ladder itself. But then what would we hold on to?

We have to wrestle with freedom as a *common good*, as something emanating from our everyday interactions with one another, with our environment and our "selves". Freedom flows not only from institutions, but also from intimate and personal relationships.

Your freedom does not begin where my freedom ends; that's an illusion based upon the underlying assumption that human beings are sealed containers, that we are individuals, indivisible atoms. But in a behavioral-scientific sense, it is clear we are *more* than individuals, that we are "dividuals" or "transindividuals", as described in Book One. **Hence, your freedom begins *not* at my imagined outward border, but at the center of my heart.**

Once you understand this, you can also see that equality is part and parcel of freedom's development as equality determines the nature and quality of our relations. So let's talk about the paradoxes of equality, and then march quickly to resolve them. I am offering an anatomy of equality and its evolution.

EQUALITY AS PARADOX

 Let me go through four fundamental paradoxes of "equality" that make the issue an eternally insolvable problem.

1. WE AREN'T ACTUALLY EQUAL

The first paradox of equality is that humans are not equals. As I labored to describe in Book One, there are great developmental differences between us, with some people advancing to higher stages of adult psychological development than others: some have more complex thinking, more universal values, more refined relationships to life and existence.

The same holds true in terms of other characteristics: some are healthier and stronger, some have more balanced personalities, some are more industrious and have greater endurance and tolerance of stress, some have higher IQ, some are more sociable, some are better looking—and some have the opposite traits. At a superficial level, this could have us think that equality in a deeper sense is not possible as our differences and variations of endowments will always manifest in our lives and our relationships. But such a defeatist stance will not serve us well; it is, after all, quite apparent that different societies have different levels of equality, and hence that equality can develop. Rather, we must venture deeper into an understanding of equality to resolve this paradox.

→ 2. THE CRUELTY OF PERFECT MERITOCRACY

A limited version of the value of equality is the idea of "meritocracy", or the "equality of opportunity". According to this ideal, the aim of pursuing equality is one of removing all obstacles for people to achieve what the traits of their character would "naturally" let them "deserve". You may remember Martin Luther King's echoing voice: "I look to a day when people will not be judged by the color of their skin, but by the content of their character." That may be a good starting point for equality, but it is certainly not the endpoint. The Martin Luther Kings of today and of the future must ask for much more. They must be much more analytically stringent and radical.

Let's say for a moment that we really achieved a society in which people are truly "judged by the content of their character". This would mean that people with more competitive traits would gain more recognition, power, resources—and ultimately happiness—than their more miserably endowed fellow citizens. And there would really be no excuses in a perfect meritocracy. You got every opportunity, and you still ended up getting the short end of the stick. You're a bloody loser and you know it. You can't blame anyone but yourself. And everybody else blames you as well. You are not judged by distinctions of class, gender or race, but you are still judged. And the entitled feel even more exalted, yet more deserving. Drawn to its logical conclusion, King's vision—so often held almost as a religious tenet of modernity—reveals an inescapably cruel and cynical side.

It's a meagre vision for society because it ignores the fact that people are not equals. Any deeper equality is not possible unless we address this issue.

3. RECOGNITION FROM THE RECOGNIZED

To a large extent, equality is about recognition, and you are recognized not only *despite* your race/gender/class, but also *because of* your abilities to produce things other people want (products, services, elicited emotions). And people will only give you recognition if they are unable to take it from you, i.e. if there is a power balance in place. Cows "give" us milk but receive no recognition because they are powerless in our bovine-oppressive society.

The meritocratic vision of equality still builds upon outdated, religious (I am tempted to say Protestant) ideas: that you have a soul, and that "God" doles out rewards depending on how pretty you are on the inside.

With King, we have—perhaps unsurprisingly—smuggled in a good dose of Luther and Calvin.

In reality, of course, no such God exists. And there is no fate that rewards good character according to a universal measure; no law of Karma, at least not in the traditional sense. People don't "deserve" anything in any deeper, cosmic sense.

As the ladder of life is strung—as society is "stratified" into higher and lower strata—people simply end up in different social positions as the result of cold, mechanical processes, some of which originate within each of us and from our own choices and actions, and some of which originate from structures lying far beyond our control. There is really no solid border between the inequality that comes from beyond ourselves, and the one that comes from within (from our psyches, personal traits and behaviors).

Naturally, not all inequality is *always* a bad thing, but up to a certain point—a rather high threshold—inequality is painful to people and detrimental to societies, whether it originates from people's inner traits or from unfair collective structures.

We are called, then, to look for an intimately *lived* and *felt* equality; one that in turn shapes our relationships in the direction of mutual respect and solidarity, caring, even love. Such equality must ultimately be based upon social **recognition**, that people's value and quality are genuinely *appreciated* and honored by others. This and similar arguments have been made by many sociologists in recent years, most notably perhaps by the social theorist Axel Honneth.[50] This line of thought goes back as far as Hegel (in *The Phenomenology of Spirit*), who viewed the struggle for recognition as a primary driver in history, and it has been theorized not only on the Left, and not only by sociologists—in 2018 none other than Francis Fukuyama published a book titled *Identity*, which also looks closely at the primacy of recognition in society.

But this striving for a *de facto* equality of recognition, espoused by Honneth and others, lands us in yet another paradox, largely missed by the theorists of recognition. It is, if possible, an even more caustic one.

All humans desire recognition—civic, social, economic, emotional and sexual. We want to be recognized as worthy citizens, as real people, as competent contributors, as good friends and family members, and as gendered and sexual beings.

But—and this is the paradox that defenders of recognition tend to miss—**we *only* want recognition from those who we *ourselves* value, from those who we ourselves "recognize" as equals or superiors, from the ones *we* respect, admire or desire**.

We don't want to be admired by the ones we look down upon, but by the ones we look up to. We don't want to be members of a community we don't respect. We don't want to have our taste and lifestyle venerated by those we deem to have poor taste and ignoble lifestyles. We don't want to be validated as beautiful and desirable by those we deem ugly and repulsive. **In short, we desire recognition from the recognized.** And it goes farther than that—we even want only the recognition of those who in turn are recognized by others we in turn recognize. Recognition is a networked tagging game; a game of performances and displays. Recognition reproduces recognition. Disdain reproduces disdain.

And the eliciting of respect and recognition is not a volitional act on behalf of the beholder. Admiration, attraction and respect are things that occur *automatically*, as a result of our emotional, social and cultural wiring. We can't help ourselves but to admire the gifted, to desire the beautiful, to clamor for the glamorous, to respect the powerful, to be dazzled by the smooth and the cool. And conversely, alas, we cannot help but feel disdain for those we perceive as stupid, ugly, delinquent, weird or immoral—disdain for the people who don't elicit positive emotional responses in us or otherwise don't provide things we value.

Sure, on a theoretical and impersonal level, we can extend our solidarity to the wretched, with citizenship and the vote and human rights. But we won't choose them as friends; we won't enter long-lasting and productive professional partnerships with them; we won't invite them to our parties; we won't miss them; we won't marry them; we won't truly love them.

That innocent wish we so often hail as universally human: "I just want to be respected, loved and desired", has an inescapable dark side, whispering under its breath: "I merely want to be respected, loved and desired… by the ones I respect, love and desire". And we often respect, love and desire someone simply because other people seem to.

Ours is a tragic universe, where universal love cannot be the simple answer. Any attempt to be genuinely loving of the unloved will prove unsustainable. Even if you let one alcoholic beggar live at your house, you will pay a significant price for doing so, and you will have to exclude the next beggar who comes knocking. And the exchange between you and the beggar will be an act of charity rather than a genuine and *mutual* offering of respect. The whole thing is set up to create large groups of the unwanted, the disrespected, the untouchable.

This cruel mechanism of social reality lays its verdict on all of us; as noted earlier, we are all winners and losers, in different contexts and to different extents. We all know both sides, and we all know the intense pain of rejection, of withheld recognition and cold indifference. And we all know, perhaps apart from the unconditional love of mothers for their children, that all that matters in life, at the most sensitive and intimate level, can be taken away from us. Hence, we cannot give our care and recognition freely.

If we play our cards wrong, if we convene with the lonely, the failures, the nerds, with those who cannot offer us new and productive outlets for life, this will not only create limited rewards for us; it will spill over and affect how others judge our status and standing in society.

Hence, we stay clear of those who have little recognition, in turn offering them no recognition so that we can gain the recognition we so desire. The wounds of the lonely and the despised are as frightening and contagious as leprosy.

4. WE ENVY ONE ANOTHER

Last, but not least, there is **the disturbing tendency of humans to *envy* those who gain the kinds of recognition we ourselves long for.** This creates another paradox of equality.

We withhold our recognition for reasons of envy. Such envy can show up for different reasons: that we feel competition for the scarce resource of attention and recognition, that we are invested in another story about reality (why should the footballer be recognized when great poets like "myself" are ignored; why should brilliant Marxists be admired when in truth libertarian economics are the best; why should great intellectuals be honored when "I" am so much kinder and more spiritual?)—or that we feel someone's recognition was acquired through undue privileges, that "the fight was fixed". Or simply that we find someone morally undeserving: why should such a wretched person be so lucky?

The strange and ubiquitous hunger of the human soul, the hunger for recognition, makes the fair and even distribution of recognition yet more acrimonious. Envy is an often underestimated force of human societies and interactions, and as discussed earlier, it generally goes unnoticed by the envier himself. It leads us to give unhelpful and unsolicited advice, to slander and diminish the gifts and beauties of one another. It works as a subtle but pervasive counterforce to human dignity and equality. It gets in the way of any struggle for deeper equality.

—

I have thus offered four paradoxical natures of equality: first, that we are not *de facto* equal; second, that even a perfect meritocracy with no structural discrimination reproduces an exacerbated felt inequality; third, that all equality is based upon viscerally felt and embodied recognition, but that we will only seek the recognition of the recognized, and thus only offer true recognition to limited segments of our social surroundings—and last, the strange and subtle presence of envy.

This might all look rather hopeless. Yet, equality varies over societies and epochs. **Equality *can* be developed; it *can* evolve.** At the most universal level, equality is deepened when the games of life are developed.

Recognition cannot be forced to be given, nor can it be redistributed like material wealth, nor can it be force-fed to the starving. But, again, **the fact that equality is paradoxical, and perhaps cannot be "achieved" in any absolute sense, doesn't mean it cannot develop and grow.**

Deeply felt equality is an emergent property of society's self-organization, of its power relations, of people's opportunities, of second chances given, of freely available information, of education and feedback processes governing people's lives, of people's degree of emotional and social intelligence, of people's physical stature, and so forth. And the depth of our equality affects all aspects of society—just as inequality harms every aspect of society and ultimately limits our freedom.

The issue is not, then, to "achieve" equality, but to tackle its paradoxes more intelligently; to work around them with wide and deep-reaching measures.

SIX DIMENSIONS OF INEQUALITY

We have noted that equality and inequality, in the last instance, are deeply *embodied* phenomena; that they are viscerally felt in all aspect of life. If we seek to increase equality in society, we must know its different dimensions. I suggest there are at least six such dimensions: **the economic, the social, the physiological, the emotional, the ecological and the informational.** Let us briefly describe them one by one.

Note that I leave aside the question of civic entitlements and equality of legal rights in this ensuing discussion, not because I find it unimportant—to the contrary, it may be the most fundamental form of inequality—but because we are dealing primarily with *future* attractors, i.e. with increasing equality in postindustrial societies where basic formal equality has already been largely achieved.

Onwards.

ECONOMIC INEQUALITY

This first and most obvious form of inequality in our days revolves around income, wealth and access to material resources; the ability to acquire goods and services from others. Because material wealth has long been the main focus of struggles for equality, it merits less discussion here. It is, of course, no less important. For instance, it is perhaps the single most widely accepted finding within social science that greater economic inequality (often measured by the so called "Gini coefficient") has a solid correlation with violent crime, much more so than poverty in itself, and that lower economic inequality is conducive to stability, social trust and a higher quality of life in society at large.

With this in mind, let us briefly mention a few central dynamics of economic inequality in the present world.

There is, in the public debate, considerable confusion regarding the question whether economic inequality has been rising or falling during recent decades. On the Left, the idea that inequality is rising remains an almost religious tenet. A famous 2013 book by Thomas Piketty, *Capital in the Twenty-First Century*, showed that a small group—the "top one percent"—has been amassing an increasingly larger portion of the wealth since the turn to neo-liberal economic policies, beginning with the Reagan-Thatcher era around 1980, and that this is largely a global trend. This trend is much more pronounced if you look at the top 0.01%, which has led many to believe that rising economic inequality is an uncontroversial fact. But there is more to the story as so often is the case with these things.

We are witnessing a few interrelated trends that have to do with economic globalization, the lack of transnational governance, rapid economic growth and technological advancement. These factors taken together create a more complex picture. Let's take a look:

- The overall economic inequality of the world is falling, with the global Gini coefficient reaching a peak around the year 2000 (the most unequal distribution of income). It has since begun to decrease somewhat, largely due to the impressive economic growth of countries like China, India and Brazil where large new middle classes have emerged. Inequality within these countries has also increased as not all members of society have been successfully included. Still, if we are to believe the forecasts of an influential 2008 Goldman Sachs report, two billion more people should have joined the global middle class by 2030, and thus far, at the time of writing, the numbers have not disappointed.[51]

- The economic inequality *within* rich countries, such as the US or the European countries, has been rising. This is largely due to the pressures of globalization where many jobs have been outsourced to low-income countries and immigration from poorer countries have created downward pressures on low-paying jobs. This means the middle and working classes of these societies have become more pressured since they are competing within a much larger world economy. Many jobs have also been automated, and countries have been less able to maintain generous welfare spending and high taxation as many corporations have become more transnational and thereby been able to move their profits and activities to countries with lower taxes. Taken together, this means the general experience of "normal people" in rich countries is that inequality is growing. As these populations still largely dominate the global discourse, "the normal Westerners", this has become the leading narrative.

- Absolute poverty (living on less than two dollars a day) has been falling sharply due to economic growth around the world. An important aspect here is also that technological advancements have made it possible to get more value for less money. For instance, getting a smartphone, which contains many empowering technologies, is much less expensive than getting a camera, a computer, a telephone, and a GPS. Writing an email is less expensive than mailing a letter, reading Wikipedia is less expensive than buying books or newspapers, and so forth. Internet trade and large retail warehouses like Walmart have also increased the efficiency of distribution and thereby made many consumer goods much cheaper. The world at large is becoming richer at an astounding pace.

- And yes, Doctor Piketty, a small proportion of the global population has been amassing a growing share of the wealth. This is the result of two fundamental factors: globalization and technological progress. Globalization (increasing trade, communication and foreign direct investments) connects all of us into one bustling economy of seven going on eight billion people. **In a smaller world, say a tribe of 150 people, you can never really get much richer than anyone else. But when there are billions of interacting people, those who gain the most central positions in the economy can become very, very rich.** This is due to what network theorists like Albert-László Barabási call "non-random networks", i.e. that the central positions always have more connections to make use of. Add to this some central technologies that are difficult to create, but many people want or need, and you have setup a cocktail for small groups to become incredibly wealthy. This is reinforced by the dynamics of the digital economy and its large platforms which tie millions of market agents to the same central nodes, which grants the advantages of "big data" to the central agents.

Thus, the interconnected world market is creating a situation where global inequality is decreasing, poverty is decreasing, *but* inequality is increasing *within* countries, and small transnational elites are becoming much, much richer than the rest of us.

You can see it all summed up in this one graph, taken from *Our World in Data:*[52]

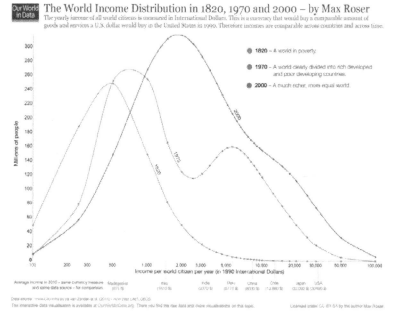

You can see how, in 1970, there were a rich world and a poor one (the two bumps on the 1970 distribution). By 2000, however, this had changed into one large, even global, pyramid with more people at the top and fewer at the very bottom. The rich countries no longer offer the same "buffer" against inequality within their borders—now we are all part of the same competitive mega-structure that is the global market.[53]

Which conclusions can be drawn from this analysis? An obvious one is that inequality is increasingly a *global* issue, and thus more of a transnational concern than a national one. This means that economic inequality—for all its importance and for all of its harmful effects—cannot readily be tackled by means of classical Left economics of redistribution within the singular state. If you raise the taxes and redistribute wealth too vigorously within one country, this does not only necessitate the exclusion of foreigners, but it also scares away global capital. Hence, we need effective global systems of redistribution. In order to reach a point where serious global redistribution is possible, we would require a larger systemic shift towards global governance.

And to get there we need significant proportions of postmodern and metamodern people around the world. And these people only show up in significant numbers within the postindustrial strata of the world economy, which makes any prospect of establishing such a world order unachievable for the foreseeable future as it won't be possible without vital economies such as China and India.

This is not to say that income redistribution is futile: Stronger economies with functional institutions can still perform relatively extensive such measures. But redistribution by means of taxes and social security is just not sufficient to counter the extremely powerful trends that drive the world economy: globalization, non-random network effects, technological advancements and unregulated transnational markets. However, as we shall now discuss, there are *other* ways to decrease the viscerally felt inequality between human beings. In fact, I would argue, that an exaggerated focus on economic inequality leaves us with an impoverished vision of what equality really is.

SOCIAL INEQUALITY

I have a younger relative who lives with schizophrenia (unfortunately not the first or only case in the family). If he doesn't take heavy medications he can hear voices, hallucinate and easily get overwhelmed. His medication makes him tired and leaves him with a short attention span, so it's difficult for him to work within an advanced economy. Living in a welfare state, he gets all he needs in terms of food, shelter, medical attention; even a little money to go to punk concerts twice a year and have a few beers now and then. Yet his life can only be described as a very difficult one. His main problem? Loneliness.

Besides his closest family, this lonely rider doesn't have any friends, let alone romantic partners. This isn't because he's not a nice person. He is quite friendly and rather intelligent, has some style going on, a somewhat rugged guy with tattoos who sometimes draws female attention. He lives on considerably more resources and money than most people during their student years, but he lacks something else: to be considered as a social equal and to be recognized as a friend.

By the look of it, this shouldn't be very difficult to fix. Can't he join a club and make some friends there? Can't he go on online dating and find a partner? But no, he cannot. All of his old friends have subtly abandoned him. They sometimes say they will call or come visit when in town, but when push comes to shove, they never do. It's just him, and his dog— every day, each day of the year, for years on end. And sometimes dinner at his mother's house, but she won't be there forever. Loneliness.

If this doesn't qualify as a severe form of inequality, I don't know what would. If this guy goes to the local pub and musters the courage to sit down with a party of strangers, he will very soon be asked "what he does". And if he doesn't want to spend his evening with odd evading answers or unsustainable lies, he will need to say he doesn't have a job. The next question that presents itself is "why". And that's even more difficult to answer: "I have schizophrenia". But that's not the end of it. If it comes out, or is intuited, that this is a lonely man with no friends, he will evoke no interest or sympathy in his interlocutors. They will physically turn their backs on him—literally speaking—and find reasons to end the conversation shortly. Rejection, rejection, rejection.

And this isn't about money. If he had the same apartment, the same financial means, even being unemployed—but had lots of friends, contacts, fun stories about what he has going on and interesting things to say, then he would be welcomed. His illness has put him in a position where he has **low social capital**. From this position he has no references to make in any new social situation he finds himself; and in this manner, his social poverty reproduces itself and isolates him from his fellow human beings.

This is of course only one example of a wider and deeper phenomenon of **social inequality**. Social capital comes in many complex forms: number of friends, in turn how well connected and popular these friends are, the depth and stability of those friendships, personal charm, good family relations, professional contacts, socio-economic status, being "cool", enjoying the trust and admiration of people, having sexual appeal, being respected for one's achievements, having many good stories to tell, being able to make fun and interesting events happen, and so forth.

Social capital of this kind can describe both a person and a society. A person who has higher social capital is one who always gets invited, who is welcome, for who doors are always open, and who can count on the support of others. A society with higher social capital can boast greater interpersonal trust, higher levels of solidarity and greater propensity to help strangers, trust in institutions and lower corruption, greater voter turnout, more cooperation and lesser destructive competition—and generally fewer people who are lonely and left to fend for themselves.

Social inequality exists not only in the human world, but can readily be observed in the animal kingdom. Different primates organize in groups where social status varies according to their species and environments, some animals being more egalitarian than others. In humans, if economic inequality doesn't show up to significant degrees in small tribes of a 150 people, *social* inequality certainly does. And it is, of course, very painful for the deprived.

In larger human societies, social inequality can have very numerous and more complex causes. It interacts, unsurprisingly, with economic inequality. If you have more contacts who trust, respect or even admire you, it becomes much easier to earn money as well. And if you earn money, it becomes easier to be an interesting friend, romantic partner and so forth. But beyond economics, social inequality also follows the larger dominator hierarchies and stratifications of society, such as ethnicity, race, gender, sexuality, class, social stigma (like disabilities) and what the sociologist Bourdieu famously called *habitus*, i.e. how you subtly express your standing in society through gestures, taste, language use and so forth. It's just easier to be a cool white male New Yorker in flashy clothes than to be a black disabled woman in a small town wearing Walmart clothes.

So this is what social inequality looks like; here's a "sociogram" of 63 Chinese children in a class of 6th graders. They can nominate other kids as friends (arrow).[54]

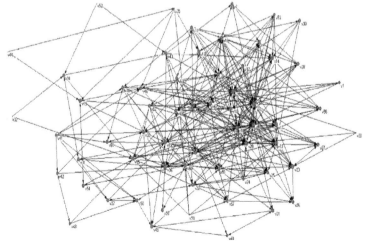

All kids nominate at least two friends, but not all kids are nominated. Far from all children who are nominated by someone nominate them back. As you can see, there is a clear pecking order where some kids are at the center and even enjoy the prestige of being friends with the popular ones, while others are sidelined all but completely. They are also at the longest distance from the most popular ones.

Such spontaneous processes self-organize automatically throughout society based on the ongoing interactions of people. And then they crystalize and reinforce themselves: The people at the center of the social clusters have innumerable advantages over those at the peripheries. What a cruel world!

It is insufficient to focus only on economic inequality when said processes of social stratification remain present. Social inequality is just as cynical and harmful—and viscerally felt—as its economic counterpart. It is not difficult to see, moreover, that social inequalities also can have far-reaching economic consequences.

In modern societies, such social inequality comes in two related but distinct flavors: the **socio-economic status** dominant in adult life, and the **micro-social status or "coolness" or "popularity"** dominant in adolescent life and youth culture. The first is of course tied to such things as professional status, success and achievement, while the second is tied to personal expression, taste, fashion and lifestyle, and it remains an important factor for social and mating success throughout one's lifespan.

Within the creative classes and other fresh, fly and funky bastions of society, coolness in terms of aesthetics, education and taste are closely tied to economic success. In postindustrial societies, "coolness" tends to become yet more pronounced—where hipsters, hackers and hippies often awake bitter resentment in the rest of the population with their flagrant displays of "refined" expressions of art, conversation topics, fashion and instagramable lifestyles.

The long-term egalitarian goal must be, of course, to make such things as fashion and taste matter less for people's social recognition and dignity. So we are not only looking to remedy the "hidden injuries of class" (as the sociologist Richard Sennett famously termed it), but also "to end the reign of cool".

Social inequality harms people. When more pronounced, we can expect a number of distortions of the games of everyday life. People are likely to become tenser and less relaxed, more scheming and strategic in their friendship formations, less likely to challenge norms and habits, more socially competitive, more prone to slander and mock one another, and more prone to take anti-social measures to check or reverse the social prestige of rivals. People will judge the ideas and opinions of one another less by merit and more by status, and there is less of a stable foundation for democratic ideals and solidarity in general. How afraid are we not of losing our social ties, or to be scorned and looked down upon? When it comes to social status, people are suckers—and for good reason, too.

Social inequality is, of course, yet more difficult to address than economic inequality. After all, money and material resources can be transferred from one person to another, but friendships, trust, respect and inclusion cannot; they are not "given", but only *elicited* through different behaviors and interactions.

However, as strange as it initially may appear, we can often do *more* about social inequality than about its economic counterpart, and such measures can often combat inequality more profoundly and effectively. We cannot change the logic of the global economic order overnight, but we *can* certainly shape and design organizations and institutions that generate a higher likelihood for social equality. In schools, we can have meditation training (which elicits more pro-social behaviors on a day-to-day basis), collaborative learning games in which all kids get to contribute to the greater whole, carefully designed (and non-sexual) massage sessions where kids touch one another in a friendly manner across the hierarchies, playgrounds designed for inclusive games, training in social and emotional intelligence, extended sexual education, and so forth.

In society at large, we can apply vaguer and corresponding measures, not least creating a layer of social support (by trained professionals) for the truly excluded ones, who can then be coached to greater social competence and be encouraged in their attempts. The sexual games can change if the average person is more socially and emotionally functional—and of course, norms can evolve towards less materialistic values, and unnecessary taboos and stigma can be breached so that people are generally more accepting of differences. For instance, in a more post-materialist culture, being "unemployed" can be less of a big deal as people can be offered a wider range of opportunities to create positive social identities beyond their employment status and profession—identities that reach deeper into the personal, civic, spiritual and aesthetic realms, echoing the words of the Young Marx:

> "Assume *man* to be *man* and his relationship to the world to be a human one: then you can exchange love only for love, trust for trust, etc. If you want to enjoy art, you must be an artistically cultivated person; if you want

to exercise influence over other people, you must be a person with a stimulating and encouraging effect on other people."[55]

Even if the Young Marx writes with the "humanist"[56] perspective of his time, and even if it smacks of romantic game denial, his vision is certainly a compelling one. Can we create a society in which people's exchanges are free from irrational and distorting hierarchies such as different levels of wealth?

Within affluent welfare societies like Sweden, the struggle for material equality is often really the struggle for *social* equality in disguise. In such societies, it is not that people are actually starving, but rather that lacking economic wealth can negatively affect their status and hinder their inclusion into social events. You even hear nurses, school teachers and police officers say: "It's not that I really need that much money. I just want my paycheck to properly validate my work and effort."

In such societies, it may well be time to more directly address the more complex, touchy—and embarrassing—issue of *social* inequality. This is not only a question of extending a vague "inclusion" of minorities and misfits, but also, and primarily, an issue of changing the games through which everyday life plays out. An important part of this is to help people become more socially competent and empowered.

Going back to my young relative with schizophrenia, he doesn't need to be included because people feel sorry for him—he needs skills, resources and occasions to be genuinely valuable to others so that they will be happy and proud to call him a friend or a lover. This, in turn, would save society a lot in terms of his worsening medical condition and by letting him be of service to others.

To conclude, here's an example of how a scale of people's social capital might look like: The richer you are, the more you can "afford" to act outside of norms, comfort zones and so forth. How many bridges can you afford to burn?

1. You can burn 90+ percent of your bridges without significant loss of subjective wellbeing, after recovering from the loss (famous people: even complete strangers will find you valuable and want to keep you alive and well).

2. You can burn more than half your bridges without significant loss of subjective wellbeing.

3. You can lose any one major field (professional, group of friends) of your life but still thrive.

4. You can lose any one major bridge within any one major field but still thrive.

5. You can lose any one major bridge but still manage at a lower level of subjective wellbeing.

6. You cannot afford to lose any major bridge without a dramatic drop in wellbeing and the risk of crisis/depression increases.

7. You have very few real bridges and must constantly worry about keeping them.

8. You have very few bridges and feel a pressing fear of losing them very often ("social precariat").

9. You lack major bridges and live in crisis ("social precariat nightmare").

10. You lack bridges and support structure to handle crisis (*pariah*, everyone shuns you, and even social workers privately look down upon you while helping).

Each stage represents a *quantitative* difference that causes a *qualitative* shift. That's how capital and inequality work. You get more of something, and once you have a certain amount, the whole game shifts and your outlook on life changes. Just shifting one or two steps on this scale puts you on a whole other map, in a different world.[57]

PHYSIOLOGICAL INEQUALITY

Let's link the social to the biological body itself.

According to a recent study published in *Science*, you can take a female rhesus monkey (or "macaque"), put her in a terrarium, then gradually add more monkeys over time, and the one who was there first will then generally have the highest social status while the newcomers will have lower status—much like in Norbert Elias' and John L. Scotson's 1965 classical sociological study of an English small-town community, *The Established and the Outsiders*. The established were often, quite simply, the people who had lived in the community the longest while the newly arrived were the outsiders.

The monkey researchers could reverse the social order of the rhesus monkeys by letting them into the terrarium in another sequence. The ethical issue of treating monkeys like this aside, the researchers made an interesting finding that was unavailable to the sociologists: **that the quality of the immune system of the monkeys depended on their position in the social hierarchy.** If you came in last, and hence had the lowest status, your immune system was much weaker. And this could be reversed if the researchers intervened to change the social order again.

In other words, the social hierarchy of the monkeys determined some of their biological characteristics, even down to the biochemical level—social stress affects the expression of almost 1,000 genes. Probably, the mechanism at play here is that lower ranking monkeys feel more stress and anxiety, which sets up their system for responses to more immediate threats (high cortisol levels and other stress responses), which then takes its toll on more long-term biological processes such as the immune system.[58] Oh, and it's not just macaques by the way—the Stanford primatologist Robert Sapolsky has found the same pattern in ethological studies of freely roaming baboons in Africa.

So if you're low status, you also get sick. Hey, I told you it's a cruel world out there.

Point being, of course, that **there is an inescapably *physiological* side to inequality. It really goes both ways—other forms of inequality, such as economic and social, can have negative physiological consequences, and disadvantageous physiological states or traits can in themselves be sources of other inequalities.** There is any number of studies to show different aspects of this, not only within the animal realm but among humans as well.

For instance, taller people make more money. People in rich countries tend to grow taller than people in poor countries. Fat people are kept at farther physical distance by slim people during everyday interactions, and distance is spontaneously kept between people of different social status. Good-looking people have happier lives. Disabled people suffer from stigma, are discriminated against, and are thus limited beyond the inherent limitations caused by their disabilities. Poor people have worse health and worse medical care, in turn affecting economic success. People with higher status are touched more, which protects from stress, which boosts health and long-term performance. People in higher social classes eat better and do more effective workout and have less physically strenuous jobs. It even seems that women's menstruation cycles fall into sync, where the dominant woman of the group leads the others (there's not quite consensus on that one). And more dominant men smell better to ovulating women, especially if the women are young, fertile and already in a stable relationship (likely because natural selection has favored moderate amounts of infidelity).

Okay, that last one gets a reference, just because.[59] You can look all of this stuff up if you like. There's lots of it.

Again, there is a physiological, deeply *embodied*, side to inequality—and it reaches all the way down to the biochemical level, affecting long-term processes that steer our lives and shape society. As biological creatures, we are not equals. Inequality, your position in the social hierarchies, sticks in your body: victories, successes and social validation are embedded in your spine, into your body posture, into your very DNA. And so are losses, failures and rejections, real or imagined. Dominance hierarchies go far back in evolutionary psychology; we can see that animals of all kinds have confrontations, and hormones change depending on who wins, with changed ensuing behaviors as a result.

Your entire *habitus* scents of dominance or submission, of confidence or insecurity, of power, pride and prestige or of tense frustration, shame and the accumulated disdain of others. **Inequality lives in and through human and animal bodies. And society's institutions can work to exa-** **cerbate or combat this inequality.**

The sociologist Catherine Hakim has even proposed that there may be such a thing as "sexual" or "erotic" capital, which suggests a corresponding form of inequality in society.[60] There is good reason to take Hakim's idea seriously as it is well known and proven that richer men end up with women of greater fecundity, and that sex and sexuality certainly play a part in the stratifications of human relations.

I do, however, feel that the categories of social, physiological and—as we shall see—emotional inequality together may give a fuller and more comprehensive account of these dynamics. In other words, I view sexual capital as an emergent subcategory of these three. But certainly, it deserves attention: How held back and beaten down are we by sexual and romantic rejections? More on this in the second part of the book.

So both economic and social inequality leave deep physiological traces; and these in turn reproduce inequalities in any number of ways. The mechanisms and causal feedback loops of physiological inequality can be many different ones, epigenetics (the ongoing activation and deactivation of genes) only being one frontier to explore.

The different forms interact. At the most basic level, malnourishment hinders optimal physical and cognitive growth, and thus perpetuates powerlessness, submission and poverty. This has been common knowledge for decades and is part and parcel of studies of economic development and foreign aid.

There are, however, also studies of affluent countries that reveal the deeply seated inherited physiological inequalities that reproduce themselves over generations. I would like to mention two such bodies of work: the so-called Whitehall studies and the Canadian studies of (epi-)genetic de-generation due to childhood adversities.

The Whitehall studies (there are two of them) looked at over 18,000 British male civil servants for a period of ten years. The first studies were conducted from the 1960s to the 1980s, but they have had follow-ups to this day, and they look especially at factors that could explain cardio-vascular diseases and mortality rates. And lo and behold, these studies heralded an entry of social science into medicine and vice versa: Men of lower rank died off more quickly than those of higher rank. Lower rank-ing grade was associated with a number of risk factors, including obesity, smoking, reduced leisure time, lower levels of physical activity, higher blood pressure and higher prevalence of underlying illness.

"Whitehall II" found that additional factors affect health across a life-span: the way work is organized, work climate, social influences from out-side of work, influences from early life, and health behaviors.

There is no escape from the marriage between social and natural or clinical science, for one thing. And there is, moreover, no escape from the physiological dimension of inequality.

The second body of work is the Canadian studies of epigenetics and population epigenomics (how genes are affected by demographic and so-cial factors). The global leadership of this field consists of a rather wide research community of senior medical scientists, more than I can name here. This wide network has been doing truly groundbreaking and pro-foundly relevant work when it comes to understanding physiological inequality. The studies suggests, among other things, that "DNA methyl-ation" (basically, our genetic aging) increases in kids whose parents were stressed out during pregnancy and/or their children's early childhoods.[61] You can look at a fifteen-year-old and see their gene expressions are dif-ferent from more privileged peers—and more like those of older people— if their parents went through some rough times when they were little. You get scarred at the *molecular* level for things that happened before you can remember.[62]

This is true not only at the individual level, but also at the level of whole schools and larger communities. And we have already seen that lower social status can stress people out, as can economic insecurity. What we may be looking at here is thus a very intricate and intimate form of inequality reproducing itself. But more research is needed—and the Cana-dians are providing it.

All of this points us towards a discussion about which measures could reasonably be taken to reduce physiological inequality. Whereas this issue is not generally on the political agenda, there have been some interesting developments during the 20th century. One simple such is that dental care was offered to many more citizens, especially in social democracies like Sweden. Social-democratic leaders took to heart the struggle to improve the teeth of poor children, and while their reforms perhaps did less to improve and equalize oral health than the simple proliferation of tooth-brushes and tooth paste, they did let all school kids flush their teeth with fluorine and largely managed to decouple shiny white teeth from distinctions of class. To this day, it is even a common measure for municipalities in Sweden to pay for entire sets of synthetic teeth for the homeless so as to improve their overall health and decrease their physiological stigma. Such measures generally get thumbs up in social work scholarship, but they are of course expensive and thus have difficulties securing sustained public funding.

The question is to which extent physiological inequalities are caused by other inequalities—of wealth and status—and to which extent the opposite is true, i.e. that physiological differences cause other inequalities. And the question is *which* physical inequalities can be changed through political and social measures and which ones remain largely immutable. We cannot, of course, make a person with Down syndrome score high on IQ tests or make a person who lost her legs in an accident suddenly grow her limbs back. But many measures *are*, indisputably, possible to take, many physiological factors and developments *can* be affected by conscious design, both on a day-to-day basis, and over the course of a lifespan—with profound implications for public health, physical and mental. And such physiological or bio-social factors hint at a wide canopy of measures that can affect and reduce the complex reproduction of inequality throughout society.

Without delving deeper into the discussion, let us simply name a few possible such measures: widespread training in posture and physiothera-peutic practices such as "basic body awareness" as proposed by Jacques Dropsy and Gertrud Roxendal; training in uses of body language (which has been shown to affect emotions and degrees of confidence and asser-tiveness); the facilitation of making healthy food choices that favor slow metabolism, stress tolerance and resilient bodies; the cultivation of a non-judgmental and non-competitive "gym culture"; the transformation of public spaces with more available outdoor facilities for physical exercise; combating stress and ergonomic strains of office life and work life in ge-neral; the expansion of physical and bodily labor rights to protect from physical harm; the increase of leisure time to pursue physical and mental training—and so forth.

All of these things can and do interact with other forms of inequality and empower millions of perpetually disempowered human bodies. And as human bodies are strengthened, so are human dignities salvaged and human potentials released.

EMOTIONAL INEQUALITY

It has been shown in a growing body of recent research that social exclusion and rejection activate similar patterns in the brain as physical pain. Social exclusion is like a slap in your face. This is a *real* thing: You subject someone even to a small slight or rejection, and not only do they experience pain, they also become more vulnerable to such pain in the future, *and* their emotional state is pushed towards vengefulness and envy—even increasing the propensity towards physical aggression.[63]

If we zoom in yet another step on the intimate and embodied processes of inequality, we find that human lives are lived in profoundly unequal emotional surroundings.

Some of us wake up relatively carefree many mornings and experience positive rewards as the results of our actions, while others live out their lives in considerably more painful and impoverished inner landscapes. This is a form of inequality: **emotional inequality**.

And, as the network sociologists Fowler and Christakis have famously shown, such emotions are collective goods, as for instance happiness and life satisfaction cluster in networks of people.[64] If your friend is happier, so are you more likely to be.

This is probably because of different mechanisms: that happy people make others happier, that people who are doing better generally are happier and have the luxury of choosing friends and partners who are also doing well (while subtly excluding the less fortunate), and that other life factors make people cluster together into happy and unhappy segments of society.

In Book One, I labored to show that people—and other living creatures—are in different subjective "states" at every moment of our lives. To be alive is to feel *like* something: stable wellbeing, or nagging discomfort, or nightmarish valleys, or even spiritual and blissful heights of subjective experience. Such states are very volatile; they can change from moment to moment, but some people certainly live in higher states than others.

The totality of our experience is never quite "neutral". Imagine the great difference, in terms of real-life outcomes, between people who live their lives in lower states and people who live in higher ones.

Would such emotional workings not be the very foundation of equality and inequality? Is not the aim of all struggles for equality, after all, to guarantee that people can live rich and wonderful inner lives, rather than impoverished and suffocating ones?

What could be a greater privilege than having a fundamental sense of "okay-ness", even a sense of meaning, enchantment and wonder, throughout one's life? And what could be a greater injustice done to us than having our lives filled with embitterment, resentment, self-hatred—or even sheer existential terror?

I also argued in Book One that "subjective states" are more fundamental than emotions. But this, of course, doesn't mean emotions don't matter. In the previous chapter we discussed that freedom is always related to emotions, consciously felt *or* lying dormant in the background but still steering our everyday actions and interactions. Society, in this view, is a vast, interconnected **fabric of suffering and bliss**, pulsating and reverberating with multitudes upon multitudes of lived experiences. Can this fabric be consciously and actively developed? Yes, it can.[65]

It is the goal of political metamodernism to extend compassion, or at least solidarity, to this whole fabric of hurt and bliss, to society in its complex entirety, to the co-emergent inner worlds of countless millions.

Let's take a look at how emotions are unevenly and unfairly distributed among human organisms (and non-human animals). If a person is happier and more energetic, this plays out in every aspect of her life. The happy person has an easier time getting things done since the reward feedback loops are more functional. This means she will be able to produce better results for herself as well as others, which means she will be more respected and gain greater recognition, attain a better self-image and thereby boosting her sense of meaning and happiness.

Conversely, the sad and depressed person doesn't get emotional rewards for performing tasks, which wrecks the positive behavioral feedback loops. In fact, she gets emotional *punishment* for most of the things she does, which makes it so much harder to make an effort to change her situation.

This very easily leads to anxiety, fear, shame, embarrassment and self-hatred—which paralyzes her and makes her strivings seem futile. And she is less fun to be around, which in turn makes her lonelier.

These proposed mechanisms are of course simplifications, but they are firmly established in behavioral science. You also have lots of folks who are very active and productive but still struggle with feelings of anxiety and lacking meaning; consider the many empty treadmills that bourgeois life can put us through.

But the point is that emotional hurt and lower states *do* have great costs over a lifespan. It has been shown, for instance, that bad parenting can knock 20 years off your life expectancy.[66]

Here's another example. In an influential 2013 book called *Scarcity*, the behavioral economists Mullainathan and Shafir presented ample evidence of a "scarcity mindset". Poverty taxes cognitive resources and causes self-control failure. We literally become dumber and make more short-sighted decisions when we are poor or under economic stress: we eat less healthy, invest less intelligently and we even score lower on IQ tests. When we feel like crap, we get stuck in a scarcity mindset. This is a form of emotional inequality.

On the flipside, you can see how affluent populations tend to develop higher value memes and post-materialist (non-consumerist, environmentalist, etc.) values over time, as has been the case in e.g. the Nordic countries. You feel good, you space out, you have the time to contemplate life, and so forth.

There is good reason to believe this principle of a scarcity mindset extends well beyond economic decision-making and that it is equally valid in other areas of life: love, dating (where dating coaches also warn of a destructive scarcity mindset, using the exact same term), social recognition, making one's opinions and values heard, and so forth. So inequality of any kind likely produces *emotions* and *general mindsets* that steer our many decisions and hence our lives. **Inner states and emotions are at the center of how inequality is reproduced across all of its dimensions.**

Our streams of thought, our very streams of consciousness, look very different from each other, often steered by emotions. How evenly is *shame* distributed in the population? What about fear and self-hatred? Frustration and bitterness?

Even if all of us experience these emotions, there are large segments of the population whose very lives are run by these. And how many of us get to feel satisfied, proud and stimulated on a daily basis? And when the insecure, the nervous and the grief-stricken encounter the laid-back, the comfortable, the happy—what are all other, more superficial, forms of equality ultimately worth? How much easier is it not to dominate, exploit and manipulate the emotionally impoverished? On the other hand, what is more empowering than peace of mind? More empowering than a heart in love with life itself?

Whereas all of these emotions of course emerge in larger contexts, in our living conditions and social-psychological circumstances as well as in our personal biological and genetic constitutions, it is not impossible to directly influence and steer the emotional development of human beings.

Even if our emotions are products of economic, social and physiological inequalities, **there are, roughly speaking, two forms of services that can be offered: 1) the eliciting and boosting of positive emotions and 2) the support towards successfully coping with, integrating and transmuting negative emotions.**

In a listening society, the deeper welfare of the future, we can and should create institutions and structures that work against emotional inequality—not, of course, by making the happy miserable to even out the playing field, but by strengthening our psyches so as to deal with difficult emotions. We should offer good emotional support, training and services to all citizens from the day they are born until their dying breath. If you care about the *real*, fundamental equality and dignity of humans, no other conclusion is possible or justifiable.

Some of the possible political measures that have been mentioned above, under social and physiological inequality, feed into the struggle for emotional equality. For instance, again, we can affect emotions by developing body postures and body language, by training social and emotional intelligence, by making sure good meditation practices are taught, and by making healthy food more available—for instance, intake of vegetables has been shown to protect against depression, as has physical exercise.

But emotions can be targeted even more directly. For example, all children could be offered simple forms of counseling during their school years, which would help many of them from being taken over by destructive emotions during their early lives and onwards. Schools could use exercises of "positive psychology", and the general framework of schooling could be designed to elicit more positive emotions. We could have greater possibilities for adults to take a year off and work on their emotional issues and concerns, with places of rest and recluse. And people could be trained to better manage conflicts and rejections, which severely affect our emotional wellbeing and development. At the national level, we could start measuring the prevalence of different emotions and present public statistics to guide public discourse.

The issue here is not to pan out all the solutions—thousands are possible, with so many social technologies that must be invented, implemented, evaluated and refined; and the sky is the limit. The issue here is only to raise awareness of the question of emotional inequality so that the political discussion can begin, and so that it can enter the political agenda.

Even if all emotions are, in some cosmic last instance, "okay", we really shouldn't wish for ourselves or our fellow citizens to be trapped by fear, shame, guilt, aggression and envy. Such emotions exacerbate inequalities and suffering in more ways than we could hope to name or think of.

ECOLOGICAL INEQUALITY

Ecological inequality includes such things as access to fresh air, clean water, lush vegetation, beautiful scenery, healthy and non-toxic food, clean living spaces—even sunlight. In many large Chinese cities, a lot of people hardly see the sun, and millions die as a result of air pollution. Many people around the world work in noisy, physically dangerous, dirty and toxic environments, like children in West Africa working on huge piles of waste from electronics, slowly poisoning themselves to retrieve valuable metals and minerals. The brunt of harm caused by environmental degradation is carried very unevenly by populations. You see this in everything from poor climate migrants, to subsistence farming damaged by global warming, to cognitive growth stunted caused by poisoned waterways.

Of course, this kind of inequality is closely tied to the global economic order. The rich can choose to live in nicer and cleaner environments, buy heathier products, go on hikes or health resorts, and so on. This, naturally, translates into other stratifications, such as race and ethnicity; for instance, in the US, in California, it has been shown that blacks and Latinos on average breathe in 40% more air pollution than whites—which naturally affects physiological equality and thus all the rest of it.[67]

And the rich parts of the world generally transpose the most environmentally destructive production processes and industries to the poorer parts. Citizens living in poor areas of urban India have fewer choices in terms of healthy food and environments. This of course in turn affects all other aspects of inequality: economic, social, physiological and emotional.

Even if the expansion of "rights" is far from always the best and most practical way of protecting people's interests, we should at least discuss the possibility of introducing **ecological rights** of citizens and/or communities. Rights can lead to rather rigid forms of governance and they are difficult to relate to in terms of cost/benefit analysis, but something along these lines may offer productive venues for future global policies.

As it is relatively easy to see and understand this aspect of inequality, I will not dwell further upon it; suffice to say it is a crucial part of equality, that it is an issue that divides the rich world from the poor, and that it interacts with differences of socio-economic class. And even if a new global order is needed for this to be seriously addressed, there is of course much that can be done at the local level.

INFORMATIONAL INEQUALITY

The sixth and last form of inequality is one we cannot miss in the Internet Age: **informational inequality**, the divide between the haves and have-nots of information and knowledge. There has been much written about the "digital divide" which privileges younger generations over older ones, digitized economies with good broadband infrastructure over poor developing countries, and so forth.

The digital divide is, however, not always a straightforward issue of "internet access". For instance, white US children spend on average 8.5 hours daily in front of a screen, while Hispanic and black children spend about 13 hours (watching more TV, playing video games, social media etc.), with obvious negative effects upon physical and mental health as well as psycho-social development. The relationship to information and IT also reinforces inequalities. Those stuck at the bottom of the "attentionalist economy" are perpetually distracted from projects of self-empowerment. The quality of their information flows and resulting worldviews deteriorates, which feeds into economic and social capital: time is "wasted" and the ability to recognize emotional cues in facial expression shrinks with excessive screen-time. Too much screen-time also seems to increase the likelihood of developing ADHD, which in itself makes it difficult for you to economize that cardinal resource: your attention.[68]

At a more fundamental level, access to useful and reliable information is one of the greatest consequences of economic inequality. Financially strong actors will know the markets, prices, tax evasion strategies and so forth to a much greater extent than the weaker ones.

The well-positioned can buy expertise and process much larger flows of information, which plays out against the weak in favor of the strong. In its most salient form, this is true of the large internet companies, who own and manage vast quantities of personal information about people—increasingly knowing not only the markets, but the behaviors of citizens and consumers, often much better than we know ourselves. Tinder can have literally 800 pages worth of very sensitive personal information if you've been on it for a few years.

Hence, informational inequality works through many different mechanisms. One such mechanism revolves around the powers of producers and large companies over consumers, with the latter by necessity having lesser access to relevant information, thus being easily manipulated in a myriad of ways.

And this dissymmetry of informational access plays out in a corresponding manner within the political arena as wealthy groups gain disproportionally large political influence and misuse state institutions to protect their interests, shaping media landscapes and curtailing the transparency of decision-making and bureaucracies.

And beyond that you have the general pattern that some people thrive in the information age, being able to critically evaluate and access vast amounts of information and creating vibrant networks of highly skilled cooperators, whereas the less complex thinkers and less technically apt fall prey to fake news, misinformation and waste their attention, time and money on things that don't accumulate good results in their lives. This mechanism exacerbates the other forms of inequality, where the less educated and more emotionally desperate are more easily exploited.

It is difficult to see how this rampant informational inequality can be curbed, but it certainly plays a part through its interactions with the other forms. We could imagine a future where internet access is readily available and free around the globe and where basic education would equip us with at least some basic informational savvy, networking skills and critical judgment. We may also envision the growth of transnationally enforced **informational rights** of world citizens.

What about cultural inequality then? For curious readers, I have reserved this discussion for an endnote.[69]

For now, let's see what deeper equality would mean.

Chapter 7

DEEPER EQUALITY

I have now presented six forms of inequality: economic, social, physiological, emotional, ecological and informational—all of which interact with each other. Or conversely, we can speak of uneven distributions of economic, social, physiological, emotional, ecological and informational *capital*. Taken together with concepts such as cultural and sexual capital, these can be said to constitute a person's or group's **total capital** (or lack thereof).

Most observers have failed to recognize total capital. And this means they have failed to defend and develop real equality. Rather, most of politics today is stuck with a helplessly superficial idea of equality; one that does, in its analytical crudeness, leave millions of children to be crushed under its wheels.

DEEPER RESONANCES

Some readers of a more classical Left persuasion may feel this multidimensional focus obscures the central issue of economic inequality, and that it may be used to provide excuses for it. Yet I would insist the opposite is true: A richer and more inclusive view of inequality serves to highlight the real mechanisms of inequality, hence giving us more and better possibilities to work for a fair and equal world order.

I would argue, moreover, that such a vision strives towards a deeper and more fundamental form of equality, one that reaches deeper into the embodied lives of humans. It doesn't take anything away from the struggle for economic equality; it just opens more venues for transformation.

Any struggle for equality worth its salt in the coming period must strive to increase equality across all six dimensions. The listening society must be deliberately and sensitively optimized to minimize inequality across all six—given of course it is achieved in a manner consistent with the principles of "game change" rather than "game denial" as discussed in chapter 2, and as long as it doesn't conflict with the development of freedom, as outlined in chapter 4 and 5. **A multidimensional equality is a more real equality, and hence a deeper equality.**

I have already suggested how to think about the interactions of the six dimensions of inequality. Let me repeat myself: "Each stage here represents a *quantitative* difference that causes a *qualitative* shift. That's how capital and inequality work. You get more of something, and once you have a certain amount, the whole game shifts and your outlook on life changes."

The same holds true, naturally, in the "meta-system" of all six forms of inequality as they interact with each other. Your access to information sets limits for your economic success, which sets limits for your physiological wellbeing, which sets limits for your emotional wellbeing, which sets limits for your social life, which sets limits for your access to information... and so on.

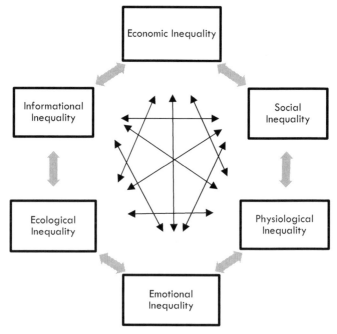

Figure: *The six dimensions of inequality. Any work to create a fair society is sure to backfire unless all six forms are taken into account and efforts are coordinated across all of them.*

These six dimensions of inequality form one great, deep pattern in society. This pattern constitutes a "meta-system", i.e. a set of interlinked and interdependent systems of inequality that can be compared to each other, but each of which also has unique and non-translatable properties that function by distinct logics and mechanisms. Deep "game change" has occurred whenever a pervasive shift in this "pattern of patterns" is effected.

This meta-system can be shifted from one pattern to another as society evolves or unravels. A useful metaphor for these fundamentally game changing "shifts" can be found in cymatics—an area of study at the cross-section of music, mathematics and the physics of waves.

The basic idea of cymatics is this: If you play a sound at a certain frequency over a fluid or a membrane with powder on it, a sound-wave induced pattern appears in the medium (the fluid or the powder on a membrane). The soundwaves are shaping the medium, upholding a certain pattern of waves. These patterns can be quite beautiful:

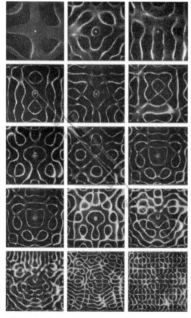

Figure: *Cymatics, here as white powder on a black vibrating disc to increasing frequencies of sound. As the frequency goes up, the pattern shifts from one equilibrium to another. I suggest that increases in multi-dimensional equality in society may effect shifts in the patterns of everyday life in a corresponding manner, shifting the dynamics from modern to metamodern life.*

The patterns change with the frequency of the sound. You go to a higher frequency, and the same pattern continues to reproduce itself, but with a finer and smaller grid of repetition. But if you increase the frequency enough, the whole pattern suddenly dissolves. And after a certain point, a new pattern emerges; *a more complex* pattern. You have reached an inherent systemic threshold. And as you increase the frequency further yet, the new pattern becomes more finely meshed until it dissolves and a new level is reached.

This is how cymatics work. You should do a web search for sassier images and videos of this mesmerizing phenomenon. At each stage, the pattern changes. And the same can be said—I would argue—of the games of everyday life: A metamodern pattern will not just be quantitatively "more of the same", more of what already exists in modern society, but something qualitatively distinct. Although this cymatics image may not be a ready "theory" of inequality, it serves as a general way to grasp how the games of life follow certain recognizable patterns and that these can shift between equilibria—between stages, if you will. The different social dimensions of life can be brought to *resonate*, as it were, with each other; a "deeper resonance" can chime through society and everyday life.

What we are looking at is a kind of social, transpersonal cymatics. The six dimensions of inequality together form an elegant but tragic pattern of human suffering and degradation. The fabric of suffering and bliss. It is by shifting the game across *all* fields of development, across *all* forms of inequality, that a new relative utopia can be realized.

EQUALITY, EQUIVALENCE, EQUANIMITY

What, then, are the farther reaches of equality? How can the overall "cymatics of equality" progress? What would a "deeper resonance" be like? The general idea would be that deeper equality is not only an issue of distribution, but also—and perhaps ultimately—a question of transformations of the eye of the beholder. Inequality is always caused by an act of measurement, by a beholder who judges the beheld as inferior, be it our "self" or one another. The deepest forms of equality must resonate not only in social structures, but also in the hearts and minds of all participant-observers.

There's a clear link to ideas of quantum physics, entanglement and enactment here: The "object" of inequality is non-local and interdependent with the observer. But let's not delve deeper into it at this point. It suffices to mention that the observer herself must be part of the equation of any deeper and more radical equality.

Instead, I would like to propose a simple stage model to address this issue. Not that the farther stages of equality are anywhere within reach in the present world, but just to understand where we might be heading long-term, *inshallah.*

Equality, stage one, is the struggle to make people more *equal,* to even out the real, visceral differences between us: the rich and the poor, the privileged and the underprivileged, the powerful and the disempowered, the enfranchised and the disenfranchised, the respected and the despised.

The six dimensions of equality all play into this struggle. There is an almost infinite amount of work to be done as obviously unjust inequalities saturate every aspect of our lives. The greatest inequality is of course the global divide between rich and poor—and thus, this must be our first and foremost focus.

In practical terms, we are so far from any form of global equality that we must *also* strive towards more local forms of equality; relative equality within the borders of countries. This is in order to curb the destructive effects of inequality upon each society so that these may develop in stable manners that serve the emergence of a transnational, global order which is fairer and more adaptive than our current morass of global governance (or lack thereof).

We need to let some societies—nations, city hubs and local communities—become nodes in the network that is the intermeshed transnational, *metamodern*, world order. Of course, this cannot happen unless people in these societies develop postmodern and metamodern values, and that can only happen if there isn't rampant inequality across all six dimensions.

Equality means making people more equal—in a sense, more alike. This is the classical understanding of equality within socialism and all modern ideologies. It is the kind of underlying assumption that still drives almost all the research into inequality—and all the practical policies towards the same end.

Equivalence goes deeper than that. It is the struggle for people to truly *feel* as equals, that we are of equal *value* or worth. After all, the very notion of equality is ridden with paradoxes. Ultimately, we cannot be equal since we are not alike. In fact, we are so *very* different from one another that even a theoretical state of "perfect equality of opportunity", a perfect meritocracy, (and the even yet more impossible "equality of information") would serve to highlight our differences and legitimize our inequalities.

Is there a way out of this paradox? There might be. What if equality could run so deeply that we genuinely feel as equals, in the sense that we are all world citizens and sentient beings? **This is *equivalence*, the genuine *sense of equal worth*.** Such an embodied sense would protect us not only from many exploitations and injustices, but also from many venues of self-blame and inferiority.

Such equivalence has already, to a certain extent, become reality through one of the great modern projects: liberal democracy, in which we are equal before the law, cast equally valid votes and so forth. Equivalence is also, in extension, the utopian or spiritual goal of socialism.

Modernity holds that people are endowed with sacred and inviolable, natural rights—unfortunately yet to be extended to other animals—and as such endowed with some kind of basic dignity.[70] We are "all humans", "all individual citizens of the state", "all workers of the people's republic", and so forth.

But in reality, the disempowered, disenfranchised, disdained and emotionally impoverished find little solace in this "formal" or legal idea of equivalence. It goes some way to make us feel like equals, but in practice, we hardly feel like dignified equals of one another.

If there could be a deeper form of equivalence, one that is felt and embodied by many more of us, this would work against the paradoxes of equality. If we genuinely felt the equal value of ourselves and others, many of the corrosive effects of inequality would certainly be mitigated. We could accept our differences and still feel as dignified equals.

Can we awaken in ourselves and one another a profound sense of dignity inherent to every human? This must be a goal that lies beyond formal, legal and material equality. Hence, equivalence is a *higher* stage than simple equality.

Equanimity goes deeper still. It is the spiritual and psychological struggle to give up our deeply seated tendency to judge and evaluate ourselves and others in the first place. You could say it's about transcending "the spectrum of judgment" (the scale of negative emotions) altogether, or to become less enthralled by the need to possess a comparatively positive self-image—an ego.

I snatched the term from Buddhist teachings in which "equanimity" is practiced as a mental stance of accepting our mental and bodily states as well as our life situations and ongoing events. As such it is linked to higher subjective and spiritual inner *states* and can only be achieved in a society in which the average inner state is much higher and the social logics of everyday life are governed as little as possible by the underlying negative emotions of the spectrum of judgment.

Equanimity doesn't mean that we give up discernment; we still need to evaluate the behaviors, ideas and efforts of one another. It just means there is a fundamental sense of "okay-ness", of **acceptance**—that our differences and inequalities no longer remain such a big deal.

And it certainly doesn't mean that we no longer care about inequalities and injustices—which Buddhism is often accused of by the Left.

In practice, true equanimity would only be conceivable in a state of profound material, emotional, social and existential abundance. So it's not really a conceivable goal for society anytime soon. It would be a society in which we obviously are not equals, but where that still—and strangely—is okay; where everyone "is okay", where people are not only tolerated but *accepted*.

Acceptance, in this sense, is the negative side of love. When we love someone fully, it is not only that we cherish their strengths and potentials, but that we *accept* their weaknesses and struggles. Such love can be found in some of the best families and long-lasting marriages.

Dare we ask of ourselves, for the future of humanity, to aspire for such an acceptance of all creatures under the sun? Here we return to the core of Christianity and other world religions. In a state of genuine non-hierarchical non-judgment, our inequalities can be treated more productively as *differences*—and nothing more.

Of course, equanimity of this kind would mean the end of that paradoxical phantom still haunting us: envy. When we no longer judge ourselves, we are no longer obsessed with the strengths and weaknesses of one another. And what lies beyond a life of fear, guilt, shame and *Sklavenmoral*; beyond hatred, judgment, disdain and envy?

There it is again, waiting for us, the crazy Nietzschean moustache: the *Übermensch*, the attractor point that draws us beyond the category of humanity and its limitations.

Perhaps, in the future, we can stumble upon it. *Inshallah*. And, as with freedom, we can begin to see that the higher goal of societal development is not so much to achieve "perfect equality", but rather **to render the very struggle for equality obsolete**.

Equality, equivalence and equanimity—**there is the progression, from leveling the unfair differences between us, to adopting a more profound sense of value for all, to letting go of our strange human obsession with impossible comparisons, ultimately rendering equality itself obsolete**.

But if the latter two are so distant, are they not merely a distraction from humanity's struggle for a more realistic equality? They can be. Why, then, have I presented them here?

Because they can still show up *momentarily*, in limited settings, for shorter periods of time, in small incubators within our personal relationships and some of the metamodern internet tribes out there. They might not stabilize or spread, but only flicker past us during our lives. But as such they can remind us of the deeper meaning of equality, and thus subtly steer the development of the world-system.

In such settings, where equanimity reigns, creativity must be held higher than equality. The longing for equality must not get in the way of creative processes that can help us achieve human flourishing in the first place. We must become lovers of the will to power—the power of ourselves *and* one another to create and to transcend.

SPIRITUALITY AS A CLASS MAGNIFIER

No discussion about inequality is complete without a consideration of "class". For brevity, however, I will not delve deeply into the question, but I should mention that distinctions of class are significantly transformed in postindustrial societies—as well as across the global world-system—and that this has repercussions not only for the struggle for deeper equality, but also for the development of the world-system as a whole.

The main issue is that the classical delineations of class, as one's relation to financial capital under the industrial mode of production, no longer act as a satisfying way to understand the stratifications of our current society. Rather, we should understand class as a complex amalgamate of different forms of capital: financial, cultural, social, emotional, physiological (including sexual) and informational. More on this new landscape of class in this endnote.[71]

To this sketchy picture I would like to add one important detail: the interactions of "class" with spirituality and self-improvement.

There has been great confusion, especially among observers on the political Left and other progressives, as to which role spirituality and related forms of self-improvement play in postindustrial society.

The most common understanding is perhaps still that spirituality, especially of the New Age kind, is a dangerous distraction from "real" societal issues and social engagement—and that self-improvement courses offer an "individualization" of societal ills and injustices. Such practices are often seen as allies to neo-liberal capitalism as "the individual" only has herself to blame and her own mind to work on: "don't protest, just go home and meditate". I should especially address the issue as my own work —which focuses much on the inner development of the population—can be subject to similar reactions.

I would suggest another understanding of the relation between spirituality and class, one that will need to remain on the hypothetical level until we can study it with relevant data: namely that **spirituality and self-improvement are in effect magnifying glasses of class distinctions**.

Here's what I mean. If you are already in a position of financial security, good access to information and cultural sensitivity to frauds and trends, you can partake in high quality meditation courses and self-development programs that are scientifically supported and help you learn new things about yourself. This will generally improve your life quality further and make you more socially, emotionally and economically proficient.

But if you are on the *opposite* end of this class spectrum—and you have little money, little access to good information, little ability to critically evaluate wild claims and promises, and generally find yourself in a more desperate situation (in a "scarcity mindset")—you are likely to be sold ineffective magic gems, expensive diet supplements, fortune teller services, astrological consulting and all manner of harmful bogus ideas (like "The Secret", the idea that you can "materialize" wealth by thinking of money, through "quantum mechanics"). All of this makes you waste valuable time, money, attention and resources on stuff that further impoverishes your life. Your spiritual beliefs simply make you vulnerable to crude exploitation.

So you have a scale of *class*—understood in its widest sense—that is *magnified* by the growth of spiritual practices and self-improvement in society. Far from all people have a rich spiritual life, but in the minority who does adopt spiritual worldviews, class differences are increased.

At the top of this scale you find what I call **integralists** (after the followers of Ken Wilber's elaborate "integral spirituality"). These folks are the relatively privileged ones who adopt difficult and esoteric teachings and subtle body practices, and drill them arduously for years—and who manage to keep a scientific worldview (uhm, *relatively*) intact in the process. Their thinking and life experience are enriched and they develop greater existential depth and higher subjective states, even to the point where they themselves can sell these services at favorable prices. They are enriched across the scale.

The middle segment we can call **the yoga bourgeoisie**. These might dabble in a little astrology and quick-fix "life-changing" courses and eat some silly supplements, but by and large they are still energized by their spiritual practices and are comfortable enough economically to do so with good conscience. They might believe in a little magic here and there, but they generally understand that they should keep such discussions to themselves and don't spoil their professional lives in the process.

And then, on the low end of the scale, we have what I call **the astrology precariat**.[72] Here the magic beliefs of desperate people result in a heightened vulnerability, which leads to a **cruel commercialization of the human soul.**

In a capitalist society, made hyper-commercialized with the advent of the internet, disempowered people are made to believe in the worst imaginable nonsense, and there really is no end to the venues of exploitation: conspiracy theories, aliens, ghosts, past lives, "healing", alternatives to vaccine, Scientology, divination—the list goes on, and there is no end to the supply side and the inhuman cynicism with which it is tooted, packaged and sold to those weathered faces lined in pain.

But the hopes and aspirations of the astrology precariat are betrayed as no quick-fixes materialize beyond some initial placebo. And then you just spent the last year paying healers to help you when what you really needed was to get your life and finances more organized. And you end up even more desperate and gullible. People in the astrology precariat very often suffer from severe mental illness and distress—and often end up in psychiatric care (psychiatrists can attest to the prevalence of people with borderline syndrome who have been exploited by quacks and con artists).

It is tempting, from a classical Left perspective, to think spirituality and self-improvement are simply nonsense and offer no path towards deeper equality. Yet I would hold that they, in fact, are keys to transforming society, even beyond equality, taking us closer to equivalence and equanimity. However, **I would be wary of any attempt to center the transformation of society on spirituality and self-improvement alone**. This would only lead to an exacerbation of inequality in its most profound and venomous sense.

Spirituality and inner self-improvement are heavy drugs; they are indeed a double-edged sword. Today, they have become a magnifying glass for inequality and class stratification; tomorrow, *inshallah*, they can become universal tools of empowerment, emancipation and universal solidarity.

Would it be so strange if, at the enigmatically silent depths of our human (or posthuman) hearts and minds, we will find deeper equality?

Chapter 8

THE EVOLUTION OF NORMS

Confused? Perturbed? Wondering where all of this is going? That's okay, I understand it's a lot to unpack, but please keep up the good work and don't feel shy to read some of the previous chapters in this book or its prequel if certain things remain unclear. I can assure you it'll be worth it.

Thus far I have presented the anatomies of order (the state), freedom and equality over an axis of development, showing that the order progresses towards an increasing intimacy of control, that freedom progresses through "emotional regimes", and that equality, through its six dimensions, progresses towards the deeper principles of equivalence and equanimity.

In Book One I also introduced the idea that humans and their societies evolve through a set of "effective value memes", from traditional to modern to postmodern to metamodern—this is briefly discussed in Appendix B of this volume. Now I will tie these things together.

But to do that, I need to introduce one more fundamental concept. Until this point, I have left one system of societal progression out of the picture—the development of **norms**, i.e. of the simple rules that guide everyday behavior by means of social rewards and penalties.

This is, luckily, a much easier concept to understand. **Norms regulate what is *normal* behavior, and thus which behaviors are repeated as habits.** To have a fuller picture of societal development, this part must also be addressed and related to the other ones (order, freedom, equality and value meme). Let us now introduce the idea of a **system of norms**, and then put it together with the other systems.

Cultural Penalties and Rewards

Norms are simple rules, injunctions, ideals and taboos that steer our behavior in everyday life, all attached with weighted penalties and rewards. Just as there are economic incentives for us to do certain things (like getting a job), so there is any number of cultural incentives for us to act in certain ways, present ourselves in certain ways, or to avoid certain behaviors, ideas or values.

These norms are not "ethical" *per se*, i.e. they don't necessarily have anything to do with a reasoned account of what is right and wrong. They are—with the words of the classical anthropologist Margaret Mead—that which divides the "pure" from the "impure". As such, the norms of different societies can seem quite arbitrary or even silly to members of other societies or cultures. Some norms are more specific to cultures; in China it's considered good behavior to (gently) burp at the dinner table, for instance. Others are almost universal, such as the incest taboo. And they arise, of course, as a result of many interrelated factors that shape our everyday interactions: power relations, beliefs, biological dispositions, economic systems and interests, and so forth.

Much could be said about different types of norms, these types arising and functioning by different logics: fashion is different from morals, which is different from eating habits, which is different from greeting rituals. But for the sake of the argument in this book, let's keep it simple and treat the system of norms as a single entity.

Examples of norms from contemporary Western societies entail such things as: don't talk about too personal or "private" things in professional settings, don't be racist, don't be a pedophile, don't have sexual relations with animals, say hello to acquaintances but not urban strangers, shave your legs if you're a woman, don't be obese, and so on. The kinds of sanctions one might expect from violating these differ greatly—one may have you labeled as a weirdo, while another can have you end up in jail—but they are all part of the same overarching norm system.

From a critical and social-scientific perspective, it is obvious that different norm systems can be more or less compatible with different societal and economic systems. For instance, democratic norms of free speech and tolerance are generally very useful to large, complex societies that need to process large amounts of information and coordinate the actions of many millions of people. Strong family norms and loyalty to one's parents can be useful in traditional agrarian societies—for increasing chances of individual and collective survival—but the same norms can be emotionally suffocating and economically constraining in large, liberal market democracies.

Hence, there is always good reason to critically evaluate the norms of ourselves and one another. But such a critique must necessarily be an endeavour pursued with great patience as the norms aren't rational, deliberate choices; norms are lived, felt and embodied, part and parcel of who we consider ourselves to be and how we see the world. Only on rare occasions, and under very favorable circumstances, can you "talk somebody out of it". And the norms exercise great power when they are followed by many. For a vegan like myself, for example, it just isn't worth it if I were to disdain and condemn everyone who contributes to the harming of animals for reasons of idle consumption and trite habit. I would simply be so outnumbered that it would cost me too much and make little if any positive difference.

All norms come with calibrated rewards and penalties of different kinds. If you cheat on your husband in the wrong culture you get disowned by your family and perhaps even stoned to death. It might even count as cheating if you were raped. In modern Western societies you're fined or sent to prison if you beat someone, but you "only" get lower social status if you display "lacking manners" or fail to present yourself as positively masculine or feminine.

But the norm systems of course change over time, and this can happen either through unconscious processes as we reflexively adapt to changing circumstances, or through consciously organized and deliberate struggles on behalf of social movements and what sociologists call "moral entrepreneurs" (folks who invest their lives into changing norms).

The simplest and clearest example of such norm development is perhaps the major shift in Western societies from homophobia to acceptance of LGBTQ+ rights. Very recently, only a few decades ago, it was viewed as embarrassing, disgusting, unnatural and even immoral to be gay. Some time around the 1990s—after decades of struggle on the behalf of social movements and moral entrepreneurs—this strangely and abruptly shifted to a situation in which *homophobia*, rather than homophilia, is viewed as deviant: as hateful, bigoted, judgmental, narrow-minded and downright evil. The norms shifted from punishing people for being gay, to punishing people for being homophobic.

This shift occurred across large parts of the Western world, in some places a little quicker than in others, but more or less everyone followed suit with astounding obedience. State bureaucracies formerly concerned with "treating perversions" suddenly became engaged with combating "discrimination against sexual minorities" and defending gay rights.

It is, from an ethical and critical perspective, not difficult to argue this was a "good" development, that it represents an expansion towards more functional and universally justifiable norms. This "development of the norm system" may in part be explained by the general shift to higher average effective value meme in the population, with more people at the modern and postmodern stages.

But the fact that almost everyone shifted so dramatically, from one polarity to another, whereas the average effective value meme demographics, after all, do not change as rapidly (there are still only about 20-25% postmodernists, from where the concern with gay rights is primarily derived, in these societies), reveals that something else must have occurred: There must have been a major shift in the norm system *itself*.

The norm system functions by doling out rewards to followers and conferring penalties to delinquents. It's a delicate power balance. If you are an open homophobe in present-day Western societies, you will be punished and held back in a large variety of ways. People will argue against you, win arguments and score points on you as you are embarrassed and demeaned in front of your peers. You won't get hired, you *will* get fired, you won't have as many friends, you probably won't get laid. And if you speak out too openly and aggressively, you can even be fined and go to prison. Talk about penalties.

How did this situation come about? **Certain groups simply managed to win a long series of *symbolic* struggles, and thus started punishing those who violated the new norms.** More and more people quickly found greater rewards in being anti-homophobic, and started mining this new gold mine for personal gain. And the disgruntled and outmaneuvered conservatives on this issue learned to keep quiet.

And before you know it, people changed not only their behaviors, but also their honest opinions and values. New norms took hold, and they began to shape not only the postmodern populations (many of whom were already pro-gay rights), but seeped deep into the modern mainstream and even found grudging compliance among many religious traditionalists. The game had shifted, and the conservatives lost the symbolic struggle as more and more people switched sides.

It's not that people suddenly became "more enlightened", or that they all advanced to a higher effective value meme, or that society itself became so much freer and equal (as we have seen, economic inequality has even grown within affluent countries during the same period). It's just that the norm system changed, and thus changed the behavioral incentives. And when incentives changed, people unconsciously changed their own deeply held values in less than a generation. **When it comes to gradual and honest inner growth, humans are slowly awakening gods. When it comes to the shifting of norms, we are lemmings.**

This account may strike some readers as cynical, but it's really just basic sociology and psychology. We know that when there are strong incentives to feel a certain way, to adopt certain values, our minds generally follow suit. You may have heard of the "Stockholm syndrome", which is when captives in a hostage situation suddenly adopt a strong affinity for their captors. Or you may bring to mind countries like the USSR or North Korea where people will worship and adore the most monstrous leaders because they live under the constant threat of being severely punished. Hell, even the detainees at concentration camps can become eager followers of their oppressors' ideology. Destructive cult leaders can rise by means of the same dynamic, using extreme peer pressure to shift people's norms and worldviews.

On a more mundane level, people will hold on to beliefs that serve their economic interests, and which procure social rewards and avoid social penalties (consider climate deniers within the fossil fuel industry). Norms follow interests and incentives.

I'm not saying that everyone is Machiavellian. People will *honestly believe* that the norms that serve their (perceived) incentives are their *own*, deeply held, values. And from there on, they (or *we*) will eagerly and sincerely defend and justify these norms. The structure of social penalties and rewards really *does* become our lived, felt and embodied norms.

This is how the norm system functions, for better or worse. **The norm system itself follows no morality and no norms, only a cold logic of penalty and reward.** But as such it can bring about norms that are more or less univeralistic, more or less functional and lead to more or less sustainable consequences under the current historical circumstances.

That is what happened as norms shifted towards anti-homophobia, towards women's suffrage and feminism, towards environmental concern, towards the abolishment of slavery, towards anti-racism and against other forms of discrimination.

As our suspicious friends on the Left like to point out, none of this was achieved by the goodness of people's hearts, but rather by the results of long and exhausting social and political struggles. Norms often shift because groups of people led by moral entrepreneurs put in lifetimes of hard work and struggle. Eventually the lemming tide can shift and we all start running in a new direction. Rats after the Pied Piper.

And the historical circumstances of course determine *which* norms are *more likely* to take hold and be victorious in the long run. Why did the gay movement eventually win out? Because it simply made more sense given all *other* social, political and economic structures of liberal, democratic societies. The right for adults to freely engage in consensual same-sex relationships follows from the secular and liberal foundation of democratic society. Hence, denying this right either puts you in a position of rejecting modern democratic values alltogether, or, one of self-contradiction—both of which increase the likelihood of losing the debate in the end.

This is a good example of how the *Realdialektik* (a concept discussed in Book One) present within the structure of language itself leads to logical outcomes: Once you have said that love is free, and you can marry whomever you like, it also follows that gay people should be allowed to love freely. It naturally follows from the same statement. It just took a hundred years or so to successfully unravel that logical sequence on a wide, collective level.

And today, even the far Right is often not against gays; criticising Islam for being homophobic and rallying around the quite flamboyantly homosexual YouTube-star Milo Yiannopoulos. A few decades ago, on the other hand, even humanist, progressive Leftwing philosophers, such as Erich Fromm, were still homophobic. Accordingly, it's not that today's far Right is of "higher effective value meme" than was Erich Fromm—it's just that the norm system has changed. This simple fact speaks volumes for the tremendous power of the norm system.

THE NORM SYSTEM AS CULTURAL STRUGGLE

For all its power and influence, the norm system is never complete. There are always cracks, loopholes and exceptions: people who don't run with the lemming tide. And there is, moreover, **always an ongoing struggle over which norms should apply** (and what penalties or rewards should be deemed suitable). Most norms we simply have to follow in order to function within society, but there is often room for challenging at least *some* norms, trying to honor new values and condemn some currently common practices.

There is, of course, no reason to believe that the norm system of today is final or that it has stopped evolving. If anything, it mutates even more rapidly in today's hyperconnected, complex world, not least as the result of an increasing interaction between conflicting norm systems.

Here are some examples of norms likely to be struggled over in the coming period:

1. **Animal rights and veganism** as we are no longer *de facto* dependent on animal exploitation for food and work and as the scientific worldview holds that humans are animals like any other. So if we have solidarity with all humans, because they're sentient, feeling beings, it's difficult to maintain that such solidarity should not be extended to other animals—but the impediments of habit and vested interests make the transition a difficult one.

2. **Pedophilia**, since we can probably prevent more kids from being molested if people aren't judged for having unwanted sexual urges and if these can be openly dealt with. Besides, it's also more humane to the circa 1% of the population who suffer from pedophile inclinations. Controversial as it is.

3. **Professional identity and work ethics.** People should have other means of acquiring social value as the professional "work" becomes more arbitrary and difficult to achieve in a postindustrial economy.

And there are of course many more, such as the rise of "post-materialist" norms, where it becomes embarrassing rather than cool to own a sports car and where displays of cultural capital and self-actualization confer prestige. Preventive and "harm reduction" stances on drugs and prostitution also come to mind.

Norm systems develop through changed historical circumstances and as the result of protracted struggles between different groups for social and moral dominance. This means that different groups and value memes can be dominant during different periods.

Casual observers sometimes think Scandinavian countries are "postmodern". The truth is, however, that only a minority can be said to function at the postmodern stage. What has *really* happened is that postmodern groups and alliances have successfully managed to influence the media and the political discourses in ways that have shaped the norm systems in these countries. Postmoderns have won the symbolic struggles. Hence, you have the rise of "political correctness" and anti-discrimination laws and the like.[73]

In the US, the struggle to define which norms should apply for society as a whole even has a name: the "culture wars". On one side we have the progressive liberals (postmodern), usually found in the big cities, and on the other we have the religious conservatives (traditionalist), who mostly reside in rural areas and small towns. This has come to define American politics to a degree where party affiliation now depends more on effective value meme than class distinctions. It cuts across all income groups with poor (mostly white) rural inhabitants and wealthy conservatives rallying behind the Republican Party, while wealthy educated urbanites along with hipsters, intellectuals and various minority groups vow for the Democrats.

And despite the fact that the majority of the American population gravitate towards the modern value meme, it is the traditionals and the postmoderns who dominate the political discourse: gay rights vs. "traditional family values", multiculturalism vs. white Christian majority culture, environmentalism vs. climate denial, feminism vs. traditional gender roles, etc.

This struggle is just as much a cultural battle as a political one, with each side seeking to establish their respective values as normative for society as a whole, and to denigrate those of their opponents. These culture wars play out in so many arenas: When liberals find support in established media houses such as CNN and The New York Times, conservatives build strongholds around rightwing upshots like Fox News and Breitbart News. And when conservatives mobilize the churches to condemn the decadence and perverted agenda of the liberals in Hollywood, popular talkshow hosts and comedians of liberal bent don't shy away from mocking the uneducated and less cosmopolitan conservatives and their elected leaders on national television.

And the result of this cultural struggle: ebbs and flows of changes to the norm system—which in turn affects how society functions as whole.

THE MAP OF CULTURAL GAME CHANGE

We are now approaching a more comprehensive model of "cultural game change". There is the development of:

1. higher effective value memes within the population,

2. the major shifts of gear between different orders of state emergence and the intimacy of control, emotional regimes (degrees of freedom), and the struggle for deeper equality, encompassing an increasing portion of the six dimensions of equality, and

3. cultural changes to the system of norms.

More "progressive" norms are the ones better suited for larger and more complex societies. These norms aren't "better" in some cosmic sense—there is no God out there who loves us more if we believe in political metamodernism rather than Christian conservatism. The norms of the former are simply better adapted to how society is currently organized.

Naturally, all of these factors interact:

1. the system of norms affects the formation of people's effective value memes,

2. the average effective value meme affects which emotional regime is instituted, and

3. the degrees of equality and freedom shape how fiercely and bitterly the penalties and rewards of norm systems are distributed.

Of course, societies develop through other mechanisms than these, such as the establishment of institutions, growth of the economy and advancement of technology and science. I am here focusing on the **cultural game change** that steers everyday life and determines our degree of equality and freedom.

So I am pointing out powerful attractors and the logic that makes them likely to manifest in the future. But this should not be mistaken for a theory of economic development or a model applicable to poor, developing countries like Afghanistan.

Rather, I am offering a vision of what higher equality and freedom means, given that sound political institutions and economic advancement are already in place. In other words, we are talking about developing higher freedom, higher equality, more advanced value memes and more progressive norm systems.

Let's try to squeeze the current argument into one of those sassy Venn diagrams (on the next page). It can be helpful to summarize what has been said thus far.

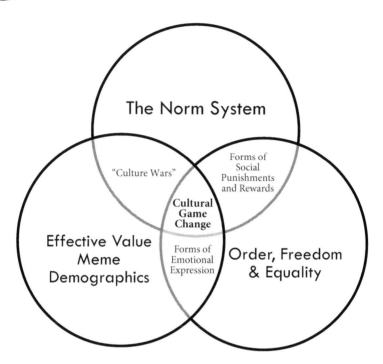

What you see in the model above is the suggested components of cultural game change, basically the stuff that determines how we live our lives within a given setting of historical circumstances. Cultural game change occurs when:

1. populations develop into higher effective value memes,
2. when there are shifts in the intimacy of control, the emotional regime and the degrees of equality, and
3. when there are shifts within the system of norms.

There are, as mentioned, many interactions between these forms of development. For one, the nature of the ongoing culture wars relates to a combination of which effective value memes different parts of the population gravitate towards, and which norms are currently dominant. In a society with universal suffrage and basic human rights, the culture wars will be waged around norms concerning things like abortion, gender relations and gender roles, gay marriage, and ecological awareness. In other societies, the struggles will look different—and they may take place by other means.

So what about the **"forms of social penalties and rewards"**? In highly unequal societies governed by earlier emotional regimes, the norms are upheld through more brutal forms of penalties and rewards: ostracism, corporal punishment, ideas about going to heaven or hell etc. In more equal and free societies, where the underlying emotional tensions are lessened, the norms are upheld with fines, definitions of psychiatric pathology, withheld social support, withheld recognition, subtle behavioral cues, ridicule and mockery, slander etc. And you can move up and down what I have termed "the spectrum of judgment" to produce different forms of punishments and rewards.

The general **"forms of emotional expression"**, (i.e. how people express themselves emotionally and interact in everyday life), are shaped by the effective value memes as well as by the underlying emotional regimes and the degree of equality. In countries such as the Nordic ones, which have a considerably high degree of freedom and equality as well as high average effective value memes, you can see the emergence of more "casual" and "sensitive" forms of emotional expression as people increasingly have the luxury of being "self-revealing" and "authentic" about their inner lives and feelings. They need to think less of "saving face" and displaying markers of prestige or honor. In these settings, it is often even taken as a sign of strength and maturity to be judiciously revealing and open about one's weaknesses, knowledge gaps and insecurities.

When these three (1. culture wars, 2. forms of social punishments and rewards, and 3. forms of emotional expression) are viewed as a totality, it becomes apparent that societies can self-organize more smoothly and intelligently if they have higher value memes, are more free and equal and have more progressive systems of norms.

But please note that purportedly "progressive" systems of norms can easily collapse and revert to "regressive" norms if they are not supported by corresponding value memes in the population—as well as by higher freedom and deeper equality. Again, Soviet communism comes to mind; the USSR had a partly progressive ideology but lacked in all the other regards (see Appendix B).

All of these factors taken together determine the nature of a society's cultural—and psychological—development. As we have seen, **it is this cultural-psychological development that must be consciously spurred, so as to match the kind of complex world-system that is emerging in the internet age**.

Culture isn't just, or even primarily, about being Japanese or Swedish, for instance. Sure, there are geographical and historical idiosyncrasies which shape collective habits, demeanors and so forth, as has been demonstrated and discussed in different ways by folks like Richard E. Nesbitt, Fons Trompenaars and Geert Hofstede. Culture is also, and I would argue *primarily*, a developmental issue.

Just as there are both different personality types and stages of *personal* psychological development, so there are types and stages of *cultural* development. And stage is a stronger factor than type. It explains more and it makes a much greater difference. The cultures of modern Japan and Sweden have more in common with each other than they do with medieval Japan and Sweden respectively.

At the very center of this model, I have placed **cultural game change**. This is the very vortex of all that has been discussed thus far—it is where all the dots connect. Metamodern politics is ultimately about building the frameworks that will evolve culture itself, that will change the games of everyday life. As an emerging global society, we must make deliberate and concerted efforts to reach higher stages of cultural development.

—

And this, my suspicious friend, concludes this first part of the book. We have now pointed out some very powerful societal attractors that describe the developmental direction of society: how the state (or order) develops, how freedom develops, how equality develops, and lastly, how the norm system develops.

Again, that's what the next stage of politics must achieve: **to create the frameworks for propelling growth into higher stages of cultural and psychological development**. That's why we need the Nordic ideology (to develop a listening society) where the innermost needs and wants of people are seen and heard; where the personal truly becomes political.

We're not supposed to follow this as a step-by-step process. The suggested developmental models show us *non-linear* attractor points. There are no guarantees we'll get to higher freedom, deeper equality, a more complex self-organized order, and "more progressive" norms. But with this in mind, we can navigate the seas of history a tad more consciously—with an ironic smile at our own self-importance… and with the trembling hearts of the cautiously faithful.

Now let's get on to the part where we start creating the institutions that can get us there. We're going to need six new forms of politics to make this happen.

PART TWO

The Plan: Metamodern Politics

Interlude to Part Two: The Plan

THE SIX NEW FORMS

> "We often want our lives to be less complicated, which is *not* the same as being less complex [...] The reality is that complexity is actually quite simple in its elegance. Optimizing complexity has the feeling and physical reality of harmony. It moves across time, space or potentialities, the flow of moments, with a phases flow that is literally what a choir singing in harmony feels like, as the individual members differentiate their voices in harmonic intervals, and then *link* them as they sing together."[74]

T he above is a quote from Daniel Siegel, the clinical professor of psychiatry who studies integration in human minds, emotions and relations. As he points out, more integrated systems can manage greater complexity, and when something manages greater complexity there is a quality of elegance and simplicity to it.

Let's see then if we can do the corresponding move for metamodern politics; let's see if we can identify the simple, underlying pattern that creates a more harmonious whole—within ourselves and within society at large.

We're now entering the second part of this book. **The Plan**. Up until this point we've been doing some real weight-lifting, but now we can begin to reap the fruits of our hard labor; we will look at the six new forms of politics, the new processes that can and should be instituted in order to make society productively transition into a metamodern stage of development.

If we manage to do that, we're talking millions of lives saved, and yet many more lives dramatically improved—and that's by a conservative estimate. If we don't, immeasurable suffering is likely to follow as the world falls apart. The fate of billions depends on a successful development of politics to match the growing complexity of the world if we are to avoid **○** social disintegration and ecological collapse. Modern politics leaves us severely underequipped at productively addressing these new life conditions that technological progress, global interconnectedness and existential threats to civilization bring about. The arena of national democracy is just too limited in scope, state legislation too feeble a tool, and governmental institutions too ill-prepared and uninformed to prevent run-amok technologies, the unrestrained powers of multinational companies and the continuous destruction of the environment from causing immense suffering and death.

Politics needs to evolve. Modern society is out of its depth; its scope is too limited and its influence too shallow to develop the cultures, psychologies and behaviors needed to keep up with its emergent structural complexity.

How dire will the consequences be if we fail? If you look across the globe, with billions of people, and over decades worth of dramatic change, is it really an exaggeration that we can save a few million lives by taking the right steps to develop our political institutions, and doing it sooner rather than later? I don't think it is. **Hence—remember: millions of lives at stake. At non-linear, long-term stake, but still.**

Not to mention if we shift the norms towards animal emancipation, against animal exploitation, where we have sixty billion land animals and over a trillion aquatic animals killed each year.

When the stakes are this high, you don't get to pretend you're the good-guy by saying you'd just rather not relate to these issues. You are not the good-guy, you cannot remain innocent.

And yet, we must remain playful, lest we are guaranteed to experience the failures that follow from fanaticism and disastrous consequences of misguided effervescence. We must strive towards coherence and harmony, but we can't force it to happen.

Let's kick-start this cold engine with a quick exposé of what has been said thus far; brace thyself.

VERY, VERY QUICK RECAP

In Book One, I described the fundamentals of a metamodern political philosophy: the rise of "cultural capital" as a self-consciously organized political power, the increasing influence of the triple-H populations (hipsters, hackers and hippies), the obsoleteness and transcendence of classical Left and Right politics, the emergence of a new meta-ideology concentrated especially in the Nordic countries (Green Social Liberalism 2.0, or "the Nordic ideology"), the re-integration of the civic, personal and professional sides of life, a general both-and perspective, a transpersonal perspective of the human being, and "the view from complexity" which sees self-organizing chaos and fractals (rather than focusing on social power structures). Phew.

All of this is based upon a developmental (and dialectical) view of humanity and society; a perspective that looks at *both* external factors (systems, technology, economics, etc.) *and* internal factors (psychology, culture, spirituality and inner states)—in effect avoiding "developmental blindness" and "inner dimensions blindness".

We saw that the psychological development of people through four dimensions (cognitive complexity, code, state and depth) largely determines their "effective value memes", and that achieving a higher average effective value meme of the population is exceedingly important for the development of healthy postindustrial, transnational, digitized societies. A new political movement is needed to put such psychological growth on the agenda.

Such a political movement is necessary not only because it can shift the psychology of the population away from the moral and psychological deficiencies of modern society, but also because we are facing a global **crisis-revolution** as technological, scientific and economic developments redefine the human condition. Global society is in a stage of transition from modernity to what comes after; a moment of untold promise and terrifying risks.

The two main agents that embody and manifest this new political philosophy are "the process-oriented political party" and "the metamodern aristocracy". The first is a more popular movement, founded upon and informed by metamodern ideas, but whose rank-and-file members are not necessarily at the Metamodern value meme. The second group, the metamodern aristocracy, is a small transnational "elite" who deeply embodies the metamodern values and ways of thinking, and who works to develop new metamodern theory and applications thereof.

Double-phew. That's a lot of background understanding to keep in mind. And then we have spent the first part of this book fleshing out a corresponding metamodern political sociology—seeing the historical directionality of the state's development, the developmental anatomy of political freedom, and the meaning of deeper equality, and how these categories steer the cultural struggles for emancipatory norms.

By the way. Why is this general understanding "metamodern"? Is anything Hanzi says "metamodern" by definition?

No. These theories are *metamodern* because they synthesize the ideas of *modern* progress through successive stages with a *postmodern*, critical sensitivity towards modern society. They offer a direction and a roadmap without relying upon a naive, materialist, linear and mechanical faith in science, rationality and humanity. There's no statue of Lenin pointing us towards a glittering future.

Rather, the metamodern view of progress takes as its point of departure the very failures, limitations and insufferable tragedies of modern life. It is born not from the glory of the modern project, but from its frailty and futility. And more; it is born not from the postmodern critique of modern society, but from the relative fruitlessness of that very critique.

If you see that it's not only modern society and its institutions that are futile, but that even the postmodern criticism of the same is equally so, you must also recognize that the postmodern **"deconstruction" must be followed by a corresponding *re*-construction**: We must create new visions and pathways towards a *relative* utopia. This is where *political* metamodernism enters the picture.

So now that we have enough understanding, hopefully, to see the greater context within which a metamodern political program makes sense, it's time to get practical. The reason I didn't rush to present this part of the work is simply that you need all the background understanding for it to make deeper sense. Taken out of its context it is not only difficult to understand, but also easy to *misunderstand* and thus misuse. And such misuses can be dangerous indeed.

You have to see that the six new forms of politics presented in the following are pieces of a greater puzzle; that they aim towards raising the prevalent stages of psychological development of the population as a whole, gearing life towards deeper freedom and equality—cultivating **the listening society**.

PROCESSES FOR DEEPER SOCIETAL COHERENCE

In the following chapters we will go through the six new forms of politics which I argue can and must emerge for society to make a successful transition from modernity to metamodernity.

You may recall from the introduction that the six form of politics proposed are:

* **Democratization Politics**
    * Aims to create ongoing processes for developing and updating the system of governance and the quality of institutions.

- *Gemeinschaft* **Politics** (politics of relationships and community)
  - Aims to improve the quality of human relationships across all aspects of society.
- **Existential Politics**
  - Aims to support all people on their life's journey and spur inner growth, mental health and strong moral integrity.
- **Emancipation Politics**
  - Aims to create ongoing processes protecting citizens from all sorts of oppression, not least from the other new forms of politics.
- **Empirical Politics**
  - Aims to evaluate all policies and institutional practices and make sure they are based on the best available evidence.
- **Politics of Theory** (or narrative)
  - Aims to create ongoing processes for developing and updating the narratives society relies upon, how it "brainwashes itself".

All of these will be introduced and discussed in this order. In a last summary chapter we will also discuss how they form a larger, coherent pattern of braided streams.

What they all have in common is that they work towards a deeper interplay of (in)dividuation and integration of human behaviors, bodies and minds. In this way, they serve the development of higher value memes and to remedy many of the sufferings and sicknesses of modern life. They work towards a more listening society in which there is greater coherence of information processes, human minds and behaviors. And all of them reach deeper into the human soul and its social, relational, physiological and cultural development.

Adding new forms of politics to the list of what is thought of as "the political" is nothing new. Governments in the 19th century naturally had fewer political areas of concern than do present-day ones. Even if the US Department of Forestry can trace its history back as early as 1875, the vast majority of environmental politics has emerged during the latter part of the 20th century. Today, there are even ministers of gender equality in countries like Sweden, and governments make significant efforts to regulate, fund and maintain sports and culture of all sorts.

If we are to cultivate six new forms of politics that should become part and parcel of the institutional framework of our societies, this means we are looking at long-term developments that include the accumulation of appropriate expertise, knowledge and frameworks over decades. The issue here is that we need to make some key processes of society's self-organization become more explicit and consciously held. We're working towards a society in which there is coherence at a deeper level.

Take a look at the diagram below. It looks similar to the six dimensions of inequality, but this one is different:

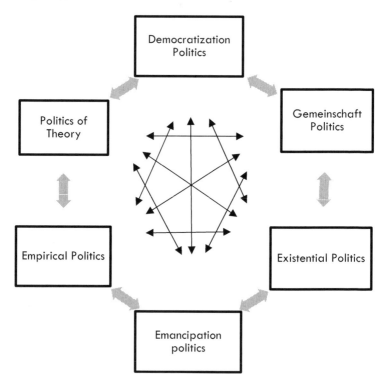

Figure: *The six new forms of politics, all part of one emergent, "intra-relational" balance: None of the six forms are fully possible without the others, and the very meaning of each new kind of politics changes depending on how the others develop.*

THREE CAVEATS

A few important notes before we delve into it. First of all, **it should be noted that none of these forms of politics are themselves *answers* to the problems of modern life in any static sense**.

Each of them is a ***process***; one that can be more or less consciously recognized and monitored; more or less clearly articulated and productively acted upon. Just like we today have ministries of finance and a host of institutions for financial regulation, this hardly guarantees good economic governance—likewise the existence of Democratization Politics does not *guarantee* a good process of democratization (and so forth with the other five forms of politics).

But it is still a good idea to have ministries of finance, and likewise it is a good idea to have a deliberately crafted politics of democratization. **The existence of these kinds of politics does not in themselves, of course, guarantee *good* politics within each field. It merely opens a host of potentials.**

The point is that these processes are ongoing in our societies either way, whether or not we have a language to describe them and political frameworks to relate to them. As these processes become consciously recognized and re-organized, we increase our ability to create a free and fair society—a great potential, but no promises made.

The manifestation of these six new processes includes several ingredients: they must become seriously considered political issues that are discussed in the public debate, they must have batteries of interventions and experts working with them, and there must be serious efforts to expand this knowledge and understanding through the social and behavioral sciences—i.e. they must become part and parcel of academic life as well. There must be educational and career paths for people who want to work with these issues, and there must be sufficient recognition of this work. That's how we get the new processes of society's self-organization going.

Why, then, is a *process* so much more powerful than any specific policy position or any one "concrete action"? It is because a process consists of a multitude of countless concrete actions that build upon and are coordinated with each other in a coherent, larger pattern. And because there is an ongoing flow of new actions taken, the process can begin to flow in new directions. It is flexible, but still has continuity and an overarching theme. If you want to build a skyscraper, it requires many people to understand roughly what a skyscraper is and what it means to build one. The same goes for large, societal processes. You need to name them, define them, discuss them, and keep developing your understanding of them.

The second point to note is that **we're *not*—at this point—taking a hard stance on whether these new forms of politics should rely upon state bureaucracy, market solutions or civil society**. The only thing that is certain, I would argue, is that the state cannot be *entirely* left out. It is going to have to involve political parties and other groups, advancing these issues in a *political* arena. But the *extent* to which markets and civil society can and should be relied upon is beyond the current scope of inquiry. No doubt, the answers to this question can and will vary across different countries and historical circumstances: some societies have more robust public institutions to build upon, other livelier civil societies, and yet others more dynamic markets.

Future deliberations about the balance between state, market and civil society will need to be specific in nature—for instance, perhaps there is more room for market agents within democratization politics than within *Gemeinschaft* politics, and perhaps the optimal mix varies over time. It is quite likely that a good mix of the three will be viable within most of these areas of concern—even if the state, and politics, is likely to play an indispensable role, simply because we are, after all, considering institutions.

The third point I wish to emphasize is that **I am here speaking of "society" in the abstract**, not necessarily as a country with a state. Given that much of society will self-organize through other means than state institutions in the coming period (with blockchain technologies, transnational corporations, NGOs, strong city regions, industry hubs, supranational organizations and so forth) there is no reason to lock down our perspective to states only.

But even beyond states, through whatever form society self-organizes, I hold that this pattern of deeper governance is relevant. So please allow me the luxury of speaking about "society" as if it were a country with a state, and you can make inferences and adaptations to other structures of governance from there. This does not mean we are adopting the state-based social engineering made famous by the Swedish sociologist couple Alva and Gunnar Myrdal in the 1930s, but rather that we are looking at wider patterns or processes, with the development of the state as one primary *example*.

After these presentations of the six new kinds of politics I will inquire into how these taken together form a **master pattern**, how they each balance each other out—and how they are instituted.

Hence, there is an element of chicken-and-egg paradox here: You need to understand all six new forms of politics to see the master pattern, but you need to see the master pattern to see how they can function and realistically be instituted within society—so that our thoughts, feelings and actions may emerge together in deeper harmonic coherence across all aspects of everyday life.

Without further ado, let us leap into the torrent. First out is Democratization Politics.

En garde!

Chapter 9

DEMOCRATIZATION

POLITICS

Is democracy a done deal? Is the form of governance prevailing in the West today the most democratic there is ever going to be? We normally think of democracy and dictatorship as a binary question: either a country is a democracy or it is not. Yet this black-and-white conception of democracy has been challenged, for instance by Freedom House's graded scale or the 2014 Princeton study which argued the US is more accurately described as a civil oligarchy than a democracy per se.[75]

To be, or not to be democratic—that isn't really the question. No, the intelligent question is the extent to which a society manages to include its citizens into the political processes; not whether a society is a democracy, but *how* democratic it has become.

So how do we determine just that? How do we define democracy and how do we measure a society's degree of democracy?

The mainstream account of democratic governance still goes along the lines of what the political scientist Robert Dahl described in the 1950s and onwards. According to Dahl, democracy shows up as a power balance between different interest groups. Such balance forces the parties into a situation in which the following five criteria must be true (this particular definition is from a 1989 book):[76]

1. **Effective participation**: Citizens must have adequate and equal opportunities to form their preference and place questions on the public agenda and express reasons for one outcome over the other.

2. **Voting equality at the decisive stage**: Each citizen must be assured their judgments will be counted as equal in weights to the judgments of others.

(ROYGBIV)

3. **Enlightened understanding**: Citizens must enjoy ample and equal opportunities for discovering and affirming which choices best serve their interests.

4. **Control of the agenda**: "The people" must have the opportunity to decide what should be actual political matters and which should be brought up for deliberation.

5. **Inclusiveness:** Equality must extend to all citizens within the state. Everyone has a legitimate stake within the political process.

It should be noted that all the states commonly held as democratic fail to truly fulfill these ideals, and that it would be more or less impossible to actually do so. Dahl's definition of democratic governance, despite being rather conventional, serves to illustrate how much democracy is more of an ideal than an actual state of affairs; that democracy remains an impossible goal worth striving towards.

Just like the socialist Eastern Bloc didn't actually consider their societies communist, but rather saw communism as the end-goal that the "actually existing socialism" was in the process of creating, true democracy remains the unrealized promise of liberal society; the equally distant utopia that the "actually existing liberalism" should be in the process of creating.

Sadly, the idea of democracy as an ongoing process—a fight for equality and liberty that never ends—has waned in favor of the belief we have already reached the end-goal of a fully democratic society. As a result, faith in democracy has eroded in recent years. Without the prospect of further democratization, those who feel disenfranchised in modern society have become more inclined to abandon democracy altogether.

As a remedy, I propose we update democracy; that we abandon the notion of democracy as a done deal and renegotiate its terms—that democracy, as it is currently realized, can only ever be a proto-synthesis; that it, by necessity, remains provisional and always subject to future revision.

UPDATING DEMOCRACY ITSELF

I thus believe we have ample reason to challenge the relative self-contentment of the world's "most democratic" societies by asking how they could become *more* democratic? Could the governance of societies like Sweden or the US be transformed and improved upon, even beyond what Dahl envisioned? Could there be future, *deeper* forms of "democracy" which are not only improvements upon the present systems, but genuinely and qualitatively different in clearly preferable ways?

From such an imagined future vantage point, could today's taken-for-granted state of affairs in contemporary "democratic" societies even be viewed as terribly undemocratic, primitive and oppressive? Are we medieval?

It is often claimed that today's democracy is under threat; that it is decaying, that it might be losing its grip or otherwise is becoming increasingly dysfunctional.[77] But such diagnoses can also be understood as a malady of modernity aging, of the modern institutions, founded a century ago or more, having become unable to effectively tackle the complexities of metamodern (postindustrial, transnational, digitized, etc.) society—a society in which the key self-organizational flows occur on a much higher order of complexity.

Thus, we are not only talking about restoring, revitalizing or "saving" democracy, but about fundamentally *updating* democracy and re-imagining its institutions. Hence, we are asking a more radical and dangerous question: How do we reinvent democracy? What kind of democracy comes after democracy?

This is an idea echoed not only in the work of Habermas, but also in the experimental political philosophy of the legal theorist Roberto Unger. Habermas points us towards a deeper form of post-liberal democracy and Unger opens the door to taking an experimental stance towards the democratic institutions—that they can and should be experimented upon under controlled and reasonable forms.

If our present political systems are in a state of relative decay, can they really be mended and saved with the currently adopted tools of democratic governance? Isn't it more realistic to imagine a path forward towards a democratic system more up to speed with today's globalized and digitized world? If our democratic institutions are working poorly due to being designed to govern a modern, industrial nation state of yesteryear—doesn't it make sense to take the issue of updating and reinventing these institutions more seriously?

The fundamental starting point of **Democratization Politics** is thus a *negative*: **There is simply no conceivable reason to believe our *current* forms of governance in modern democratic societies would be the only possible and best forms of governance for all posterity.** If all other forms of governance have emerged in historical time, have had beginnings and endings, is it really a feasible supposition that liberal parliamentary democracy is an exception?

No, democracy is not a done deal. Why would it be? It is a developmental process like everything else, just one that stabilizes around relatively fixed equilibria (or "local maxima") because institutional changes require such great investments and create path dependencies. With "path dependency" I mean that, basically, once a society has opted for a certain form of governance, it is very "expensive" and difficult to change the structure.

The fact that liberal democracy has been stably operational for a good while, that is has outcompeted its modern alternatives, such as communism and fascism, and that it remains very difficult to change—even to imagine a credible alternative—can create the illusion that democracy in its current form is "the natural order of things". But of course, it isn't.

Luckily there are hacks; there are ways to get around this bottleneck and to open developmental paths that lie beyond liberal democracy.

First of all, a society can expend resources, time and effort in smaller settings to experiment with potentially better forms of governance, e.g. in "experimental zones", as proposed by Roberto Unger. Secondly, a society can orchestrate a large number of democratic technologies and innovations in governance which seek to enhance democracy incrementally. If enough incremental change has occurred, eventually the system itself will have shifted from one stage to another.

And here's another way of seeing it: Given the sacred status of democracy, isn't it strange that no late modern economies are making serious, concerted and patient efforts to develop it and improve upon its quality? By treating democracy as a given, are we not failing to take our own democratic values seriously?

THE TRUE NORTH: COLLECTIVE INTELLIGENCE

Let's begin by plunging into this question by identifying a few general historical trends. What does it mean for democracy to develop? How did it emerge, and why? And what were the attractors that brought democracy into being?

I'd like to suggest that there are some deep and sturdy historical patterns which—again—don't *determine* where things are going, but certainly hint us towards some long-term attractor points, i.e. the direction towards which things potentially *can* go.

If democracy is not a binary variable, not a question of either-or, but a developmental matter, a direction—can we then know and recognize its "true north"? Can we know when democracy becomes deeper, retains higher quality, becomes truer to its own principles and ideals?

And if we go far enough in this direction, will democracy inevitably look like "more of the same", or will there be qualitative shifts from one stage to another that will make democracy look like something completely different, perhaps event warranting a new word? What if liberal parliamentary democracy isn't "democratic enough" for governing metamodern society?

To traverse the dangerous territory such questions lead us towards, we'd better have a good sense of a "true north" lest we can get lost and end up inventing new forms of oppression, tyranny, or political disintegration and collapse. Let's look for such a true north.

One undeniable trend is **the increasing dispersion of leadership and decision-making**. If we go back in history it becomes perfectly clear that pre-modern and early modern monarchical leadership was more concentrated, more arbitrarily wielded and relying more upon the good nature and talent of specific rulers than what is the case in present-day parliamentary democracies. Today, more people partake in decision-making at all levels of society, and wider groups of citizens can be elected.

But even nowadays, the world-system, as a whole, places incredible responsibility and power in e.g. the US President, which must be viewed as a very high-risk strategy for governance. If this one person has significant flaws—as we all do—this leads to great costs for people all around the world. As such, there still remain pockets of irrationally and inefficiently concentrated power in contemporary democracies.

Another undeniable trend has to do with **the increased total volume of active decision-making, i.e. the sheer volume of information processed by organs of governance, and the complexity of the processes deliberately shaped by governance.**

When viewed as a very long historical trend, it becomes obvious that governance has become "more powerful" over the centuries. Governments simply have much greater capacities to interfere in the lives of citizens than in the past. I have already pointed out that the taxation capacities of modern societies, even while limited in practice due to corruption and the flight of transnational corporate capital, are staggering compared to anything that came before. Strong states levy high taxes, and they penetrate society more thoroughly in a variety of ways. As we have discussed, Foucault pointed out that modern "free" society requires many additional layers of control.

Naturally, it is not that a system with greater total power is more democratic in itself, as it is easy to name totalitarian states with high degrees of organization. But there certainly is a correlation between the quantity of self-organization and the growth of democratic forms of governance around the world. And even if libertarianism is a strong current in many present-day democracies (seeking to minimize state power), even the most libertarian ones in the world today are highly organized by historical standards.

Thus, as democracy has progressed, it has begun to organize greater amounts of money in the public sphere and otherwise regulating exchanges on the market. Money, of course, isn't a concrete "thing" "the state" can "take" and then "spend". That would just be a childish way of seeing things. No, money is a measure of people's coordinated efforts to extract resources from the environment as well as their degree of coordination of agency with one another.

The point, then, is that democratic governance has come to dominate both greater material or natural resources, and it has begun to coordinate more human actions: longer stretches of time of people's lives (in terms of time, effort and attention), in more minute details, playing parts in more abstract patterns of information, for more abstract shared goals. This means many more decisions must be made, much greater amounts of information organized. Hence, there is a move towards bureaucratization and digitization—anything that can cost-effectively monitor and control larger quantities of more varied (and specialized) human agency.

A third long-term trend is that democracy has evolved **more checks and balances against arbitrary uses of power; hence there has been an increased accountability of decision-making**.

This one is difficult to spot in recent decades, as democratic development has stagnated and come to a halt. But if we look over the centuries of modern history, the pattern is obvious. There are more laws restricting the use of power, the power of office is decoupled from the office-holder —legally, if not socially—and there are greater demands for transparency and motivation of decisions made. Moreover, there are more institutions —state-run as well as in the media and civil sphere—which actively seek to uncover failures of governments, elected officials, the bureaucracy, the courts and the legal system at large. There is even an increasing number of critical social scientists who spend years laying bare problems in just one sub-section of governance, be it concentration of power in informal networks of elites, shady conflicts of interest, or structural malfunctions that elude casual observers.

These many forms of checks and balances increase the inter-subjective verification of legitimacy, or indeed, the inter-subjective falsification of claims to power. This does not mean that democracy functions by the same premises as does modern science, which also ideally works by inter-subjective verification/falsification—far from—but it suggests a vague, tentative approximation of the scientific ideals.

This, in turn, entails that the self-organization of society gradually begins to rest upon a deeper and more intricate web of verifications and falsifications. And even these verifications and falsifications are themselves subjected to increased scrutiny as more voices join the fray.

We may sometimes nostalgically look back at the times of Athenian democracy, of English coffee houses (17th and 18th centuries), of French salons (18th and 19th centuries), of worker socialist collectives (19th and early 20th centuries), or even the youthful energy of 1968. "Ah, those were the days", we say, "when people *cared*, when everyone engaged in the political, in the public, in the civil sphere. Back then, folks were citizens, not merely idle consumers". But we often forget that these expressions of political enfranchisement only reached small cliques of the overall population: Athenian democracy excluded all women, slaves and non-Athenians; English coffee houses catered to urban well-to-do citizens; French salons were meeting places for the upper bourgeoisie and the radicalized parts of the nobility; more comprehensive worker collectives showed up during key moments and events rather than being a permanent state of affairs; and even in 1968 (with the hopeful, radical students) we must remember that university and college admissions were considerably smaller than today. It is true that there have been beautiful and inspiring nexuses in historical space-time, and it is true that such beauties have waxed and waned —but this should not blind us to the obvious macro-historical process: that checks and balances have increased over time as democracy has grown into its current variety of forms.

This leads us to a fourth long-term directionality; namely that **democratic participation has thickened and deepened**. Even if the younger generation of today appears to have a lower level of interest in public life (at least conventional politics), and even if many democratic institutions and practices have become subjected to different degrees of market logic (where voters are viewed as "customers" or "clients"), largely due to the impact of the so scorned cultural and political currents of "neoliberalism" and "new public management" in recent decades—it still remains true that today's citizens have more venues of participation than in the past.

Not only do larger groups of people have greater access to media and more time and resources to inform themselves. People also have more concrete channels of participation: in advisory boards and citizens' councils, feedback channels for public institutions such as schools and hospitals, direct links by email to elected officials and a higher number of representatives. And then there's a dramatic increase in the number of interest groups and civil society agents who defend the interests of many groups—from the ethnic minorities to the sports' clubs to the animal rights activists to the people suffering from sclerosis and, increasingly, metamodern groups (yay!) who seek to enhance the quality of public dialogue, and so on.

Seen as a totality—and if we put the partly negative trend of neoliberal watering-down of public enfranchisement of recent decades into a greater historical context—there can be little doubt that public enfranchisement has *increased* dramatically. This does not have to mean that more citizens spend their time doing things public and political; it simply means that there are many venues and that many and diverse interests crop up and organize.

Lastly, a fifth long-term trend has to do with **the growth of democratic culture and values**. Yes, Sweden was indeed a democracy even in the 1920s and the 1950s if we consider its institutions. But in the 1920s, a husband could still legally rape his wife, it was considered inappropriate to speak too openly against religion, people talked to one another differently depending on social status and title, and so forth. Up until the early 1960s, you could beat children, not only at home but also in schools. In short, culture was considerably more authoritarian, less tolerant, less multi-perspectival, less egalitarian and overall less democratic than today. If you go back to the late 1800s the issue becomes even clearer, with a majority of the constituency being against not only women's suffrage, but also against racial equality, equality of different social classes (or "estates") and free speech.

Earlier in this book we discussed that values evolve in recognizable patterns as societies develop, and in Book One I mentioned the research of the huge World Values Survey (WVS) which indicates that the Nordic countries have the "most progressive" values in the world. As Christian Welzel, the boss of WVS, notes, it is clear these values play well together with the development and maintenance of democratic institutions. When "progressive" values decrease—for reasons of economic turmoil or otherwise—it often leads to direct attacks on democratic institutions, as has recently been the case in Turkey, Russia and the Philippines.

What I am getting at here is that democracy in itself is not only a matter of institutional frameworks, but also of cultural development where the values, sentiments and behaviors of people can be more or less in line with democratic ideals and their collective democratic functionality.

The recent rise of **co-development** ideals in the most progressive countries bears witness to this tendency. Co-development is the process of improving the *quality* of debate, dialogue and deliberation throughout all of society and across the political spectrum. It works from the supposition that we can't possibly be right about "everything" and hence always need to learn from one another, friend or foe; if nothing else just to see where they're coming from. This, of course, is a deeper democratic ideal and an early sign of a further deepening of democracy.

All changes of institutional and constitutional frameworks must ultimately rest upon the values and cultural realities of real people. It is within this cultural realm that challenges to the existing equilibrium stage of governance ("liberal democracy") can grow.

Thus, I have suggested five dimensions of what a deeper democracy may entail:

1. increased dispersion of leadership;

2. increased volume, complexity and efficiency of information processing;

3. increased accountability and balancing of powers, putting greater demands upon the verifiability of decision-making;

4. a deepening and thickening of *de jure* and *de facto* participation and popular support in processes of decision-making and opinion formation; and

5. the growth of democratic, egalitarian and multi-perspectival culture and values.

If you like, you can call these five dimensions a way of increasing the **collective intelligence** of a given society; a means to "deepen" democratic participation.

In this regard, **a deeper democracy is one that lets solutions of higher orders of complexity emerge and gain legitimacy, thereby allowing for more complex forms of society to exist and thrive**.

If more real problems are solved, if public support of and consent to decisions are better, if the decision processes run more smoothly, if there are fewer unwanted and unexpected consequences of decisions made—

and so on—*then* we can say that democracy has been developed, that it has been deepened.

These five dimensions give us a kind of "true north" of democratic development, a map that can guide us towards a more democratic democracy. Today's democratic institutions are better than their historical predecessors not because they in-and-of-themselves are a God-given "correct" form of governance, but simply because they fulfill these five criteria more adequately as compared to earlier forms of governance.

FALSE DEFENDERS OF DEMOCRACY

When we "defend democracy", this can mean two very different things: We can *either* defend the progression and development of these democratic ideals and their manifestation in society (which is good)—*or* we may be defending the current, increasingly outdated *institutional form* of modern "liberal democracy" from the metamodern currents of renewal and refinement. In the latter case, we may think of ourselves as heroic defenders of democracy, raging against the dying of the light, but we are in fact waging a war against the core values of democratic development because we mistake the current forms of governance for a sacred entity—for instance, by being overly defensive about "the constitution". The latter is as enlightened as holding sharia laws to be the only true and God-given way of organizing society. It makes us medieval.

Because democracy in its current form is seldom regarded with a sober and secular gaze, and often as a kind of sacred value-in-itself, the majority of the population may in effect be on the anti-democratic side of the developmental tide—much like when most folks in the past were against women's suffrage and gay rights. Habits, outdated norms and investments in the *status quo* all work to uphold social inertia, an immunity to change. In this case, we end up fighting off necessary developments of governance and thus of our collective intelligence. The majority position, then, is that of the **false defenders of democracy**.

The majority is wrong. Always were. Then again, what else should we expect? The point with democracy isn't that the majority is always right. **The point is that there is a process of free and sufficiently systematized truth-seeking and dialogue going on for small groups to be able to prove the rest of us wrong, again and again, so that values, opinions and laws can evolve and adapt.** That's how democracy works—you can't "vote" about the truth; the idea is that the truth offers a powerful attractor point so that, in the long run, more truth than falsehood will win out, and that this, on average, will have better consequences.

The true north of democratic development can and will lead us bey- ○ **ond the institutional forms of modern society.** We are, of course, still struggling with the taboo of asking such questions, about what might lie beyond liberal democracy (with a capitalist market), because the two major alternatives of the 20ᵗʰ century—communism and fascism—turned out to be such terrible mistakes.

However, this compass could actually help us steer clear of new treats of totalitarianism that may show up in new, seductive, postindustrial, digital-age guises. With a good compass, and with a critical sensitivity towards the directionality of historical development (seeing the stages of development and how these constitute historical attractor points), we may be nearing a point in history in which we are compelled not to take any form of governance for granted—and in which we must begin to dream dangerous dreams of future forms of governance.

THE FOUR DEMOCRATIC FORMS

Fundamentally, then, governance is just another word for the self-organization of society (shaping the development of people's psychologies, who in turn consciously participate in the organization of society). To develop democracy as we know it is a way to tackle this issue of self-organization.

In this view, then, "liberal democracy" with its parliamentary party politics is only a train station on a longer developmental railroad that has stopped at several earlier forms of governance. True, we have stayed here for a hundred years or so, which is a long time. But we stayed at monarchic and varieties of feudal rule for much longer. And then we moved on.

It's normal for the train to stop for a while. The system needs to stabilize and the costs of getting to the next station are high. But the train does move on, sooner or later. As I said, there is no reason to suppose that democratic governance will—or *should*—look the same during the entirety of the 21ˢᵗ century as it did in the 20ᵗʰ.

Let us, before we go ahead to describe what Democratization Politics may look like on a state level, do an inventory of a few key concepts that may serve as building blocks as we begin to construct metamodern forms ₵ of governance. First out are the four forms of democracy and their inter-relations: direct, representative, participatory, and deliberative democracy. These four forms of democracy are most famously discussed by David

Held, but they have been treated by many other prominent political scientists as well. I'll touch briefly upon them and try to cut to their core essence.

Direct democracy is when people—"the whole population"—vote directly on decisions for laws, regulations, taxes and public projects. In extension, all non-autocratic governance rests upon a foundation of direct democracy. In theory, a population, "demos", must be able to oust any representatives, revoke or reverse any decisions made, change any laws, rewrite any constitution. The idea of democracy is simply that the power belongs to the people, the people being whoever is governed by a monopolized use of force. Thus, any "in-direct" democracy must, in the last instance, reference a direct democratic rule, lest it loses any and all democratic legitimacy.

Representative democracy is when people elect representatives who make decisions for them (within certain designated areas of common concern) in "free and fair" elections. In this system, people who want to get elected generally organize into lists of names on the ballot with others who they tend to agree with, and these lists are the political parties. These parties often gain a life of their own. It is, goes without saying, the main system of most democracies in the world today.

Participatory democracy is when people—i.e. the constituents themselves—get to participate directly in decision-making, carrying out decisions made, fulfill advisory functions and so forth. The idea here is to increase the pathways into the exercise of power, in effect broadening how many people get to really partake in governance and have a real relationship to the common, to the political.

Deliberative democracy is democratic decision-making based upon "deliberation", i.e. carefully facilitated discussions between the stakeholders. People are invited to panels or councils and the discussion goes on in organized and curated manners until some kind of common ground can be reached. The common ground is thus taken to be the decision. The idea here is that people often need to learn from one another and listen to many arguments and perspectives before they make an informed decision, and that there are often non-obvious alternatives that are not only watered-down compromises but actually synthesize different positions so that a "better" position or "higher ground" is reached.

The most prominent scholar to advocate deliberative democracy is, again—and of course—Habermas, a.k.a. the patron saint of the EU and social philosopher of communication. But the topic is increasingly popular academically and otherwise, and has been growing as an ideal in the early 21th century. We can see a staggering growth of "facilitation techniques" such as Art of Hosting, Deep Democracy and Otto Scharmer's Theory U as well as organizational forms which build upon deliberative ideals, such as Sociocracy, Holacracy and Frédéric Laloux's phenomenally popular "Teal Organizations". These are really all over the place, from NGOs to tech startups to international meetings that gather philanthropists and activists.

Anyway, so we have these four forms of democracy, and I would like to specify the relationship between them, as this has not been quite properly done to my knowledge.

Let's start with the completely *wrong* way of thinking about this (and, regrettably, the by far most common one). The completely wrong way is to view each of the four democratic ideal types as "a system" which can "be instituted" at a certain time in history and from there on "functions" according to the logic of that same system.

So you will hear people coming from this perspective—when reacting to the mentioning of democratic development—saying things like: "I don't think *that* is a good idea, as it would lead to mob rule" or "Today's society is already *too* democratic; we shouldn't make it more so."

What are these people missing? Why is this *not* a fruitful way to think about and discuss this topic? I think there are *three* points that must be stressed.

1. They don't see that these four forms of democracy aren't coherent pre-existing systems set in stone which can "be instituted" at any given point. Rather, they are each a general principle which must continuously be developed in exchange with the other ones. *All* existing democracies incorporate at least *some* of these elements. Hence, it's not a question of "implementing" one "system" or another, but rather of pushing the boundaries for democratic development and cultivating new and deeper layers of governance. Within each of the four forms of democracy there are of course also many different shapes and ways to go about, for instance different ballot techniques as we shall briefly discuss shortly. So it is a question of *continuous enrichment* of the existing system by means of delimited experimentation, systematic evaluation and of an ongoing discussion regarding which criteria we should use to measure a "better democracy". Such quality markers could be better decision-making (that decisions actually have the intended effects), higher collective intelligence, more public psychological ownership of the decisions made (and higher compliance to rules and regulations), efficacy, transparency, degree of inclusivity, and other criteria that may yet need to be invented and agreed upon.

2. People don't recognize that these four forms of democracy—the possibilities for them—cannot be accepted or dismissed with eternally and universally valid arguments. They are, of course, context dependent. The context within which they emerge includes the value meme demographics of a society, the available technological tools of communication, the degree of cultural democratic development, the amount of accumulated human experience with a certain kind of system, the surrounding bureaucratic framework, the strength and stability of the state, the kind of economy that must be governed, the size of the governed society and the availability of social and psychological innovations of dialogue and decision-making—and so forth.

3. People don't recognize that there is an inherently logical relationship between the four different forms of democracy, and that they do in fact make up a coherent pattern of a greater whole. This is a pattern that includes both a developmental directionality and a manner in which the four forms counter the inherent weaknesses of each other.

Okay, hopefully you can see that it's not a simple matter of being "for" or "against" any of these democratic forms. This incorrect way of thinking shuts down the entire discussion and any fruitful development of a deeper democracy. Either we're invested in a "pies in the sky" model that never gets tested in real life and has any number of problems once we try it, *or* we simply get stuck with the current *status quo* and fail to make adjustments that are both possible and necessary, because we don't see "how *that* system would work".

INTERCONNECTING THE FOUR

Let us now then zoom in on the last of the three points made above. What are the interrelations between the four forms of democracy?

First of all, **there is a progression from the most basic and fundamental form to the most advanced and complex one**. Direct democracy is the foundation of all democratic decision-making, ensuring that the governed have a say in the decisions made, which is the basis of all democratic legitimacy.

Representative democracy puts some of this decision-making into the hands of smaller groups of people who in turn are elected by means of direct votes.

Participatory democracy creates paths for non-elected people to reenter and enrich the decision processes and execution of decisions made, which thus builds upon an established representative democracy.

And deliberative democracy creates venues for deeper discussions through which people's participatory understandings themselves can be enriched and more aptly coordinated. Deliberative democracy builds upon a foundation of the participation of relevant stakeholders.

Secondly, you can see that this progression also plays out as a historical sequence of how democracy and democratic theory have developed. Direct democracy, naturally, is the basic form that evolved already in ancient Athens and to which we all return whenever a group of people say "let's give it a vote".

Representative democracy grew through various forms of republicanism in antiquity and early modernity, taking stronger and more systematic hold as representation grew after the 1688 Glorious Revolution in England and corresponding developments elsewhere—becoming fully manifested after the French and American revolutions.

Participatory democracy has existed only in a full modern form in some socialist contexts, such as during the Spanish Civil War 1936-1938, in which the Spanish Republican anarchist factions were governed with participatory principles. And then it played a significant role during the utopian leftwing surges and intellectual currents of the 1960s.

And deliberative democracy has bloomed chiefly as an academic concept, being taught at universities since a few decades back. In its concrete forms it exists only on a micro scale, within experimental companies, local citizen inclusion projects, committees and so forth.

Thirdly, there is an inherently *logical* relationship between each of the four. Direct democracy is of course democracy "in and of itself", its purest form, which is hence the elemental substance of all democratic governance. The fundamental measure of all consensual and contractual governance structures must ultimately be that the governed govern.

But this is of course always impossible in practice: Not only are there minors and others who cannot partake as equals, but as soon as the coordinated political unit is above a certain size, this requires representation in order to reduce the costs of managing the complexity of decision making. In an advanced economy with significant division of labor, it simply doesn't make sense to have everyone expend much time and effort making decisions about the minutiae of all public matters.

The larger and more complex the economy, the greater the need for representative democracy; for politicians, civil servants, parliaments, cabinets and parties. Representative democracy can also curtail some of the good old stubbornness of the people, letting those with stronger arguments win in central arenas. The fact that direct-democratic Switzerland only got the vote for women in 1971 (the last canton resisted until 1990 and had to be forced by court decision), reveals the fact that even the most necessary adjustments can be held back by the social inertia of the population. Rousseau famously idealized the Swiss mode of governance, but in practice it often tilts the political game in a conservative rather than a progressive direction, quite unlike what Rousseau romantically imagined. (This being said, the Confederation of Switzerland still has much to teach other countries in terms of effective democratic governance.)

The larger the political unit, the more complexity must be managed by means of representation—and hence the less viable direct democracy becomes. This creates an increasing distance between the governing processes and the constituency itself; i.e. there is by necessity a growing gap between the citizens and their leaders. Today it is common to talk about this phenomenon as "the democratic deficit"; a discussion held particularly in regard to the EU and other forms of transnational governance. The distance between a G7 summit and ordinary citizens, for instance, is simply so vast that it hardly can be called democratic in any real sense.

Hence, the role of participatory democracy is to re-conquer these representative structures, subjecting them to the wills and perspectives of relevant stakeholders and "common people" without bogging it all down with the impossibility of mass votes on each and every technical question. Participatory democracy is the process of enriching the cold machinery of bureaucracy and professionalized politics with warm hands, reconnecting the governing bodies to the governed.

And deliberative democracy is the practice of refining the processes through which many perspectives are formed and coordinated, so that participation can be fruitful and relevant. The more stakeholders are included at every level of decision making, the greater the risk they clog up the relevant decision-making processes and in effect hinder the actions of one another. Hence, the issue emerges of creating smoother processes through which thoughts, perspectives and actions are coordinated on a deeper and more complex level—the need for thoughtfully designed, curated and facilitated processes of deliberation. Three researchers, Zelma Bone, Judith Crockett and Sandra Hodge, suggested in 2006 the table on the next page to distinguish between debate, dialogue and deliberation.[78]

SHAPES OF POLITICAL DISCOURSE (adopted from Bone, Crockett and Hodge, 2006)		
Debate	Dialogue	Deliberation
Compete	Exchange	Weigh
Argue	Discuss	Choose
Promote opinion	Build relationships	Make choices
Seek majority	Understand	Seek overlap
Persuade	Seek understanding	Seek common ground
Dig in	Reach across	Framed to make choices
Tight structure	Loose structure	Flexible structure
Express	Listen	Learn
Win/lose	No decision	Common ground

I think it summarizes well how deliberative democracy aims for a distinct form of communication: not just "debate", where the issue is to "win", not just "dialogue", where the issue is to "understand one another" but *deliberation*, where the aim is to create something new together and to find out how to do what's best given the circumstances.

If we put this table in a wider developmental context, we can see that we go from a pre-democratic state of settling issues by force, to a direct democratic vote where people just arbitrarily take a majority stance, to a debate within central arenas of representative democracy, to a dialogue of participatory democracy, to the deliberation pertaining of course to deliberative democracy. There is an inherent developmental sequence here, paralleled in part by the value memes (*modern* debate, *postmodern* dialogue, *metamodern* deliberation).

Of course, the later stages of this developmental sequence require higher levels of interpersonal trust and are more suitable for handling issues of increased complexity—in which it may be difficult to delineate your interest from mine, or even to define and weigh my very own interests. We'll get back to the issue of generating deeper trust under *Gemeinschaft* Politics.

The point we need to see now is simply that deliberative democracy facilitates the listening, learning and understanding processes that make participation possible; and participation makes representation legitimate; and representation makes democratic governance manageable; and direct voting makes democracy legitimate in the first place. Deepening deliberation is key to what I call "co-development", but deliberation must be used in harmonious tandem with the other forms of democracy.

The fourth **and last connection between the four forms of democracy is that they each come in degenerated and pathological shapes, each constituting a distinct kind of tyranny**. An important element of why each form of democratic governance can be derailed is that necessary balances with the three other forms fail.

Direct democracy was of course critiqued already during antiquity by Plato and others for its way of creating a crude majority rule, a tyranny of the majority. Naturally, there is no reason to assume that the majority position is always, or even very often, the best one. This tyrannical degeneration is echoed in authoritarian communist regimes with a "dictatorship of the proletariat". Such regimes generally claim to be a kind of direct democracy, as the Soviet system did to a significant extent. There is thus a super-concentration of power (with no division of powers *à la* Montesquieu or Locke) and massification of party membership, with no division of powers as "the people" are thought to rule by decree. In practice, of course, a small group or single leader can snatch the reigns, as Napoleon did. As the communist rule progressed, the lack of proper mechanisms of representation meant that information feedback processes were bottlenecked and systemic imbalances grew. All of this harkens back, of course, to Rousseau's famous words: "We will force you to be free!"

Authoritarian capitalist societies like Singapore, Egypt or Pinochet's Chile—or in our days, to some extent even China—lack even this pretension of being a "people's republic". A small elite simply claims to represent the country as a whole and that they know what's best. This representation is decoupled from any direct democratic basis, which means that it lacks any democratic legitimacy. This doesn't in itself mean that its governance must be unsuccessful—just that it may be difficult to develop deeper forms of democratic self-organization, as these societies are necessarily built upon frail monopolies of power.

Fascist "corporativism" that grew in Mussolini's Italy is a society organized around professional categories, industry interest groups, or a modern equivalent of medieval "guilds". This can be said to be a perverse form of participatory democracy: If you base governance upon member participation, but with no direct vote and no effective representation mechanisms, people become deeply involved but still have few means of curbing tyranny and misuse of power. So you can get a lot of people to coordinate their actions very intensely for a while, but the lack of both democratic legitimacy, power balance and representation will ensure that the system has low social sustainability. Fascism, and corporativism especially, thus constitute a deranged form of participatory democracy.

Pathological versions of deliberative democracy have yet to emerge on a larger scale—the history of the 20th century doesn't give us any examples of a "deliberative tyranny", after all. But we can certainly see derailed attempts at deliberation in smaller "progressive" organizations, which easily take on smothering ideals about "sensitivity", "humility", "listening" and so forth, to the extent that people get stuck in complicated and icky social relations while striving for an impossible consensus, accusing one another of being passive aggressive and so on. Because co-development and deeper deliberation is such a powerful attractor as society progresses into a more complex, postindustrial and global order, we are bound to become more and more acquainted with the pathologies pertaining to deliberative democracy and its particular and yet largely unknown forms of tyranny. To be sure, it will have something to do with subtle transgressions of the personal integrity of people, overstretched subtle nudges and manipulations, and the kind of social-psychological mechanisms that can play a part in "group-think".

Because we need so much deliberation, because we are compelled towards co-development, we must face the darker sides of deliberation. The logic of this progression—from direct, to representative, to participatory, to deliberative democracy (and then back again in different combinations and iterations between them)—points in a certain direction of increased capability for co-development and complex self-organization of society. But it also portends that new and subtler kinds of tyranny and oppression may emerge during the 21st century.

And new sources of oppression can emerge where we least expect it: in the circles *most* committed to democratic ideals and to deepening democracy. When everyone is committed to the process and to developing their own positions, the divisions of party politics can break down and hence new and subtler concentrations of power and new methods of manipulation can emerge.

What has been said thus far can be summarized in the table on the next page:

FORMS OF DEMOCRACY			
	Direct	**Representative**	**Participatory**	**Deliberative**

	Direct	Representative	Participatory	Deliberative
Basic role	Basis of democratic legitimacy	Manages complexity and issues of scale	Re-introduces stakeholder perspectives	Facilitates the coordination & development of perspectives
How complex?	Least complex	Second least complex	Second most complex	Most complex
Developmental stage	Ancient governance, smaller units	Modern governance, larger units	Critical re-appropriation of modern governance	Making critical appropriation possible in practice
Pathology	Tyranny of the majority, communism	Distant and unaccountable bureaucracy	Fascist corporativism	Subtle smothering, manipulation and group-think

There is a deep connection between these democratic forms of govern-ance, and not any one of them is in-and-of-itself "the best". The issue is rather that the different forms connect to each other and create a coherent whole, and that the developmental possibilities of any given system of governance must be continuously evaluated and developed.

—

Democracy can never be a question of arriving at the best deal once and for all. The terms of governance and political participation must remain open to continual renegotiation to be considered truly democratic, and only through processes of further democratization can the faith in demo-cracy be kept alive. Democracy, it's not a thing; it's a process.

Indeed, democracy isn't real. It doesn't exist, and never will. Demo-cracy is forever destined to be a fairytale in a land of nowhere, a utopia we'll never actually reach. **Only *democratization* is really real, and only higher or lower levels of democratization can be said to exist.**

Democratization Politics can thus never make reality of the utopian vision of a society governed by the people, but it can bring into existence the relative utopias that strive towards the attractor point of increased collective intelligence—the true north of democratic development.

Chapter 10

EVOLVING DEMOCRACY

G iven that representative democracy has hitherto been the most successful form of governance, the main task ahead is to attempt an **enrichment** of the representative form by means of introducing direct, participatory and deliberative democracy within limited settings.

This chapter is here to consider some pathways for such enrichments
and some of the surrounding tools: the development of voting systems,
uses of internet democracy, and Unger's institutional experimentalism.
We also take a look at what Democratization Politics can look like in
practice.

Voting Systems and Internet Democracy

Even countries less democratic according to measures such as Freedom
House can start from somewhere and build newer and deeper forms of
democracy—even China can democratize its institutions, albeit from
another starting point and through other paths than Western societies.

Democracy is not, as we observed, a binary variable. It is a graded scale
pertaining to the level of collective intelligence within the systems of
governance, the results of which can be measured by agreed-upon universal principles, and there may be different pathways to its development.

So we need to try new paths ahead for governance, until we find which
forms prove effective and satisfactory, at which levels of governance, within which sectors, and according to which criteria. It is not a question of
scrapping representative democracy and replacing it wholesale; it is a question of learning where today's system can grow, how it can be refined,
and how it can be deepened.

There are of course many paths ahead within each of the forms, many
methods to explore within direct, representative, participatory and deliberative democracy. In deliberative democracy you have different ways of

facilitating, different ways of delineating the topics discussed, ways to distribute speaking time and attentions, etc.; in participatory democracy you
have different ways of letting people take part—in advisory functions, partaking in executive functions, sharing or rotating leadership roles, and so
on.

When it comes to direct and representative democracy, you always
need some kind of ballot, vote or election, and these can take on a number
of different shapes, which have been explored by theorists of elections as
well as in practice. For elections of representatives, the following systems
all give different dynamics:

- **First past the post**: You count the votes and whoever gets the most
  votes wins.

- **Ranked voting, "instant runoff"**: Voters rank the alternatives, and
  then you eliminate the least popular candidate until someone has 50%
  of the remaining votes, and then they win. Used in Ireland and Austria.

- **Ranked voting, "Borda count"**: Voters rank all the candidates, and
  whoever has the lowest score wins (you get a "1" if you're someone's
  first choice). Used in Slovenia and on some Micronesian Islands.

- **Ranked voting, "Condorcet method"**: Run a theoretical election
  between each of the candidates, until one candidate has beaten all
  others based on their voter rankings. To date not used in any existing
  country.

- **Approval voting**: Voters can check boxes for whom they approve of.
  Whoever gets most approval wins.

- **Score voting**: Voters score the candidates on a scale; highest added
  score wins.

And of course, there are other possible variations. Each voting system
produces different dynamics and different forms of fairness, just like it is
with the classical distinction between majority vote systems and proportional votes. Some systems lead to more strategic voting ("my candidate
can't win either way"), some produce more compromises that have fewer
strong supporters and so forth.

The point here is not to discuss the implications of the different ballot
systems, but simply to point out that this is another arena within which
experimentation of democratic development is possible.

In a similar vein, it should be pointed out that there are plenty of possibilities to explore digital forms of voting, decision making, participation
and deliberation. The first idea that comes to people's minds is usually

that there could be an internet-run direct democracy, through which citizens are themselves asked to vote on different issues. In practice, of course, such a system would still need facilitation and some forms of representation, and it would likely be a poor form of governance as people would vote on many issues with little background knowledge.

Looking at our five suggested dimensions of a "true north" of democratic development (last chapter), it is only clear how a straightforwardly defined internet direct democracy might do some good in the first dimension. It would almost certainly be harmful to the second one, and its effect in the other three would be doubtful at best—just look down the list again and think:

1. Increased dispersion of leadership;
2. increased volume, complexity and efficiency of information processing;
3. increased accountability and balancing of powers, putting greater demands upon the verifiability of decision making;
4. a deepening and thickening of *de jure* and *de facto* participation and popular support in processes of decision-making and opinion formation;
5. the growth of democratic, egalitarian and multi-perspectival culture and values.

Again, the issue is not to envision *one* certain system to replace the current one wholesale, but rather to envision a *path* that lets us experiment with and enrich the existing system in a multiplicity of ways, so as to improve the legitimacy, quality, reach and efficiency of governance.

The point I want to make is that there is today—thanks to the help of online tools—a significant window of opportunity to experiment with new forms of governance. Public institutions must be established with the task of evaluating and developing these new forms, and to spread the best practices.

The research on internet democracy (or so-called "e-democracy", electronic democracy) and the knowledge base about online deliberation and digital citizen engagement is actually quite large—the body of research and practical experience has grown immensely since the early 2000s. Within this tradition of research there are plenty of people with a deep background in social science, theories of communication, psychology and network theory.

There are some innovative thought-leaders such as Tim O'Reilly and Clay Shirky—who write about the emergent possibilities of participatory online tools, as well as the transformations of digital society at large—and there are academics who spend their entire careers researching these and similar topics, such as Martin Hilbert (but this field seems to remain within in highly academic circles), and there are plenty of online tools out there, such as Loomio, Delib and GlassFrog, designed and marketed by countless companies, small and large. And there are—last but not least—so many projects of online citizenship polling, petitions, deliberation and citizen feedback from all around the world, usually at the local and regional levels of governance, from India to Denmark to the UK to California. And within party politics the Pirate Party (most famously the German one) has tried something they call "liquid democracy", which is an early form of crowdsourced online politics, and the Italian Five Star Movement has had electoral successes by using simpler forms of online citizen activation. The EU Commission has shown significant interest in these issues, and public officials are generally positive towards these trends of deepening democracy by means of online tools.

BOTTOM-UP AND TOP-DOWN

Given the strength and spread of these trends, why aren't we seeing a major transition in terms of systems of governance happening around the world? I'd like to suggest, again, that these developments are up against too strong forces of social and political inertia inherent to the existing structures of governance for them to spread, take hold and begin a true journey of iterative improvement. **It is simply too heavy, difficult and, in a general sense, "expensive" to shift the systems of governance for any rich plethora of small actors to succeed in doing so.**

The sheer volume of people's actions that have to be re-coordinated for a shift to be effected is simply too large. This is why we have yet to see an effective accumulation of knowledge about e-governance and implementations thereof; only a thousand loose threads and forgotten trails spread across the globe.

My suggestion is that the hitherto dominant bottom-up approach must be matched by a coordinating and centralized effort. After all, major infrastructure projects, such as high-speed rail services, satellite systems and public universities, rarely emerge solely through grass-root initiatives. Why should we expect a major update of democracy itself to emerge only through bottom-up processes?

We are hence left with what appears to be a paradox of developing the systems of governance: Any centrally planned top-down effort is likely to miss out on the complexities of everyday life and be built without real contact with human needs and experiences. They tend to be large, clunky and "fragile", rather than flexible and resilient, as economist Nassim Nicholas Taleb put it in his famous 2012 book *Antifragile*.

But any small-scale bottom-up effort is likely to be drowned in the already existing and more pertinent structures of society. We must hence strive for a synthesis between the two: a proper metamodern "both-and". **There must be central planning which coordinates and strengthens a genuine multiplicity of experimental, iterative emergences, including local and private initiatives.**

Free bottom-up emergence works fine outside such arenas as governance and basic infrastructure. On the free market and in civil society we see the growth of social media, citizen journalism, Open Data and all sorts of collective and collaborative processes of "Web 2.0". There are even new shared forms of encryptions and accounting that allow for blockchain based crypto-currencies; things that may eventually fundamentally transform how finance works. All this is miles ahead of any corresponding development in the political realm. The best we have in the public realm thus far is perhaps the movement towards "open data", which increases transparency and the ability of the public to use official bodies of information.

Despite the fact that the world is brimming with interesting and useful initiatives within deeper democracy and software solutions to this end, the high hopes of the cyber-utopians of the 1990s and early 2000s have hardly been met. In the midst of a hurricane of digital transformations of society, the political system has remained much like before the internet. This is a worrying inertia.

As long as the state remains passive in this field and its key agents make no substantive efforts to support these new experiments, to evaluate the best practices, and to spread and apply such practices, we are simply too far away from a tipping point where the current systems of governance start to give way to a wave of institutional innovation and renewal.

INSTITUTIONAL EXPERIMENTS

The conclusion must be clear: an institutional experimentalism is needed, much akin to Unger's ideas about "experimental zones".

There must be instituted a central agency which helps to fund, develop, evaluate, as well as gather and share information about all forms of democratic innovation—be they digital tools, new voting systems, panel and deliberation programs, decision feedback systems, pathways to citizen involvement, or conflict resolution and mediation efforts: everything that aids the quality, efficiency, reach, transparency and fairness of governance.

This is the essence of Democratization Politics: **The idea is that *the state itself* and its democratic governance in many layers, from the local to the transnational, becomes a developmental project, continuously discussed and improved upon.**

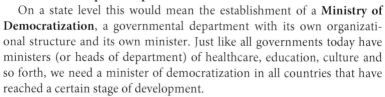

On a state level this would mean the establishment of a **Ministry of Democratization**, a governmental department with its own organizational structure and its own minister. Just like all governments today have ministers (or heads of department) of healthcare, education, culture and so forth, we need a minister of democratization in all countries that have reached a certain stage of development.

The Ministry of Democratization is the hub in a larger de-centralized multiplicity of ongoing democratic experiments. All cities, municipalities and counties should be allowed a certain budget for trying to improve upon their democratic system through a variety of projects invented at the local level; projects built upon civil society, solutions purchased from companies within the field and so on. These projects experiment with new forms of elections within delineated decision processes (different ballot systems etc.), new forms of citizen feedback, new ways of enriching the representative system with subcategories of direct votes, participation and deliberation.

The ministry should be responsible for supporting, in part funding, evaluating and documenting these projects and spreading best practices. Hence, there is a cycle of experimenting with new forms of governance, evaluating and pruning these, and continuously updating actual governance on all levels. When enough knowledge, experience and expertise has been gathered—not least in the form of an international plethora of innovative democratic tech companies—larger experiments can be conducted on state and even transnational levels.

This is Democratization Politics: **It's bottom-up-top-down *and* top-down-bottom-up.**

It builds upon what is actually existing and real to the people involved, *and* it takes the potentialities and visions seriously. It works *both* to revolutionize the political system, *and* it builds upon a slow, conservative development which respects the culture and values of people on the ground. It works *both* with short-term projects that solve tangible here-and-now problems, *and* it works on a long-term scale with cycles of decades or longer of updating the institutional code of society.

As democratic society is designed today, it is simply not built to withstand the sheer rapidity, force and disruptiveness of social and technological change. We have states which can change their laws as society evolves **—but we do not have states with built-in mechanisms at the meta-level, where the way we propose laws and make decisions is itself continuously developed**. We hold democratic governance as our most cherished value, and yet we fail to take it seriously enough to ensure that democracy is updated and rejuvenated in pace with the development of a postindustrial, digital and globalized world.

A little crutch from biology might be appropriate here. Denis Noble, a biologist and Professor Emeritus of cardiovascular physiology at Oxford, has written a book called *The Music of Life*. He argues that living systems self-organize not only in a reductionist bottom-up manner, but that there are a multiplicity of processes which emerge at higher levels of self-organization, which also create feedback processes on lower levels of emergence. A cell, can, for instance, include emergent properties which affect chemical processes at the molecular level, and so forth. In other words, if we are to believe this old Brit, there is good reason to think in a bottom-up-top-down *and* top-down-bottom-up manner when seeking to understand how a whole system emerges and remains healthy.

Regardless of how we rate Noble's understanding from a natural-scientific perspective, I certainly feel it may be the right way to think about democratic development from the micro interactions between two people, to the governance of the world-system. Below is a model borrowed from Noble's 2006 book:

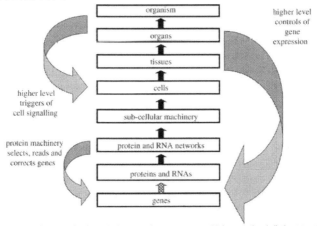

Figure: *Adopted from Oxford cardiology professor Denis Noble's 2006 book "The Music of Life".*

Would it be so strange if the emergence of governance could work in a corresponding manner? Could there be a deeper coherence, a music of social life? It does make sense that higher levels of governance can and should have a lively interaction with the lower levels, and that lower level emergences should in turn enrich and reshape the higher levels.

Where to start? We would need, then, to work at the *middle level*—the level of institutions—in order to spur a deeper development across the whole spectrum of governance, from the local to the global.

Think about it—all latter-day social science points to the simple fact that **the quality of a state's institutions has a larger impact on the stability of a society, its economic development and the wellbeing of its citizens than any other factor.** Why is Costa Rica doing okay and Venezuela not? Institutions. Why is Denmark a highly functional and competitive economy and Greece not? Institutions.

Macrosociology, the sociology of large structures, cultures and classes, has largely been a disappointment. Microsociology, understanding processes of interaction, socialization and alienation, has also largely failed to produce strong, predictive theories. *Meso*sociology, however, is different. This boring grey mouse of the social sciences, which looks at technical details of institutions and organizations, has proven to be a goldmine: Not only do the structures of organizations reveal why companies thrive or stagnate, but the institutional frameworks of states seem to explain more about societies and human lives than almost anything else.

Would it be a bad idea if late modern society would expend perhaps half a percent of its GDP on ongoing serious experiments of governance? Upon continuously cultivating and updating its own institutional framework? Probably not. Would it make sense to educate a number of new professionals who are not only democracy experts, but facilitators, communication coaches, counselors, organizers, organizational developers, democratic software developers, theorists, evaluators and democratic project designers? Could we "make an effort to make an effort" to improve democracy itself, until one day, perhaps, it looks completely different from when we started?

I think it would be unwise to go ahead with outmoded systems of governance into an entirely new technological age without even beginning the search for new forms of governance. We should buy the insurance.

And I think we need to start now.

FINAL COUNTDOWN FOR DEMOCRACY

It may not be an exaggeration to claim that we are approaching a final countdown for democracy. The pressures for transnational and regional (like the EU) and global governance are simply mounting with such rapidity and force that we will necessarily see the growth of impenetrably thick layers of top-down governance at a supra-state level in the coming decades. Because all the most pressing issues are global and transnational, they must be dealt with and regulated at the corresponding level. ✳

This will place most real power at a hopelessly long distance from the common citizen of the world. A person goes about her life and casts a vote in India or Brazil, but the decisions governing her life conditions are made in a closed room on the other side of the planet by people she's never heard about and may not even know exist.

As things stand today, that's where we're headed—faster than a cannonball. And how hard will it then not be for democratic forms of governance to maintain their legitimacy under circumstances where all meaningful decision-making is so distant, abstract and foreign?

The clock is ticking. If the pressures for transnational solutions push us into supranational structures of governance without a corresponding rejuvenation of democratic life and participation at all levels of society, supported by—but not limited to—new digital forms of democracy, we will come to a point at which we suddenly live in a global order that is distinctly non-democratic. Global non-democracy.

Democracy will have died the slow heat death. It will not have been killed, simply dispersed under its own entropy, being superseded in all but rhetoric by a global technocratic elite from which we can expect only a very limited amount of accountability. Transparency will be lost, and for all practical purposes, democracy will be lost—globally and, for the foreseeable future, permanently.

Again: the clock is ticking. **Either we begin the slow and cumbersome process of continuously reinventing and updating democracy, or it simply drifts away into space.** If people are engaged and sufficiently empowered to partake in governance on all levels, and live in a richly democratic culture, and if accountability is expanded and autonomy grows from the bottom up, then perhaps democratic forms of governance can conquer their way to the top, and we can see the emergence of a deeply democratic global order in the 21st century.

Where do we start? **We start at the meso-level**, the middle level of institutions, organizations and regional clusters of innovation (based around a "triple-helix" of companies, city administrations and universities) so often overlooked. We use the state to spur bottom-up democratic innovation, which then besieges the distant towers of patronizing state technocracy.

From that position we struggle on, non-linearly, to democratically shape the processes of the emergent world order. **We start at the meso-level and then we use the increasing organizational and institutional leeway to gradually go back and forth between the micro- and macro-levels.** Development starts at the middle and bounces its way up and down in increasing magnitude: from changing people's ideas and habits, to changing national, transnational and supranational structures of governance. Democratic development *oscillates*.

Will global governance be a monolith that follows the lowest common denominator, a frail autocratic colossus on clay feet; *or* will it be a rich, robust and effective ecology of institutional innovations? Beneath our feet the ground is giving way, a silent abyss of tyranny and decay opening. Above us, the skies are calling us to a greater potential, to higher forms of self-organization, to deeper democracy.

Ladies and gentlemen—Democratization Politics.

Aux armes, citoyens! To arms, citizens.[79]

Chapter 11

GEMEINSCHAFT POLITICS

> "Today we are faced with the preeminent fact that, if civilization is to survive, we must cultivate the science of human relationships—the ability of all peoples, of all kinds, to live together and work together, in the same world, at peace".
>
> —Franklin D. Roosevelt, in an undelivered address for Jefferson Day, intended for April 13th, 1945.

The quality of ordinary citizens' relations with one another can make or break a country. Societies characterized by a strong sense of community, high levels of trust and mutual respect and understanding tend to be richer, less corrupt and more peaceful. Countries with weak communal bonds, widespread distrust and little sense of belonging often fall apart, sometimes violently. That's why *Gemeinschaft* matters.

If a country fails badly enough at *Gemeinschaft* you get Yugoslavia or Iraq, if it succeeds, you get Denmark or Japan.

So what is meant by *Gemeinschaft*? The German sociologist Ferdinand Tönnies made the important distinction between *Gesellschaft* and *Gemeinschaft*. The former refers to the formal system of rules and regulations of a society, the latter to the more personal and informal bonds between people. Whereas *Gesellschaft* can be roughly translated into "society", *Gemeinschaft* does not have a satisfying equivalent in the English language. It is often translated into "community", but that sounds more like we're talking about a local neighborhood or a soccer club. And since we furthermore don't want to imply it is the same as the political philosophy of "communitarianism", we will use the original German word which moreover has become accepted in social science among English speakers.

We could also use the Swedish word, *gemenskap*, which has the same origin and meaning as the German term, better fitting "the Nordic Ideology". Or the Danish word *fællesskab* or the Norwegian *fellesskap*, both of which have the same meaning as *Gemeinschaft*, but instead share origins with the English word "fellowship". Over the centuries, however, "fellowship" has come to mean something slightly different than *Gemeinschaft*— but at least it gets us closer than "community".

So we're getting at a "politics of fellowship", if you will, a strand of politics which actively and deliberately seeks to improve the sense of fellowship among citizens and other aspects of our general relatedness to one another. A politics, perhaps even, of friendship. To cultivate a society based more upon friendship, camaraderie, collaboration. A call to an expansion of personal relationships as well as universal, impersonal love.

A CALL TO FELLOWSHIP

Whereas Democratization Politics is the politics of developing our formal relations, our governance (corresponding to Tönnies' *Gesellschaft*), **Gemeinschaft Politics is the politics of developing our *informal* relations; the many personal and civic relationships so vital to every aspect of a good and sustainable society.**

Gemeinschaft Politics is about human relationships, including: those between residents in local communities, cultural and sports activities and other forms of volunteering in civil society, how well community builders and local leaders are treated and supported, how class distinctions play out, relations between different ethnic groups, the integration of immigrants, relations at work, gender relations and sexual and romantic interplays, family relations, domestic conflict and violence, relations in school, how much loneliness there is, how much bullying there is, how much peer pressure there is, cross-generational relations, social safety nets for old age and disability, the quality and prevalence of friendships, acquaintance network relations, distributions of social capital and status, levels of interpersonal trust, levels of average interpersonal care and solidarity, the degree to which people are willing to help strangers, norms for treating one another in public spaces and in general, the level of kindness and understanding people show one another, how judgmental or forgiving we are towards each other, how people reject one another and handle normbreakers and delinquents, how many grudges and perceived "enemies" we have, what resources there are for conflict resolution, which taboos we can't talk about, how good we are at social perspective taking.

Et cetera.

Relations. Relationships. Amen.

In a word: *Gemeinschaft.*

We need to apply scientific knowledge to improve the quality of human relations, long-term, at all levels of society—just like Franklin D. Roosevelt said it.[80] The value of social bonds and relationships is of course immeasurable. Yet, besides this value-in-itself, the quality of human relationships is a source of unimaginable wealth or poverty.

I have already underscored that there in today's affluent societies are almost no real material or economic problems left—pretty much *none* of the fundamental problems of late modern society are due to a *de facto* lack of economic resources. Once a postindustrial level of affluence has been achieved, with an annual per capita GDP above 25,000 US dollars, the reason people suffer is no longer because of an actual lack of material resources. **The main source of society's ailments is that people's behaviors, psychologies and social relations don't function properly.** In late modern society, suffering is *social* rather than economic.

If you look at an issue like unemployment, the challenge isn't really to feed and shelter the unemployed, but rather to provide them with social status, meaning, dignity, activities and a daily rhythm—to prevent *social* decay. When it comes to rising housing prices that can burst into market bubbles, the issue is greatly exacerbated by the growth of single households, the need for people to protect their private spaces from intrusions by insensitive others who would disturb their peace. A society in which everyone is nicer to be around—where folks are more socially functional—and where there is greater mutual trust, would be one where people need less distance from one another and thus one of greater living space efficiency, hence with lesser living space competition, and hence with lower housing prices and rents.

If you look at issues like overconsumption and ecological footprints, it is not difficult to see that a society in which people have less reason to feel insecure about their social status would also be one in which a more postmaterialist culture could flourish and people could more easily make sustainable choices.

In a society where people communicate better and are less violent, there is less reason for inter-ethnic fear and resentment to grow, and hence lesser reason for discrimination, and hence lesser reason for racism and ethnic populism. It also means security costs become lower across the board, meaning more resources can be pooled into preventive social measures, meaning society becomes less repressive.

When it comes to issues of mental health, psychological development, how personalities develop, the degree of prosocial behavior to be expected from a population, what personal issues people have that steer their motivations, the prevalence of delinquency and crime—it must be obvious that each of them is shaped and defined by people's relationships.

These are just a few examples of how the nature of people's everyday relationships shapes society. Point being: it's social, stupid.

DEVELOPING THE DEMOS

Gemeinschaft Politics is closely linked to Democratization Politics. Democracy implies that there is a "demos", a people that governs society. But for there to be a people, there must be a certain something to bind citizens together; a feeling of communal togetherness, a sense of fellowship, a reason why we should belong to the same society to begin with. In short, if you don't have *Gemeinschaft*, you'll struggle to get a *Gesellschaft*—i.e. to get sound and sustainable institutions.

In the past, a shared religion and the myth about the ruler's divinity sufficed to maintain a minimum of social coherence. But with the transition to modernity, it became increasingly urgent that people shared the same culture and language. A sense of fellowship was needed to ensure peaceful and productive relations between different classes and people from culturally distinct provinces who now lived side-by-side in crowded industrial cities. The nation-building projects of the 19th century can thus be seen as an early version of *Gemeinschaft* Politics.

The modern nation state gave rise to what we commonly refer to as "civil society"; the non-governmental and non-commercial arenas where people can organize and act together in pursuit of shared interests, purposes and values. A strong civil society is in turn required for liberal democracy to function because the arenas of civil society are where citizens can organize themselves in ways to ensure rulers rule in accordance with the will of the "people", the "demos". But people won't necessarily see, or even accept, one another as members of a demos just because the state grants them citizenship and equality before the law. The demos can only exist if its alleged members experience mutual feelings of fellowship with one another, and a democracy can only function if the demos feels their shared destiny is tied to the state. The state can create the legal conditions that define the formal relations between citizens, and between citizens and the state, but the fellowship needed for people to accept one another as equal members of society can only be cultivated within civil society. Democracy thus also needs a civil society because this is where its demos is developed.

The development of a demos can occur within the borders of a state and justify its existence by a shared citizenship as in the case of France or the US, or it can develop from shared cultural ties stretching beyond state borders as in the case with the formation of Germany or Italy. It is, however, within the many arenas of civil society (clubs, newspapers, organizations of all sorts etc.) that discourses develop about who is to be included in the demos and thus be considered entitled to citizenship and equal status, and who is to be excluded from the *Gemeinschaft*.

This, however, does not mean states did not play a vital role in the formation of national identities and the cultivation of civic and democratic manners. It merely means that states could not develop the demos through the legal instruments of governance alone since the informal relations determining the demos per definition cannot be legislated about. Yet, this did not prevent the state from using other means to further the nation-building project. Since civil society was where the action was, the state put great care into ensuring that civil society enjoyed favorable conditions to blossom and that the clubs and organizations that favored the national agenda received additional funding.

FROM PUBLIC TO DOMESTIC TO PRIVATE

Modern society required informal relations of a more delicate nature than in the past in order to make the wheels of industry and bureaucracy run smoothly. People had to engage in productive relations with strangers from more varied backgrounds and classes than what they had been used to, and they had to follow new intricate codes of conduct in their relations at work and towards authorities. Former peasants had to learn how to avoid bickering and misunderstandings when interacting with the many strangers in the densely populated urban environments, and they had to accustom themselves to the role as factory workers and the instrumental nature of the relationship between workers and factory owners. The state thus took measures to teach its citizens to read and write and speak the same language so that they could better understand one another. Literacy also made it possible to read the national papers. This gave them access to the discourses of civil society that could teach them about their new living conditions in a modern society, and this made them part of a larger public so as to mold them into the national *Gemeinschaft*.

The elite was also compelled to adapt to the new societal relations by revising their manners when interacting with the lower classes in public. Verbal and physical abuse could not be tolerated in a modern society.

First of all because the poor had the same legal status as the rich, at least on paper; formally, workers and employers were equals who freely exchanged labor for wages. The ethos of liberalism thus demanded everyone was to be treated with the same amount of politeness and respect. In practice, however, the demand for higher levels of politeness and respect was a societal necessity to prevent daily conflicts from interfering in production and to avoid stirring up tensions that could easily erupt into uprisings among an already embittered working class.

The new ideal of the ruling classes, the "gentleman", thus became widely promoted in newspapers and magazines and within the salons and clubs where the bourgeoisie gathered. In fact, everyone had to behave nicer and with greater consideration towards others as stress and tensions among thousands of strangers cramped into small spaces made people more susceptible to go off. Consequently, a culture of politeness and strict etiquettes of public behavior emerged within civil society, and people began to address strangers as "mister" and "madam", poor as rich, and say "please" when asking for something as a way of showing that they acknowledged one another as equals and free citizens who could not be arbitrarily expected to follow an order.

The many new ways the informal relations within the public sphere got adjusted to life and work in an industrial economy would largely develop without direct governmental interference. The state merely made sure that people understood they were equal citizens of the nation state and that public discourse within civil society was sufficiently equipped to develop the demos. This can as mentioned be seen as an early variant of *Gemeinschaft* Politics. **All of these changes remained, however, within the public domain.** How you treated your wife wasn't part of the state's political project. Domestic and personal issues were left out.

As we saw in Chapter 3, this would change—dramatically—with the late modern consumer society of the 20th century. As Western societies democratized, the demands for civil society to cultivate evermore refined informal relations went up accordingly. The democratic developments of the *Gesellschaft* prompted corresponding developments within the *Gemeinschaft* to avoid alienation, and to ensure the *informal* relations between people would match the increasingly complex *formal* relations. There are just so many subtle and minor things that cannot be put into a code of laws. We need to regulate ourselves in all the day-to-day affairs that constitute the minute parts in an increasingly complex society.

So in order to ensure people would relate to one another as equal citizens and pursue their political interests in democratic ways as they entered the political battlefields of the *Gesellschaft*, Western governments made great efforts to support their civil societies to cultivate democratic notions of *Gemeinschaft*. The welfare state's growing expenditures on everything from public radio and television, over culture and sports, to afterschool activities for children and local community projects can all be seen as measures to generate positive emotions of fellowship between citizens and make them feel as equal participants in a democratic society.

However, as the notions of the *Gemeinschaft* became more democratic and cosmopolitan, the *Gesellschaft* also had to develop to match the new level of *Gemeinschaft*. The two go hand in hand in a dialectical process where one cannot successfully develop without the other. Social inequalities and injustices get harder to tolerate when people start seeing themselves and others as peers. Social measures within the domestic sphere (unemployment aid, health insurance, pensions etc.) had been implemented in some countries since the 19th century, but mostly as a way to curb socialism, not as a measure of *Gemeinschaft* Politics. This changed during the 20th century. To maintain public faith in the institutions of government and to ensure social stability in a democratically inclined late-modern society, new measures were needed to increase social mobility and limit the extent of social problems. Affecting behavior in the public domain wasn't enough. **Gemeinschaft Politics had to go domestic**.

The material welfare of underprivileged families became a societal concern so as to prevent poverty, poor health and lack of education, all of which hinder children from becoming productive members of society. Even such seemingly private matters as what people ought to eat and how to avoid sexually transmitted diseases became a concern for the expanding welfare state. But the state also began to interfere in more intimate affairs such as child neglect, substance abuse, domestic violence, divorce rights, abortion and so on, so as to avoid the marginalizing effects of dysfunctional social relations at home. New legal measures were put in place to protect the wellbeing of citizens in the domestic domain. Yet, alterations of the formal relations between citizens, and between citizens and the state, were not sufficient to improve the informal relations in domestic life. Only through changed attitudes about gender relations and what is to be considered acceptable behaviors among family members, could domestic relations be improved. And this in turn required another change of attitude: that domestic affairs should become political issues.

The attitude that it's no one's business if a man gets drunk and beats his wife and children every Tuesday, or the idea that women should shut up and obey their husbands, won't change much just because the state says it's wrong. It is mainly within civil society that any substantial changes to such discourses can come about. So just like in the 19th century, the *Gemeinschaft* politics of the 20th were conducted with the help of civil society. The welfare state began to fund a multitude of non-governmental initiatives seeking to cultivate more democratic and benign relations in the domestic domain. Everything from private drug and alcohol rehabilitation programs, over child protection agencies, domestic violence awareness groups and women's rights organizations, to local community efforts among youths to counter loneliness, bullying and idleness, can thus be seen as the expansion of *Gemeinschaft* Politics into the domestic domain. New civil societal initiatives pertaining to the further development of *Gemeinschaft* Politics within the *public* domain were also added, such as anti-racism campaigns, LGBT+ and ethnic minority rights organizations and so on. But the defining feature of the *Gemeinschaft* Politics of the welfare state was the expansion into ever more intimate aspects of the social relations within the domestic domain.

The mission of the welfare state was not only to curb poverty and disease, but to create a just social order people could identify with and view as their home. The fact that the Swedish welfare state was referred to as *folkhemmet*, "the people's home", is thus no coincidence. The massive welfare programs of the post-war era, that literally entered people's homes, can thereby be seen as the next stage of *Gemeinschaft* Politics that was needed to match the developments of increasing democratization in late-modern consumer society.

So, what would be the next step?

A developmental sequence towards increasingly intimate aspects of the scope of *Gemeinschaft* Politics has already become visible: from the public, to the domestic, to the… my suggestion is: the **personal**.

Then, what could *Gemeinschaft* Politics look like in the global, hyper-complex, multicultural, information society of the 21st century? As the world grows ever more complex, citizens will find it harder to avoid confusion and alienation and society will find it increasingly challenging to maintain high levels of belonging and togetherness—to maintain pro-social behavior and trust in others. At the same time, the demand for even better relations between citizens goes up. That all the king's subjects didn't share the same cultural understanding was hardly a problem in medieval times, but in the industrial age it would break the kingdom apart. In the times of Charles Dickens, governments could safely ignore that common people were too poor to give their children a safe and happy upbringing, but in the massive social housing projects of today's metropolises, a group of disgruntled and alienated Oliver Twists can turn a city into a war zone.

Providing a sense of *Gemeinschaft* to a factory worker in an industrial city is more demanding than it is to do the same for a peasant in a medieval village—and providing *Gemeinschaft* to a modern consumer in a service economy is more demanding than for a 19th century factory worker. It thus hardly needs to be said that *Gemeinschaft* Politics gets even trickier when we are dealing with a new generation of digitally connected millennials who have to come to grips with one another in a globalized information economy. And if our children are to survive, they will need to experience higher levels of *Gemeinschaft* than any generation before. Their relations with one another will need to be of a much higher quality than what is typical today. Our future civilization depends on fellowship, higher levels of love and friendship. If Oliver Twist could ravage a city center today, he could blow up the world tomorrow.

Gemeinschaft Politics needs to get personal.

ENTER CREEPY POLITICS

Again—Democratization Politics, the politicization of the development of our *formal* relations in the public sphere, must naturally be matched by a corresponding development of the *informal* and personal relations between all citizens across all spheres of life.

After all, does not each and every vote cast depend precisely upon the relations people experience in their everyday life? Does not every debate, dialogue or deliberation depend upon the level of trust and the social skills of the parties involved? Does not the very will to want the best for not only ourselves, but for the public and for all citizens, depend upon our experience of these same people we meet? Deeper democratization is only possible if there is a solid foundation of *Gemeinschaft*. Ultimately, the political always rests upon a personal foundation, and this foundation is always relational.

We need *Gemeinschaft* Politics. As I have argued, for a society to actively and deliberately cultivate and promote the quality of all human relations, the personal must become a *political* issue. This drives us towards the frightening conclusion that even the love affairs of teenagers are of political concern, that how many friends an average old drunk has is a political issue. It is a matter of public interest, because it affects all of us. In order for society to self-organize at a new and higher level, the realm of the political must expand; the political must dive into the human soul, crawl in under our very skins.

This can and will of course get creepy as hell—*unless* a corresponding deepening of democracy has occurred, so that it is not an expert committee who subtly nudges and shapes the rest of us, but rather a free, transparent and fair debate is had about how citizens want to shape the generative preconditions for rich and functional relations to thrive. And there are other restraints that keep creepy at bay, as you will see in the coming chapters. Just as deeper democracy requires deeper *Gemeinschaft*, so does *Gemeinschaft* Politics require a successful expansion of Democratization Politics if it is to be in the service of higher order, freedom and equality.

For now, bear with me. This is going to get creepy. **But remember that this perceived creepiness is a symptom of *not* working with all the six dimensions of new politics together, of *failing* to get the new "Montesquieu balance" up and running.**

If society is going to work at all in the future, we have to go deeper in our coordination of human agency and cognition, and we thus need deeper politics. All else is toothless crap. To believe that you can rearrange things without going deeper is what I call the position of "the liberal innocent", a figure we solemnly sentenced to death in Book One. The liberal innocent is a false defender of freedom.

Let us then go beyond the liberal innocent. Let us dive into deeper politics, one that seeps into so many more relations, one that dares to go where the truth leads us: towards the intimate. Because it's the only way ahead; if we don't reshape human psychology, we don't stand a chance. And in order to do so we must travel down a sensitive and risky path.

We're taking these risks. That's why political metamodernism is a revolutionary and dangerous movement. We must live and breathe dangerous dreams.

AN ORWELLIAN "MINISTRY OF LOVE"?

Just how dangerous can these dreams get? Ask your nightmares.

As you may know from George Orwell's nightmarish political sci-fi dystopia *1984*, the Ministry of Love was the ministry of interior affairs, enforcing loyalty to Big Brother—the personification of the ruling party— through tremendously extensive surveillance, manipulation, networks of informants, brainwashing and good old torture. The notorious Thought Police are part of the Ministry of Love.

The protagonist Winston Smith is brought to "Room 101" to encounter his deepest fear, his phobia of rats, in order to make him give up his love of a woman who has inspired rebellious and independent thoughts in him. His tormentors are successful; his emotions are extinguished as he betrays her to be spared from his greatest horror. Here is a government and a political realm that respects no personal boundaries, no privacy and no integrity—and which subdues the domain of private emotions and relationships to its own logic of political self-preservation.

In the last instance every trace of human meaning and spontaneity are effaced under the blind logic of power. The bad-guy in the book, O'Brien, who works at the Ministry of Love, says in earnest that there is nothing left of life, but at least he and others can have the consolation of tormenting the weak. When Winston desperately inquires for a last shred of resistance and hope, O'Brien says to his prisoner:

> "But always—do not forget this, Winston—always there will be the intoxication of power, constantly increasing and constantly growing subtler. Always, at every moment, there will be the thrill of victory, the sensation of trampling on an enemy who is helpless. If you want a picture of the future, imagine a boot stamping on a human face—for ever."

Dang. So this, there is good reason to believe, is basically what is at stake if we go ahead to create an expansion of the political realm into the private and personal. An eternity of a boot up our faces. The very opposite of Emmanuel Levinas' idea of a surrender to the helpless visage of the other, or Buber's relatedness to the sacred Thou.

I fully agree that this is a real risk. And yet—as I have labored to show in this book and the last—it is only by dealing with these inner and relational issues of all citizens that we can have any hope of resolving the problems of modernity and reach a new island of "relative utopia" before it is too late. We must evolve, before civilization itself crashes under the weight of developmental imbalances as the world-system is shocked by the emergence of new super-technologies for which we are socially, psychologically and politically unprepared. I know I am repeating myself here, but I believe it is with good reason.

And on a more mundane level, again, most of today's problems in society are not of an economic nature, but of a social, emotional and relational one. Most of us—in the rich parts of the world, at least—are limited, thwarted and harmed so much more by relationships gone awry, in so many ways, than by actual poverty. Even those who do suffer actual poverty very often do so, in practice, because too many social and emotional problems have amassed in their lives. And even when economic inequality does hurt us, it is often by negatively distorting our social relationships, making us feel unwelcome and inferior. In short, society is a relational affair through-and-through. To think that you can meaningfully manage and sustain society (let alone transform it in a positive direction) without managing the rich multiplicity of intimate human relationships is non-sensical.

I have worked hard to make this point before: We are now reaching a point in world history in which sustaining society *means* transforming it. **Rebirth or bust.** Metamodern Renaissance.

And this, again, compels us to delve into the all-too-human great web of relations. It's the right thing to do, no matter how revolting the idea may seem to the conventional modern mind. Again, you need all six new forms of politics for this to make any sense.

The modern mind—and its conventional compass—is wrong. It was built for another time, for another social and political landscape.

DOING *GEMEINSCHAFT* POLITICS

How, then, could *Gemeinschaft* Politics be any different from a degenera-ted form of Orwellian governmental super-surveillance, manipulation, over-reach and smothering? What, concretely, would the **Ministry of Gemeinschaft** be doing?

First of all, **the Ministry of *Gemeinschaft* would lead the ongoing pro-duction of high quality, detailed censuses of people's lives** over months, years and entire lifespans: how much loneliness, how much issues of trust among our friends, how often we feel the need to lie to one another and in what spheres of life (personally, professionally), what deeper insecurities drive us, how functional and satisfying our relationships are, how much we identify with ethnic or political groupings—and so forth.

Today's governments do monitor public health and some social indica-tors. But what we are considering here would be a much larger project—more systematic, more detailed and frequent and publicized as relevant self-reflection for the public.

This major thrust into sociological issues would produce a vast bank of open data upon which people can reflect, credible arguments can be made in political debates, and which social movements or civil society may react upon—or even private enterprise for that matter. Supported by big data, such a databank would not only be fertile soil for the applied social scien-ces, for invaluable empirical research into society's workings, but it would enable the public debate to process and handle issues that are today far beyond the scope of the political realm.

Such issues concern all of the many aspects and dimensions of social life and relations throughout society—personal, professional, sexual, ethnic, civic, class-related, and so forth. The general collective knowledge base, our collective ability to talk about, understand and tackle such issues, increases over time as relevant statistics and information is continuously made public: Has loneliness seen a sharp increase in older rural men lately? Or in young urban women, especially in this or that city? Do people in the education sector feel they have a harder time relating to students? How strong is the trend? Have quantities and qualities of friendships been improving or deteriorating? What is the distribution of positive attention and support? Which groups are getting too little affection from others? Do people feel sexually harassed, which groups and under what circumstances? How many people feel they have access to arenas in which they can honestly and safely express their views? Is online bullying on the rise? Online gaming or gambling addiction?

All of this can be engaging news material and lay the grounds for entirely new ways for society at large to seeing itself, for new public discussions and for political leaders and others to offer suggestions about how the issues may be addressed.

A second area of concern for the Ministry of *Gemeinschaft* would be **to devise, implement and evaluate social innovations, practices and institutions with the aim to advance the generative conditions for *Gemeinschaft* throughout society**. In the last instance it would of course be up to political leaders and "the people" (read: the processes of democratic self-organization) to suggest and validate such practices. But as is always the case when new forms of politics emerge, a corresponding organizational structure with professional expertise needs to be created. This would of course require the proliferation of university educations geared towards this end as well as a rich plethora of private companies, public-private partnerships, public support of civil society and volunteering and a host of social entrepreneurs and other so-called "fourth sector"[81] actors. Any successful *Gemeinschaft* Politics must be supported by a rich ecosystem of partnerships, as it obviously depends upon the close and intimate participation of warm hands and localized perspectives. It cannot be purely top-down, as no person can be ordered or paid to feel fellowship and solidarity or to not be lonely. These qualities must be cultivated; they must emerge.

This being said, it still does make sense to task the Ministry of *Gemeinschaft* with overviewing, evaluating, comparing and publicizing the results of different measures and programs, their cost-effectiveness, their centrality for explaining other factors, the quality of certain programs—and so on—in order to direct resources and to inform decision makers and the public. This in turn would form a basis for the ongoing political debates, dialogues and deliberations of political leaders, parties, the media and the public.

Do we want a program for conflict resolution and mediation between neighbors to reduce the great costs of eviction cases in courts? Are the end results preferable? Is it a better idea to support kids at age four from bad family conditions than to support them at fourteen as their criminal careers begin? Are single-person targeting programs preferable to programs which work with whole populations, or vice versa? Which are the best strategies to get people to share living spaces more? How can the loneliness of old age be combated; does it work to pay teenagers pocket money to hang out with their elders? Which of these solutions work best with private-public partnerships? You get the picture.

There will be a myriad of such initiatives across a given society. Let us then make sure these are systematically evaluated and supported—and that best practices become part and parcel of the ongoing political discourse.

A sociological sensitivity to the relations of everyday life must grow and become self-evident to the public; it must be incorporated into the very fabric of our institutions. Can authorities become better at communicating with and listening to the citizens? Can the citizens acquire higher social, emotional and collective intelligence? Can trust and social capital proliferate?

Any political movement or party of the future will need to give their vision of how to systematically improve upon and develop the relations of society. *Gemeinschaft* Politics is being born. It is already being performed; I simply suggest it should be done more deliberately, transparently and systematically.

FOUR EXAMPLES OF *GEMEINSCHAFT* POLITICS

Let us now examine four examples of what *Gemeinschaft* Politics might look like in terms of concrete, implemented programs. Without taking a hard stance on how highly these suggestions should be prioritized—if, indeed, at all—I'd like to outline these ideas in order to get across the general mode of thinking that *Gemeinschaft* Politics entails. In order of appearance, they are 1) measures to train emotional, social and collective intelligence, 2) organized community housing for families and the elderly, 3) support for local citizen discussion clubs led by professional facilitators, and 4) making room for civil society projects in public spaces.

Measures to train emotional, social and collective intelligence: The modern school system somehow expects that we figure out the most important and difficult aspect of life all by ourselves: how to form productive and loving relations to others. Schools put great efforts into teaching our children about chemistry and the correct use of grammar, but good social skills are more crucial to a happy and successful life as an adult. Sadly, how good we become at interacting with others is largely left to chance and many leave the education system as emotional and social illiterates.

Measures to increase the emotional, social and collective intelligence of children could include training sessions in school to successfully read facial expressions and body language, guessing the hidden motivations of others, participating in games of perspective taking (in which you need to take others' perspective of oneself in order to succeed), training team formations and task delegation to compete against other groups in tasks of collective intelligence—and so forth. All of these interventions must first be tested in lab settings, then on populations with control groups, then in society, and then be comparatively evaluated for benefits as compared to other measures.

Over time and as the expertise and implementation skills grow, there could be significant shifts in these qualities in a whole generation. Emotional intelligence would mean more self-regulation of behaviors and less conflict; social intelligence would mean people maneuver better in work and family environments and have an easier time finding ways to help one another out; and collective intelligence would increase the ability of people to find their respective strengths and cooperate in more complex and dynamic patterns of teams, organizations and so forth. If such programs were successful, we would see an improvement of human relations across the board—with gains untold.

Organized community housing for families and the elderly: Housing in late-modern society remains sociologically, economically and ecologically a deeply irrational endeavor. As things stand today, young families invest in buying expensive houses and hence drive up housing prices while amassing large debts throughout the economy, creating recurring price bubbles and plenty of leeway for system abuses of the kind revealed in the wake of the 2008 financial crisis. This also messes up economic incentives (speculation rather than work and save) and creates plenty of leverage for the already-rich and not-so-desperate; a huge lottery except the odds are rigged against the poor and needing. Even if villas, condos and apartments provide a basis of security and comfort in many people's lives, there is indeed little reason to believe that the current system opti-mally meets personal and societal needs. Today's "one-villa-one-family" housing system leads to unnecessarily large resource consumption, to loneliness and to social, economic and physical precarity in old age, to distance between the generations, to psychological pressure on the nucle-ar family, to distance between neighbors and diminished local communi-ty, to smaller support networks more generally—and of course to higher living costs, which in turn pressures people economically.

It would make more sense to have housing systems which are hybrids between private homes and shared spaces. These would form medium-sized communities with a variety of different apartments. Elderly citizens could move to shared spaces that are safe for frail and weak bodies, letting families with children move into their houses rather than the seniors hol-ding on to them, partaking in shared gardening projects, sharing some burdens of cooking, baby-sitting and so forth. There would be a facilitated framework for democratic decision-making and partly shared ownership —with relevant training offered to key people.

Social isolation would drop, psychological health would improve, social skills and intelligence would go up, and people would live more sustain-ably. The economy would be stabilized. People would retain personal free-dom but still have a communal context.

The degree to which such housing projects are possible does not only depend upon the knowledge and perspectives of the people who create them, but also—and perhaps primarily—upon the average emotional and social intelligence of the population. If people generally are nicer and more pleasant to have around, there is also less incentives for "private islands" to protect and shelter us from one another. Remember: The high costs we spend on social work, policing and security are derived from people displaying anti-social and dysfunctional behaviors. On a more gen-eral level, the average sociality of people—their mental health, personal development and social skills—sets the limits for how the economy itself functions, including core issues such as housing. One kind of *Gemein-schaft* Politics thus builds upon another.

Support for local citizen discussion clubs led by professional facilita-tors: Modern parliamentarism and the traditional civil organizations of class and special interests are severely underequipped for meeting the demand for democratic participation in today's society. New arenas for public deliberation are needed and more people should be trained and equipped to become local leaders and facilitators of such meeting places.

I have worked in such civil society organizations myself, facilitating citizen discussions at libraries and local club houses, and I can only say that the demand is huge for spaces in which people can be "general citizens" and speak their minds on current events and pressing topics and listen to the perspectives of others. When well facilitated, such initiatives seem to be able to cross boundaries of class, age, ethnicity and political persuasion.

If such initiatives for small-scale co-development and citizen engagement were present across society as a normal part of life, the gains could be immense: People would hear more perspectives, develop their own opinions and quite generally be more robust in their roles as citizens. It would also offer a platform for friendships and acquaintances to be formed on a civic basis, away from the pressures of family and professional life. If citizens could sign up for a professional facilitation training and could be afforded small budgets or just meeting venues, this could improve society's overall social capital (interpersonal connection and trust) and its collective intelligence in many ways. Again, this feeds into the two earlier suggestions for *Gemeinschaft* Politics. And, of course, it creates a much stronger basis for Democratization Politics.

Making room for civil society projects in public spaces: It is somehow taken for granted that most of the public spaces of a modern consumer society should be reserved for commercial activities. Busy shops in the center of town have long been considered the yardstick of a thriving community, and local municipalities make great efforts to encourage people to go shopping when businesses close down. Yet, such priorities simply don't make sense in today's affluent societies. Idle store clerks are hardly a greater concern than ecological collapse caused by overconsumption.

I believe it is a sign of modernity's lacking imagination when we struggle to come up with any better uses for the natural meeting points in our city centers. Couldn't we use the spaces for something more useful than idle consumption? Most of our public space has been claimed by commercial interests, but at least some of these spaces can and should be taken from the market forces and be brought into the service of the *Gemeinschaft*. People and organizations should be able to book public areas that are frequented by many fellow citizens and use them as meeting places and platforms for artistic, cultural or social ends. This would enrich society in a myriad of ways and work against the over-instrumentalization and commercialization of the public space. And, again, it would work in tandem with all of the above-mentioned suggestions.

The point isn't to stare ourselves blind at these particular suggestions. I'm sure you can come up with better ones, or challenge and improve upon the ones I've mentioned. I am simply trying to put some flesh on the bones of this skeletal structure. I am trying to get across a feeling for what *Gemeinschaft* Politics could look like and how it would work in practice.

But you can come up with more ideas. A corps of professional "listeners" in public service institutions and in healthcare? A concerted effort to improve the conflict management and mediation skills in work-life? Programs for intergenerational mentorships?

The heart's the limit.

Chapter 12

TRANSFORMATIONS OF

EVERYDAY LIFE

N ow it is time to dig deeper into some of the core issues of *Gemein-schaft* Politics: key insights on ethnicity, gender, and the transformation of everyday life.

As the metamodern ideas spread and take hold in society's institutions, political parties from across the political spectrum will adopt different forms of *Gemeinschaft* Politics, just as they will different forms of Democratization Politics. But, of course, some political movements and perspectives are more likely to be complex and powerful—and more in tune with political metamodernism—than others.

Before we go on to Existential Politics, then, let us take a good look at some general metamodern stances on how to create a friendlier society.

Hello? Transformation central, please.

REDUCING ETHNIC TENSIONS

Ethnic tensions are almost unavoidable in societies containing groups of people with different cultural, linguistic and religious identities. Reducing such tensions has become an ever more delicate task as societal complexity has increased, and the guiding principles to address the issue of ethnicity must be properly reexamined.

Throughout history, we can see a clear progression: from the **nationalism** of the 19th century, which sought to erase ethnic differences and promote a shared national identity in order to avoid political disintegration; to the **non-nationalism** of the 20th century, which sought to downplay ethnic differences and promote civic identities in order to prevent sectarian affiliations from overruling the degree to which societal participation was aligned according to wider civic categories; to the multiculturalism, or, with a more suitable term, **inter-culturalism,** of the present, which seeks to respect and embrace all identities and promote diversity in order to eliminate racism and ensure that everyone feels included. To, what I believe will be the only way of productively handling and developing ethnic identities in a transnational world order of increased global inter-connectedness, **trans-culturalism.**

The intelligent reader may already have noticed how each of the four positions seem to correlate with effective value meme: **postfaustianists**, or traditional conservatives, usually favor nationalism; **modernists**, the mainstream in most Western societies, tend to gravitate towards the more civic stance of non-nationalism; **postmodernists**, the "politically correct" elite, are almost always devoted multiculturalists who unanimously defend the position of inter-culturalism. And if you agree with most of the section below on trans-culturalism, then it's a good indication that you're **metamodern**. But before you test your metamodern inclinations, let's go through each of the positions in a bit more detail.

NATIONALISM

Nationalism is the position that defends what is perceived as one's "own" nationality, state and ethnicity from the perceived threat of other cultural units. To the extent that immigrants are seen as acceptable, they should only be welcomed *if* they show allegiance to the majority culture and if they make real efforts to be assimilated. This position does make sense in historical phases when nation states are being formed and an ethnos— "the people"—is being constructed as a shared imagined idea in tandem with the birth of the nation. For instance, it is to be expected from the birthing Kurdish nation, or even the Catalonians, to display rather far-reaching forms of nationalist sentiment.

Unfortunately, however, this process of national cohesion can also be reactivated in existing national populations when these feel threatened or shamed—contemporary examples of which we see not only in European right populism and American Trumpism, but also in countries like Russia, Turkey, Brazil and India. Conservatism tends to have a perpetual flirt with nationalism, saying stuff like "we have to learn to stand up for *our* values". I say "unfortunately" because nationalism as a reactionary movement does not really offer any credible paths to creating a regulated and functional transnational order, and it tends to feed conflicts and mis-understandings.

NON-NATIONALISM

Non-nationalism is what I call the reliance upon the modernist project—in its capitalist or communist forms—to simply supersede and eventually efface the ethnic differences between people. If immigrants only get a job, if people are respected as individuals, if people are free to make money and buy stuff and trade freely—the libertarians tell us—they will soon get over their petty parochial quarrels and live in peace. Maybe not everyone will love everyone else, but that's okay, as long as people show each other a minimum level of tolerance and respect. Enlightened self-interest: You won't go after people whose goods, services and capital you rely upon. And the free market can make that happen.

Communists will tend towards a corresponding vision: If people see their shared class interests, ethic differences will dissolve as ethnicity is and remains an epiphenomenon, ultimately reducible to class. A fair society in which material gains are fairly distributed will have fewer ethnic conflicts.

This idea of course fails to take ethnicity, identity and culture nearly as seriously as they should. It fails to see and take into account that culture matters, and that culture is a real, behavioral force with real explanatory value—which has shown itself time and again, historically speaking. Ethnicity (based on any combination of race, language, nationality, cultural customs, or religious and sometimes even political affiliations) is a force that can at times topple states and governments, and thereby efface whatever free markets or planned economies that exist under their rule.

INTER-CULTURALISM

Inter-culturalism (or multiculturalism) comes in different forms. You have multicultural state ideologies, which emphasize the importance of inclusion and diversity, claiming that the more diverse cultures you have, the better. You have corresponding anti-discrimination and pro-diversity policies in companies. You have "inter-faith dialogue" movements, which seek to find common ground and mutual respect among believers of different faiths. You have "affirmative action" programs, international children's summer camps, the peace movement, political correctness seeking to ban whatever words have become racist slurs—and so forth. Among theorists you find such thinkers as the philosopher Charles Taylor, who emphasizes the importance of ethnic minority groups having "rights" to the preservation of their culture.

The general idea here is that ethnic tensions are to be resolved through a high degree of exposure of ethnic groups to each other, and that more diversity is almost always preferable to less.

The problem with multiculturalism is of course that it does not qualify *which* kinds of diversity are good, in what quantities, and under what circumstances. It's just that diversity is good in-and-of-itself, which is then taken as a dogma, and it is often seen as unethical to even question this assumption: multiculturalism is good, period. This naturally leaves the field open to all sorts of dysfunctional social and cultural practices to be defended in the name of ethnic or cultural diversity, be it forced marriages, brainwashing and scaring children with *de facto* ghost stories, or female circumcision.

Inter-culturalism has important roots in anthropology and ethnology. What anthropologists have found time and again is that the modern project—its bureaucracy, market and "civilization"—has oppressed and destroyed the life-worlds of smaller societies, disrespecting their ways of seeing the world and ruining their societal dynamics. In our days, this view is perhaps most famously represented by the anthropologist James C. Scott, who has argued in *Seeing Like a State* (1998) and *Against the Grain* (2017) that all development from agriculture and onwards may be a mistake. Anthropologists hang out with animist cultures and notice that life there isn't so bad. They notice there are many "beauties lost", and that there is a profound richness and diversity which is tragically effaced by modern civilization. So the stance generally becomes to defend the minority cultures against discrimination and oppression from the majority. A defense of understanding, multiplicity, diversity—and a critical distance to one's own culture.

On a strictly logical level, the inter-culturalist idea doesn't really work. It emphasizes that all cultures are equal, and that each of them has a right to exist, but it is still somehow preferable with *more* different cultures rather than fewer. This leads to self-contradictions: a) If all cultures are equal, this means that cultures which work against multiculturalism and seek to retain isolation and purity should also be seen as equal; b) if all cultures have a right to be preserved, they must also be allowed to defend themselves from subcultures splitting off, which then works against a greater diversity; and c) if all cultures should be exposed to one another, this leads to monoculture, which often effaces cultural differences in the first place.

TRANS-CULTURALISM

Trans-culturalism is a multi-perspectival *and* developmental view of cultures and ethnicities; it sees all of these as being in constant flux. In a way, it is the synthesis of the three former perspectives.

Cultures and ethnic identities can *always* be transformed, and they *should* be transformed to be the best versions of themselves, whenever this is possible without destabilizing people's lives too much. Even if humans *do* need cultures, shared imaginaries, narratives, histories, customs, traditions and other vital aspects of *Gemeinschaft*—this does not mean that *all current* cultural forms and expressions are necessarily good and conducive to sustainable human flourishing, or that all combinations of cultures are mutually enriching under all circumstances.

It is an empirical matter of *when* cultures spur development and exchange with each other, or when they create pathological dissonances that breed conflict, confusion, insecurity and resentment. The answer, naturally, differs from case to case. And it is a matter of cultural discourse and exchange to determine which values should—in the long run—trump which other values. Is freedom better than chastity? Under the circumstances of modern life, yes! Are human rights better than respecting the logic of caste systems? Yes. Is equality better than slavery? Yes. Is peace-loving better than war? Yes. Is gender equality better than patriarchy? Yes. Are animal rights (or some other version of caring for all sentient beings) better than anthropocentrism? Yes. This does not mean that these values should be defended at *all* costs, that they should be forced upon all people under all circumstances. It is simply not worth the rapid breakdown of someone else's world, or an ethnic cleansing, or an inquisition, or a Thought Police. **But given the choice, given the chance, we can and should evolve cultures.**

Cultures have a right to exist, but it is not an absolute right. And in the last instance, all cultures will change and evolve either way, so we might as well have some ideas regarding in which direction they should develop.

But that does not mean certain cultures have infinite rights to impose their values upon others; it just means the more universal and functional values should be allowed to win in a longer Darwinian struggle, and that such victories should be secured in the least painful and detrimental way possible. Cultures generally have *something* to learn from one another—and the aim of trans-culturalism is to make sure that this exchange is genuinely enriching, sustainable and conducive to human flourishing.

Trans-culturalism corresponds to a more metamodern take on ethnicity. In academia you can find early beginnings of a trans-culturalist perspective among sociologists, such as Michael O. Emerson's and George Yancey's 2010 book, *Transcending Racial Barriers: Toward a Mutual Obligations Approach.*

The best example I know of trans-culturalism in action is in the Belgian town of Mechelen, under the ingenious mayor Bart Somers, who also received a "World Mayor Prize 2016" for his efforts. Belgium was the European country with the largest per capita outflow of ISIS fighters. But Mechelen, with a population of some 85,000, has had no such registered cases. A couple of decades ago, the town had plenty of ethnic tensions, a large group of alienated immigrant inhabitants and growing nationalist and racist sentiments. All of this was turned around by a number of policies and practices under the leadership of Somers. Initially, the city established a much stronger police presence on the streets so that people could feel safe. Hence, housing prices stopped falling in "unsafe areas" and segregation was curbed. Then, they had forceful information campaigns against discrimination and racism, urging tolerance and openness as civic obligations of all citizens, creating a common civic identity around such values. Then the municipality officials talked the white middle-class families into putting their kids back into the schools with many children of immigrants, family by family—hundreds of them—by giving them specific guarantees of how the quality of their kids' education would be preserved. Then they put higher pressure on dysfunctional immigrant families to fulfill their social obligations and live up to their increased status in society, offering to support the civic actors who played important parts in this. And then—this is where it gets really radical—they sent Muslim kids on special study trips to Córdoba, Spain, where they learned about the era when Islam was a dignified European power and Córdoba was a center of science and tolerance, a multicultural society ahead of its time. The kids were thereby presented with a positive narrative of what it means to be Muslim: to be a pinnacle of enlightened civilization, as the Caliphate of Córdoba was in the 10th century AD.

You see what they did there? Mayor Somers and his crew took a majority culture and pushed it towards tolerance, *and* they took a minority culture and gently pushed for its transformation in a progressive direction. That's trans-culturalism in action, and it is also the beginnings of meta-modern *Gemeinschaft* Politics—and the beginnings of the listening society. How cool is that? [82]

All of this is an example of what smart *Gemeinschaft* Politics might look like. Imagine if what Mayor Somers is doing was already part and parcel of how societies diffuse ethnic tensions. And could it be further developed? Maybe there could be meeting places and settings that provide facilitated exchanges between different ethnicities? Wouldn't that dramatically improve society, lessen ethnic tensions and create a firmer basis for a transnational global community?

Yes, it's an increased level of the intimacy of control. But is it oppressive and manipulative? Or is it just constructive and liberating? Should sociological, cultural and ethnic issues really be beyond the scope of the political realm?

Stupid forms of *Gemeinschaft* Politics will be nationalist, non-nationalist, or inter-culturalist. Smart *Gemeinschaft* Politics will be trans-culturalist.

POST-FEMINISM AND GENDER ANTAGONISM

Another *Gemeinschaft* topic that would deserve a book, or at least a chapter, of its own, is gender relations and feminism. But we'll have to do with a measly subchapter in this book since we've got so much ground to cover if we ever want to establish what metamodern politics is—so that we can begin conspiring about how to non-linearly save those millions of lives.

There's just no limit to how central gender relations are to society. It's just *that* important. I mean, if you miss this perspective, and gender relations get screwed up, you seriously screw over every other aspect of society.

Consider the following:

* Sexuality is ever-present in our psyches, affecting our moods, feelings, decisions, behaviors and relations in every moment.

* We stay within our gender identities at all times, and these also affect a very significant part of our economic and political behaviors. A very large part of all things we do are somehow related to having, keeping or managing spouses, partners or just the possibilities of these.

* Gender relations and roles are at the center of sexual and romantic relations, which are the deepest and strongest relations in most people's lives and the foundation for family formation.

* As the sociologist Francesco Alberoni famously observed, falling in love is central to the transformations of our personalities, and thus to our developmental psychologies. Falling in love connects our carnal lust and animal body to our highest spiritual strivings—it's an "all-level affair". And falling in love, and how this plays out, has everything to do with the interactions between the genders.

- As the classical psychologist Erik Erikson observed, erotic and romantic relations are at the center of certain universal life phases, and are thus either conducive to our mental health or our ruin.

- Family formations, in turn, are the basis of secure attachment patterns and good upbringing, which are instrumental to all human growth and flourishing.

- When people are sexually and romantically rejected, dissatisfied and humiliated, this translates into a profound bitterness that easily combines with destructive ethnic or political identities, as well as criminality and delinquency.

- By far most psychological issues that people have are about relations to other people, and the largest category of related problems have to do with love, eroticism and sexuality.

- If people are less satisfied and more insecure in their gender identities and love lives, this undermines trust between people. They will simply be much more prepared to betray one another to satisfy their sad, aching hearts.

- If people have gender identities which are not acknowledged by their surroundings, this causes immense suffering and confusion. Trans-gender people, for instance, frequently display mental health issues and have high suicide rates.

- In many contemplative traditions—not only tantric and yogic ones—sexuality is used as a transformative practice, as there are always strong currents of sexual and sensual impulses flowing through us.

- Gender inequalities are interlinked with gender roles and identities and with the games of love and family relations, and they underpin many of the most destructive inequalities in the world. Discrimination of women is a major hindrance to economic growth in poor countries and a major source to gendered and sexualized violence.

- Men are also discriminated against, being seen as more expendable than women, and more pressured to "be a success", which often makes them unable to be honest and vulnerable.

- During good sex, some people experience their "highest" moments in life, meaning the highest subjective states, as discussed in Book One. This means it is here they breach their boundaries for what they know is possible in life and existence.

- The first thing anthropologists study when they try to describe how a certain foreign society works is how the system of marriage, sexual reproduction and inheritance works—as this is the basis of a society's social logic and its self-preservation.

* Most sad songs and poems are about love.

Right, so if you think you can create a good and healthy society without dealing with what I will here call "**the gender-sexuality-family-formation complex**", (to catch all of these interrelated issues under one banner) you are just not being realistic.

Gender and sex issues are at the very heart of society. If you mess them up, you mess up society in very profound and far-reaching ways. Any *Gemeinschaft* Politics worth its salt should actively and deliberately seek to heal and develop the gender relations of society.

At this point I will refrain from giving the whole list (from a traditionalist gender politics, to a modern one, to a postmodern one) and just jump right to the metamodern perspective.

A smart *Gemeinschaft* Politics would work from a **post-feminist perspective**, applying a developmental-behavioral understanding, evolving the very **landscapes of desire**, and seeking to reduce **gender antagonism** in society. A very important contributor to the apparent ubiquity of societal problems in the realm of sex, love and reproduction are the **paradoxes of love and desire** which seem built into the human psyche.

POST-FEMINISM

Basically, the post-feminist position is one that accepts the "queer feminist" idea that gender roles change with historical circumstances and culture, and that ideas about genders and their interactions can and should continuously be critically reconstructed to optimize for new circumstances—but *doesn't* buy the feminist idea that there is one "toxic" mainstream ideal of masculinity (which is pitted against the feminine underdog), and that if "patriarchy is crushed" then people will become free from gender roles and their oppression.

Post-feminism gets its name by transcending and including feminism: Once we have accepted the basic feminist tenets, then what? What comes after? Post-feminism is a both-and position: *both* feminism *and* **masculism**. *Both* women's issues (sexual harassment, lower wages, lesser political power, pressures to conform to body ideals, slut-shaming, etc.) *and* men's issues (expendability, having dangerous jobs, easily being considered losers when asking for help, homelessness, higher suicide rates, crime and incarceration, more physical violence, etc.). *Both* anti-discrimination of sexual minorities, *and* the facilitation of positive heterosexual relations and secure attachment patterns for family formation. *Both* teaching men how to become more successful at dating and picking up sexual partners, *and* to respect sexual boundaries and not sexually objectify women. *Both* defending the right to be a hipster beta-male, *and* to be a tough masculine guy; *both* a butch, *and* a pink girlie-girl. *Both* solidarity with the jaw-dropping babes, *and* with the chronically unfuckable.

There is a scale from classically masculine to feminine values, demeanors and behaviors. Post-feminism defends the whole scale: the right for people to move freely and explore across all of it. It doesn't defend the androgynous at the expense of sexual polarities, or vice versa. It defends all points of the scale; the entire richness of human gender and sexual expression. This means, some people will settle for traditional gender roles while others will be queer shape-shifters. All should be defended.

SHIFTING THE LANDSCAPES OF DESIRE

This defense of "the whole scale of genders and sexualities", and all dimensions of it, is made possible by taking a *developmental* view of the gender-sexuality-family-formation complex. Post-feminists recognize that the problems is not—as classical feminists and queer feminists believe— "that evil patriarchal oppression", assuming that people would be free to express their sexualities openly and fairly if it went away.

It's that people are *insufficiently developed* to tackle these sensitive issues productively. It's that we are too poor at taking the perspectives of one another across genders and sexualities; it's that we are too insecure about our own positive gender identities; it's that we have lacking social skills to entertain and seduce one another in playful and respectful ways; it's that we know too little about the social dynamics between the sexes; it's that we carry too much subtle dissatisfaction and bitterness; it's that we simply have had too few and insufficiently instructive sexual experiences; it's that we feel good romantic and sexual relations are scarce rather than abundant in our lives; it's that we have too few reliable friends with whom we can really talk about these issues; it's that we don't feel safe and comfortable enough to express our needs and insecurities to one another; that we are unable to listen and take it in when others talk about intimate and sensitive matters; that we're not good enough in setting and maintaining healthy social boundaries; that we don't manage to show sufficient respect for one another's boundaries; that we have insufficient self-knowledge about our innermost needs in the first place; that we don't feel we can afford brutal and direct honesty—the list goes on.

Do you see it? **It's not some evil structure out there. It's our own lacking development. We—as human beings, as biological, behavioral**

organisms—lack the right properties to interact in good enough ways. And we all suffer for it. Men are left with that strange hunger and those somber thoughts at the outer rims of our minds, things that rumble deep inside and seldom give us peace. Women are left with a sense of funda-mental unsafety and resentment, a subtle sense of betrayal. It goes on everywhere, all the time. It affects all aspects of society.

If a smart *Gemeinschaft* Politics was in place, it would actively and deli-berately deal with all of these issues on a long-term demographic level. People would be supported through the educational system and through-out life in a wide variety of ways to grow in sexual, emotional, romantic and relational skill and self-knowledge. If the average personal develop-ment of a population shifts—if we all act less insecurely, greedily, imma-turely and defensively—then the whole game of life changes.

Game change. Not game denial. Not game acceptance. But game chan-ge. Sexual game change. Gender game change. Think about it: How many fewer broken hearts would there be? How many more people would grow up with secure psychological attachment patterns, thereby being better partners and lovers once they grow up? How many of us would stop taking advantage of professional relations? How many false promises would be made to procure sex or consolation? How much more relaxed and functional would our bodies and minds be?

Socially constructed *gender* and biological *sex* do saturate each other to a large extent, so it is more or less impossible to divide them into two distinct categories. Humans are sexual and gendered beings, yes, but this is both a cultural and a biological fact. If ideas about masculinity have us pumping iron at the gym, this of course affects our biology, which affects our mind and others' bodily responses to us. The point is that both the cultural and the biological basis of gender/sex can and should be develop-ed and optimized in ways that generate conditions for human happiness and thrivability. An effective *Gemeinschaft* Politics would develop peo-ple's "gender abilities" to create and uphold healthy identities, relation-ships and sexual practices both through culture, psychology and biology.

All of this is a matter of **shifting the landscapes of desire**. Even if we seldom talk about it, some lingering aspects of sexual desire are always present in everyday life. Even as we just walk down the street, and even if we have been married for years, we still tend to casually assess the attract-iveness of random pedestrians. The landscapes of desire, the realms of sexuality, are vastly greater and more pervasive than actual sexual en-counters and activities. Drives, innuendos, fantasies, stray thoughts, erotic tensions, dreams, "energies" felt throughout the body and mind, sexual interplays that require polite distance to be balanced with taking social risks, scenarios of possible futures, of what could have been—these are all present in so many moments and situations of life. Invisible worlds, ever present, nagging at the fringes of the mind, at the core of our hearts and bellies. In our lives we always travel across an intimate inner landscape of vulnerability, of secrets—one that underpins many or most of our every-day interactions.

Today, in liberal societies, we see that people in general can be viewed as interesting and attractive in a wider variety of ways than in the past. Scandinavian men are to a lesser degree held to macho ideals and standards of professional success than was earlier the case (and is still the case in most other societies) and have a wider range of positive masculinities available which can still be viewed as attractive. People can be gay, have metrosexual styles, be more childlike, more androgynous and so forth. People can hook up around weirder fetishes than before. And people can form a wider variety of love relationships and family constellations. And people who were too shy to pick one another up at night clubs can write an email. People can even share racy fantasies over the web. The landscapes of desire have shifted, which is part good, part bad (part really, really bad).

Shifting the landscapes of desire is not *only* about changing people's skills, perspectives and behaviors, but *also* about evolving our openness to a wider range of potential partners, lifestyles and erotic or emotional exchanges. **Desire is not only a vulnerability; it is also a strange and potent faculty.** As such it can be developed. We can transform not only the interplay of need and desire, but also the quality of the object of desire and the gaze of desire itself.

I'm not saying people should be brainwashed to be bisexual and more sexually active—as Georg Lukács infamously tried to make happen in Hungary when he was Minister of Culture during the brief anti-Stalinist communist regime of 1956. But just as people can become better at perspective taking and conflict resolution, so can they be more or less narrowminded about whom to have sex with and which relationships to form. To sum up, we can work for game change in the realm of sex and gender by:

- Raising the abilities of men and women to be seductive and sexually competent, thus increasing the level of abundance and satisfaction in their lives.

- And that in itself means there will be many more satisfying men and women around for all parties, which makes underlying tensions and games of competition less fierce and desperate, just as it will put less pressure on new relationships, as there will be more good potential partners or liaisons available.

* And this will create more fair games of love and sex, which means people are generally treated better, and that people act from a greater inner space of safety, affecting all aspects of their lives.

* And this will reduce the number of strange repressed desires, thoughts, drives and dreams, clearing people's inner emotional lives for more productive engagements with existence.

* And this will let people become freer in their sexual and gender experimentation, which means they will consider partnerships and liaisons across more social and cultural boundaries and identities.

* And this will create a more profound integration of all walks of life and more stable family relations, which improves the socialization of all children in society.

* And this will lead to higher mental and physical health, not least as the sexual undercurrents of everyday life shift and harmonize, relatively speaking.

Sex is transformative. Gender is creative. The landscapes of desire can be made safer, easier to traverse; their many peaks and valleys better connected. If we are more skilled, secure and satisfied—and we can expect the average other person to be so too—we can trust one another more, and the entire inner secret landscape can be developed; everyday life can be transformed at a deep, visceral level.

GENDER ANTAGONISM

At the very heart of the gender-sexuality-family-formation complex lies something I like to call "gender antagonism". This term was initially discussed by the anthropologist (of a feminist structuralist brand) Sherry Ortner in her studies of gender relations of indigenous groups in Papua New Guinea back in the 1970s. I, however, use the term in a slightly different manner:

* **"Gender antagonism" denotes a measure of the *prevalence* and *intensity* of *resentment* that people within a certain population feel towards any generalized ideas of gender categories.**

Or, simply put, how bitter women are with men and how hateful men are towards women. But of course, people can hate their own gender, or any other gender category: "those lifeless and bland feminist bitches", "those slimy, toxic macho men", "those wet noodle excuses for hipster gay men", "those filthy, power-hungry, deceptive sluts" and so forth. It's not just bitterness and resentment, but also contempt, frustration and collective or generalized blame.

We need to understand that gender antagonism corresponds more or less to racism and ethnic conflict, except that it is an antagonism between real or imagined categories of genders. Naturally, gender antagonism grows as an emergent pattern of the whole gender-sexuality-family-formation complex.

Here's an example. So if a girl has a bad dad (who because of his insecurities treats her and her mother poorly), and then gets a lousy boyfriend who just uses her for sex (because he wasn't really in love with her, just really pressured to get rid of his stigmatized virginity and desperate to gain sexual experience and she was all he could catch), then she's quite likely to not like men in general very much. And then she'll reject approaching guys at bars very contemptuously, cold and blank behind her smile, hence feeding into the bitterness of these trembling souls who had been trying to work up the courage to go and talk to someone like her for over a year…

And so on, and so forth. Gender antagonism breeds gender antagonism. It causes shitloads of harm to people's softest inner places, and it mutilates our inner developments, stunting us in our growth as human beings. And it mixes with issues of everything from economic and political stability, to ethnic conflicts, class relations, and pretty much any issue you can think of. It sucks, leaving us wasted and wounded.

The level of gender antagonism can be reduced *only* by changing the games of everyday life, by developing people's abilities to give themselves and one another what they need. If our anti-heroine above met a really sweet guy, who deeply satisfied her needs, after a few years perhaps her shields might go down and she might feel less bitter about men. And then she will stop feeding into this slugfest of resentment between the sexes.

Or imagine if the first guy she dated would have been much better trained at seducing women, so that he wouldn't have had to "settle" for her, because he wasn't in a scarcity mindset about sexual validation, and if he were less pressured to get sexual experience at any cost. If he had a rich smorgasbord of women to choose from, he would have gone for someone else for whom he had more authentic positive emotions. And perhaps he would have had more healthy and secure attachment patterns in the first place, more easily falling in love. And she would have had more satisfying experiences with the other guys she dated, and she would have ended up with a guy who really loved her. And their relation would have been better. Everyone would have saved lots of time and effort, everyone would have been spared a load of misery, and the beasts of resentment would not have been fed with the fresh blood of young hearts.

Gender antagonism not only undermines other relations, such as ethnic or professional ones—it also, quite sneakily, poisons emancipatory movements. Feminism becomes a mindless carrier of gender antagonism. Women who deeply hate men and feel bitter resentment towards them as a group find outlets in feminist groups and ideologies. Men who despise women become "Men's Rights Activists" and gather around obviously virulent female-bashing gurus. And so forth. Gender antagonism and other forms of group hatred such as racism—while understandable and explicable—tend to dress up as your only friend in this dark world. But of course, they aren't your friends. Gender antagonism breeds "bad" feminism (or masculism), a fight for gender equality that chronically leaves out relevant dynamics or perspectives, and hence only serves to worsen the situation.

I'm not saying that anger is never good. **I'm just saying that gender antagonism sneaks in and ruins whatever emancipatory potential feminism and masculism might have.** Being bitter and resentful makes people stupid.[83]

Want real, effective feminism? Then find ways to reduce gender antagonism. Want to reduce sexual violence against women? Reduce gender antagonism. Want to reduce male suicide? Reduce gender antagonism. Want to create freer gender roles in professional life? Reduce gender antagonism. Want to improve the quality and stability of family relations? You get the picture.

THE PAINFUL PARADOXES OF LOVE

A certain degree of gender antagonism is unavoidable in any society since the very territory of love and desire is inherently wrought with paradoxes, meaning that our hearts and minds always put ourselves and the people around us in impossible dilemmas of various nasty sorts. And these are often frustrating, sometimes infuriating—at times even fatal.

For now, let's stay with only analyzing some properties of what some of our friends like to call "the heterosexual matrix" (i.e. not gay relations, etc.).[84] If we look at desire and the search for love between men and women, there are quite a few nasty paradoxes bound to mess people up.

First of all, consider the fact that men get nervous around women they genuinely desire and would like to invest in long-term, and that women are attracted to confident men. This means that men very seldom get the women they have the strongest and most sincere attraction towards. This leads them to often being less happy in their relations, still being haunted by those strange ghosts of desire, which means they are more likely to stray or try to "upgrade" (dump their wife) given the opportunity. Resentment mass produced. Ouch, what a hot mess.

Here's another one. Both men and women will generally want to catch a mate slightly above their own self-perceived status in the mating hierarchy. This will lead them to invest time and effort in folks they cannot get or cannot keep, which sets them up for repeated failures, which sets them up for bitterness and distrust, which sabotages their relationships.

Another one. Women like men who are assertive and have great social prestige, and men dramatically increase their seductiveness if they display these qualities. Consequently, men need to take social risks in order to gain the attention of women. If they are not sufficiently seductive and they are rejected in public, they risk that others (men and women alike) will perceive them with contempt. And if they are too sexually assertive, they risk that their approaches spill over into boundary breaching and sexual harassment. Women feel angry for having been put in a situation where they have to either impolitely turn someone down, or quietly shut up and feel used and manipulated. Men feel that women are insincere about what they want: They don't give you a chance if you're a "nice guy" and they accuse you of being predatorial if you make advances, or being fake macho if you try to show your tough side. Resentment grows.

Another one. Species who live in groups are generally divided into "tournament species" where one alpha male gets all the *punani* after violently dethroning the former leader, and "pair-bonding species", where males and females pair up in families and males compete by being good providers and caretakers. This pattern has repeatedly been found, from birds to primates. The males are bigger than the females in all tournament species. Among primates, gorillas are tournament and the bonobo chimps are pair-bonding. If you look at the physiology and behavior of humans, we are somewhere in between, perhaps a bit more on the pair-bonding side. Accordingly, both of these deeply ingrained behavioral patterns exist simultaneously in humans, competing with each other. So even if you happen to find happy, stable love, a part of you will often want rough sex with an attractive stranger. And even if you're Elvis and can get all the ladies you want, you will still feel a bit empty inside for lack of authentic connection and companionship. We're coded to be slightly dissatisfied. And this breeds—are you ahead of me?—frustration, which in turn breeds gender antagonism.

Or how about this one. Women learn they're too slutty if they have sex with many men in too fun ways. They always stand to lose their status if they fuck the wrong guy under the wrong circumstances.[85] *But*—if they *don't* let loose and get really slutty with their men, the men are likely to feel frustrated and not wanting to stay around, which puts women back on the slutty single market where they started. And even if a woman does "everything he wants" and really lets loose, she might find that he loses interest and moves on. Or if the relationship breaks down, his bitterness towards women may cause him to post revenge porn online. And hell ensues for the woman.

Or here's another one for the ladies. All your life has been about being pretty. Pretty, pretty, pretty, hot, hot, beautiful, beautiful, feminine, feminine. It's everywhere: clothing, makeup, commercials, how you're treated by strangers, if guys fall in love with you and "woo" you or not, your standing in the local girls' group, your career chances—even starting with Barbie dolls when you're a kid. If you fail to present a beautiful appearance according to increasingly impossible standards, you pay an enormous price. *But*, dear ladies, if you *do* manage to be pretty, it suddenly takes all the attention from everything else that you do, and everyone around you insists on responding only to this one part of yourself: your looks. Your new boss says he can't listen to you because you're too hot, all your guy friends and colleagues have secret agendas, women are bitchy and competitive, quietly holding you back. If you go on TV and say something important, or even win a gold medal, people talk about your hair and your cleavage. And if you lose your beauty, you stand to lose everything, including the man who pledged to be by your side. If that doesn't breed resentment, I don't know what would.

And one last favorite. Men and women have different patterns of sexual lust. When a man and a woman enter a serious monogamous relationship, at first both want to have a lot of sex, but after a short while—on average, according to research—the woman's sexual desire drops to a much lower level, and the man's stays elevated for a much longer period.[86] As such, many a man is in for lots of rejection and disappointment at the very point in his life when he has just committed to not going after other women, which in itself is a high price to pay. There is even a growing sexual deficit in males that can be observed at a global scale: guys simply don't get as much as they'd like.[87] This of course leads to resentment and spurs infidelity. Likewise, men seem to have a much lower "cuddle-bonding" impulse after sexual intercourse than women, which means that sex can often leave women feeling emotionally vulnerable and abandoned, which then of course undermines the sense of trust in the relationship. And then there's always the whole thing about women wanting reliable men but still having a secret garden with a host of furious fancies (searching for online porn such as "extreme brutal gangbang" and "rape" more frequently than guys, as compared to their overall porn searches, and about 62% having at least some sexy thoughts about forced sex, according to one study[88]). Mix this with the fact that men really want to be seen as tough but still need someone to take care of their scared inner little boy and that this boy just isn't part of the female sexual fantasies—all of which results in confusion and disappointment for all parties involved. All of it breeds gender antagonism.

I could name many more. But let's get back on track.

Ah, the paradoxes of sex, love and gender! What a relentless production plant of human angst and desolation! How elusive that inner peace, that simple sense of aliveness and safety, that sensual and embodied fullness of being alive! If you're not very clear-sighted and well-informed on this one, you will tend towards a simple explanation for all the suffering you've been through: "it's patriarchy" or "it's those rabid bitches".

But it's not those rabid bitches. It's a complex host of emergent properties of the games of everyday life. We are mutilated not by an evil patriarchal structure, but by a blind and meaningless chaos engine, which is incidentally also the source of all goodness and beauty of life.

And we can hardly do ourselves a greater disservice than denying the existence of these games (crime 1: game denial) or accepting them in their current, cruel forms (crime 2: game acceptance). These paradoxes of love indeed constitute a vast killing ground of the human spirit. But it is also on these fields of battle and suffering that we grow the most as human beings—it is here we find the most fertile ground for inner transformations. Could society be geared towards making us much better equipped for managing these paradoxes and relating to them more productively? The answer is yes. Inner progress grows from the manure of human trouble.

These paradoxes and problems cannot really be "solved". They will be around whether we like it or not, at least until we change the very behavioral biology of humans. What we *can* do, however, is to change how well they are understood and productively related to, and thus how pathologically they play out in society at large.

Erich Fromm once wrote that for society to prosper, we need not more distant intellect, but "men and women who are in love with life". **But to be in love with life, we must also successfully fall in love with one another.**

How many of us will get to have genuinely happy love in our lives? I mean *really*? There are few greater tragedies in life than our inability to awaken deep positive emotions in others, our inability to have our trembling hearts and aching bodies met with genuine love and desire. And how cruel is not the opposite, to be loved and included but that our hearts respond only with coldness and inertia—when we are unable to genuinely love and respond to others' emotions?

How important are not these issues to society, how central to human misery and happiness? How fundamental to any qualitatively rich notion of freedom and equality? How many souls are we unnecessarily condemning to lonely lifetimes of cold and darkness? How many broken hearts are we generating? How many failed attempts at BDSM?

Can we really afford to keep this issue outside of politics, outside the ongoing discussing about the conscious self-organization of society?

We must, as a society, cultivate higher likelihoods for better relationships, developing people's sexual faculties and reducing gender antagonism. That's what a metamodern post-feminist *Gemeinschaft* Politics would aim to do.

Let us evolve the game of love. Let us shift the landscapes of desire.

EMPTY RITUALS AND UNRITUALIZED EMOTIONS

When people are emotionally stunted and existentially mutilated by the emergent deformities of everyday life, we can often find ourselves having other emotions than those that are "appropriate" to the situations we find ourselves in. Or we can feel a growing emotional distance to everyday life for any number of other reasons.

There is a distance between what is going on around us and what we are really feeling. This is the essence of alienation. We become "imposters", strangers in our own lives. Life flows, and we participate, but we don't quite *feel* it.

The party. Christmas evening. Our wedding. The birth of our own child. What happens if you don't feel what you're "supposed to"? There is a quiet, subtle betrayal of all our social bonds—emotions of anxiety, dissatisfaction, indifference, estrangement, alienation, disenchantment. In the folds and wizenings of everyday life, there is a subtle resistance. But sometimes, at least in the lives of most of us, we really *do* feel it. Something really fits, and we're suddenly intensely alive.

An effective *Gemeinschaft* Politics must work to increase the likelihood of such **"inner world / life situation fits"** occurring. It must work to enact (or make possible for civil society to enact) transformations of everyday life itself—so that our true emotions can be present in our manifest lives, and our manifest lives can play out in harmonic resonance with our innermost thoughts and feelings.

The subtle transformations of relations in everyday life are of course not only ethnic and gendered/sexual. They make up pretty much all of life. Everywhere we go there are norms, customs, habits and more or less formal regulations telling us what are the appropriate behaviors and feelings in each situation. We're quiet at libraries, energized at parties, aloof in elevators, sweet on romantic outings, professional at the office, and so forth.

As countless sociologists have pointed out, the most prominent ones perhaps being Erving Goffman and nowadays Randall Collins, everyday life is organized around rituals specific to each situation. But not only are street-walking, library visiting and beer drinking at pubs ritualized—so are all the major markers of human relationships. We marry by having weddings (ritual), we put our new employee's name on the office door (ritual), we have school graduations (ritual), we have birthday parties (ritual), we have Christmas celebrations (ritual), we have funerals (ritual). From birth to death, our lives are ritualized.

Rituals charge spaces, roles, titles and relations with *meaning*. Without rituals, we are lost in a formless void in which events are not delineated and organized. All resonance, all concerted action pertaining to a shared human world of meaning, break down.

We are ritual creatures and we create social reality by means of rituals. These rituals may have more or less specific liturgies, but the rituals certainly are powerful behavioral mechanisms that coordinate human beings. It is when a ritual breaks down that people feel an intense confusion and a host of extremely negative emotions: If a respectable lecturer sets off contemptuous laughter in the students who then begin to throw tomatoes at him/her, that's traumatic. If someone disrespects the bride or groom at a wedding… you get the picture.

Rituals of course also create and uphold all sorts of wider social and political identities: from constructing the majesty of Her Majesty, to the fervor, unity and obedience of the North Korean people as they dance and march for the glory of the Supreme Leader—none of this is possible without the proper rituals. In fact, there aren't so many commonly understood and accepted social realities that do not depend upon the performance of rituals.

Within mainstream sociology, the analysis generally stops right about here, at this pointing out of the ubiquity and importance of rituals. Then sociologists usually go on to try to enumerate rituals and describe their specifics. That can be an interesting exercise, but it's not that relevant in this context.

What we should look for, if we wish to transform society in a positive direction, is **the relationship *between* the rituals of everyday life *and* the authentic emotions people experience**.

There are so many rituals that go on throughout our lives which many of us don't quite "feel". Ever went to a school graduation that just felt like a boring formality, anyone? Spent a vacation eating good food but not really enjoying yourself? Had a romantic evening where you more or less just played along?

Luckily, with the late modern proliferation of subcultures, people who find it hard to get into the Christmas spirit can find a group of fellow Satanists who like to dress up in black rubber and get a good whipping, or they can find a punk scene in which sad, hopeful songs are sung by folks who drink beer, quote Noam Chomsky and imagine revolution or at least a romantic resistance to capitalist consumerism. There's even a growing mermaid community in Seattle. Such venues offer sorely needed outlets for many of us. There is a greater variety of social scenes, more rituals to gather around. People can shop around and see which ones "work" for them.

Still, however, it does remain a fact that for many of us, a lot of the time, life doesn't really resonate. Something is subtly off. Alienation is there. The rituals we partake in feel empty; they don't match our emotions.

Can you see what an enormous loss of value that is? Think about the resources put into, say, a New Year's Eve celebration. Just the fireworks make up a large chunk of humanity's global yearly release of led into the atmosphere. If you don't "feel the sparkles", it was all for nothing—and it may even have made people more miserable and estranged as the ritual wasn't successful and felt meaningless. When other people around us seem to happily participate in something that doesn't awaken the corresponding emotions in ourselves, we can't help but feel a growing subtle resentment.

On the other hand, people whose minds and inner subjective experiences are less conflicted and broken—people in more harmonic, "higher" states as discussed in Book One—tend to resonate more deeply with a wider range of rituals. People in high states can notice the sparkle in a lover's eye, the subtly present sense of togetherness at a mundane lunch diner, and so on. When we frequent the higher inner states, there is a fundamental sense of "okayness" and we have an easier time resonating with the rituals and situations around us.

Hence, creating a deeper and more harmonious resonance in everyday life is not only a matter of critically reconstructing the rituals, but also of increasing our ability to genuinely participate in them.

And then there are the lowest inner states, the darker depths. These are naturally more difficult to gather around in commonly shared rituals. How, after all, do we create a shared ritual experience of failure and humiliation, to take one example? There are so many rituals concerned with the successes of life, with celebrations of small victories or progress. **But all the emotions of rejection and failure constantly go unrecognized and never get to take their place as shared, manifest, ritual social reality.**

What about anxiety, angst, the fear of freedom? These dark inner worlds are harbored secretly by most of us. What about confusion about reality itself and our place in it?

And then there are the highest and subtlest states, with emotions such as greatness, vastness, cosmic love and majesty. Can these be shared in productive and non-oppressive or non-forced ways?

Just as there are many empty rituals, so are there many **unritualized emotions**, ever present at the fringes of our conscious minds, throughout society. These are the untidy, dark basement rooms of our culture. They show themselves in our dreams and those deviant thoughts that keep coming back. And on the positive end, there are the unearthly heights of existence, the subtle beauties and wonders that never quite seem to fit in but which we deep down know are possible and real.

Just as the body is the seat of the soul, so is society. Can we then make society become a proper home for the soul? Can we recreate society and its rituals of everyday life so as to let our souls feel at home in society, at home in the socially constructed universe? That would be a central—and most difficult—task of *Gemeinschaft* Politics.

GOLDEN KEYS

As *Gemeinschaft* Politics grows into an organic part of society—saturating more aspects of everyday life, redressing and evolving the nature of human relations across all sectors—the shared knowledge will grow about "what affects what" in the realm of social relations. In other words; as a society, we will grow wiser when it comes to understanding what the **key variables** are and how to improve upon them.

There will be an accumulation of the depth of our understanding regarding what these variables *really* mean. Sometimes, one variable will be shown to be explained by others. Different composites will catch different essential patterns, and tell stories back to us.

What is "trust", really? Is more of it always better? Can it be improved upon? What is the average "security of a family"? Does it cause trust, or the other way around? What buttons are there to push, what levers to pull? Or is there a third variable which can explain both of these, such as the emotional intelligence of a population, or the "degree of flatness of informal peer group status hierarchies"? And how does all of this interact with a conventional variable like the unemployment rate? These are, naturally, not matters of simple statistics—but need to be crunched as big data by AI so that we can see patterns we couldn't have thought of. But there *are* patterns, and they can be used to create generative conditions for humans thriving together, as relational beings.

The point is not to have all the answers; we can't really expect to find "once-and-for-all" answers to these questions. The point is merely, that if a proper ongoing process of *Gemeinschaft* Politics were in place, such knowledge—and its many situation-depended practical applications—would grow and take roots throughout society.

I think that we, as a society, should explore this field of development. There are certainly risks, but I believe we would come out wiser, stronger and healthier. We will find key variables and use them; golden keys to unlock the hearts of women and men, to unlock the dormant potentials of fellowship, solidarity and love.

Go on, find the golden keys.

Chapter 13

EXISTENTIAL POLITICS

> "To see the universal and all-pervading Spirit of Truth face to face, one must be able to love the meanest of creation as oneself. And a man who aspires after that cannot afford to keep out of any field of life. That is why my devotion to Truth has drawn me into the field of politics; and I can say without the slightest hesitation, and yet in all humility, that those who say that religion has nothing to do with politics do not know what religion means".[89]
>
> —Gandhi

To base a political ideology or program on an entirely "rational" or "secular" foundation is and remains a fool's errand.

Pure rationality can never answer *what* politics ultimately should be about, only *how* we're most likely to achieve what we set out to do. The *means* of politics can be more or less rational; yes, there are ways of organizing society which are more well-reasoned than others, but it remains utterly beyond the scope of rationality to determine *which goals* are worth striving for in the first place.

EXISTENTIAL ISSUES DETERMINE THE GOALS OF POLITICS

What we cherish most in life determines the goals we set for society. Politics is thus deeply subjective. I dare to say that it is *inherently existential*, since how we relate to the world, one another and ourselves determine what we believe to be just and ethical. The political thus cannot be reduced to a purely secular and objective affair.

Reason is forever destined to be the slave of passion, as David Hume once famously argued. So as rational creatures, we're stuck with serving the will of the political animal.

We are emotional creatures, first and foremost, and what we feel determines what's rational to do. We are also ideological creatures, whose ideas about society are always dependent upon that same society and our position within it. And we are religious creatures, who always adhere to some overarching narrative about reality, some kind of religion in the most general sense of the word. And, we are existential creatures; beings that can only *be* by somehow relating to "what is".

That the aim of politics, then, should be to find rational objectives, in-and-of-themselves, free of any beliefs and assumptions about what's just and beautiful, must remain a fairytale.

Rationality can only be applied to *factual* truths claims; it can establish how well-reasoned a particular line of action is in regards to the objective it is to address. How well-reasoned the objective itself may or may not be, however, can only be established by:

1. Weighing the *subjective* truth claims about its perceived value with

2. the *intersubjective* truth claims about its justness.

Hence, what's rational to do is simply senseless to ask without first having established what's beautiful and just. And in turn, what's beautiful and just depends on our narratives about the world, which in turn are the result of how we relate to existence as such.

Politics is thus a deeply existential affair. It is and will always remain utterly impossible to detach the political from the huge diversity of different personal experiences of being-in-the-world and the ways in which we relate to existence accordingly.

As such, **if the political is *already* undeniably existential, does it then make sense to leave the existential permanently beyond the political; confined to the personal or "private" realm?** Doesn't that leave the whole realm of the political—the arena of human self-organization into a society—completely subjected to the inner processes and deep psychologies that determine why we act as we do, why we want what we want? Should we really shut down all processes of openly discussing how we can support one another to reach, in a deep sense, more productive fundamental relations to ourselves and our place in the universe?

Such questions drive us beyond conventional, instrumental rationality and into the realm of a deeper, second layer of shared, spiritual rationality; if you like, into the realm of **transrationality**. What we are looking for, then, is to create a society that is, yes, more rational and secular, but *also*—and perhaps primarily—**more transrational** and secular in a deeper sense. This second secularism, which I described in Book One, does not take the modern rationality and its gods for granted.

Schopenhauer once wrote that "Man can do what he wills. But he cannot will what he wills."[90] But that is true only on an individual level of analysis. There is crushing and conclusive evidence that our wills, hopes and desires are shaped by sociological circumstances—and these circumstances, in turn, can be affected by deliberate human agency. Wouldn't it make sense, then, to try to collectively develop what "man wills" in the first place?

Doesn't the future of life and civilization depend upon what wants and hopes guide human activity? Jeremy Rifkin has made a similar case in his 2010 work *The Empathic Civilization*. I feel Rifkin is on to an important trail, but he doesn't quite see the distinct features of *Gemeinschaft* Politics and Existential Politics. He misses the mark: an existential civilization.

Is and Is Not

Existential Politics is the practice of making the foundational existential relationship that all of us have to reality itself into a *political* question, into an issue that can be openly discussed, so that measures can be taken to develop it. To develop the subjective states of human experience, to clear the depths of the human soul.

This invisible depth is always-already there in all of us. We relate to our "self", and the self is always defined in terms set by society. Existential Politics is about creating a framework, and a language, for tackling these issues.

Before I go on to explore this topic, I'd like to point out what Existential Politics is *not*. It isn't reading "existentialists" as in philosophers commonly considered representatives of the "existentialist school" (from Kierkegaard to Schopenhauer to Heidegger and Sartre) and to somehow try to base one's political ideology on these. That would be silly, and not very productive.

Nor is Existential Politics the practice of being "deep and existential" when talking about political issues. It's *not* about turning politicians into quietly smiling Buddha statues. It's not about "being profound" while engaging in politics. It's not about making all of politics about spirituality or New Age stuff. Please note the negation, dear reader.

The point is that the politics of the future must grasp greater complexity *and* depth. If we are to rise as an existentially mature civilization, we must find ways of engaging the inner depths of human beings.

Existential Politics is about creating better structures to support people in the long, treacherous inner journey that is life. In the last instance, we are all alone on this path and we have to make our own choices; we have to relate to ourselves and to "what is", to existence itself. But some ways of relating may be less productive and beneficial to ourselves and society than others—and hence nothing is more political than your inner-most relation to existence.

SUPPORTING INNER GROWTH

Yes, we are all alone.

If you remember the discussion about inner subjective states from Book One, we noted that each self-organizing conscious being is always in some kind of inner state or subjective experience. I am, I feel. Existence.

These inner states constitute some kind of unity-of-experience, some kind of integrated whole that is the experience horizon of each creature, and this vast inner landscape is never entirely indifferent; it flows, soars and falls, rejoices and suffers.

In this inner world, we are alone. If there is a terrible infection eating away at our nervous system in a manner that causes sheer madness and hell, no amount of happiness of others will console us. *This* subjective world, *this* universe of mine, is still pure anguish and pain. My experience and all I know is still an unfathomably great darkness and terror. It's just me, all alone, with what appears to be inescapable and never-ending suffering itself.

This predicament creates an irreducible fundamental relation in reality: **the relationship of the self to the self**. Or if we dig deeper yet: the relation between the universe experiencing itself and the quality or content of that same experience viewed as an entirety. Being relating to being itself in 1st person.

The eye of the I.

No matter how thoroughly we kill off "the individual" as a *political* idea, and no matter how well we recognize the co-created nature of reality—the transpersonal nature of all of society's ailments—reality always splices off into a multiplicity of singular experiences, into you and me and everyone else.

It is true, that my experience this moment may have more in common—more connections and more ways of interacting and sharing experiences—with yours, than it does with my own four-year-old former self. But unless we find a way of physically connecting our nervous systems, we are still separate. If I truly suffer, no expanse of heavenly bliss in your world will help me.

And yet—it is *also* true that these inner horizons are structured by society, by circumstance, by nature itself. Society can create preconditions for strong, healthy psyches that can deal with the adversities of life, who can act with wisdom[91] and composure in confusing and pressing life situations. It can work to create bodies and minds that ring with harmony, with maturity and contentment of old age. Or it can churn out armies of wounded, stunted and confused souls who lack the support to make it through difficult transitions—bent out of shape from society's pliers.

Society can be designed so as to support what Joseph Campbell famously called "the hero's journey", the transitions between life phases; the difficult times we all know are coming for us. Structures, norms and institutions can help us grow and turn our painful misfortunes into meaningful lessons learned and an awakened awareness of the suffering of the world, and they can help us rise to a capacity to act upon such a sense of tragedy. Or society can be designed with so many trapdoors and impossible paradoxes that life itself seems to turn into a cruel joke at our expense.

In the last instance, we are all alone in this mysterious journey. We are the sole seers with these eyes, the sole feelers of these worlds of emotions, the sole cosmic address of this inner spaciousness within which thoughts flow and all things arise. In the last instance, life is up to "me". I am here alone, writing a book. I will never read it with your eyes, never hear your thoughts—my work is necessarily cast across time, space and perspective, intersecting another universe.

Alone. But only in the last instance. There is hardly a word in this book I have come up with myself. Everything I do rings with something larger, something beyond me. Up until that last instance, up until the hour of death, I am thus not-alone. My existential predicament is set by the gods, yes. But my ability to respond is granted by you and your treatment of me from my first day onwards, by society, by the comfort of this great wooden chalet, its jacuzzi and the majesty of the mountains—or the relative deprivation of such support structures.

Will I rise to the challenge or will I fold over a thousand times and lace the steel-hard truth with velvet lies and excuses? Will you? Will we retreat into fear and hide in the crowd, turn away from our life's greatest mission?

The answers to these questions depend upon our existential strength, health and development. Will society consist of people following profound dreams, ideals and moral aspirations—or will it consist of excuses for lives unlived, for creators dead-born?

These are the fundamental questions of Existential Politics. It seeks to make open what was locked in, to let out what was suffocated, to cross out the taboos, to rid of the shame, to emancipate human beings in all of our gory, messy, beautiful, vulnerable purity.

We need to support the inner growth of human beings.

EXISTENTIAL STATISTICS AND A MINISTRY OF EXISTENTIAL AFFAIRS

I know what you're thinking, dear modernist mind:

> "Outrageous! Existential and spiritual issues are and must remain purely private concerns. The separation of church and state is a core principle of modern democracy that cannot be compromised lest we are to revert back to the dogmatic narrow-mindedness of the Dark Ages. How can you in all seriousness propose that such an unquantifiable and hard-to-define issue as *existence* should become a societal concern? And have you no sense of privacy!"

Well, *for starters*, existential angst or deep-felt alienation is hardly more private than drug abuse or domestic violence. How our fellow citizens are feeling deep down concerns us all whether we like it or not. Stunted personal growth makes its way into crime statistics and suicide rates; the angry kid who steals your car, your neighbor's daughter with a belly full of valium.

Secondly, let's have no illusions about the separation of church and state. It's not that governments suddenly realized it is wrong to meddle in the existential affairs of citizens. Traditional religion was simply abandoned in favor of new sacraments that more effectively could shape the spirit of people in the modern age: "the altars of television", through which the daily sermons of saintly news anchors help us make sense of an otherwise confusing world; "the pulpits of university halls", from where a new clergy of intellectuals preach the gospel of science and liberal democracy; "the cathedrals of fine art and culture", in which the prophets of artistic expression seek to expand the boundaries of the human soul; and "the holy church of sports", whose zealous devotees from various congregations carry out the divine mission of boosting national morale and strengthening the character of school children. All of these sacred institutions of modernity have formed close ties with the state, and the overall purpose has largely been of an existential nature: to offer a firm foundation of meaningfulness in people's lives, credible narratives about reality, something to believe in—faith, in one way or the other.

That we live in a fully secular society is and has always been a myth. As such, the intelligent question is not whether existential matters should be political concerns or not. They already are. Rather, the question is why we shouldn't have a more explicit discussion about how the instruments of politics are used to shape our relation to existence, and why we shouldn't make it a deliberate goal to support the personal growth of as many as possible?

It would thus make good sense to have a **Ministry of Existential Affairs** whose purpose should be to monitor, understand and affect issues pertaining to the existential foundations of everyday life—in sensitive, respectful and transparent ways, of course—so that more of us can develop fruitful ways of relating to life.

Thirdly. Is the spiritual wellbeing of ordinary citizens really so far beyond the scope of any quantifiable inquiries that we will never be able to make informed decisions about how to improve upon it? I don't think so. Useful data about how we, as a society, are doing deep down, how we relate to the ultimate issues of life, could be gathered if we began to ask the right questions, such as:

* How many people honestly feel they are following their dreams?

* How many are tormented by the existential crisis that seems epidemic to early adulthood, and how seriously?

* How many and how fundamental lies do we tell one another? To what extent do we live with truths that cannot be told to our nearest and dearest?

* How large inconsistencies and sources of self-deceit can be detected in our moral reasoning and actions?

* How many of us do things that are counter to our moral intuitions in our professional lives?

* How many of us feel a pervasive lack of meaning?

* How afraid are we of death, and how does this fear shape our lives?

* How many have strong, transformative experiences of a spiritual nature, and how often, and who?

* How many of us feel genuinely identified with the ecosphere, future generations and the animals?

* How many people get stuck in untreated traumas, so that deep wounds are never healed and greater inner depths never fully integrated into our personalities?

* How many live our lives with a nagging sense of anxiety in the background (Book One: subjective states 6 and 7) and how many live with a general sense of safety and basic goodness (subjective state 8)?[92]

- To what extent do we define ourselves, our identities, in terms of material wealth and worldly success versus in terms of inner qualities?

- How do we reason about the highest ethical principles and how do we relate to paradoxes and dilemmas?

- How many of us are on serious spiritual paths, or otherwise trained in introspection, meta-cognition, inner self-scrutiny and useful forms of meditation?

- How accurately and dispassionately are we able to describe our own behaviors, strengths, weaknesses and vices?

- How many of us have profound regrets on our deathbeds?

Inquiries like these could be conducted in a sound, scientific manner just like we nowadays routinely survey overall life satisfaction and happiness, what people consider most important in life, whether reality meets our expectations, and so on. So in the same way we have national agencies to gather and publicize statistics on economic performance to ensure informed decisions are made within the departments of finance, a census bureau of **Existential Statistics** could be established to provide the Ministry of Existential Affairs with much needed data about how we're doing—how we're *really* doing, deep down.

—

Truthfulness, bravery, inner self-discipline, spiritual wellbeing, self-knowledge, existential ways of relating. These are important things, in and of themselves for each person, and for society as a whole.

Am I overstretching here? Is this too much to ask of our society, that we together should relate to these questions?

I don't think it's too much. I think it would be profoundly irresponsible for us, as a global civilization, to enter an epoch of such towering complex challenges and hitherto unimaginable technological powers to generate suffering and bliss, *without* properly addressing these issues in a wide-reaching and systematic manner.

VIA CONTEMPLATIVA

Existential Politics should organize investments into new support structures for personal growth. I would like to suggest that we reintroduce—on a wide, societal level—the medieval notion of the *via contemplativa*, the contemplative life path.

The term *vita contemplativa* (*vita*, with a "t") is more commonly used —most famously in Hannah Arendt's *The Human Condition* from 1958— and means "the contemplative *life*". But here I'd like to stay with discussing the contemplative *path* and how it could be made part and parcel of day-to-day society and politics. The issue is not that society needs us to become monks and nuns, but that more of us are supported through the inner journeys of life.

First of all, let's not get carried away by nostalgia. I am not claiming medieval times were "better" than modern times, or that everyone walked around being super-spiritual back then, concerning themselves with high-minded things like life's inner journey all the time. And I am not claiming everything from early modernity—the Renaissance and its *via activa* (or *vita activa*) which broke off with the medieval scholastic and monastic tradition—and onwards represents a mistake.[93]

As you probably know from this book and other writings, Hanzi Freinacht is a developmentalist. I don't think present society has "fallen from grace", from any primordial state of innocence, wisdom or bliss—but that modern society directly follows from the principles of traditional society: Once people have agreed to the idea that one highest principle of truth should guide society ("God" or any other highest principle in traditional or what I call "postfaustian" societies), sooner or later people will also have to agree that this absolute truth must be subject to open inquiry and to intersubjective verification—which is the essence of modernity. Modern life is born from the dialectics inherent to postfaustian society. Development sometimes runs into dead ends, tying knots on itself, like in Nazi Germany. But it would be a mistake to think that modernity *itself* is such a dead end.

And yet, it would be conceited to believe *nothing* could *ever* be learned from earlier stages of society, from the rich varieties of historical experience. Even if modernity is an "attractor point" towards which postfaustian society ultimately points, we noted in the introduction that there is always a price to be paid for development; there are always "beauties lost".

The *via contemplativa* may be such a beauty lost. The medieval system was basically designed to produce good monks (and, to a lesser extent, nuns). To be a learned person was to be versed in biblical studies, theology, philosophy, contemplative practice and prayer, and some practical skills pertaining to monastic life, such as being a good scribe. Theoretical subjects were highly esteemed. In the medieval scholastic system, people entered education and were taught the first three liberal arts, *trivium* (grammar, logic and rhetoric), then advancing to the four "higher" liberal arts, *quadrivium* (arithmetic, geometry, music and astronomy). Only after versing oneself in these seven arts could one partake in lectures on philosophy and theology. This created an impressive pan-European network of Latin-speaking scholars who could converse about the nature of God and reality.

As the intellectual mission of the late Middle Ages was all about trying to find the highest principle of truth and align society with it, its educational system aimed to produce people who could refine their hearts and minds so as to find God and to serve Him. In short: The system of learning and teaching prepared people for the *via contemplativa*.

The Renaissance—the period of cultural blossoming that heralded modernity—changed the medieval educational system around considerably. Casting an eye on the proto-modern societies of high antiquity (Hellenic and Roman), and building on vital Islamic influences, the few thousand people who made the Renaissance happen redesigned education to better fit a *via activa*. It prepared people for becoming politicians, merchants, military leaders and—to some extent—artists and engineers.[94] Rhetorics, politics and history became important, and *trivium* was seen as much more "trivial" (from which we have derived the word "trivial"). Since that time, as modernity has progressed and disclosed its radically transformative powers, accelerating over the centuries, greater portions of the population have been educated for longer periods of time, and more of us have been offered a *via activa* as citizens, entrepreneurs, scientists and so forth.

Religion, reflection, self-knowledge and contemplation have—even if they still exist—undeniably taken a back seat in modern society as a whole. *Via contemplativa* is thought of as something exceptional, something for the few rather than the many. Skyscrapers have dwarfed the once dominant cathedrals in their taller shadows. Skiing resorts, exotic safaris and wet summer fuckfests on Ibiza have replaced pilgrimages and periods of monastic seclusion. People such as myself, who like spending time alone walking in the Alps for no other reason than to contemplate existence, are often seen as eccentric, disconnected or even frivolous.

During the emergence of modernity, this "life-affirming" attitude may very well have made sense: With so much to do, so much to be achieved, and yet no major risks of systemic and civilizational collapse on the horizon, it may be a good thing that people primarily focus on creating worldly things. *Useful* things. And then you may just as well savor the hedonic, Dionysian richness of what modern life has to offer while you're at it.

After all, what good is staring at a wall (to come to terms with the blissful but terrifying meaninglessness of Emptiness) when you could be out there making sure more kids get polio vaccine, or take part in any other of the seemingly infinite growth potentials of the modern world?

We are, however, now reaching a point in history where our very survival depends upon our collective inner development. In today's late modern society, in which the potentials of our technologies are so incomprehensively vast, the consumption of one single human so staggeringly impactful, the consequences of our actions so global, the possibility of ecological collapse so present, the acceleration of our changing life conditions so dizzying—we may need to reintroduce the *via contemplativa*, an updated and recycled version of monastic practices. On a very serious, collective—yet deeply personal—level we may have to stop and think, quiet as the snow.

And breathe. And reflect.

Consider. Reconsider. Doubt.

Rest. Concentrate. Heal. Suffer. Digest. Grow.

Rise.

We may have to take the issue of life as a contemplative path very seriously, meaning **that we, as a society, should be prepared to expend considerable time and economic resources on inner growth.**

Inner growth. Being with oneself. Introspection. These activities may come off as less manifest, tangible or visible than "going to work", "playing football" or "winning". But they are *verbs* nonetheless: breathe, reflect and so on—they are actions, flows, processes and events. The inner journey is something that really *happens*, something that counts for something, a difference that makes a difference. Tectonic shifts of our lives may occur, shifts of our perspectives, of our beings, aspirations, motives and life-goals. Such inner shifts of the heart reverberate across the larger patterns of our life-spans, and thus they affect the world in a thousand subtle ways.

This way of thinking is not only counterintuitive to the modern mind. It is downright offensive:

> "Should people spend *more* time in idle solitude? But what about the growth of the economy! What about climate change, an issue that requires action, *now*! What about all the social problems! And you want people to meditate and contemplate in the stillness of their minds? And how could we *afford* such a thing!"

But it is a simple fact—despite the pervading sense that we are busier than ever—that many or most of our daily activities and life goals

are quite poorly thought-out, rather shallow, and often quite unneces-
sary. We pursue shallow life goals, because we get stuck on relatively simple and basic inner needs that still "have us by the balls".[95] The goals of
our actions are themselves "ineffective" (transrationally speaking), our
motivations and drives hardly conducive to sustainable human flourishing, development, love and lasting happiness. And in these days of exponentially growing human power, the failure to pursue deeply worthwhile
goals in as many people's lives as possible, can and will be nothing short
of catastrophic. And the only way to get many more of us to develop
much more global and worthwhile goals is to support our genuine inner
development. Global scale calamities are likely to follow pretty soon, unless we start looking inwards.

   In other words, it may be a *very* sound investment—in terms of "the
economy of happiness"—to put much, much more of society's time, ef-
fort, resources and attention to people's inner worlds, to the existential
journey of each of us.

   Take a moment to consider this: All that really "is" and all that we
genuinely care about revolves around the conscious, inner experience of
humans—and animals for that matter. What is a theme park without the
ability to have fun? What is ice cream without the ability to enjoy? What is
music without the bewondered listener? What, indeed, are family and
friendship without love? What is even truth and enlightenment without
the profound recognition of the observing mind?

   The vast inner landscapes of subjective experience are not a fringe
issue, not a small detail.

   They are everything.

   They are all that we will ever have. Inner experience is all that society
ultimately produces and all it ultimately relies upon. It's what all of it ultimately is about.

   What madness, then, to build a civilization that does *not* work actively
and seriously with the development of inner experience! Whatever else we
change or build or create or develop, it all has zero value without the eye,
the mind, the heart and the soul of the observer, of the experiencer, of the
participating co-creator. We're always-already *here*, cast into being, meeting the universe half-way.

   Nothing explains more about what humanity creates than her innermost relatedness to existence. Will we create prisons, conflicts and collapse, or will we manage to respond productively to the great challenges
ahead of us—a struggle reborn as play?

Contemporary commentators like to point out that this is an existential question: "Will we fall on our own sword, or rise to the challenge?" What they generally fail to mention, however, is that this existential question itself depends upon how the inner path of each human being is supported and scaffolded—or thwarted and undermined—by the structures of society. They fail to see the political and transpersonal nature of the existential questions, and they fail to offer bids for a renewed *via contemplativa*.

A metamodern politics would need to reintegrate key aspects of all the former value memes, which means that even some aspects of post-faustian society and its traditional religions should be re-examined and judiciously reinvented. We may need to co-create a more existential civilization, one that values inner growth and earnest spiritual exploration considerably higher than today's late modern society.

LIFE CRISIS AND DEVELOPMENT

How, then, could a *via contemplativa* be properly reintroduced in a metamodern context, in the context of an advanced welfare system we call the "listening society"?

One way to go about this is to endow all citizens with the "right" or "positive freedom" to, once or twice in a lifetime, take a longer time off from work (or whatever they're doing)—for half a year, maybe a year—in order to go through a supported period of practice, learning, contemplation and self-scrutiny.

It is safe to assume there is much to be won, in a myriad of non-linear ways, if a large part of the population successfully and productively manages to deal with one or more of the different "crises" that pertain to a normal life course: the existential crisis of early adulthood (which has been growing in recent years), the major stress breakdowns many of us suffer during our professionally active years, or the crises of death, illness and bereavement that all of us must face towards the end of our lives.[96]

Add to this the fact that people can have all sorts of other crises that don't pertain directly to one of the Eriksonian life phase transitions: there are family crises, failures in life, crises due to unemployment and other structural shifts in society. Then add the fact that we *collectively* respond to crises at a societal level in more or less composed and productive (versus reactive and destructive) manners. Each of all these mentioned instances of crisis can either lead to tragic collapse, painful stagnation, or to higher stages of development and flourishing.

We all have such turning points in our lives, and our ability to manage them largely determine our adult personal development, which in turn collectively determines how our leaders govern society and how society collectively responds to challenges.

As things currently stand, most of us respond only so-so to the crises that inevitably show up in our lives. And then we walk on, wounded, hurt, numbed and stunted in our growth as adult human beings. And that shapes all of our lives, the lives of those around us, our children, and society at large.

The word "crisis"—as so many like to point out these days—is both a moment of great difficulty *and* an opportunity for "purification", for resolving long-standing issues or tensions, or for transitioning to new stages of development. In scientific terms, crisis only ever shows up in "complex systems", never in non-complex ones; so you have an "economic crisis" or an "identity crisis", but never a "crisis of the car engine". Etymologically, the word goes back to the ancient Greek word for "decision". The crisis is the moment of *decision.* It's when the shit hits the fan—and the whole thing either collapses or pays the painful price to reorganize and grow.

When it comes to existential issues such as handling the deep crises of life, it is common to think in terms of moral purity and innate character. Some people, we like to tell ourselves, are the ones who really have the courage and heart to muddle through, the composure and self-control to see clearly in stormy weather, the faith in our... blah, blah, blah. And then we like to assume that *we* are those people and people we don't particularly like or who don't share our values are weaker and less worthy at the innermost level. We must recognize this line of reasoning for what it is—namely moralism: i.e. the judgmental and self-congratulatory bullshit of our habitual minds.

Truly metamodern Existential Politics departs from a very different starting point: Whether or not a person pulls through during a moment of crisis is *not* a matter of God-given moral character, but simply a question of behavioral psychology and the extent to which she has the necessary resources available.

So the issue becomes, not to judge or congratulate, but to soberly and effectively strengthen those inner resources and societal support structures available throughout the population.

Just as a society will have a certain GDP growth over a period of years, and just as every society reproduces its murder and suicide rates with frightening precision from year to year—so must every society have a specific number of shattered dreams, a number of broken hearts, a percentage of lifetime spent in subtle self-doubt, a number of crises successfully passed (or not), a number of psychological stage transitions that occur harmoniously or in wrenching agony. Is it unreasonable to ask how each of these numbers can be studied and improved upon?

That's Existential Politics: reducing the number of shattered minds and broken souls while increasing the number of inner phoenixes rising.

Chapter 14

THE AWAKENED PUBLIC

"I want to live,
I want to give
I've been a miner
For a heart of gold.
It's these expressions
I never give
That keep me searching
For a heart of gold
And I'm getting old."[97]

—Neil Young

It is as though civilization itself is getting too old. And with age follows either decay, dementia and despair—or wisdom and self-knowledge. Can then modernity, the present world-system, begin to know itself?

This would be the *meta*-modern mission: to create a deeply self-reflective modernity; a modernity operating not only upon nature and the environment, but one that reexamines its own perspective, its own choices—if you will—its own soul.

Modernity did peer into the soul of individual human beings, under the auspices of psychiatry. But it never developed a full process for looking into its own existential foundations and to treat the maladies of civilization.

Modern society has, as Foucault famously argued, been profoundly marked by "the birth of the clinic". Metamodern society and its existential civilization must usher in "the rebirth of the monastery", echoing and carefully recycling some of the finest aspects of medieval society.

SECULAR MONASTERIES

The purpose of metamodern monasteries would be to offer all citizens necessary periods of seclusion (and/or community) and concentrated honing of inner skills, such as healing from trauma, making crucial life decisions or transitions, learning new life philosophies, practicing meditation and taking care of the body, forgiving people who hurt us, sorting out ethical dilemmas, and other transformational practices. We all have a few toys in the attic to deal with.

It would make sense to create a great network of secular monasteries, properly equipped with teachers, coaches, therapists, libraries, gardens, gyms and simple accommodation. People would be trained in one or more wisdom traditions, be supported in making necessary changes of habits, face their traumas and so on. Instead of an authoritative priesthood like in traditional religions, the main agent would be a professional group of "existential social workers", trained to deal with people's different life crises and to act as advisors. They should be highly skilled in one or more mindfulness and meditation techniques, in turn scrutinized by scientific studies.

An important aspect of such a neo-monastic societal infrastructure would be to include different kinds of bodywork and "subtle body practices", refining the skills of dealing with direct bodily experiences and sensations and developing the general wellness of our bodies. Such development is not only of great value for its own sake, but also a necessary tool for strengthening our overall body-mind systems so we can handle the difficulties inherent to life's crises and the stage transitions of personal development.

So we're looking at a major project of the listening society, one that is indeed comparable to the construction of the welfare state. You need new facilities, new infrastructure, new groups of professionals, new educational and career paths (which can generate quite a few new and very cool jobs by the way), and new institutions to govern, evaluate and develop the whole endeavor. It's going to take decades to build and/or cultivate, and yet it will produce few tangible, manifest things. But it will produce a more listening society, and an existentially mature civilization. Millions of people will untie subtle knots in their inner worlds and manage their lives more compassionately and skillfully. If the listening society is to fulfill its promise—a society where everyone is genuinely seen and heard—it must rest upon a foundation of inwards listening.

All of these services should be backed up on a collective level so that people are guaranteed a year off from work and be guaranteed a basic livelihood during the period. Hopefully, it could be possible even for parents of children to attend such periods of seclusion, just switching their day-time work for monastic life.

"What's the point of all this? And, again, can we afford it? Should we really be sucking our thumbs and navel-gazing when there are so many issues to attend and so much suffering in the world?"

Still not following, modernist mind? Sigh.

The point is that it is **only by seriously helping people to get what they really need and want from life—by supporting serious adult development, development of the mind and the personality as a whole—that we can raise the level of behavioral functioning throughout society and the level of mental health throughout all social groups.** It is in this manner we can raise the average "effective value meme" of the population above the modern stage.

And, just to remind you of the stakes: Without a deep and lasting change towards higher effective value meme, we're pretty much all going to die in a horrible car crash as we enter this age of super-technologies without a corresponding shift of psychological and cultural development.

So it's not that we can't afford to do it, it's that we can't afford *not* to. "Can't afford" a medicine that will save your life from an aggressive disease? Well, then, too bad, you'll just have to suffer and die.

Existential Politics isn't navel-gazing. Things are only navel-gazing if they are not conducive to growth and social change. If something *does* prevent oceans of human suffering, improves lives in so many ways, and saves society from collapse because it spurs human growth into deeper maturity—then it's not navel-gazing.

As things stand today, many of those who belong to the social groups I have called the Yoga Bourgeoisie, the Triple-H Population and the Integralists already find ways of getting support for growth during transitional periods: they go to workshops and retreats, do shadow-work (busting your own bullshit with a therapist) and whatnot.

But there are several problems with this privatized and individualized approach of present-day spiritual seeking. One thing is that it's only really available to these privileged segments of the population. So it's missing where it's needed the most. Another problem is that the norms of society aren't really up to speed: Most people think it's a waste of time, too idle and boring. Society as a whole should make sure more people see the profound value of prolonged, serious inner work. And a third problem is that there is no concerted effort on society's behalf to guarantee the quality, reliability and safety of such practices, which enables all kinds of swindlers and quacks to prey upon the Astrology Precariat (chapter 7). Making this a priority of Existential Politics would work to remedy many of these issues.

A neo-monastic institution, offering its support to the wider population, should of course also be linked to activities such as criminal rehabilitation, psychiatry, social work, palliative care (of the terminally ill), the development of more customized and meaningful funeral ceremonies—and of course to education, where the opportunities for psychological and existential support should not only be a background structure as it is today, but a central and prioritized feature of life in schools and universities. Not to mention healthcare more generally; most present-day healthcare systems are bogged down with people seeking medical attention when they in fact have social, emotional and existential problems—as any general practitioner can attest to. So often will people come in with a headache or stomachache but soon start crying about their life problems.

It should be a societal goal that 18-year-olds enter adult life with a sense of inner responsibility and self-love, which sadly is far from the case in today's educational system. As argued in Book One, **all children can and should be offered therapeutic talks with a trusted adult professional throughout their years in school.** How many life courses could that change; and how profoundly? Very many, and quite profoundly indeed—seeing as you get a cumulative, collective effect as the children and youth interact with one another.

If we are to turn the tide of spiritual poverty and alienation inherent to modern life, we must begin to nourish the souls of millions. Only then can we develop a metamodern society, a society that takes its own development—interior and exterior—into its own hands. If there is one thing that characterizes the emerging meta-ideology I call the Nordic ideology, it is this: **a systematic and deliberate nourishing of the human soul throughout the life course; a clarion call for adult development.**

How to get there is far from obvious, but without an explicitly formulated and manifested Existential Politics, and without proper societal processes to address these concerns, we are unlikely to achieve any such goals.

MEDITATION AND SOCIETY

We are thus imagining a future in which we as a society find ways of monitoring the development of a number of key issues that pertain to the inner growth and existential wellbeing of all members of society—then offering support to all citizens during key transitional periods of their lives in accordance with their needs and longings.

This will lead to significantly less social and economic fallout of people's periods of crisis, and it will seriously boost the number of highly functional and mentally healthy people.

In a similar vein Existential Politics should work to develop the *meditation skills* and the level of introspection and meta-cognition in society at large, as well as raising the average inner "subjective state" experienced by people in everyday life.

So basically, it should be a long-term goal to train everybody in contemplation, self-observation and meditation, starting from early childhood when our brains are especially malleable. If we transform not only the content of people's minds and the nature of our human relations, but the very base structure by which our minds function, we transform society.

Meditation and society. There are two different ways to think about this, one of them wrong and the other correct and productive. As so often is the case with these things, almost all observers and practitioners think about it in the wrong way.

Let's start with the incorrect, stupid way of thinking about this. It goes something like this: "Because meditation is good for you and has a bunch of benefits, people should do more of it, and if we get everyone to do lots of it, then all things will be much better."

There is *some* truth to this statement—indeed, if one advanced society has everyone above age nine meditating for 20 minutes per day and another society doesn't, all things equal, the first is likely to be somewhat better off in terms of how people feel and behave—but that really is just a piss in the Mississippi, and there are no guarantees. The problem is that we're viewing meditation as:

1. a specific, delineated activity,
2. as a binary question of either-or,
3. as a static "thing" that can be "added", and
4. as something to instrumentally do for the sake of other benefits.

With this kind of thinking, meditation so often becomes an unexamined prop taken to have semi-magical properties, or it is scorned as a cheap trick, or subjected to a one-time evaluation trial and then either rejected wholesale or used in other, unrelated contexts.

The reason people think this way about meditation is of course that they have limited knowledge of and/or experience with it, or that there is some kind of seduction to the idea of this black box fix-it-all. But while understandable and forgivable, this way of thinking about meditation simply is not what can and will transform society.

The second and correct way of viewing meditation-in-society becomes apparent once you zoom in on the phenomenon—experientially, analytically and scientifically. **Meditation turns out not to be a convenient black box or a nifty add-on, but** *a whole continent.*

Think about it, how huge isn't your inner landscape? It truly is a vast continent. When we talk about meditation and the inner work of consciously examining and affecting these inner landscapes—are we looking at certain techniques for concentration, or inner familiarization with which emotions arise and how, *or* direct inquiries into what consciousness itself is, or techniques to calm *or* quiet the mind, *or* techniques to increase the subtlety and sharpness of our perceptions of sensations throughout the body, *or* the practice of not reacting negatively to unpleasant sensations but only responding with equanimity, *or* the perception and work with subtle inner experienced flows through our guts, *or* the deliberate efforts to shift to alternate mental states, *or* the contemplation of deep mysteries or koans, *or* staring at white walls, *or* walking or moving our bodies very mindfully, *or* looking very mindfully at a certain object of beauty until all thoughts fade away, *or* meticulously studying one's thought structures and their phenomenological underpinnings, *or* cultivating certain attitudes or emotions like loving-kindness and compassion, *or* contemplating our greatest fears to try to get over our aversions towards them, *or* contemplating our most eager desires to try to transcend our attachments, *or* trying to remind ourselves of some profound truths to guide us, *or* are we just sitting down with no expectation, *or* doing something else that has to do with wordless relations beyond any and all "techniques", *or* the listening to a soothing sound, *or* the visualization of a peaceful place, *or* a radical dive into the very moment of Now, *or* the subtle exploration of the topology of the inner horizon—i.e. how our inner landscape is shaped as space—*or* using self-suggestion and mantras, *or* lying down and exploring the edges of sleep and being awake and the possibilities of "lucid dreaming" (when we dream but we know it), *or* actively using our breath as a mood regulator, *or* trying to purify our minds from old mental toxins by means of processes of identifying with the things we don't like and see that they were really parts of ourselves all along…

You see where I'm going. Each of these forms of meditation and countless others I didn't mention are, in turn, not singular "things"; each of them is a rich process with trapdoors and potentials. Each of them can take a lifetime to learn and explore. Simply: Since the inner world is vast, when awareness and attention are brought to operate upon consciousness itself, there are thousands or millions of actions that can be taken, millions of mental events that can occur.

Add to this that each of these forms of meditation can be 1) taught and explained in different ways, 2) practiced for different lengths of time and at different times of the day with different intervals, 3) practiced in very different social contexts and situations, 4) used for different age groups or other forms of calibrations, 5) used or learned in any sequence or combination of different techniques, 6) studied empirically and evaluated and spread in accordance with best practices, 7) evaluated by different criteria of success or failure, such as preventing mental illness, reducing stress, increasing subjective state or successfully integrating traumatic experiences, and 8) interacting with any number of psychological, neurological or psychiatric variables, including possible risks and adverse effects.

All things said and done, it should be understood that "meditation and society" is *not* a straightforward relationship. It is a rich field which holds many subtle but profound possibilities of societal transformation.

A good comparison can be made to other basic skills, namely reading, writing and arithmetic. If you teach a kid to read and write, it doesn't necessarily make them much smarter, and it doesn't in itself guarantee a good life. It all depends, of course, on what this person will be reading and writing. If they read Nazi propaganda and poorly spelled snuff porn all day, only breaking off to write hate emails to members of their local minority population, they would perhaps have been better off without literacy after all.

The point is that literacy is a whole world, a whole continent. It's not this "one thing" that can be "implemented" and should or should not be done 20 minutes per day.

And yet, literacy is fundamental to our society. **To metamodern society, meditation—contemplation, introspection, phenomenological exploration—is *that* fundamental.** The human mind is running haywire and diving right into a global super-nano-robotics-AI-bio-digitized economy galore, and you want to leave our minds unchecked, unexamined and without proper tools for self-scrutiny and self-knowledge? That, my friend, would be as crazy as trying to run a modern society without literacy and arithmetic. Meditation is *that* fundamental. It's self-observation and self-reflection, a higher layer of self-organization.

If we had told a peasant in the 1700s that their children should stop working the fields to go learn something called "chemistry" and "physics" by looking at letters and numbers, this would indeed have seemed very abstract and as a waste of time. To the modern mind, investments in developing the inner world necessarily appear wasteful and frivolous in a corresponding manner. Not only is the modern mind focused on outward progress and achievement, but its very sense of reality is built around intersubjective verification. Hence, turning inwards to what cannot be seen and shown in the intersubjective realm appears as a way of turning away from reality itself.

There are some promising beginnings in the work of secular Buddhists such as Robert Wright and Sam Harris, just as there is plenty of research, neurological and other, in prominent scientists such as Richard Davidson, Tania Singer, Olga Klimecki, Daniel Siegel and others who would deserve mentioning—many of whom work with experienced meditators and do indeed confirm they have unusually happy and healthy brains (and even vagus nerves, how about that). Long story short, meditation is a real thing.

One obstacle to getting anywhere in terms of meditation-in-society is that it deals with a hypercomplex entity: the brain, or our nervous system as a whole with interacting physiological systems. As such it is difficult to generalize knowledge about it: I may experience bliss and healing doing one type of meditation, but you might find the same exercise boring or even harmful. (Whatever theories, models or metaphors we can glean about the nature of meditation and inner experience, these must, for the foreseeable future, remain pale "shadows on the wall", recognized facets of surface phenomena, as compared to the actual intricacies of what is actually going on.)

Too often people will have a very good experience with one technique and then try to evangelize it to the world; "oh, if only everyone did *exactly* this one thing, in this particular sequence!"[98] But in reality, patterns of inner growth and experience are very hard to generalize, even to ourselves over time. We are so, so far away from an exact predictive science in this field, even if there are certainly compelling research results. And the same goes for psychology, really. All psychological theories and traditions are in fact pale shadows of the complexity and depth of the actual mind.

This, of course, leaves plenty of room for Existential Politics to pool considerable resources into learning how the inner landscapes of humans can be developed, and which practices can be taught and how, when, where etc. Research, implementation, professional roles, countering adverse effects of training, ethics… We need a real, institutional platform for the administration of long-term inner development. We require an ongoing process in society to take meditation as seriously as reading and writing.

TRANSPERSONAL INTEGRITY

I realize this subchapter title sounds a bit conceited. After all, who am I to tell you what "integrity" means? To have integrity means to stand up for oneself and one's beliefs, to be reliable, honest and straightforward! To live up to our own standards—and so on.

I will now take a four-page detour to talk about integrity so that we can get to the point relevant to Existential Politics and how it connects to the rebirth of the monastery.

These days you can find any number of commentators—even among the most highly esteemed scholars—who will claim that "a good society is built upon the integrity of the individual". And the integrity of the individual is taken to mean some kind of true moral inner worth—being reliable and forthright. It is taken to be some sort of residual essence of goodness, residing in the heart of the individual person.

I agree that, if we were indeed talking about "integrity" in the above and mainstream sense, it would be a conceited endeavor to define it and say there should be more of it. That's just taking our own narrow frame of a "good person" and trying to force other people to conform to it, subtly judging them if they don't. And it requires at least some kind of "God" as to give a final say on who has the prettiest soul. It's just an advanced version of Snow White's evil witch stepmother: "Mirror, mirror on the wall, who has the prettiest soul of all?" All of this requires a fundamental reliance upon what I have called "the guilt regime".

To the metamodern mind, integrity looks very different.

First of all, a true metamodernist "killed God". (And then we killed the modern residual God, and then killed the yet subtler residual postmodern God, and pissed and spat on their graves. And then we revived God on the third day as a co-created meta-pattern of a self-organizing multiplicity of perspectives, which includes the said three dead Gods… But that's another story, so let's not get carried away with theology, fun as it is). Point being: If there is no God to serve as ultimate umpire, there can be no final goodness or badness of a soul, not even circumscribed as the "integrity" of a person. There are only different descriptive variables, and perspectives or methodologies from which these can be known, and different comparisons that can be made to evaluate these.

Secondly, the metamodern perspective is fundamentally **non-judg-mental**. In other words, it is based upon a radical acceptance of "reality-as-it-is", which necessarily includes any "evil that men do" and whatever "integrity" people may have or not. Without non-judgment there can be no metamodern "solidarity with all perspectives", which is the corner-stone of metamodern ethics.

And thirdly, the metamodern perspective is **transpersonal**. It sees that even if different organisms do indeed have different behavioral properties, they do not have any core "essence" or "self" that can be pinned down, and their behaviors must always emerge through the interplay of so many other factors interacting non-locally (across time, space and through diff-erent dimensions of analysis).

Still with me? Okay, let's go on then.

So the question becomes, then, *not* to judge the integrity of the indivi-dual and to explain society as based upon an imagined sum of such inte-grity, but to see how people's inner lives and behaviors co-emerge in a greater and deeper transpersonal space. And if you have *that* starting point, it makes perfect sense to talk about integrity.

So what is integrity?

It's *not* how honest and steadfast you are. Those are only surface phe-nomena indicating a deeper structure of the psyche.

Here it is:

* **Integrity is a measure of how and to what extent the different parts of your psyche—be it thoughts, beliefs, emotions, habits, reflexes, assumptions, perceptions, evaluations, intentions, motives, or identities—contradict and undermine each other, and/or how well they reinforce and strengthen one another.**

* **Integrity is the measure of how well your psyche is *integrated*.**

That's it. Lack of integrity is when different parts of us contradict or fail to meet. Hannah Arendt famously wrote about "the banality of evil" when she reported on the trials of Adolf Eichmann in 1961. She held that the most demonic evil could often be understood by studying surprisingly ba-nal processes, actions and events. If we are to believe her, we should also see that the forces of good, of human integrity, solidarity and reason, are equally banal. The banality, if you will, of virtue.

The reason you let your kids down is that your planning and schedu-ling abilities didn't rhyme with your promises and intentions as a parent. The reason you found yourself lying about a slightly embellished past was that your self-image didn't rhyme with your expectations of others' treatment and reverence of you. The reason you ripped the living heart out of that nice young lady was that your sexual drives weren't integrated with your attachment patterns.

Even two "good" qualities can give rise to "bad" emergent properties if they happen to marry poorly. Let's say you are honest and kind: Your honest feedback to another person made them see a bad pattern in their life, but then you were to kind to push harshly for a needed change. In the end, this left the other person confused and unhappy, stuck between two life patterns. The different parts of you were not *integrated*. It's that banal.

Transpersonal integrity, in turn, builds upon not only how well the different parts of our inner selves are integrated, but how well all of us jive with one another, and how all of us jive with society around us. And all of this involves some pretty uncompromising soul-searching on the behalf of everyone. With a transpersonal perspective, it is clear that *you* can often see unconscious motives and drives in *me* and affect my actions outside of my own awareness—and vice versa. We are not autonomous, sealed containers, each with a God-given will of our own, but open and multilayered systems. Hence, in the last instance, what counts is not *personal* integrity (because that will always only be a surface phenomenon) but *transpersonal* integrity: our shared and intersecting inner depths.

Point being: **we'll never have a harmonious, kind and functional society without extensive inner work being done by many or most of us on a regular basis**. And this is where the neo-monastic institutions would be of help: At major transit stations and periods of crisis in life, people would be supported to do the hard work that inner integration requires.

Seriously. It's hard work. It takes time, effort and resources. I woke up in the middle of the night a few days ago. There was a terrifying emptiness in my heart that had somehow snuck up upon me during sleep. There was a kind of inner storm cloud, a chaos I couldn't grasp or even see the beginning or the end of. In my mind lingered the memory of a strangely violent dream in which I had been stopped from calling an ambulance after somebody had been struck down. I felt deeply disoriented; drifting in an imageless field. Everything around me felt *unreal* somehow, and I feared that madness might creep up on me, as it has on others in my family. Yet, the experience was eerily familiar. I sensed how this confusion had made itself known earlier, in waking states, as a subtle tinge on the fringe of my awareness. I spent a good portion of the following day away from writing and studies, meditating and exploring what appeared to be an old wound that had opened in my mind. Today, a few days later, my mind is clear and open as a cloudless sky, the love of life resting softly in my chest.

I cherish these peaceful moments, as I know they too will pass, sooner or later.

How does one reel in such chaotic states of mind and integrate them with one's everyday self? Daniel Siegel has argued that a healthy mind is an "integrated" mind (and shown plenty of evidence to back this fundamental principle up). In his vocabulary, that means a balance between successfully "differentiating" mental phenomena from each other and then "linking" them together in more organized ways, seeing their interrelations. This line of thinking of course has a lot in common with the developmental perspective proposed in this book and its prequel.

To have integrity, one's different inner drives, beliefs and habits must harmonize with each other without causing mental turmoil due to inner contradictions as one impulse must be repressed because it happens to be on a crash course with another. They must be successfully "integrated" in Siegel's sense of the word.

This, again, requires time and effort. On a societal level, it requires resources. Money. It needs to be taken very seriously. It's either that or bad bosses until the end of days, because good leadership is well integrated leadership and poor leadership is a lack of development and/or integration.

Some of us are fortunate to have relatively few such inner contradictions and thus need less inner work to maintain our mental health. Others have many, and thereby "less integrity". But note that the person of "lesser integrity" can still be more empathic, more concerned with others, have more stringent morality, be more unwilling to tell lies, and so forth. The point is that the latter person's behavior will be less reliable and predictable for herself and others because there are greater inner contradictions to reconcile.

As we go up in "effective value meme", the demands on our integrity increase proportionally for us to be socially functional and have good mental health. If you're a nazi (low effective value meme), it is relatively simple to be consequential about your values and actions: you are pro this group and against that one, etc. If you try to live up to the ideal of solidarity with all sentient beings and a corresponding solidarity with their perspectives (high effective value meme), you are more likely to run into performative self-contradictions.

More complex societies need higher effective value memes in their population to sustain themselves. So if people are supported to do extensive inner work within a neo-monastic structure, we are—all taken together—much more likely to successfully maintain the transpersonal integrity necessary to uphold higher effective value memes. The failures of higher value memes to be backed up by a corresponding integrity in people—on a deep, transpersonal level—lead to these often being recognized as hollow and hypocritical, which turns many people away from caring about high-minded and idealistic purposes. And that's a tragedy.

DEATH, TRUTH AND DISCOURSE

Hypocrisy. Let's stay there for a moment.

Just as the value of money can be deflated[99] **in the material economy, so can the honest search for truth in the public domain of ideas and morals**. The truth, or the signaled truth-seeking of people, can be viewed as increasingly hollow and cheap when their claims aren't matched by actual behaviors and sacrifices made. In a society where people use idealistic claims and truth-seeking to boost their own identities, idealism always appears to reek of hypocrisy.

If we don't deal with our deeper existential issues and our underlying fear of death, we tend to invest more emotions in, and cling more eagerly to, our "ego"; our sense of being a separate and righteous "self". Because a lot of our ego identity is built on having the right opinions, being on the right side of moral struggles and being righteous, we thus have profound inner stakes set against any proposition that could seriously challenge our moral or political standpoints.

As mentioned earlier, it has been shown by students of the psychology of death that even a subtle reminder of our mortality can make us more selective and prone to confirmation biases and less receptive to information which would disprove the positions we currently identify with.[100] In other words: Our underlying fear of death makes us clasp to our ego, which in turn makes us resistant to truth and to honest conversations about central topics.

I should mention that there are empirical findings suggesting that people who develop higher "emotional complexity" (a personality measure closely related to higher stages of self-development) tend to have much lesser anxieties in relation to death and aging.[101] This suggests we can support inner peace by supporting personal development, and that this in turn supports truth in society—or rather, its truthfulness.

Hence, the inner insecurities we all bear with us deflate the perceived value of truth-seeking on a massive scale. Given that society is becoming more complex and people are required to have more coordinated, abstract and correct opinions about more matters than ever, this is nothing short of catastrophic for the self-organization of society. The discourse becomes poisoned as we are all limited by our own identifications and hopes.

Of course, we can't just "get rid of the ego" and be done with it. Everybody needs to have a sense of self and maintain a reasonably positive self-image to feel okay as they go about their day. But we are staring at a very crucial correlation here, one that is possibly instrumental to the very survival of our civilization. It goes something like this:

- The average underlying fear of death in society is proportional to the identification with the ego, refusing the stiff procession to the grave.

- The identification with the ego is proportional to our tendency to identify with certain moral and political conclusions, which curtails any attempts to challenge these notions.

- Forms of inner work that let us deal with the fear of death and help us to disidentify with the ego, such as serious meditation practice, will—on average, over time and as a collective—help us maintain a more functional and sane discourse in which people more honestly seek to know the truth.[102]

Can you see it, dear reader? It's **the deflation of truth.**

Can you see how cheap the truth has become since we all prefer being right over being wrong (and enjoy proving others wrong, never giving them space to save face) just a little too much? Can you see how this is linked to an underlying insecurity we all share? Can you see that this deflation of the truth is a deeply **transpersonal** phenomenon (meaning that it resides both deep inside each of us and in our relations), as any conversation you will ever be in can and will have its very parameters set by the willingness of all parties involved to entertain the possibility that they're wrong about something? Can you see how "the ego" has hijacked truth-seeking in all aspects of politics and society, even within yourself?

Again, the point isn't to "transcend the ego" so that we "can all see the truth". That would be silly. The point is that society—and its members—can be more or less emotionally and existentially mature, more or less invested in identities, political or otherwise.

This hijacking of our strivings, this massive devaluation of all the most precious gems of existence, does not stop at the search for truth. Take any other of the central human endeavors: moral struggle, the creation and expression of beauty, spiritual attainment, the cultivation of love—all of these are hijacked in a corresponding manner. You see a bunch of kids struggling against injustice, and you just know deep down and instinctively that their moral outrage is likely to be more about self-inflating identity-seeking than about genuine moral concerns; their less-than-exemplary behaviors, intellectual inconsistencies and eagerness to accept simple and judgmental ideas all belie that morality is being remote-controlled by the ego and its struggle to place itself at the center of the universe and above others. Beauty becomes pretentious "artsy art" or the impulse to possess and display the beautiful as something indicative of our own splendor. Spiritual seeking becomes a smokescreen for the display of the superiority of our pure soul—a claim that conveniently enough cannot be disproven and takes no effort on our behalf. Even love becomes reduced to a grim game of exchange and power relations.

And what a loss all of this is; what a ubiquitous tragedy! The deflation of truth and of all the greatest values in life.

The cynics of the world are proven right again and again: don't trust idealism to save the environment and moral conviction in the face of injustice (it's "virtue signaling"), don't believe the sensitive heart of the artist (it's all posturing), don't believe the people who claim that spiritual goals are more important than worldly ones (it's just a strategy to score points without making an effort), and don't even live for love. All of it always turns out to be a lie, at least in part. And as things stand, the cynics, for all their crudeness and stupidity, often turn out to be right.

But the point is that—even as these things *are* indeed often based on lies, even if they are conceited and steeped in falsehood—they are still the greatest values of existence: the true, the good and the beautiful. **Due to our collective existential immaturity, however, we perpetuate a situation in which people's strivings for these noble ends cannot be trusted.** This existential immaturity is not an eternal or necessary quality, however; it is something that can and must be challenged and outgrown. And it's not binary; through contemplative practice, self-knowledge and self-acceptance we can reduce the grip that ego identification has on all of us. It's a *scale*— and together we can climb the scale towards higher collective freedom.

That's the ultimate goal of Existential Politics: to see that ego identification can be rolled back, that the fear of death can be eased at the deepest level. Thus the genuine striving for the good, the true and the beautiful can be unleashed in our lives and beyond—to see that truth and idealism can be sought with the metamodern rebel wisdom we have called informed naivety.

Many can handle the truth, but how many of us can handle the truth about the truth? With Existential Politics, we can build a bridge across our fears.

MADNESS AND CIVILIZATION

There have been many versions and nuances of the idea that there may in fact be an intimate relationship between madness and civilization; that civilization itself is bound to growing existential challenges and an escalating inner chaos: Marx's *alienation*; Durkheim's *anomie*; Weber's *iron cage* and *disenchantment*; Freud's idea that civilization forces us to lock up sexual and aggressive urges, which leads us to lives of perpetual *neurosis* and *discontent*; Fromm's idea that technological progress makes the *sane society* increasingly difficult to achieve, which results in an *escape from freedom*; Foucault's idea that "madness" is itself an invention of the modern mind, the purpose of which is to sweep its own dark side under the rug (hence his 1964 book title *Madness and Civilization*); Habermas' *fragmentation* of life and *colonization of the lifeworld by the "system"*; Deleuze and Guattari's *deterritorialization*; Sennett's *corrosion of character*—and many others. In recent years it has become abundantly clear that there is a rising problem of mental health issues among adolescents and young adults in the most advanced economies of the world—even as crime and alcohol use generally have decreased. We become civilized and we subtly go batshit crazy.

Of course, there are many aspects of this intimate connection between madness and civilization. I would suggest that the role of Existential Politics is to grapple this complex relationship, not only as a matter of "psychiatric care" and "mental health", but as a fundamental issue involving all of us—so as to curb the lingering madness of everyday life itself. And what a daunting task that is.

We're not looking only at the tip of the iceberg, so to speak, but at the entirety of a mostly subsumed mountain of ice. Our relatively innocent little neuroses, our innocuous inner grueling, our bitter silent comparisons with the fortunes of others—all of these realities are continuous not only with the prevalence of serious psychiatric illness and cases of social drudgery, but also with the games of everyday life and the workings of the economy and politics.

What is it that puts more and more of us, and increasingly often, face to face with madness? On a more general level of analysis, I would argue, it is not so much "civilization" or "modernity", as the classics suggest, nor "the postmodern condition" or a variety thereof, as the analysts of today assert. Rather, it is the staggering increase of complexity itself. As society becomes so much more complex, so quickly, it simply becomes more difficult for the mind to reach a somewhat stable "local maximum" or "equilibrium". It's just more difficult to know who I am, what's right and wrong, and what's really real in the first place. Even as we are richer and more secure than earlier generations, there are also countless social and psychological adaptations that have to be made, and the problems we do have are less tangible and direct. I've said it before, and I'll say it again: We're not built for this kind of complexity. The rewards are too great, the immediate gratifications too readily available, the threats too nebulous, the world and its horizons too vast. The mysterious relationship between madness and civilization has a name: increasing complexity. Late at night we wake up and face the creeping horror: that life itself as we know it is a social construction, one that ultimately cannot be real, only a fragment on top of an infinite abyss.

And handling greater complexity in the world requires not only new ideas; it requires a kind of *spiritual* development of the average person. It should hence be a societal goal to develop not only higher subjective states in each of us, but also to help more of us develop and integrate greater inner depths, and—if possible—to develop our ability to think more abstract thoughts, to cognitively grasp and relate to more complex realities. This can be described in the following graph:

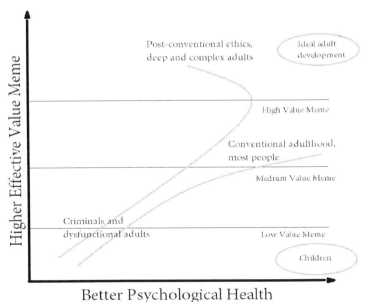

Graph: *Effective value meme versus psychological health. High value meme people often have less stable mental health and functionality, as they are more often in "far from equilibrium states".*

The graph may need some further explanation. It is a summary of the developmental traits of a general population, with higher value meme (the intersection of cognitive complexity, code, state and depth) on the vertical axis and "better psychological health" on the horizontal axis. "Psychological health" can here be understood not only as the absence of psychiatric diagnoses and mental illness but also one's general wellbeing and the freshness and integrity of one's mind overall. If you like, you can imagine one axis as one's "stage" and the other as an agglomerate of how well you have managed to pass through the Eriksonian life phases you have thus far been through (did your mother treat you kindly, did you make friends as a six-year-old, did you form an identity as a teenager and so forth).

As you can see, in this admittedly schematic graph, many or most children have low effective value meme but relatively "good" psychological health. Of course, children also have mental health problems, but at least infants have less of them and young children have much lower rates than e.g. young adults. In childhood, there's often that directness or freshness of experience that in some primary sense is "healthy".

Between the two grey lines on the graph you find most adults. The greatest number of people develop to "conventional adulthood", which means some loss in mental health as compared to the aliveness and simplicity of childhood, but the achievement of an average value meme and stage of development (e.g. the Modern value meme). A minority have their development stunted and remain at low value memes while their mental health deteriorates—and that's where you find many or most dysfunctional and criminal people. Up until the development of conventional stages, people's value memes seem to largely follow the psychological health and functionality of a person: it's just difficult to become a reasonable person who internalizes the norms of society if you feel too bitter, confused or miserable and your social relations and habits are a mess.

High value meme is to some extent *also* tied to mental imbalance and dysfunctionality. A minority of adults develop to higher value memes (e.g. Postmodern and Metamodern) but must thereby also face greater inner obstacles. Many of those who develop exceptionally high complexity and great depth have minds oscillating in "far from equilibrium states". I don't have the data to prove it, but just by looking around my own circle and the people who respond to metamodernism, there is a striking pattern: very high intelligence, Mensa-level is standard, very high prevalence of ADD and ADHD, some autism (especially among the most gifted), dyslexia, very high prevalence of depression, some people who have very extreme personalities if not necessarily diagnosable, high prevalence of strong spiritual experiences, high prevalence of psychedelic experiences, high prevalence of psychotic breakdowns and so forth. In my own family, there is schizophrenia, epilepsy, depression, anxiety and chronic pain due to nerve diseases just as there are highly intelligent and creative people. And among post-conventional thinkers you find lots of gay people and folks with non-binary gender identities and polyamorous lifestyles, however that fits in. Shine on you crazy diamond.

You get the point, right? There seems to be a pattern here: **exceptionally high value meme seems to correlate with a lower level of mental health and stability, and in some sense "unusual minds" or atypical neurological structures**. If you look at the biographies of spiritual masters, like Jiddu Krishnamurti and Eckhart Tolle, a similar pattern appears. Before their "awakenings" to recurring higher states, these people went through extreme inner turmoil—the edge of madness.

As my friend Nick Duffell has argued in his studies of British elite boarding schools, each society and subgroup have their own "**psychohistory**", a collection of social conditions that affect the psychological development and personalities of the group.[103] In sociology, similar arguments have been made, not least in the study of generations (from Karl Mannheim and onwards) and "cultural trauma" (Jeffrey C. Alexander).[104]

Different demographics seem to have specific psychohistories, and the generative conditions for people's life-shaping events can be affected. There appear to be social and genetic factors that cause the high value meme folks to *also* have greater mental vulnerability. I don't pretend to understand the intricacies of this relationship, but I do believe the relationship is factual. The "most civilized" people, in a sense, tend to be slightly bonkers.

If this is correct, the conclusion should be clear: We need a society that helps more of us to marry high effective value meme to inner peace and stability, to mental health. In some few select people, you have the marriage of exceptional development with childlike purity of experience, mind and emotions. This, of course, is what society can and should strive to support, knowing fully well this is a tricky ride: A more complex civilization requires higher effective value memes, which seem to require greater inner obstacles to be surmounted, which is married to a greater propensity for losing grip on reality.

The only hope for civilization is found, thus, on the brink of madness. Think about it: informed naivety, magical realism, the crossroads between fact and fiction, the transpersonal perspective, the hall of mirrors, sincere irony—doesn't it all reflect the madness of a psychotic episode? A few slips, and you're suddenly mad as a hatter. When we open up reality to be co-created in a transpersonal space, is this not an act of enlightened madness?

What kind of person can dive into madness and come out a deeper and more complex thinker? The kind of person we need. The metamodern mind, ideally speaking. **Applied Existential Politics should support the spontaneous emergence of higher subjective states and greater existential depths in the population as well as a greater psychological robustness.**

The acceleration of the developing world-system is a dizzying ride. As new and increasingly phantasmagoric and bizarre and subtle and complicated and mind-blowing phenomena press themselves upon us, life becomes a rollercoaster of an unearthly height—even touching the stars—and deeper valleys as nightmares crawl through the television screens and enter our living rooms. Not to mention social media and smartphones hijacking our limited attention spans. Subtler and more multidimensional games are played for higher spiritual stakes. More of us try to surf the waves of this madness, in the service of higher ideals. Those of us who try psychedelic drugs less often do so in the context of Dionysian "partying" and more often as serious Apollonian "soul-searching".

Something lurks at the back of our minds. And we wake up at night. And the ground shakes and our heads spin and the skies crack open. Utter and profound confusion. Even a scent of madness; but also an opportunity to change our socially constructed universe, to shift our maps of meaning.

The question is not—as Fromm and many other humanist Marxists believed—how to create "a sane society" once and for all. That's just not going to happen. Because madness is civilization's shadow. And now as we're crashing into a whole new level of civilizational complexity, we'll get a whole new level of crazy to go with it. Hey, I told you it's a tragic universe.

The question is, rather, how to create a society where a sufficient number of us develop the resilience to hold on during this crazy ride. That's why we need an ongoing process that supports the development of higher states *and* the successful integration of greater inner depths. This process serves to cultivate an awakened public.

Messieurs dames—let's give a warm welcoming hand for Existential Politics.

Chapter 15

EMANCIPATION POLITICS

N ow we are shifting to a higher gear of complexity in thinking. The first three forms of politics—Democratization, *Gemeinschaft* and Existential—serve to spur subtle but pervasive transformations of society and everyday life, until we reach a higher equilibrium of human well-being, as we achieve a listening society. As I argued in the first part of this book, this follows a long-term historical trend of increasing *intimacy of control*: larger and larger parts of our minds, behaviors and bodies are co-ordinated in more complex and deliberate ways.

Emancipation politics, the politics of defending (in)dividual rights and increasing the degrees of freedom, seeks to counteract the new forms of oppression that can and will occur as the *intimacy of control* increases.

You may recall that we noted an intrinsic connection between any "holistic" view of society and the "totalitarian" impulses of many movements, the two words mirroring one another. If we want a society whose different parts harmonize and create coherence rather than nasty paradoxes and contradictions that wreck people's lives (and civilization itself), we must deal with the inherent risks of relating to society in a more holistic manner.

Emancipation Politics must be animated by the earnest grasping for "another kind of freedom", for the highest reaches of what it means to be free. It must want more for all of us than the rather superficial and unevenly distributed freedom in today's liberal societies: to climb the spectrum of judgment, to transcend the emotional regimes, to go beyond the hidden negative emotions that control us.

As I have pointed out several times already, it is insufficient to simply denounce all holism and deeper integration as totalitarian and cast ourselves as defenders of freedom, pitched against "those control freaks". As soon as people get what they want and enjoy freedom, new things emerge and thus complexity increases; and as complexity increases, there is a renewed need to coordinate behaviors and organize things—and that's control, whoever or whatever system may instantiate and exercise it.

Higher freedom is paradoxically married to greater and more intricate forms of control. If you throw out all complex coordination of behaviors, you don't get absolute freedom, but simply fragmentation and alienation; things painfully falling apart.

That being said, society must counter its processes of governance and integration with corresponding and principled defenses of the singular person, her uniqueness, her lived experience, her rights. In modern liberal democracies, this is guaranteed by the rule of law and independent courts —in theory, powerful citizens cannot trample even the meekest beggar because her rights will be protected by the courts. In theory.

New Sources of Oppression

But can the "legal rights" of the modern division of powers really protect us against the subtler forms of oppression that can and will arise from the new forms of politics as the intimacy of control increases? Here are some examples of such subtler forms of oppression:

- You go through school as a child and the staff use all kinds of psychological tests and diagnostics to see your likely developmental trajectory, and many of them think of you as a future criminal, which subtly but noticeably affects their treatment of you negatively. Adults talk behind your back, "What's your major malfunction?" they ask. And you are surveilled and judged beforehand, resulting in a vague but pervasive sense of having been violated and betrayed. This sense follows you throughout life.

- You partake in a culture where people generally value deep authenticity of emotional bonds, mutual openness about vulnerability and spiritual goals in life—but you can't quite "feel it". Whenever people share deep emotions or talk about their spiritual or meditative experiences, which happens a bit all over the place, you feel pressured to do likewise, but it often leaves you with a sense of numbness, and you notice that people seem to disapprove of you whenever you honestly say you're not quite feeling all that stuff they're talking about. You then end up embellishing the truth just to fit in, which in turn leaves you with an icky feeling that follows you throughout life.

- You are part of a society in which self-governance and participation is highly valued and you are pressured to partake in any number of panels, ballots and committees, even if you don't enjoy it or think it's very meaningful. Deep down, you know you're wasting your time and not making a difference, but at least the people around you seem content. A part of you whispers that you should break free from all of these tokens of responsibility and cultivate your own unique skills and projects, but these inner doubts are squashed under the weight of peer pressure to be a good democratic citizen. A subtle sense of disempowerment takes hold and follows you throughout life.

- You go to work but your ideas and values are somewhat different than those of the people around you, including some of the nice and well-meaning leaders. It's just that you know you have other ideas and talents that would take a longer time to explain and would require others to listen to you. But they control the money and decision-making, so you go for years and years and never quite act on your deeper intuitions and intentions.

You get the point. I'm sure we can come up with a multitude of nasty scenarios that are more or less plausible and could affect different parts of the population in different aspects of their lives. The common denominator would be that people are somehow subtly *oppressed*, in the sense they are being held back, pressured into things, feel suffocated and manipulated, or just aren't treated in a dignified manner. It is important to understand that such oppression is not only a theoretical future risk, but something that goes on in all contemporary societies. We're just not very used to thinking of these things in terms of oppression, but we will become more acquainted with them as the intimacy of control increases. With more intricate forms of social self-organization come new sources of oppression.

Except for such subtle and indirect forms of oppression, we are of course likely to see renewed oppression in obvious and gross forms as the means for state surveillance and manipulation increase with abundant surveillance cameras, advanced AI systems for facial recognition, online activity monitoring, DNA tracking, new forms of censorship, you name it. In criminology, Gresham Sykes and David Matza famously formulated the "neutralization and drift" theory of delinquency and crime, in 1957. Basically, they argued that people become criminal offenders by inventing a large number of excuses or "neutralizations" for their behaviors and that they "drift" into increasingly criminal behaviors and criminal social environments. With today's explosive development of technological means for surveillance and manipulation, it is not difficult to see pathways towards criminal and oppressive governance that go via "neutralizations", trivializing breaches of personal integrity and "drifting" towards full-fledged oppression of dissenting opinions, practices and ideas.

New subtle oppressions derived from a new layer of "metamodern" politics *and* new forms of gross oppression pertaining to the technological properties of the information age—these are two categories of human misery that make necessary a corresponding level of emancipatory struggles.

The idea of Emancipation Politics is to create a permanent framework for society's ongoing debate and dialogue about freedom and oppression: If new forms of oppression emerge, in whatever subtle or obvious guise, there should be a forum for bringing this to the public eye and a framework within which new solutions and responses can be discussed and devised.

Rights Reloaded

There is a profound connection between emancipation at this abstract and subtle level and the ongoing negotiation of negative human rights in society—*and* corresponding responsibilities (because your rights are inevitably my responsibilities and *vice versa*).

"Negative" human rights (or negative freedoms), as we have seen, include such things as not being arbitrarily imprisoned, freedom of speech, freedom of movement, freedom of religion, profession, trade, etc. These freedoms or negative rights were relatively straightforward when applied to the powers of early modern states: don't tell people what to believe in terms of religion, don't threaten them, don't throw them in jail and torture them, don't crack down on the press, and so forth. And as we have seen, from there on—from the establishment of the modern state—the complicated and difficult questions in established democracies have to do more with delineating sound *social* rights or *positive* freedoms: should someone have the right not to starve, even if they don't work, or right to education, right to have a job? Modern politics of Left and Right have largely been about finding a reasonable and sustainable level of social rights, whereas only extremists and totalitarians have seriously sought to infringe upon the negative rights.

As we begin to understand the new political landscapes of the globalized, digitized and postindustrial era, the discussion of negative rights is reborn, if you will, on a new and higher level of abstraction. We can all agree that we, as citizens, should be free from threats of violence on behalf of the state if we speak out against some perceived injustice. But what about the vague but real threat of Islamist extremist terrorists, *or* the right not to have our "free will" manipulated by technocrats and special interests, *or* the right not to be brought into social situations in which we are "out-depthed" and feel utterly confused and horrified as a result, *or* the right not to be subtly held back by narrow-minded definitions of the societal system, *or* the right to not have our attention span invaded by a thousand addictive smartphone apps and commercials?

This is where a renewed and revitalized discussion of rights is in order. And not only should there be such a discussion in the civil sphere, but there must also be a strengthened institutional framework to define and/or contest claims for such rights. There must be clearly defined arenas in which we can defend such rights, try to understand which boundaries are being trespassed in what ways—where we can design counter-measures that will *either* hold people and authorities, companies and employers directly responsible, *or* (more likely and more often) remedy the harm that has been done, while preventing further harm from occurring.

In short…

a) as society's complexity increases,
b) this also creates pressures to increase the reach and density of governance,
c) and this creates new sources of oppression (both the increased complexity of society at large *and* the new layers of governance),
d) and this creates an increased need to expand negative human rights and freedoms, i.e. the right *not* to be subjected to a host of new oppressions,
e) and as these new negative rights must be of a subtler and more abstract nature, they will be harder to define, defend and make sound and socially sustainable,
f) which thus makes necessary an ongoing political process through which information is gathered, rights and obligations are perpetually discussed and tested, and new institutions are created in order to defend people against new forms of oppression.

And *that* process (point f), is Emancipation Politics.

It's not a binary "thing" that you can do to "guarantee freedom". People aren't either free, or not. As we have noted, freedom is a scale, both at the level of the single person and for society as a whole—and it develops together with order and equality. Even new (in)dividuation will eventually lead to new forms of oppression.

And since society's development is full of uncanny paradoxes and contradictions, it is unavoidable that efforts to improve the human condition can and will create new forms of oppression. The point is that this emergence of new oppression should be preempted in the best possible manner and be made visible and a subject of public debate and political agency.

That's what would be going on at the **Ministry of Emancipation**: All forms of oppression that people experience in their lives would be gathered as data and analyzed. There would be public discussions about the interpretation of these data, and there would be an ongoing debate about what can be done to defend people, according to what rights. Human rights will no longer be enshrined and taken as religious absolutes, but be recognized for the social constructions and social *deals* they really are. What rights do you have, and whose obligation is it to uphold these rights, under what circumstances? This will become an ongoing and central discussion in metamodern society.

Just as a key difference between modern and metamodern society is that in the former, the system of governance is a given, and in the latter, it is an ongoing developmental process, so it is with human rights and civil liberties—in modern societies these are seen as naturally given and immutable background variables, in the latter they are seen as a productive field of expansion, development and critical restraint. This is human rights reloaded.

In today's society we are already slipping into this redefinition of rights within many areas: culture wars, identity politics, issues of migration, expensive healthcare (do we have the right to medications that cost millions, if these save lives?), nudging, environmental impact, basic income, free speech and false information; all of these seep into every part of politics and the media—who has what rights, who is oppressed and in what ways, and who has what obligations. But as things stand today, there are only weak and haphazard institutional frameworks for dealing productively and systematically with these issues, which results in a host of pathologies: liberal politicians pursuing untenable expansions of people's "rights", single court decisions getting too much power over major societal issues, people being attracted to extremist positions on both ends of the political spectrum.

Our societies need a "human rights 2.0", an ongoing updating of which rights apply in which contexts, and an ongoing cultivation of frameworks which counter any new forms of oppression that may arise as society progresses into a metamodern stage. Consider this: You have the "great stretching out" of value memes, i.e. more people encountering one another across all of the different value memes than ever before, under the increased ability to monitor and control one another, not only technologically but also psychologically. Do you really think that a static set of given "individual rights" can and will protect everyone from oppression in all of its forms and guises? That would be a terribly naive belief.

As we create a new layer of **dividual rights** or **transpersonal rights**, these will need to be less static than the human rights of e.g. the UN Declaration: "No one shall be held in slavery or servitude; slavery and the slave trade shall be prohibited in all their forms", etc. They will be less formulated as rules and more a "**meta-rights**", and they will need to be more case sensitive. I will leave examples aside at this point, but I hope to discuss the matter in future Hanzi books.[105]

The cultivation of such Emancipation Politics—and the gathering and coordination of emancipatory and libertarian forces of society—is a necessary counterweight to the integrative forces of the other forms of politics. *Gemeinschaft* Politics, Existential Politics—just imagine how wrong these things can go. And yet, necessary they are.

For metamodern society to materialize, it must ultimately always prioritize higher freedom and creativity over equality. But such a priority can never be a concluded affair. The ghost of totalitarianism can and will show its face again and again in the coming period, in increasingly subtle and seductive guises, within ourselves and in the cracks of our reasoning.

It may be tempting to claim that we, as humanity, will find freedom *beyond* the political realm. But even in such utopias, if they were credible, people would still need to coordinate their actions on a large scale, and to do so successfully would require inescapably subtle forms of self-organization: coordinating deeper and deeper parts of our psyches.

The answer, then, is not to avoid deeper integration of human agency and further development of the intimacy of control, but to put the struggle for deep emancipation—a principled defense of dividual rights—at the heart of this development. Failure to do so can and will set us on a drifting course towards totalitarianism.

Integration and (in)dividuation are in a perpetual dance. Emancipation Politics can never *by itself* create higher (in)dividuation. You can't "do politics" on someone and make them advance to a higher stage of personal development. Such processes of development must always belong to the person or group themselves who find new ways of acting, thinking or feeling independently. As such, (in)dividuation can only occur spontaneously at so many local and unique sites, at specific historical micro-events. Micro-revolutions—acts or insights that reassert autonomy—happen in people's lives much like falling stars appear in the night sky. Such things cannot be controlled or governed.

But Emancipation Politics can stop *the systemic suffocation of* such instances of (in)dividuation. If people are failing to find their inner voices of conscience or to develop their unique talents because they are being pressured or manipulated or made invisible or systematically ignored—this can be made visible for the public and measures can be taken to counteract the forces of oppression.

LA RÉSISTANCE, DIRECT AND INDIRECT

We have mentioned that Emancipation Politics can, in practice, take two distinct forms in terms of measures taken: direct and indirect defenses of freedom. Let us examine what Emancipation Politics can look like more generally and these two forms of defense specifically.

The Ministry of Emancipation should monitor trends of experienced oppression in society, publicize its data for public discussion, gather expertise about the possible sources of such oppression and organize fora in which different competing interpretations can be put forward.

Such monitoring can take three different forms: 1) quantitative data gathered through surveys, web analysis of big data and the like, 2) qualitative data gathered through ethnographies and undercover participatory studies, analyses of current discourses in society and so forth, and—most importantly 3) people's own filed complaints. This last instance would be made possible by a new public framework of civil service, which has the obligation to listen to complaints and try to see if their experienced oppression can be resolved. So: measure, define, publicize, discuss, remeasure, compare trends over time, discuss reasonable solutions, remeasure…

Somewhere in that seemingly tedious process, awaits higher freedom, ready to bloom—more so than on top of any barricades I can think of.

Questions that must be answered on a yearly basis are such as:

• What unhealthy and unwanted dependencies do people feel control their lives?

• In what contexts are people afraid to speak their honest opinions, and for what reasons?

• In what contexts are people being held back from legitimate initiatives and through what means does such holding back take place?

• What levels of personal (in)dividual freedom do different groups of the population have, if we use the 1-9 scale suggested in chapter 5 of this book?

• What hooks and points of leverage do people have upon one another and how do these things play out in their lives?

• In what contexts are people being limited by bureaucracy and red tape?

- In what contexts have single persons or small groups been rolled over by collective or stronger group interests?

- In what contexts do people show obvious unwillingness to take personal responsibility, and what are the mechanisms causing such learned helplessness?

- What uses of authority can and should be questioned within policing, criminal care, healthcare, psychiatry, education and social work?

- In what contexts are people being manipulated and treated as means to an end?

- In what contexts do people feel pressured by civil society and family relations, and what are the consequences?

As a society, we should have institutions, arenas and fora for collectively thinking about freedom and oppression in society—and for implementing solutions to reduce oppression and increase the degrees of freedom. That requires the development of a *language* for speaking about these matters and a strong basis of knowledge and expertise about the sources of oppression. That's what Emancipation Politics would aim to provide: an improved collective awareness of freedom and oppression throughout society, a richer shared self-understanding.

The *direct* defenses of freedom would have to do with citizens' legal rights and things that can be treated by courts. If someone steals our information, subjects us to unjustifiable surveillance, *or* excises undue medical authority, *or* limits our speech through forms of censorship, *or* actively threatens us to adopt social or political views lest we lose our unrelated job, *or* if someone unfairly has manipulated the stream of information that reaches you; such matters—at least some of them—should be able to be treated by courts or similar (e.g. a hospital might have its own system for receiving and dealing with complaints).

If the "new layer of negative rights" is defined too sloppily or widely, this will quickly devolve into a society bogged down with ridiculous amounts of legal cases, as everyone will feel oppressed by everyone else. The main issue here must remain that people should have at least some lines of defense against the growing powers of states and corporations as these gain ever greater access to technology. But to begin with, we must institute Emancipation Politics so that a discussion can be held about what such new rights should entail in the first place. Again, we're talking about a developmental process, not a set destination.

The *indirect* defenses of freedom are all *other* measures that are taken to support citizens and hinder oppression: regulations, supportive services, scrapping regulations, changing governmental practices, trying to strengthen weaker groups, increasing the monitoring of those who have power over others, increasing transparency and accountability, limiting the powers of authorities—and so on.

Any suggestion motivated by an attempt to hinder some kind of oppression that has been identified in society—governmental or not—and which does not specifically bestow people with rights they can then use in order to take others to courts or file direct complaints to be rectified, is an *indirect* form of Emancipation Politics. Sometimes emancipation can be as simple as lowering a tax rate or removing a regulation—but it often won't be that simple and will require elaborate plans.

It is not easy to know beforehand how all of these policies and practices should look like and work because it is all so contextual and must build upon gathered data, expertise and public dialogues. But we *can* know that without a serious and ongoing such process, many new oppressions will sneak in and wreak havoc as society develops, and many opportunities for empowering and emancipating people will be missed. If we're serious about raising the average level of (in)dividual and collective freedom beyond what has been known to modern societies, we must make emancipation a central concern to metamodern politics.

FOUR DIMENSIONS OF OPPRESSION

Lastly, I would like to offer a simple map of four categories of oppression within which new emancipations will be necessary in the future. Being oppressed can mean quite different things, and the different forms of oppression should be treated and prevented in different ways—the four dimensions, if you will, of Emancipation Politics.

The *first* category has to do with being **oppressed by external state and/or market structures**, and this is perhaps how we conventionally think of oppression. If someone hinders you from expressing your opinions, spies on you, forces you to say words you don't believe in, or unfairly drives you into poverty and degradation by ruining your means of income, all of these things are different forms of direct oppression *by* the system or the collective, *of* you as a single person. You are being violated or suffocated by the formal systems of society. In such cases, negative rights should be there and be defined clearly enough so that you can fight back against your oppressors. But not only can the singular person be oppressed by the system—the *system itself* can also be oppressed, when it is hindered from functioning according to its key principles of universality.

So we need to look beyond the old narrative of innocent individuals stuck in a big nasty system; that's not necessarily the case. Many forms of systemic oppression stem from the fact that the system is hindered in its functioning. A lack of good accounting and the disorder it causes also creates leeway for many unfair power relations to emerge, and hence for oppression to show up in unexpected guises.

The *second* category has to do with the **limits of everyday life interactions**, the cultural forms of oppression. For instance, if you are of a disdained minority group and people habitually ignore or downplay your perspectives, opinions and interests, this is also a form of oppression. Or if you are of a lower effective value meme than most of society and you are pressured to take on a straightjacket of morality requiring an inner depth and cognitive complexity that you simply lack, this feels like oppression. You try to be a good person, but even if you try your best, people keep attacking and degrading you for being shallow and evil, and you never quite see it coming. In such cases, you are being *culturally* oppressed. Of course, higher value memes can be oppressed by lower ones as well, like when the Nazis went after "degenerate art" or when today's speciesist society penalize people who don't think we should torture two-year-old toddlers to death (vegans being against factory farming).

Cultural oppression includes such things as language structures: Words have connotations (consider "a fat nigger" or "a cheap slut" and a lot of unflattering things about our culture come to the fore). Language can also be too poorly developed; we may lack the words, expressions and social rituals to express certain commonly held experiences or feelings. As I have mentioned, there are empty rituals as well as unritualized emotions. In these cases, *culture itself is oppressed*. Here, much of the emancipatory potential may lie in the arts and other forms of experimental cultural expression. And some may lie in critical resistance to the discourse (as proposed by e.g. Chantal Mouffe and Ernesto Laclau).

The *third* category of oppression has to do with **other people and their behaviors more directly standing in your way**. On the crudest level, this means things like someone forcing you to live at their apartment and have sex with them, but there are any number of oppressive relations that come in different levels of directness and severity.

Ideally "your freedom should end where mine begins", but—as I have argued earlier—in actual social reality, people and their everyday lives are always layered in social relations: parents have power over their kids, larger family groups over single persons, bosses over employees, teachers over pupils, bossy and manipulative peers over peers. Your freedom doesn't start at my outer border, but at the center of my heart. You try to express a new interest or idea, but you're pushed aside, ridiculed, threatened or silenced. You try to affirm your autonomy, but people use whatever leverage they have over you to put you in your place. You try to start a business, but your competition sabotages your efforts. All of these are direct, interpersonal forms of oppression. They cannot be viewed as originating from the system, or from culture at large (even if they do of course interact with these categories), but simply from the behaviors of others— from specific bullies in all their forms and guises. A society full of bullies and oppressors is, naturally, less free than one in which we don't play such roles in the lives of one another. An Emancipation Politics worth its name should work to reduce the prevalence and severity of such bullying and oppression throughout all of society.

The *fourth* and last category of oppression has to do with **our own inner oppression of ourselves**. In the last instance, freedom is always dependent upon us having sufficient skills and faculties to act freely and make use of what resources we have for the benefit of ourselves and others. For instance, if we cannot recognize what emotions and deeper motives arise within ourselves, we will be slaves to motives that lie beyond our conscious awareness—often being stuff such as greed, envy, power hunger, or an unreasonable sense of insecurity. And others will have greater leeway to manipulate our perceived needs, wants and motives to serve interests that we may not even be aware of.

Or on an even more basic level: If our minds spin and we can find no inner peace, we cannot be happy and feel free even if we have all the riches in the world at our disposal. And when people have trampled our wills and pride many times over, eventually we will stop ourselves from acting upon our higher impulses and deeper wishes; we internalize the oppression of others and begin to oppress ourselves. This last category links us right back to Existential Politics: Obviously, there is an intrinsic connection between our relationship to existence and the deeper freedom in our lives.[106]

Political metamodernism holds within itself the best means to defeat the other strands of political metamodernism. Be the power—fight the power! Both and. Let the struggle for higher freedom commence, *and* may we defeat the demons of oppression that a deeper and more intimate politics unavoidably brings to life.

Chapter 16

EMPIRICAL POLITICS

"Never in the history of human scholarship has so much been written by so many to the benefit of so few."[107]

O ur work, as metamodern philosophers and scientists, is to rewrite the very fabric of what is real, as our participatory perspectives express higher truths, as they mirror more profound insights—and land us in a vast landscape of reflections, gazing deeper into the abyss.

Science is the process of building upon what we know, which ultimately always tears down the previously known. It is a dance of consciousness, always delving into a deeper mystery. We don't live in a universe where "science" tells us "the truth". We live in a universe where the truth always lies beyond us as we plunge into its mystery.

This part of the story is relatively straightforward—and yet it is far from. On the one hand, the aim of Empirical Politics is something that is already an accepted norm in pretty much all societies—simply that policies, regulations and practices can and should be based upon the best available information and empirically tested knowledge. For instance, if patients are granted the right to get Cognitive Behavioral Therapy for depression, it is in the interest of most everyone involved that CBT can be shown to work to reduce depression. Nobody would argue with that.

On the other hand—and this is where things get interesting—defining what is "good science" and what level of empirical foundations can reasonably be expected within each field of decision-making, and how such empirical support should be cultivated, is difficult. It is, one could say, a whole science in its own right.

Not Obvious, Not Naive

And that's exactly why we need Empirical Politics; we require an ongoing, deliberate and explicitly planned process for making society *more* scientifically driven and empirically tested.

If making society as empirically solid as possible was an easy or obvious thing, we could "just do it" and be done. But since it is such a highly abstract and difficult thing, we need a wide-reaching process through which different paths to validity, reliability, consequentiality and truthfulness are suggested and tested against each other.

We need to perpetually answer and re-answer questions about practices in society. This points us towards more reliable empirical results.

For example, which kind of didactics should be used for which kids in school when they learn to read? Given that we can agree on some basic aims (high information retention, concentration, good reading speed, good awareness of one's own reading style, etc.)—it's an empirical question. How should we use policing and social work to reduce crime rates? Empirical question. What level of social welfare optimizes security without being financially untenable? Empirical question. How do we improve the quality of democratic deliberation and the average political engagement of citizens? Empirical question. How do we reduce the level of false information and increase people's ability to critically evaluate sources of information (as well as one's own beliefs and presuppositions)? Empirical question.

You get the idea. The core issue of Empirical Politics is how to optimize the process of getting the best possible empirical knowledge and to get all parts of society to commit to using that knowledge. And that, my suspicious friend, is far from a no-brainer.

The societal value of empirical science and knowledge cannot be overstated. Even if we get a deeper form of democracy, people will still need to base their shared decisions upon as sound evidence as possible. The whole point of having a better decision-making process is to come closer to a shared truth; so in the last instance you will still be dependent on evaluations, cost-benefit analyses, facts, second opinions, additional tests and so forth. What does "an opinion" help, or someone's "feelings" for that matter, if the facts speak against it? Should we treat people with vaccines? Are GMOs dangerous? Are the Jews conspiring against our race? Does imprisonment of convicted criminals help; if so, whom, how and under what circumstances? Whatever feelings or gut reactions we may have towards these issues, it is in our common interest that the most valid and reliable data are produced, presented and rigorously (but not conclusively) interpreted for us.

Precisely *because* a completely science-driven politics can only ever be a naive fantasy, we must continuously bombard the entirety of politics and bureaucracy with new and critical empirical evidence. "Ideological positions" in the bad sense of the word (holding on to simple, preconceived suppositions about complex issues, where our ideas about empirical truth follow our values rather than the other way around) are often due not only to our cognitive biases, as discussed under Existential Politics, but also simply to lacking empirical data and a rigorous discussion of all relevant information. As empirical knowledge grows, and the demands to cast one's arguments in verified facts increase, the inner pressure to adopt ready-made template ideologies decreases. It should be pointed out that, at some level, most atrocities have relied upon false assumptions about *factual* affairs: the Jews weren't *actually* conspiring against Germany, and no socialist utopia emerged if you just whacked the kulak farmers hard enough by forcing them to collectivization, and you couldn't actually reshape human nature at will by brainwashing folks. These were false assumptions about *factual* matters.

If you look at the great theorists of science, from the logical positivists of the Vienna Circle, to Steven Jay Gould's witty histories, to Thomas Kuhn's and Karl Popper's philosophies, to Richard Feynman's ingenious commentary, to Steven Pinker's recent book *Enlightenment Now*, to all the critical voices from the sociology of knowledge and ethnographic studies of science as a social practice—at the very least all of these agree that science isn't straightforward, that it must be upheld, maintained, defended and renewed. Achieving a scientific society isn't easy.

In advanced late modern countries, politics is already to some extent data- and science-driven. When national politicians are asked what they are going to do about this or that complex problem, a common reply is that they are going to pay a bunch of university professors to initiate an investigation into the matter and come up with suggestions. Then the parliamentarians, sooner or later, usually follow through on these suggestions, often in broad consensus from left to right. Likewise, more and more of decision-making is delegated to meritocratically selected but unelected experts, consultants and technocrats. In a way, then, such societies are already slipping into an early form of Empirical Politics—often, however, partly at the expense of democratic legitimacy and transparency. As the systems of governance are tasked with tackling greater complexity and more issues that require technical detail, they tend to slide towards technocracy.

Empirical Politics is the process through which the long and tricky path to a scientifically sound society is discovered and traveled. **It should be obvious, after all, that today's society is still largely unscientific**: Massive institutional practices are kept alive without a shred of evidence for them being the best alternative, most people are relatively poor at scientific reasoning and critical thinking, and the politics of the major parties are largely based upon loose "opinions". Most of life goes unexamined (Socrates turns in his grave) and the unexamined life gets away with it— most fatefully, perhaps, the criminal justice system. Given the very powerful technological forces that are about to be unleashed upon the world, the failure to seriously upgrade the level of scientificness in society is dangerous, bordering on suicidal.

Yet, societies of today are, in a variety of ways, "more scientific" than those of a century ago. Still we should make certain that it is an explicit and prioritized goal to make tomorrow's society yet more scientific than today's. Do we know that this kind of schooling is the best in terms of securing long-term human happiness? Do we know that this prison time for this crime is appropriate and leads to the most desirable consequences? The truth is that most of the time we simply don't know and we're pretty much guessing as we go along.

Empirical Politics may sound drier and less exciting than the Politics of Democratization, *Gemeinschaft*, Existence and Emancipation. But what is any radical transformation of governance worth without a solid relationship to the truth? What is freedom without an intimate connection to the falsifiable search for truth? What is the inner growth of the population, if it cannot be shown to exist? In fact, I could argue that Empirical Politics is the most radical of all that have hitherto been mentioned—the politics, if you will, of truth itself.

What could be a wilder ride than to align society with the verifiable regularities of the cosmos? After all, scientific discovery always surprises us in so many and so earthshattering ways. If madness is civilization's shadow, our only hope for sanity may lie in increasing our ability to cross-check and falsify the propositions of one another. It's not obvious and it's not naive.

HIGHER LEVELS OF TRUTH?

So what does it mean for society to be "more truthful" or "more scientific"? Here's what it *doesn't* mean: It doesn't mean that there is one category of "serious, academic, scientific, rational, empirical, logical and rigorous" inquiry and another of "weak, emotionally driven, woo-woo, sloppy" category, and that the first should displace the second in the highest degree possible. In the minds of a lot of stupid people, the first category is good, strong and respectable, while the second is despicable and feeble. And "I" am of course, always and forever, on the first side, because I have the guts to stand up straight and sober and see society for what it damn well is! And those others are delusional and cowardly. Yeah! If only everyone were like me, all would be scientific!

What is wrong with that supposition? As we saw in Book One when we discussed the different systems of symbolic code (Modern, Postmodern and Metamodern), the fundamental feature of modern science is *intersubjectivity*, meaning that science progresses by the act of people verifying or falsifying the findings of one another. Is there an elephant in the room or not; or a rhinoceros, as Bertrand Russell and Ludwig Wittgenstein once discussed in a Cambridge office? Do you see it too? By what method can we reasonably find out? How sure can we be? And have we asked the right question to begin with? All of these questions each offer a step at which others can come in and burst our bubbles and perhaps convince the audience that we are wrong—even showing ourselves that we are mistaken.

The level of "scientificness", then, is not about people thinking more like yourself. How would we know exactly who is that super-scientific and critically minded respectable person that we all believe ourselves to be? I mean, I know that *you* are, but how do you convince all those other buckos of that obvious fact? They all seem to believe—preposterously and arrogantly—that *they* are the scientific and empirical ones! But without a God as ultimate umpire, the only claim for universality and truth can come through having the most power. And if it turns out that Stalin has the most power, his truth will reign—and we will all be reading his *Dialectical and Historical Materialism,* clapping resplendently until our hands swell.

No, the **level of scientificness of society can only be measured by the density and complexity of the meshwork of *intersubjective* verification and falsification**. Fundamentally, that's what it means: the degree to which we—collectively as a society consisting of a network of people referring back and forth to one another—manage to check, double-check and triple-check the information, suppositions, methods, claims and ideas of one another, and the quality, efficiency and systemic optimization of said checks. A peer-reviewed society? Yes, why not—given that the peer-review system itself is criticized and upgraded.

I have already argued that freedom is a collective good, as are the higher reaches of human freedom—well, so is truth. Truth is not due to your intelligence or the honesty of your beautiful soul. It depends on how hard and often and fairly and efficiently and rigorously you are checked for bullshit and mistakes, and how often and well those that check you in turn are checked themselves, and how often the checkers of the checkers are checked—and so on. The finer and more optimized and harmonic this resonance of intersubjective verification and/or falsification is throughout society, the closer society is to the truth.

Is our present society close to the truth? To get an idea, we can take a look at the field of science itself. There are about 50 million published "scientific" studies at the time of writing, with about 2 million being added every year. On average, only 40% of these seem to produce replicable results (and that varies across fields; social psychology is dismally low). And if you look at how many of these research findings are "triangulated" (meaning that you can see the same finding by use of another, independent method, as to avoid any biases due to your way of measuring), you understand that much of science amounts to rather faulty towers. Critical social science and humanities are even worse off. Of all papers published in the humanities, in peer-reviewed journals, only about 20% are ever cited. The rest just pile up. Many are only ever *read* once or twice; whole careers go on like that.[108]

We seem to have reached a systemic limit in terms of sheer "knowledge production". As an emerging global society we need to start thinking about how to corroborate and solidify knowledge, how to make it travel across disciplines and social settings so that it lands in the right place, how to invent new applications and combinations of knowledge—how to increase the quality of knowledge in a general sense. Most likely, this would involve lowering the (relative) number of pure researchers and increasing the auxiliary professional functions.

The fact that science and truth are shaky is a serious matter. The greatest terrors and the darkest nights of history are born from jammed information feedback systems, when glaring truths are systematically suppressed and ignored. Communism, fascism, the animal slavery of today—these evils are, fundamentally, direct consequences of unchecked hypotheses, of terrible transfigurations of the processes of truth-seeking, of intersubjectivity violated.

From an informational perspective, the very reason democracy works (somewhat) is the same reason science works in the first place: It allows for ideas and claims to be intersubjectively scrutinized and checked. The developmental direction, in terms of attractors and "relative utopia", could not be clearer than in this case: **The society of the future, meta-modern society, must be a society closer to the approachable but always unattainable truth.**

Yes, we live in a universe of multiplicity, a universe of perspective. Yes, there is a multiplicity even of truth itself. Yes, actualities and facts are always but thin slices of a greater pie of potentialities that make up reality in the absolute. And yes, our truths are always relative, dependent upon language games, and we can never speak to the word of God, to an ultimate point of reference.

But that doesn't leave us in darkness. On the contrary, the radical insight that all truths are constructed, relative and multifaceted leads us towards a more profound relatedness to the collective seeking of truth: The ability of a society to manage, evaluate and coordinate the greatest possible number of injunctions into the truth is a measure of how truthful that society is.

Some societies are more empirical than others. Which ones? It's an empirical question. How do we find out? It's an analytical question. How do we organize a process of finding out how to be more empirical? It's a political question.

AN APPALLING STATE OF AFFAIRS

Just *how* unscientific are we, really?

Compared to an imagined future vantage point, we can be seen as living in medieval times in which people think irrationally and superstitiously, in which we know too little about most anything. We take all sorts of *ad hoc* decisions with huge consequences and most of our activities are never seriously scrutinized. The idea is to change that situation, gradually but forcefully. And this process of "truthing" society relies not upon doing what this or that "designated smart person" thinks, but by increasing the overall capacity of society for intersubjective verification.

Think about it. Each of us are very limited in scope, time, attention, patience and capability, so in almost everything we "know", we must rely upon the expertise of others. In any and all matters where such expertise does not exist, is scantily clad, or where enough people dispute it, we're simply left guessing. And *still* we manage to believe ourselves while we're making all these horrendously unqualified guesses!

It is often held that supporters of the populist Right are "fact resistant" when it comes to climate change, while they in turn say that the Left denies obvious facts about links between e.g. criminality and immigration from the Middle East into Europe. What has happened in these cases is that the civil sphere has been fractured: Different segments of the population with different sets of values (and interests) refer to different "authorities and experts" who reinforce certain worldviews and preconceived notions. Let's face it—you and I do believe in climate change, but it's not because we can figure it out ourselves, but because we believe in people who are seen as authorities by *other* people we respect and trust. In the world of the populist Right, another set of people are trusted and cross-referenced, so they can feel safe that they're right about their worldview. Science outside of the research itself is fundamentally a *reference system*, and if enough distrust polarizes civil society at large, it will fracture whatever can be seen as "scientific consensus" as well. That's what's going on.

But the appalling unscientificness of e.g. Trump voters is just the tip of the iceberg. The rest of us aren't doing much better. In fact, the differences are marginal if you look at the big picture. Take these (simplified) 2013 forecasts published in *Science*: If we are to globally make the climate goal of keeping the temperature below a 2°C increase (which is still possibly catastrophic, as we'll have more carbon in the atmosphere than for millions of years), we need to reduce our carbon emissions by something to the tune of 25 billion tons per year before 2060 (as compared to the "business as usual" scenario). Now imagine this. Reducing with *one* (!) billion tons would require *either* doubling the world's nuclear power output, *or* expanding our wind power output by 50 times (some two million new mills), *or* expanding solar power by a factor of 700, *or* using a sixth of all globally available arable land to grow biofuels to replace fossil fuels... And if we do all four (linearly increasing the output over the period 2013-2060), we are still only done with a small fraction of the overall necessary carbon reduction; four out of the necessary 25 billion tons reduced. And as things stand today, carbon emissions are still growing according to the "business as usual" scenario.[109]

Most people aren't responding to this, to the sheer quantitative immensity of the task and its rising stakes. They don't care, they don't understand, they don't inform themselves because they're not incentivized to; they don't politically support serious decisive action and they don't adjust their lifestyles. Many people I talk to really don't worry about it. Travel by flight is booming globally, as is meat consumption. None of the political parties, including the Greens, are advancing anywhere near the necessary measures. The media talk about trivialities such as making "conscious choices" and not throwing away good food. This amounts to just another splash of piss in the Mississippi.

That, my suspicious friend, is catastrophically *unscientific* behavior— and it's not a few hillbillies on the red hills of Georgia. It's the establishment; most people you will meet. It is an indication, if anything, that we live in an unscientific society—leading lives far, far removed from empirical science. It is, frankly, an appalling state of affairs.

And yet, science itself doesn't point us towards appealing to human rationality as the best means for transitioning to sustainability. Within disciplines such as environmental psychology and behavioral economics, it is becoming abundantly clear that emotional and personal development evolves our values, habits and goals in terms of sustainability. Consequently, science itself seems to point us beyond "rationality", and towards a meta-rationality that includes our emotions, relations and narratives. A scientific society would not only change our minds, but also our hearts.[110]

Breathe it in. We are far, far, *far* away from a truly scientific society. We are medieval.

THE TEN-FOLD PATH TO ENLIGHTENMENT (2.0)

So much for the Enlightenment and its modern project. In short, we must "truth" society. It must be properly truthed. It needs a good and thorough truthing. I give you… the ten-fold path to enlightenment! Enlightenment 2.0, that is.

As with so many other things this is not a binary matter, a matter of either-or, but a developmental matter, a matter of society advancing to higher stages of empiricism and critical self-scrutiny. The radicality of this process lies not so much in the general idea that polices should be "evidence-based", but in the thrust to make it an ongoing *political* project to make society more scientific in a wide and pervasive sense.

Here and there, proto versions of Empirical Politics are cropping up. In 2018, the French president Emmanuel Macron announced that his country will combat "fake news". This, of course, begs the question about who knows the truth, and who gets to say what's fake, and how fake it has to be? His taken path is much too linear, much too naive and bound to produce self-contradictions and censorship, perhaps in the hands of less liberal powers. Clearly, he does not see that truthing society is a long-term non-linear process. You can't just "press the truth button". Like I said, Empirical Politics is not obvious, not even to the prodigies of progressive European politics. And in cases like Macron's, it does get naive.

What, then, are the major areas of Empirical Politics? What exactly would our **Ministry of Empirical Politics**—or maybe just the Ministry of Science or something similar (Orwell's *1984* had a "Ministry of Truth")— be up to? I'd like to mention ten categories of things to do. We won't discuss them in detail because expanding them is itself part of the political process, and because there's ten of them. The ten-fold path.

Numero uno: The Ministry of Empirical Politics would evaluate, survey, rate and publicize the degree of evidence-based practice in all areas of public sector work and civil service. This would include everything from education to healthcare to social work to policing and forensic practices to environmental protection to all of the other forms of politics that we have mentioned thus far. What can be shown to function in a replicable manner, and what cannot? How can big data be accumulated and analyzed in each of these cases? In which areas are we driving in the dark? Together with people on all levels of society, the ministry should also be charged with making plans for how to improve the empirical rigidity of what is going on. Step by step, all public activities should become more knowledge-driven and well-informed—meaning they should be intersubjectively scrutinized, again and again.

Number two: Empirical Politics would aim to improve the quality, relevance and reliability of science, throughout all branches. It is an uncontroversial fact that universities and other institutions generally function far from optimally. Society as a whole has a lot of science out there, and this entity, viewed as a massive entirety of enough frontiers to explode any human brain, can of course be more or less efficient, well-coordinated and in line with human needs and goals. It's not just a question of how much funding science gets; it's a question of what level of *quality* science—this most crucial of society's projects—has. There is a *lot* of low-quality research that is just too sloppily made, made for show, never reproduced or double-checked, and simply never read by anyone. And there is so much stuff which needs to be done but never is, "because we don't have the resources". Science and research of course require a good amount of autonomy to function: Naturally, we want evidence-based policy, not policy-based evidence! But even that is a question of Empirical Politics: If we want a society informed by the best possible knowledge, how do we make certain that such knowledge is produced autonomously and reliably?

Number three: a cultivation and development of the critical meta-discussion about science and its role in society. Basically, if we are to have a society where things are always evaluated against the benchmarks set by scientific inquiry, we should better make certain that science as a whole and our "politics of science" are properly critiqued from as many and systematic angles as possible. This is where activities such as the philosophy of science, the sociology of knowledge (and of science, and of philosophy), applied cognitive science and the discipline that is sometimes called "social epistemology" (pioneered by Steven Fuller) are granted plenty of resources and a central role in society. This concerns such things as seeing which trends and norms are dominating within the sciences—and why—and how this spills over into society at large; or how politics and economic interests may be undermining the autonomy and validity of science; or how certain sciences unduly get more resources and attention than others; or how certain research programs may be built on shaky premises in the first place; or how certain ethical codes are not being observed... You get the picture. There's really no limit to how deep you can go on this one. Under the umbrella of all projects we think of as "sciences" (and humanities) there is just so much crazy and unfair and irrational tunnel vision stuff going on that we must make certain there is a proper critical discussion about science-in-society. Science is *not* a straightforward affair, something "obvious" that you can "just do" and then "get knowledge". It never was and never will be. New questions always arise: what is worth knowing, why, and how highly should it be prioritized, and by what processes should we decide, and how should the research be organized... Tough questions.

Bruno Latour, the philosopher and anthropologist who wrote *Laboratory Life: The Construction of Scientific Facts* in 1979 (with Steve Woolgar) pioneered the practice of studying the everyday life of scientists and their research tools and environments; today Latour's tradition is called "Actor-Network Theory": scientists whose specialty is to study scientists. People like to joke—sometimes scornfully—that then there are scientists who write about scientists who study scientists, and scientists who write about scientists-scientists-scientists, and so on. But yes, that's pretty much the direction society must take: a peer-reviewed society. It's no joke. Society must be scientific, and science itself, viewed soberly as a part of society, must also be under constant critical siege from a rich multiplicity of intersecting perspectives. Science isn't too sacred to be scrutinized: It *becomes* sacred through scrutiny. An intelligent Empirical Politics would fund and cultivate such a process of the sociology of knowledge throughout society.

Number four: We should increase the number of networked contacts and exchanges between the scientific fields—there's that magic word interdisciplinarity (or crossdisciplinarity)—as well as between the sciences and the industries, both private companies, social entrepreneurs, the public sector and other agents. You may recognize this line of thinking in economic geography, where people study things like innovation clusters, triple-helix models (the synergy of university, business and city administration) and incubators for high-tech industries. The point is that if an economy specializes within some branches of science in the global knowledge economy, say solar power or nanotech, it should also try to create pathways to putting this knowledge into the right contexts and uses. Science is one thing, science-in-society is another; it's the rich ecosystem that feeds upon the juices of discovery and in turn creates fertile soil for further research. Not only should science be improved upon and optimized, so should science-in-society. These knowledge ecosystems should be improved upon, and that requires smart Empirical Politics.

Number five: increasing the average ability for critical thinking and logical reasoning in the general population. There are, naturally, many ways of doing this. One way is standardized tests in schools that include techniques of "fooling" the minds of students, so that they must be confronted with how they bought into an illusion, an apparent surface phenomenon or a case of downright trickery. Creative projects that cultivate the public's logical and critical thinking could be funded, e.g. by means of prize contests and so forth. Coaches in logic and critical thinking could be educated and be employed as teachers or advisors within many fields. If more people identify as critically minded and "logical", this will make such norms more pervasive—and hence quackery and false inferences will be more difficult to get away with within all fields of society. Not only should more people be more apt at busting bullshit arguments—this being a skill we generally lack to a truly deplorable degree—but more of us should cultivate a deeper search for truth. This includes increased inner self-awareness; that we are trained, for instance, to catch our own minds making false implicit inferences ("this person is bad at playing the violin, so he's probably a shallow person" and all other sorts of things we make false assumptions about).

It has been shown that it is not enough to inform people of our own biases; we must be actively trained to catch ourselves before such biases curtail our reasoning. Our fundamental relatedness to reality as a *mystery* is one of the forms of inner personal depth that we discussed in Book

One; and by finding ways to awaken this spark within more of us, we can bring into being a more profoundly truthful society.

Let's speed up.

Number six: the founding of crosschecking media institutes. When President Macron wants to combat disinformation and fake news, he is not entirely off mark. But the way to increase the reliability of the media and the general discourse long-term is through cross-referenced reviews of the quality of reporting and journalism. Media outlets, journalists and writers should be checked for factuality, reasoning and presentation and be given rates and rankings. Low quality journalism should not receive public support. Again: a peer-reviewed society. How to do this in a depoliticized, fair and "objective" manner is a question of Empirical Politics. May the best suggestions win.

Number seven: the support of a **co-developmental** political culture. We don't want the sneakiest and most loudmouthed to rule us and gain power; we want the best possible common truths and solutions to emerge through the rich processes of competition, understanding and deliberation. So we need our political culture and debate to take on more civil and respectful forms. There is a tendency in all of us to admire the dashing, the confident, the winners of exchanges of clever retorts. But in an advanced and complex society, such competitions are little more than a signal interference in the information-processing that makes up society's self-organization. We need to find ways to develop beyond it, to develop political culture itself; from snide remarks and sly competition, to earnest co-development. I'm not saying it's easy, I'm saying do it or die trying.

Number eight: We could support the development of popular culture in an empirically correct direction. Whereas the arts must always remain free, it should be noted that blockbuster movies and popular outlets play a crucial role in forming people's background understanding of reality. If physics and history are presented with glaring faults in movies and books, this certainly affects the overall level of realism that can be expected from the public. Efforts could be made to support the proliferation of more factually correct stories. If people are soaked in preposterous movies 24/7, should we be so shocked that many don't react when leading politicians deny climate change?

Nine: the development of the precision and reliability of everyday language. Since so much of our lived and shared reality is mediated through language, many of our political problems, conflicts and misunderstandings stem from linguistic imprecisions and the vagueness of words. It could be a long-term project to make language more coherent, exhaustive and precise. It's one of those things that's almost impossible to measure, but the impact of which must undeniably be vast.

Ten. Phew. This one links back to Existential Politics: support of the "ontological security" of the population. Ontological security is a term coined by the sociologist Anthony Giddens, and usually refers to "the sense of order and continuity in regard to an individual's experience". The point here is, as noted earlier, that our commitment to truth and our ability to challenge our own opinions and conceptions depend upon how *safe* we all fundamentally feel in the universe. By strengthening this sense of security, we serve truth-in-society at its most essential level.

—

Ten things, my suspicious friend. Feel free to add more, or to exchange this list for a better one. But the issue remains: We need to find ways to be better at sticking to empirically sound assessments of reality.

Ice-cream does not make machinery work better, not even computers, I am not Napoleon, vaccines don't cause autism, climate change is not a hoax. If we're wrong about these things and if we make the wrong predictions, we pay an enormous price. It's *that* fundamental. All things tend to work poorly without good predictive models of reality. And yet we are *always* at some distance from knowing any number of very relevant, life-changing truths.

But you're getting the drift, aren't you? The point is that if you do these ten things in a smart and organized manner, and you coordinate all of them with each other, and you love them long-time, you will wake up one morning to a more truthful society. And I hope I've shown you that this isn't an "obvious" thing that "we're already doing". It isn't and we're not.

We really need to kill off all the excuses our lazy minds can come up with for not being scientific and committed to truth. I am not proposing scientism or crude reductionism; I'm talking about finding the best possible explanations and solutions and using them in all parts of society. There isn't a place in the world, not even within the arts, psychedelic trips or spirituality, where the truth has no relevance.

In metamodern society, "truth is God" (Gandhi said it). The point is not to obsess about "hard, rational empiricism!" with those strict eyebrows of a narrow-minded modernist, or to reduce the richness of life and existence to hard, crunchy data and chew it like a jawbreaker until the end of days. To the conventional modernist mind, truth is binary: To them, there is "the real world" and then there's the cheap copout fluff of weaker and dumber spirits. This stance is sometimes called "scientism", sometimes "naive realism".

That's not what metamodern Empirical Politics is about. **The point is to *gradually* increase society's capacity for information processing and event prediction by developing our collective capacity for intersubjective crosschecking**. This must happen at all levels of society.

Although we must all bow before the dazzling elegance of science, it doesn't offer us a safe "ground of reality", just a strange space that tunnels in all directions. Yet, in this magnificent and frightening hall of mirrors we must still latch on to the best models of reality, and we must still respect the authority of science, but only if it can be questioned by yet more universal authorities of science creation.

Empirical Politics is the cultivation of our shared commitment to an honest exploration of the mysteries of reality. Imagine waking up in a world truly committed to science on a new and higher level.

And what a wonderful world that would be.

Chapter 17

POLITICS OF THEORY

> "Once you learn to discern the voice of Mother Culture humming in the background, telling her story over and over again to the people of your culture, you'll never stop being conscious of it. Wherever you go for the rest of your life, you'll be tempted to say to the people around you, 'how can you listen to this stuff and not recognize it for what it is?'"
>
> —From *Ishmael* (the name of the telepathic gorilla guru who silently speaks these words), novel by Daniel Quinn

The last of the six new forms of politics is the strangest, the most radical and the most complex. It, more than any of the previously discussed ones, builds upon the successful implementation of the other five. If you don't have all the other ones in place, this one can and will flip out in every conceivable manner. And yet, in a way, it constitutes the very essence of metamodern politics. It is the most dangerous of all the ideas in this book. Time for a chapter of dangerous dreams, on the edge of madness, at the crossroads of fact and fiction.

At first this chapter touches on some rather general philosophical perspectives, then we get into some more nitty-gritty detail, both theory and practice. Bear with me; we're approaching the heart of the sun.

CULTURE INTO OUR OWN HANDS

The basic idea of Politics of Theory (or "of Narrative") is to monitor, steer and regulate the fundamental "theory of everything" that people subscribe to; our shared narrative or worldview. Straight talk: It's the politics of massive population brainwashing.

I realize how this sounds. But hold on just a second.

All societies more or less brainwash their citizens into a certain story (or set of competing stories) about reality, society, humanity and life. We are all socialized into a certain identity, ideology and ontology—ideas about our "self" and our place in the universe, about what's right and wrong, and about what's really real in the first place. We imbue the cultural code of our society; we are bathed in it, fed with it, marinated in it, drowned in it. Every person who speaks a language and is above a certain cognitive stage of development will have *some* kind of answers to the fundamental questions of life, and most of these originate from their social context. It's in the air we breathe.

The modern conception of a historical development towards higher levels of individual autonomy in thinking (they used to tell people to believe in Jesus, but now we're free to believe what we want) is manifestly wrong. Or, at least, it is "true but partial". As we discussed in chapter 3, the modern project and its reach for freedom is undergirded by a corresponding growth of intimate mechanisms of control, mechanisms through which minds, bodies and behaviors are controlled and coordinated to an unprecedented degree. The most obvious of these mechanisms is schooling: "Society" takes all kids at age six and indoctrinates them for twelve years. If that isn't brainwashing of an astronomical magnitude, I don't know what is: millions of people, shaped, trained, drilled, molded, taught, disciplined, controlled.

No matter how much we may tell ourselves that our educational system is "liberal" and only brings out "what wants to flourish within each person", it is obvious that such socialization must always be structured somehow, meaning, it must build on certain premises and ideals. And that in turn molds our bodies and minds. School in present-day capitalist digitized democracies isn't the same as school in 20th century communist Poland or Franco's Spain.

So the question, then, is not "should we have massive and extensive brainwashing of millions?"—we already do, and we probably must: Modern society relies upon an educational system, and all societies rely upon shared narratives and intricate coordination of people's perspectives and streams-of-action.

Rather, the question is, "should this underlying theory of everything be brought under continuous, explicit, democratic scrutiny, or should it remain beyond our reach in terms of democratic governance"?

You see—what initially may seem as the libertarian, "liberal" or democratic good-guy response: "we should let everyone make up their own minds!" is *actually* the authoritarian response. Listen to yourself:

> "NAY! Millions of people should be brainwashed and no discussion or common discourse should be held about what that entails, or why! All of us

should be taught what is thought of as common sense and no comprehensive democratic discussion should be held about it! This is freedom!"

Freedom of thought? Doesn't sound like it to me. Sounds like oppression, like authoritarianism.

No. The freedom-loving response, and the only responsible response, is to say that we will make the massive brainwashing of everyone visible rather than invisible, explicit rather than implicit, transparent rather than opaque, thought-through and well-argued rather than customary and habitual, subject to public scrutiny rather than to quiet consent, in the hands of the many rather than the few.

The initial negative response most people have to the idea of a Politics of Theory is that of "the liberal innocent". Remember this character, the one we went after in Book One? The liberal innocent is the mindset that thinks you can just take any one position within the normal Left-Right spectrum, live a "normal life" and that you will be the good guy, and that there is no blood on your hands for all the good suggestions you ignore or for all the critical discussions you suffocate. But, of course, there are no such positions of innocence. If your complacency kills, you are guilty as charged: This is either "game denial" or "game acceptance" as you have blocked real and possible "game change".

Or, as we have said earlier in the present volume, these defenders of freedom turn out to be the "false defenders of democracy".

The fact is that the massive brainwashing is already happening. People are brainwashed, for instance, to think of animals as less worth than humans and that they can be tortured for the most trivial of human concerns. What the "liberal" response implies, then, is a *preclusion* of further discussion of the most important thing of all: the social construction of reality and everyday life. That, my suspicious friend, is anything but innocent. Seriously—who's the Stalinist here?

So, yes, I am saying we should use political means to brainwash the population. And yes, I do recognize this is a dangerous idea. But the point is we're already doing it. All I am saying is that we should add a democratic discussion about it and call it for what it is. Is that more or less imprudent than the current system? Is it more or less democratic? More or less fanatic?

Should the massive, ongoing brainwashing be brought under democratic control or not? The main difference, the deepest difference, between modern and metamodern society lies in the answer to this question.

Modern society and its project of enlightenment and progress uses science and economic growth to reshape *nature* in accordance with the inner projections of the human mind—but it does not see its *own* culture and fundamental worldview as subject to change. It doesn't recognize that not only does our knowledge of the world evolve, but so does our *perspective* of our knowledge of the world. Our own thinking and our viewing of the world are believed to simply rest in the background; they are a constant, as "man" progresses through the universe over the millennia!

The postmodern critique of the modern world revealed that the underlying patterns of thought and ideas governing the lives of people can be questioned, analyzed, deconstructed, unveiled. It led intellectuals to question the universality of the modern project in its entirety.

Metamodern society takes that fundamental code, our very own perspectives, into its own hands, and shapes it, just as it shapes nature; metamodernism is the historical point when society becomes conscious of itself.

So if modern "man" boldly rode out to conquer outer space, metamodern society takes into account that the very concept of "man" and its underlying presuppositions will only last for a while and is already being replaced by other ideas of the fundamental protagonist in the universe: self-organization and consciousness, categories beyond any anthropocentric and humanistic biases. And then it—"it" being the metamodern mind as a pattern of human agency—works to reshape not only outer space, but the very perspective, the very maps from which that reorganizing is to occur. It is the conquest, if you will, of inner space.

Just as our maps of the universe, our scientific maps, are always limited in scope, reliability and applicability, so are our maps of meaning, our discourses, our narratives, our mythologies, our language structures, our "imaginaries" and "imagined communities", our cognitive schema—our social construction of reality. And, given different circumstances, some maps are better than others, and our maps must be reshaped to fit whatever conditions life throws at us, as (in)dividual persons, as states, as an emerging global civilization.

To the modern mind, *nature is the object*, the "great it" and *culture is the subject*, the "great me" who acts upon a silent cosmos. **To the metamodern mind, culture and nature are *both* part of the object, whereas the subject is the transpersonal developmental process itself.** Just as nature must be governed, regulated and controlled for modern civilization to exist, so must culture itself be governed, regulated and controlled for a metamodern society to emerge and be sustained.

"Metamodern society" is defined as a society where the modern ailments—ecological unsustainability, excess inequality and alienation—are extinguished, for all practical purposes; a relative utopia. If we want to achieve relative utopia, we're going to have to consciously and deliberately develop culture itself.

A Serpent Biting Its Own Tail

Society's cultural development and narratives about reality set the frameworks, goals and limitations for the actual applications of the natural sciences and technology. Our perspective of reality shapes how we use the forces of nature.

Today we can create all sorts of bizarre little mutants by means of genetic manipulation (there are, for instance, frogs with eyes on the back of their head created by researchers at Tuft's University, and the nerves of the frog's third eye lead to the part of the brain that registers hearing). And we can, soon enough, transform the global ecosystems and human biology itself, including the brain and hence the inner worlds of experience. We will be able to create new life and new conscious experience: extremely high and low inner states. If anything goes wrong, we can all but literally create hell.

We're talking about transformations of sentient life itself—a notion popularized by the physicist and AI theoretician Max Tegmark as "life 3.0". This life can not only reproduce itself (life 1.0), nor just change its culture (life 2.0) but can change its own hardware, its own physical properties (life 3.0).

But according to which ideals should such transformations take place? Within which frameworks, according to which goals, with which constraints? The answers to all of these questions depend on our culture. And who decides how to develop culture?

Simply put: Who gets to brainwash who, and on what grounds?

The transformation of nature is accelerated and deepened in our time; and since nature is transformed by the logics of culture, we must begin to think of how culture itself can be transformed—before it irrevocably transforms nature into something undesirable, such as unimaginable amounts of suffering that would make the Second World War seem like a walk in the park. Point being: More advanced technology requires more advanced narratives; in some sense, "better" narratives.

Yes, some worldviews and narratives are likely to be "better" than others, given certain technological/historical circumstances, and thus it is of utmost concern that the "best" narratives come to the fore and take hold.

But here's the paradox: **We can of course *only* evaluate what might be a "good" narrative from *inside* of the confines of whatever narrative we already subscribe to!** In one narrative the greatest good for the greatest number is the goal, in another it is to get people to wake up to the truth of Jesus being our savior and the son of God, literally speaking (lest they go to hell for eternity, which is serious business after all), and so on. Each of them will have us transform nature and culture in different directions, according to different premises.

Yet, again, how do we know *which* one of all the possible worldviews we should pick, given that they themselves can only be evaluated as seen from inside of another worldview? We don't, after all, have access to "the eyes of God", and so we can't see all the worldviews "from the outside". We're stuck, seemingly.

Or are we?

When our culture begins to create institutions of Politics of Theory, it takes a view of itself that is necessarily culturally and historically *situated*; culture considers how to develop *itself*. Culture becomes both object *and* subject, both the change-maker and the clay in the potter's hands. A potter made of clay (as the first man by God in the biblical Genesis), who in turn makes another potter of clay. A fractal of infinite depth. And when we begin to recreate life itself by means of bio-engineering, this takes on a whole new dimension: culture recreating nature, recreating consciousness, recreating culture, recreating nature, and so on… We are dissolving the boundary between nature and culture and diving into the depths of development.

There is no clear beginning or end to the relationship of culture to culture/nature itself: It is like a serpent in a ring, biting its own tail, an ancient symbol also called the "the ouroboros" (sometimes it's a dragon biting its tail). The Klein bottle is another image that comes to mind (the mathematical image of a "bottle containing itself" first presented in 1882 by Felix Klein). Or, if you like another image less imbued with occult or mathematical symbolism: a dog chasing its own tail.

So if we try to have a discussion about which culture is better and which worldview should be taught at schools and be upheld in everyday life, we will necessarily be like the serpent biting its own tail. Nevertheless, we have to do it, because if we fail to develop our culture and worldviews in deliberate and intelligent ways, we won't optimize the people's worldviews, and the world can and will be governed from frameworks and narratives that will prove to be incompatible with our new-won powers over nature and ourselves.

Where, then, does this leave us? Does it leave us saying that all that can be done is that all members of society will have to fight it out by arguing that their worldview is the best, and then we'll just have to hope the best player wins in a Darwinian struggle between memes? Not quite.

If Politics of Theory entails taking the development of our culture and shared narratives into our own hands, it makes a whole lot of difference *how* the dog chases its own tail. Is it stumbling about cluelessly or is it an elegant, self-conscious and playful swirl of a dance? We should create institutions that improve the possibilities of different worldviews to meet and argue about the proper balance between them.

Under the best possible settings and circumstances there is an increased likelihood that the more complex, universal, nuanced and (in a deep sense of the word) *secularized* worldviews and value-systems eventually will win out. The "more advanced" worldviews are likely to win because they tend to beat the simpler ones on their own terms. But again—that is only true over a large number of repeated iterations, under the proper circumstances of free and fair exchanges, minimally distorted by power games, rhetoric, social dominance hierarchies and so forth.[111]

Under the current historical conditions, we have democratic institutions; rights and liberties that enshrine a somewhat free and fair "market of ideas", even if distortions and manipulations necessarily occur. What we *don't* have is a proper set of institutions with the *explicit* goal of monitoring and steering the worldviews of the population. Politics of Theory would offer just that: an institutional framework for our stories about the world to come together, and for the best narrative—or meta-narrative with a set of sub-narratives—to be explored, developed and spread.

The difference between this way of thinking and the major brainwashing programs set in motion by the authoritarian communists of the 20th century is that the latter never created a framework that could let through other ideas than their own. They already thought they knew "what's right" and simply proceeded to the brainwashing part.

What I am suggesting is different: **The brainwashing should be democratically up for grabs by all contenders, and all political actors will need to specify which worldview they would like to spread and why—which means all worldviews become subject to greater self-scrutiny.**

What you get then is not that one monolithic idea someone read in this or that book gets shoved down everyone's throat, but a richer "diffraction" of many different perspectives. You know, diffraction is when sound-waves cross one another and create new patterns. We should get the best possible cultural pattern-of-patterns, and make certain it is spread in a fair and transparent manner.

That's what Politics of Theory is about; it wants your brain.

THEORY IN PRACTICE

Let's bring this down a notch and try to look at some ways Politics of Theory may be practiced. And as always, remember there's nothing more practical than a good theory, especially a theory shared by millions and touted in a thousand ways by all institutions of society.

So let's say there is a **Ministry of Theory**. An important function of this institution would be to gather rich and complex data about what people really believe about the world, trying to understand the internal structures of these worldviews, and to present these data on a regular basis—for public discussion. More on the methods for doing so below.

This institution would build up a large number of small agencies throughout society, particularly within all layers of education, and these would convey and explain certain key ideas and basic suppositions that have been democratically agreed upon. In the end it will always be up to each person what they believe or agree with, but society certainly does set up a norm-system which promotes and rewards certain beliefs and not others. This should be a transparent process.

Questions might be: Should society support democratic and tolerant values; how intolerant should it be to intolerance? Should there be a multicultural backdrop or a trans-cultural one? Should natural science be coupled with an appreciation for the humanities and for spiritual concerns? Should we have a materialistic-reductionistic or holistic-emergentist "default ontology" (the first is today's mainstream)? How anthropocentric should our worldview be? (current discourse: very!) What general timeframes should we identify with: here and now, or ten years, or a century, or even longer? Each of these questions can be answered at multiple levels; what ranges of answers should be taught and discussed, and to what extent?

These underlying suppositions—including and especially the metaphysical ones—will affect news reporting, the arts, our pastime interests, our basic frameworks for political thinking, which questions that can be asked and seriously discussed in respectable settings, and so forth. Remember the norm-system we discussed earlier? Well from now on it won't be up to power struggles in the shadows to decide upon their evolution. It will have become a conscious process.

In Book One I discussed four different developmental dimensions: cognitive complexity, subjective state, inner depth and cultural code. What we are dealing with here is the active and purposeful development and adjustment of our shared cultural code. Code systems come in different "symbol-stages" (assigned letters A-G, such as E Modern, F Postmodern and G Metamodern) but each symbol-stage can of course take many different forms, hence "developing" such code doesn't always mean to try to get to a "higher" stage.

Bluntly put, today's society brainwashes people to accept symbol-stage E Modern and, at some university campuses, F Postmodern, whereas future society should brainwash us with some symbol-stage G Metamodern stuff to go with that.

In practice, of course, people will disagree vehemently about how to rank different worldviews in a developmental sequence, or whether or not such ranking is possible in the first place, or what it means for a certain worldview to be developed. And that's alright.

The point isn't that there should be an elite of metamodernists who read a few Hanzi books and then brainwash everybody else; the point is that this process of deliberate discussion of our worldviews gets to materialize in the first place. From there on, it's up to all storytellers of society to try their best to make their story about reality the one supported by the public and its institutions. Today we certainly have stories that are supported by society's institutions, but we *don not* have organs to deal with such deep and fundamental issues in an open and transparent manner. We lack a Politics of Theory.

If such a process were to exist, this would dramatically increase our collective capacity to critically reflect upon our own worldviews, upon those of one another, and upon finding ways to co-exist and ideally develop together. All political parties would need to specify which worldview they subscribe to, and this would spur a much greater philosophical depth throughout the political discourse. Politics gets married to philosophy. In a very non-linear way, we will have vindicated Plato's old adage "until philosophers become kings":

> "There will be no end to the troubles of states, or of humanity itself, till philosophers become kings in this world, or till those we now call kings and rulers really and truly become philosophers, and political power and philosophy thus come into the same hands".[112]

Or rather, through the process of self-organization and deeper governance "the people" *become* philosophers, and in that instance, we also become kings. We begin to deliberate at a new level; we open the doors of collective perception, and we become masters of our own culture, and the fractal of mind-and-self-and-society cracks open to us as a co-created process of conscious evolution.

Doing this is risky because such institutions can be used by reactionary and anti-scientific forces (let's say Trump or Erdogan gets to brainwash the rest of us), but it is necessary as our technology and environment change at an accelerating pace, and that raises the stakes of life accordingly. If we don't find ways of becoming nimble self-transformers at a deep, collective level, we are bound to be stuck in the stories of yesteryear and get hit by an endless cascade of catastrophes as we are always one step behind the society we ourselves have created. If we recreate our environment, we must also recreate our culture and ourselves.

Seriously—**we need to have institutions that make culture itself transformable because our life conditions will change again and again.** So it's not about finding "the right answers" about life, the universe and everything (let's say we come with the answer "42") and teach it to everyone. It's about finding ways of tearing down culture again and again, to always see what lies underneath and beyond. It's about making our shared narratives more adaptable and more flexible to changing life conditions.

EXAMPLE: BIG HISTORY IN SCHOOLS

So, what would be a good place to start if we were to develop our shared narratives about the world? How about the way history is taught in our educational system? After all, our understanding of the past determines how we make sense of the present, and how we intend on shaping the future; our sense of what kind of society we live in, and where it ought to go.

It is therefore no coincidence that historiography remains one of the most hotly contested fields of all the sciences and frequently has become subject to political interference. In the past, history curriculums were largely concerned with Biblical accounts and the good deeds and glorious victories of kings and nobles so as to ensure people became good Christians and loyal subjects of the monarch. Later, as part of the nation-building effort, school curriculums came to focus more on the histories of the nation and the state. And as societies democratized, past struggles for political emancipation and victories over authoritarian dictatorships were highlighted in these national narratives so that pupils would become good, democratic citizens. Such nation-state centered narratives still remain dominant in most schools today.

But despite its many merits, this kind of history teaching has increasingly begun to be at odds with the interests of our emerging global civilization. It teaches us to think too much in accordance with linear and periodical history; it fails to emphasize the truly global aspects of societal and technological development; it overemphasizes the construction of national identities and mythologies; it overemphasizes the role of states and ethnicities in our present era; and it provides too limited understandings of the interactions between humans and the rest of the biosphere.

In recent years, postmodernism, mostly in universities, has challenged the national approach to history by focusing on topics such as the lives and histories of those who have been largely ignored or been subject to the biased perspectives of the powerful: ethnic and religious minorities, indigenous populations, women and sexual minorities, the colonized, the enslaved, the vanquished souls who never got a chance to write their perspectives into our history books.

This is arguably more in tune with the multicultural societies of today's post-colonial, global world, but it still suffers from a number of inadequacies: it's overly preoccupied with details and smaller histories, more concerned with picking apart established conceptions than creating new ones, and it offers little help to navigate a hypercomplex, ever more technological advanced and increasingly interconnected global civilization on the brink of ecological collapse.

Although postmodern historiography is better than the conventional, nation-centered one, as it does acknowledge different histories and perspectives, it has no principle by which it can coordinate and compare this multitude of histories. It simply "smashes" them together. This is obviously more inclusive than just favoring one history or one perspective, but the postmodern "smash approach" leaves us with a "history in pieces". It urgently lacks meta-narratives to link the many pieces together.

Unfortunately, the "smash perspective" seems deeply embedded in the postmodern DNA. Jean-François Lyotard once wrote that "Simplifying to the extreme, I define postmodern as incredulity towards metanarratives",[113] by which he meant teleological stories that guide or structure our explanations of social reality. And truth be told, postmodernists tend to passionately dislike all such grand overarching explanation models—be they religion, modern science, liberal democracy and whatnot. After all, haven't all such narratives eventually proved erroneous, if not downright evil; nothing more than deceptive means to oppress the weak?

But without any meta-narratives, we are left with is a fragmented and parochial view of history, too absorbed in details and devoid of any attempts at fitting them together into a greater, coherent worldview; in effect rendering history lessons into a random presentation of ODTAA, "one-damned-thing-after-another"[114], to quote the historian Arnold Toynbee—which makes it difficult to explain why anyone should bother studying history at all. How is all of this connected to my life? one may ask. One learns history, but does not develop one's relationship to history as a whole.

This can be harmful since it creates a fragmented and estranged view of ones place in the world that may contribute to a subtle but pervasive feeling of disorientation and not "fitting in", what Émile Durkheim refers to as "anomie" (the breakdown of social bonds between the individual and her community).

A way of tackling this lacking sense of belonging and direction, and a more suitable approach to history teaching in today's world—one more in tune with the emergence of a metamodern society—is, I believe, what has been proposed by David Christian, Fred Spier and Cynthia Stokes Brown as **Big History**.[115]

Big History is an emerging historiographical discipline that spans the entire history of the universe: from the big bang, to the creation of stars and planets, to the origins of life and on to humankind and the present. And as such, it is a multidisciplinary approach that seeks to present a more universal and seamless narrative that bridges traditional world history with both archaeology and anthropology, as well as natural sciences like physics, cosmology, evolutionary biology, climatology and environmental studies, all viewed as historical sciences.

Big History is thus an attempt to overcome the perceived division between humans and the natural world prevailing in both modern and postmodern thinking. Whereas postmodernism does avoid the nation-centrism of conventional historiography, it is still, for the most part, largely anthropocentric. Big History, however, sees human culture as part of nature, not separated from it. It strives for a **world-centric** perspective that emphasizes universal themes and patterns without a sharp distinction between the human experience and the earlier and ongoing evolution of the physical and biological world.

In Big History, humans do not take the center stage. The central agents are the patterns of self-organization that occur both in nature and culture. Hence, it is not we who are to be seen as the driving force behind change, but rather the patterns of change *per se* which simply manifest themselves through human beings and their culture. Big History thus expands the reach of historiography: It sees nature in history and it treats the natural world as a historical development.

This cosmological approach to history is capable of giving students a more secular, scientific and above all a more comprehensive and inter-connected view of life and society than most history courses can offer; and it permits asking the very large questions and encourages searching for greater meaning in the past.

According to David Christian, the ambition of Big History is to assem-ble all the disconnected fragments of science into a coherent and accessi-ble account of origins, "a modern creation myth" in his words. *Both* science *and* myth. I take it the good professor is being ironic and sincere at the same time. How very metamodern of him. Yet, is there any better way to provide us with an overarching narrative of creation itself?

Postmodernism has taken us to the end of the road in terms of diffe-rentiation and reductionism. Modern science became such a powerful tool of explanation by reducing the objective world to its smallest and most easily comprehensible parts. This development of increasing analytic differentiation continued with postmodernism by chopping reality down to even smaller pieces by ripping the formerly coherent neutral observer apart. What we ended up with was an extraordinary understanding of the pieces themselves, and a critical stance towards the subjective observer, but at the expense of grasping the whole. We have successfully decon-structed the world like a kid taking apart a tape recorder in order to understand how it works, but we are yet to engage with the task of putting it together again so as to hear the enchanted tones it once used to play.

In view of this postmodern condition, David Christian has argued that "construction must precede deconstruction."[116] This is not far from the metamodern dictum, that reconstruction must follow deconstruction. But to achieve this, we must accept the postmodern critique, namely that we will never obtain the truth in any absolute meaning of the term. The quest for truth can only be stated in provisional, playful terms: only a **Proto-Synthesis** is possible. The attempt to (re)construct a coherent and mean-ingful overview of world history in a cosmological context can only gene-rate a provisional synthesis, a synthesis that can never be considered final or as absolute truth. So Big History grasps this proto-synthesis and holds it with self-conscious naivety.

Does a "creation myth of our time" sound a bit naive and fantastical? Perhaps, but at least we are dealing with "informed naivety" and "magical realism"—at "the crossroads of fact and fiction". The endeavor to con-struct a new meta-narrative, stated in mythic form, is as idealistic as it is pragmatic. After all, despite all our modern knowledge and reasoning, we still seem utterly incapable of eradicating the poorly composed myths that each of us spontaneously constructs nevertheless. So why not deliberately create a better myth and have it out in the open so that we can criticize it and improve upon it?

It is a relevant question to ask if this kind of historical understanding should replace the prominent position of national histories. Would that affect political opinion and the deep frameworks of understanding shared by generations? Yes, certainly. Is it a good idea? Probably, but there is much that needs to be tried and discussed. It is no mere question of educational politics, it is more than that: it is Politics of Theory.

You can go on with similar questions: What about environmental awareness and systems' views of life? Should panpsychism (the idea that competes with materialism, arguing that consciousness is ubiquitous in the universe) be discussed in school? Or how about animal rights? We can set the stage for how people will create their worldviews. Let's make sure we do this well, and that we arrive at the "best" (or least bad) solution through the best possible communicative processes.

Of course, some people are going to think we should eliminate all traditional religion and superstition. Some are going to think that we should make everyone believe in Jesus as our savior. Some will think that everybody should be supported in critical thinking and resistance against capitalist power structures. And that's fair enough; there will remain any number of worldviews side by side in society, and people will cling to these narratives. In a democratic, free and fair process of Politics of Theory, these factions will need to fight it out in a civilized manner and affect the overall sanctioned narrative.

Those who disagree with the prevailing narrative and its balance between different worldviews will at least get to relate to an open, transparent structure, and they will be offered democratic means to state their case and to change it.

METHODS FOR WORLDVIEWING

You can't have empirical results without theory; you can't interpret data without theory; you can't have scientific method without (methodological) theory. Nor is pure theory much good without empirical knowledge. Empirical Politics cannot stand alone—ultimately it must have a Politics of Theory to dance with. Takes two to tango.

Science will always rely upon the theories of everyday life and vice versa, and so we must make certain that we as a society have the best possible understanding of our own theoretical understanding. I will be keeping this one short so as not to get overly theoretical. But I should at least list some ideas, research traditions and key concepts that may be relevant to describing how people's "theories about reality" may be studied—and which a Politics of Theory could draw upon, if and when such a thing materializes.

If there were a Ministry of Theory, it should gather expertise within:

* *Weltanschauung* (worldviewing), as first described by the Prussian philologist Wilhelm von Humboldt in the early 19th century. Basically, you try to map and study the internal logic and structure of a person or a group's worldview, particularly a certain linguistic or ethnic community. Such descriptions should be as free from one's own biases as possible and be describable to people who subscribe to other worldviews.

* **Study of value memes (and metamemes)**. People tend to stabilize their worldviews and values around certain discernable equilibria I call "value memes". These, in turn, depend upon both social (or environmental) and psychological factors, which can be studied as large patterns or "metamemes" (modernity, postmodernity and so on). There should be good data about which value memes are present in the population and what seems to drive different developments. This is a difficult and contentious issue, naturally, so it will require both a strong empirical program and cultural sensitivity.

* **Social constructionism**, as described by the sociologist Peter L. Berger and Thomas Luckmann in 1966 (or its closely related strand social constructivism), describes how people are socialized into and maintain socially constructed universes—from everyday habits to explicit theories. These socialization processes and acts of maintenance should be studied and brought under public scrutiny.

* **Mythologies and archetypes**, as described in Jungian psychology and made famous by the mythologist Joseph Campbell, and intuitively described in Daniel Quinn's 1992 novel *Ishmael* (in which a telepathic gorilla guru teaches the protagonist about the mythical and limited nature of the stories that "modern, rational man" tells himself). The idea here is that there are certain recurring mythologies, creation myths, symbols and basic ideas we all share, and that the structure of these can be elucidated and developed.

* **Narrative analysis** is a big thing in humanities and qualitative critical social science. Whenever anyone writes a text, for instance, they rely

upon a larger underlying narrative; assumptions that may be unconscious but make up necessary struts and beams for the narrative to make sense. Such underlying narratives can be studied, mapped and compared to each other.

- **Discourse analysis** is a more critical, left-leaning version of the former, based upon the tradition of Foucault. This kind of method works to see underlying patterns regarding society's power relations and whether they somehow distort how truth claims and everyday social facts are made. Hint: Usually, we're pretty unfair and biased.

- **Hermeneutics** and **the hermeneutic circle**, is a rich tradition of interpretative methods and philosophies in which one's own understanding of the world is viewed as affected by the act of studying a foreign world of understandings.

- **Ethnomethodology** (invented by Harold Garfinkel) is the study of a group's underlying assumptions and "hinted at" shared realities that make the abbreviated forms of everyday life possible. How does someone "indicate" they are a police officer, a hipster, a professor, and so on? All of this builds upon concepts that are shared and always reconstructed real-time by a large number of implicit references made.

- **Imaginaries**, a concept coined by the Canadian philosopher Charles Taylor. You can study whole inner worlds of imagined things, and how these reflect into people's behaviors, relations and society at large.

- **Studies of cultural values**, such as the World Values Survey or Hofstede's studies of the organizational culture in different countries. This is important to see bigger structures of how people think and what they value.

We could go on for much longer, naming more research traditions and pathways to create a shared knowledge and understanding about the worldviews prevalent in society—and for creating frameworks for discussing how they could be developed, spread or tweaked to become more internally coherent and harmonize better with each other. A whole book could be written about it. Many books.[117]

But let's stay with this conclusion: **There are already lots of useful** *methods* **for studying the "theories of reality" prevalent in society; we just need to start doing it at scale, in a more coordinated fashion and link it to the world of politics and democratic governance.** That's all. From there on we will have begun to take the very development of culture itself into our hands. It's easier said than done, but it's doable.

We will move *from* simply being ruled by culture, *to both* governing culture *and* being governed by it—thereby reshaping the direction of the evolution of all life on our planet.

—

That was Politics of Theory, so close to the kernel of political metamodernism. It only truly makes sense in the context of a metamodern outlook on life. Politics of Theory requires us to be ironically sincere. It is the essence of always suggesting a proto-synthesis, of cocreating a meta-narrative.

Six new forms of politics. Six new processes. Now let's take a look at how all of this fits together.

Chapter 18

THE MASTER PATTERN

"The very nature of materiality is an entanglement. Matter itself is always already open to, or rather entangled with, the 'Other.' The intra-actively emergent 'parts' of phenomena are coconstituted. Not only subjects but also objects are permeated through and through with their entangled kin; the other is not just in one's skin, but in one's bones, in one's belly, in one's heart, in one's nucleus, in one's past and future. This is as true for electrons as it is for brittlestars as it is for the differentially constituted human [...] What is on the other side of the agential cut is not separate from us—agential separability is not individuation. Ethics is therefore not about right response to a radically exterior/ized other, but about responsibility and accountability for the lively relationalities of becoming of which we are a part."

Well said, dear Karen Barad, theoretical physicist, philosopher and writer of the above quoted 2007 book, *Meeting the Universe Halfway*, in which she marries quantum physics to critical feminism and presents her view of the fundamentally relational nature of reality.

Of course, Professor Barad says it in an intricate and nuanced manner, but she cuts right to the heart of what I am proposing in this book: namely, **that society and our perspectives of it, in large part, are one and the same thing**. It is only by developing our perspective of society that we can change it, and it is only by changing society we can change ourselves in lasting and meaningful manners as society sets the limits of our perspectives.

And that's what political metamodernism does; **it develops our shared capacity to hold, coordinate and use perspectives**. That's the Nordic ideology, thus far only vaguely emerging in the Nordic countries and a few other places. These faint glimmers will grow to sparks which light flames that spread like bonfires throughout the central nodes of the global world-system.

In this somewhat longer chapter, we explore the "master pattern" of the Nordic ideology and how it connects to the listening society and how it can emerge in actual reality (through the process-oriented party and its practice of co-development).

Once you've read this chapter, you will know exactly what political metamodernism is; the goal we set out at the beginning of Book One. Feel free to open a bottle of champagne.

Let's admit it; it's been quite a journey. May your feet not fail you now; let them take you to the finish line.

RESONANZ, BITTE!

At the heart of the emergence of metamodern society lies *neither* the object ("society", the thing we're changing) *nor* the subject ("we, humanity", doing the changing). At the heart of it all lies a transpersonal process of emergence. This process can be harmonious or disharmonious; it can have greater or lesser **resonance** or dissonance.

A harmonious development of society has little to do with "harmony" as in perfumed massage parlors with relaxing elevator music—and everything to do with how well and how deeply all parts of society fit together, and thus how each one of us comes into existence as a sensing and breathing world citizen.

It's the universal problem of coordination, of *fit*. In this broken universe, most of the time, most things don't fit: people with circumstances, people with people, different parts and layers of our inner selves with each other, society with the biosphere, and so on. So we have to work to improve the fit of things so that they can evolve until they don't fit again. Ours is a broken universe, always perturbed, always striving for deeper resonance—as patterns of cymatics (sound made visible, see chapter 7) that are broken again and again only to produce more intricate weaves.

Resonance. This has become a growing theme among leading thinkers and researchers of our day, from Nancy S. Love's 2007 book on political theory, *Musical Democracy*; to Barbara Fredrickson's neurological studies of interpersonal resonance where people's affection and trust are shown to grow as they successfully and repeatedly resonate in terms of brain activity while interacting with one another (popularized in her book *Love 2.0*); to Daniel Siegel's theory of inner health and growth; to the rise of studies of complex systems and ecologies. And then there's the parallel discussion about *coherence*, which touches upon similar themes. I could go on; it's a thing, and it's emerging across the sciences.

In social science, the place to look is the German sociologist Hartmut Rosa's magisterial 2016 work *Resonanz*,[118] a thick and potent book that works its way through many aspects of what it means for a human being to "resonate": alone, together with others, as a part of society or even as a part of nature. One of Rosa's main points is that, in an ever-accelerating society of global capitalism, such spontaneous resonance becomes more difficult to achieve, and our lives become subtly impoverished as a result: His is a theory of alienation and subtle societal decay. We need to find our way back to a deeper resonance.[119]

So—by looking differently at society, can we change it? Can we offer a perspective (or set of perspectives) to resonate with the living conditions of the internet age?

Here's what I believe: The fundamental pattern of our emerging transnational society is that it is no longer modern (even if we still live in what may be called a "late modern" society); the emerging digitized postindustrial society is metamodern in its memetic DNA. We're shifting from one pattern, one societal creature, to another. And as long as we conceive of society, the world, and our place in it, from a distinctly modern perspective, we will have mounting dissonance until our ears bleed. A postmodern perspective helps us see this dissonance and perhaps remedy some of it, but it doesn't bring harmony. In many ways, it even adds to the cacophony.

My claim is that a metamodern politics—one that takes a self-critical but developmental perspective on humanity and society and its institutions—can bring us-as-society into greater resonance and manifest a deeper form of society than has hitherto existed: new forms of governance, economy and welfare. New forms of emergent networks of dividuals.

Just as with cymatics—or the structure of snowflakes, for that matter, as these form different crystals depending on temperature, etc.—you find that different developmental stages resonate differently. Now—today—we need to find the politics that resonates with the life conditions of the internet age.

All of the six new forms of politics deal with actively and deliberately creating and maintaining resonance throughout society. But not only do they address the new demands created by the life conditions of the globalized internet age; they also *resonate with each other*. They balance each other out. They hold each other in check.

They constitute a pattern; the emergent **master pattern**, I hold, of metamodern politics. To celebrate the achievements of German sociology, we can call it *ze Master Pattern*.

Here it is again, in its simplified graphic form. Behold its splendor:

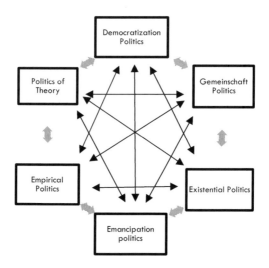

MONTESQUIEU 2.0

My suspicious friend, as you no doubt have heard, the road to hell is paved with good intentions. We need to remember that cocreating a metamodern society is risky business.

I have said it before, but it can hardly be overstated: **Each of the six new forms of politics is, taken by themselves, deeply harmful and destructive.** Each of them will lead to worse clusterfucks than we could reasonably imagine—*unless* they emerge, and develop, *together*. They are a symphony. Play it wrong and the phantom of the opera is let loose. Being the good guy or having the best intentions isn't enough, or even such a big deal. You have to get it right—your understanding and cocreation of society, that is.

This is because each of these political processes is an aspect of political *metamodernism*. In the environment of a distinctly *modern* society, each of them will mix poorly with existing institutions and cause all sorts of developmental imbalances. It's like we're on one cliff and need to make a decisive jump to the next. It's not impossible; we just need to know what we're doing before we take the leap.

There's a sequence to these six. You can start by only doing Democratization Politics, for pragmatic reasons—the world and our current society may not be ready for all at once. But before long, you must add another of the six processes, in the right sequence, until you get to Politics of Theory. Only then will you have set in motion the transformational whirlwind that is political metamodernism. And to be clear, the sequence is:

Democratization, *Gemeinschaft*, Existential, Emancipation, Empirical and Theory.

The reason I didn't tell you about all of this earlier in the book, or even in Book One, is that you first needed to know what each of the six political processes really mean, just as you needed a clear idea of the attractors ahead in terms of value memes, state formation, freedom, equality, and norms. Plus you needed to get a taste of the general metamodern philosophy. Now you can see that we're going somewhere: towards higher personal development in the population and a new layer of society. These two things go hand in hand.

Think about that when you try to communicate this stuff to others; if they hear you talking about one of the forms, Existential Politics for instance, they'll most often assume you're being naive and failing to understand some basics about the current state of affairs; that your idea of such a political process just isn't realistic. They don't see there is a new wider context within which this makes sense, and that it's only stupid and naive when viewed from within the framework of today's society.

Let's take a look at some examples of how these six forms of politics balance each other out, much like Montesquieu's separation of powers (legislative, executive and judiciary), albeit at a more indirect and abstract level—which is to be expected, as we are talking about a more complex and advanced stage of society. We'll just do a general crisscross, so you get the picture, without exhausting all combinations.

Here goes:

* If society gets "democratized" (through Democratization Politics) without there being a corresponding development of people's sense of real, embodied *Gemeinschaft*, we will gain more and more intimate control over one another while failing to actually identify with and trust one another. We will feel that the participatory and deliberative developments are not nice freedoms, but rather burdens, as we don't really "feel it" and, frankly, don't really care that much about common and public matters. We will get stuck in many more discussions and debates that fundamentally stem from lacking trust as well as lacking social and emotional intelligence. Rather than collective intelligence, we'll get collective stupidity: the whole being dumber than its parts, let alone their sum. This is the highway to hell.

* If we were to cultivate an expansive *Gemeinschaft* Politics, this would quickly get very creepy unless there are *also* deeper forms of

democratic governance. We don't want groups of distant elites to redesign the intimate dynamics of our sexual relations; such deeper power must be owned by the public, meaning that it would require a much deeper form of democracy than is presently available in modern societies.

- The same can definitely be said about Existential Politics: It must be held in place by Empirical Politics and it must be a democratically owned, open-ended and transparent process. Just imagine the avenues of New Age woo-woo taking over society with meditation, coaching, bodily practices and dumb explanations for most anything in the name of crystals, glitter and acid. I once gave a talk about Existential Politics and the discussions that followed were promptly taken over by people who thought all citizens should be given a proper astrological reading. True story.

- *Gemeinschaft* Politics must also be matched by a functioning Emancipation Politics in order to combat the new sources of oppression stemming from a deepening *Gemeinschaft*. It also requires Politics of Theory so that we can develop the underlying narrative around which *Gemeinschaft* is cultivated. And it must be complemented by Empirical Politics to ensure the many ways of improving human relations actually work in measurable, repeatable and tangible ways. Whatever we agree upon, empirical reality always slaps us back with a cascade of candor.

- For Emancipation Politics to work we must have much deeper and more embodied democratic institutions (Democratization) so that we can actually discuss and deal with all the vague and complex issues regarding boundaries of social rights and the different dimensions of personal integrity and privacy. And we need much higher standards on the truth claims—experiential and factual—in such a discussion, which necessitates Empirical Politics.

- Empirical Politics that would make everything "evidence based" would amount to a coldhearted technocracy without much legitimacy unless it is matched by a corresponding democratization, and it would be alienating and dysfunctional unless it resonates with the embodied *Gemeinschaft* of society and the shared narratives about reality (Politics of Theory). You can't have truth and empiricism without shared theories and narratives about what that means. In whatever way we may try to collectively approach the truth as a society, we will always be limited by the narratives and worldviews that we share, or don't share, and this unfailingly leads Empirical Politics to its deeper source: Politics of Theory.

• Politics of Theory, the most complex and profound of all the open-ended processes of political metamodernism, must be coordinated with the real, embodied communities that exist in society (*Gemeinschaft*) and be held in check by verifiable factual claims (Empirical), and any attempt to force perspectives down people's throats must be challenged and counteracted (Emancipation), and it must be reconnected to a transparent democratic process (Democratization), and whatever narratives and value memes are strengthened through this process must be matched by the inner development of the population (Existential). It needs all five other processes up and running in order to emerge in a functional, healthy way.

Okay, ya get it? Democratization needs *Gemeinschaft* needs Existential needs Emancipation needs Empirical needs Politics of Theory and so on. None of these are "the most important one", or "the most fundamental"; they are all part of one six-dimensional open-ended process—ze Master Pattern. Montesquieu 2.0.

Of course, these different processes balance each other out in a more abstract and indirect manner than do Montesquieu's three powers. Each of them pushes for a certain form of development, and the long-term quality of each dimension is guaranteed by the other five intersecting and challenging it. If one ring rules them all, you get either totalitarianism or fragmentation—possibly sharp swings between both.

All of this rests upon a central paradox: These are six different forces that, to a significant extent, work *against* each other! Emancipation Politics is out to get *Gemeinschaft* Politics, and Existential Politics is out to get Empirical Politics and vice versa. They aren't friends. They are enemies; they are different competing forces, just as capital and labor. The master pattern is not brought to life through one harmonizing totalizing "plan", but through a number of processes pushing against each other, refining, challenging and defeating each other. That's dialectics for you: *Realdialektik*, as we said in Book One—there is a logical, recognizable sequence to this development, and a recognizable shape to it.

This process sets in motion the generation of a self-aware and self-organizationing political culture, the hallmarks of metamodern society; a society that gazes deeper into its own structures, its own becoming, its own citizens, its own future and place in the universe. And this master pattern is self-reinforcing; it is already an attractor on the maps of history. Not because I said so, but because it makes sense.

INHERENT SEMIOTIC STRUCTURE

Semiotics, as you may know, is the study of signs and symbols and their use or interpretation. It's about, among other things, how symbols such as words are used to reference or point to objects around us: a chair, this chair, chairs in general, the picture of a chair, the chairness of chairs, something that could serve as a chair but isn't quite, and so forth.

One of the key findings of semiotics as a discipline is that there are certain structures, a certain form of logic, to symbols and their referenced objects that seem to hold true across languages and cultures. And an important and recurring theme within semiotics is the study of 1st, 2nd and 3rd person perspectives: I, you, he/she/it. That's the important part here.

I claim there is an inherent semiotic structure to the master pattern that unveils a *logic* for why it *must* be this particular pattern of interrelated political processes that emerge together.

Take a look at this:

- **Existential Politics** develops the relationship of me to myself, my subjective inner world, the relationship between 1st person and 1st person.

- ***Gemeinschaft* Politics** develops the relationship between us and us, between people in general, relating to another as a "you", in 2nd person.

- **Democratization Politics** develops the relationship of the single "me" to society, to all other people, empowering my participation and so forth.

- **Emancipation Politics** develops the relation of society to me, of how I have the right to be treated or not treated by society as a whole, by all of you.

- **Empirical Politics** puts 3rd person constraints upon what forms of relations can be had between self and society (all of the four above relations between 1st and 2nd person); it is thus the relationship between 3rd person reality and the self/society relation.

- **Politics of Theory** develops the relationship of self/society *to reality as a whole*, i.e. to reality in 3rd person. It is thus the relationship of all the first four processes (1st and 2nd person) to a commonly constructed 3rd person view.

It's a bit technical, I know. But there is a simple elegance to it: We must develop the relationship to ourselves, to one another, between self and society, between ourselves and objective reality—and make certain we stay within the boundaries of objective reality while never failing to see and act upon real potentials that may always lie beyond our current conceptions thereof.

We should be wary of being seduced by simple elegance, it's true. But sometimes, if something seemingly complicated comes to the fore in a unifying simple pattern, it means we're onto something. And today might just be that day—the day we're approaching a self-reinforcing attractor. Here it is again, presented schematically, ze Master Pattern:

1p means 1ˢᵗ person, 2p means 2ⁿᵈ person and 3p means 3ʳᵈ person, and 1&2p means both 1ˢᵗ and 2ⁿᵈ person and their mutual interrelations.

Existential Politics	$1p \rightarrow 1p$
***Gemeinschaft* Politics**	$2p \rightarrow 2p$
Democratization Politics	$1p \rightarrow 2p$
Emancipation Politics	$2p \rightarrow 1p$
Empirical Politics	$3p \rightarrow (1\&2p)$
Politics of Theory	$(1\&2p) \rightarrow 3p$

I wasn't joking when I put all of these six processes in a hexagon; they really do fit together. We certainly do need to develop society across all of these semiotic relations if it is to function at a new and more complex stage. You can't cherry-pick these processes, each of them calls forth the others—just as the structures of our language and its relation to reality call forth a me, a you and a shared world of he/she/it—1ˢᵗ, 2ⁿᵈ and 3ʳᵈ person perspective.

This is the underlying structure of the attractor point of metamodern politics. You see there's an inherent symmetry to it, which makes resonance all the more likely to occur. It doesn't mean we're determined on a set course of history or that we must submit to the ideas in this particular book. But it does mean there is something we can and should relate to; these relations are there either way, whether we like it or not. That's how historical attractor points work. I believe we're looking at one.

So there has been a common thread all through this second part of the book, even though we have covered seemingly distant and only vaguely related areas. But it's not potpourri. There is an elegant and simple order beneath the surface. Relate to it and use it creatively.

What Must Be Done

Okay, so now we're really closing in on the point: You have six new forms of politics, and these function, over the long-term, *together* or not at all, and they reinforce each other and they are already emerging in society.

But *who* then makes it happen, and how? If you've been a good reader, you already know the answer to this question. Then again, everyone might need a reminder from time to time, and there are still a few blanks to fill in.

You have two main agents in this world-saving drama: 1. **the metamodern aristocracy** and 2. **the process-oriented party**, both described in Book One. The metamodern aristocracy is the transnational networks of people who understand and embody the Metamodern value meme (and the symbol-stage Metamodern G). They also happen to have the time, energy and resources available to commit themselves more or less fulltime to working for a more conscious society. They play a key role in affecting the arts, academia, media, global institutions, political discourses and industries in a metamodern direction—whether or not they explicitly think of themselves as "metamodernists" in my terms.

You can spot metamodern aristocrats among some leading people and some less noticeable "garden gnomes" (folks who stay in the background and quietly lift a great and complex burden, largely unbeknownst to most) within the process-oriented parties that are beginning to crop up in the Nordic countries.[120] The metamodern aristocracy has a relatively clear understanding of the developmental map and the attractors ahead of us. They combine high cognitive complexity with inner depth and are relatively psychologically and physically functional and healthy. But such people remain rare. It's simply unlikely for them to emerge in great numbers in any given society.

Metamodern aristocrats play key roles and plant the seeds. But most of political metamodernism must be brought into being by wider movements. Such movements don't necessarily have to be very large in terms of numbers of participants, but they have to be strong enough to be able to meaningfully participate in the political arena.

And that's where the process-oriented political party comes in; its role is to be a vehicle for infecting the whole political spectrum with the metamodern virus. The process-oriented party gathers wider ranges of people from the triple-H population (hipsters, hackers and hippies) and what I have called "the yoga bourgeoisie", and it acts to slowly but surely spread metamodern structures throughout the political system.

Here's how it works.

The process-oriented party pries its way into the conventional spectrum somehow; this can happen in any number of ways: by taking over key positions within centrist or center-right or center-left parties; by taking the initiative within green movements, for example The Alternative in Denmark; by riding on a wave of radical newcomers such as the pirates (as in the Pirate Party in places like Germany, Iceland, Sweden or the Czech Republic) or feminists—or simply by forming its own party structure when the time is ready (the only example I know of being a small thing called "The Initiative" in Sweden). It is more difficult to imagine this thing happening from the basis of a classical Left party, a hardliner libertarian party, or a nationalist anti-immigration party. Somehow, the process-oriented party must be able to draw upon an accumulation of cultural capital (innovation, creativity, ability to manage relationships and draw attention, command over status symbols and so forth) and hence the interests and worldviews of the triple-H populations and what is sometimes called "the creative class". You need to be able to build upon the dominant ideology of Green Social Liberalism and work your way towards some version of a Green Social Liberalism 2.0.

In today's world, 2019, we have some basic elements of process-oriented politics in France's *En Marche* under Emmanuel Macron, Italy's *Five Star Movement* and Spain's *Podemos*—but they all lack a clearly metamodern political foundation (such as an underlying theory presented in this book) and none of them act within the space of a sufficiently high value meme population. Hence, they can only be premonitions of the metamodern process-oriented party and its emergence as a transnational network at the center of the emerging global polity.

So first, the process-oriented party pries its way into politics wherever it can. From there on, it begins to transform public democratic discourse by taking the moral and rhetorical high-ground in terms of how to treat others' arguments, how they stick to rules of relative transparency and how they commit to ideals of **co-development**. As we saw in Book One, co-development means you take a transpersonal, dialectical, and developmental view on politics: If you get the best possible processes for debate, dialogue and deliberation, you get the best possible politics, even as people have conflicting interests and values. It also engages more people more deeply by more systematically trying out ways for setting up meetings, idea workshops, feedback processes, deliberations and all the rest of it—hence building a versatile platform for citizen engagement.

It is hard work to get co-development right, but if you do this as your top priority, you eventually hit a nerve in every functional late-modern democratic society and the process-oriented party gains a central position.

The process-oriented party focuses primarily on the *political process* and on keeping very high standards of behavior. That doesn't win mass votes and quick landslide elections, but it makes it become the most trusted and respected of all parties—or, seen differently, the least hated by all other positions on the spectrum. It does not maximize quantitative success (number of votes), but becomes part and parcel of the most central nodes of society—respected by public actors, industries and civil society.

The party branches out, working within these different categories. It gets to the center of the network of power and it keeps up very high standards of behavioral conduct, having solidarity with the perspectives of others.

"The center of the network of power", aye? What does that mean? It *doesn't* mean that political metamodernism takes a "centrist" position. It means, because it has solidarity will all other perspectives and the people who embody them, and their partial truths—and because it works deliberately to co-develop **transpartially** with all of them, and because it attracts higher average cognitive stage folks who are more able to do so— **political metamodernism has the shortest *average* distance to all other positions**. It is closer to socialism than the conservatives, closer to conservatism than the ecologists, closer to ecologism than the libertarians, closer to liberalism than the social democrats, and even closer to the political fringes than the center and vice versa. **It is not the most popular of positions, but it is the *least hated*.** It is thus, in a sense, the *opposite* of cheap-scoring populism—and yet it can approach and deal with populism more easily than does conventional centrism and liberalism. Populism sounds exciting but is boring in terms of its potentials. Co-developmental politics sounds boring, even goes out of its way to look harmless, but it is truly radical and transformative.

So the question is not to have one strong relation or alliance. It is to have **many weak ties**, and to compete by having the most such weak ties. In network terms, you thereby reach the **highest centrality**; you are more connected than all the other positions. And as you have co-developmental ties and processes with all other positions, you also gain higher "gravity", i.e. you pull them a little more than they pull you, not least because you always have more contacts to draw upon.

The centrality and gravity of power is most concentrated to "bridges" in the network. And as metamodernism is itself often an expression of reintegrations of the three spheres of life that modernity differentiated—the professional, the political and the personal—this also means that the people it attracts are more likely to have contacts across various economic, political and cultural spheres of life. This also facilitates the concentration of power into the hands of political metamodernism.

Who would vote for such a party? In Appendix B in this book under the section titled "Too Dumb for Complex Societies?" you can read how IQ scores tend to line up neatly along the axis of the value memes represented by the political parties. If a co-developmental party shows up, the same pattern will show: You will get the smartest and highest stage constituency, and you will integrate them in a more multidimensional manner, meaning that your metamodern movement gains a disproportionately large degree of agency in politics, media, public discourse, industries, academia and civil society.

And it can and will attract people with higher cultural capital, which is itself taking an increasingly dominant position within society and the economy. You get the triple-H population and creative class on your side, combined with the higher stage populations.

Ideally, such a process-oriented party should be able to balance the "liberal" minds with the "conservative" ones in terms of what people are attracted to. As you may know, it has been shown and widely discussed during the last ten years or so, that people's personalities are at least partly genetically determined. Personality types have different biological blueprints, gearing the levels of sensitivity to negative emotions, the degree of empathy, one's orderliness and so forth. And these different blueprints turn out to be strong predictors of people being leftwing "liberals" or rightwing "conservatives". Liberal minds tend to really dislike unfairness and restraints to personal freedom and creativity, whereas conservative minds tend to really dislike disorder, crime, cheating and loafing, wastefulness, and so forth. Liberal is high openness on the Big Five personality scale, and conservative is high conscientiousness. This has been said by more people the last ten years than I could name, perhaps most famously by Jonathan Haidt.

So even if you can see a good ten points of average IQ difference between the UK Greens and nationalists,[121] for example, this doesn't mean that being more conservative in terms of personality is in itself correlated with being less intelligent; in fact, there have been many studies to suggest there is no significant difference. The essential thing to do is to marry the high stage conservatives to the high stage liberals. This isn't so easy to do, as the "triple-H populations" from where you draw the members and whose interests you represent often have *very* liberal minds, which skews the recruitment and alienates the conservative types. **But orderliness and creativity fit together; they need each other—especially in metamodern politics.** If you get this mix right, you will have a very powerful potion.

What do you do with that power? You introduce "stealable" ideas, and do so by "show it, don't tell it". You start advancing the six new forms of politics, one by one. First, you say you want to revitalize democracy (as *En Marche*, Five Stars, Podemos, Pirates and others have already been doing, only without much of a theory behind it or a larger perspective), showing everyone that Democratization Politics is a thing. As this is a powerful and competitive idea in late modern societies with semi-bankrupted political party systems, others will follow suit. Some of the Green, centrist and leftwing parties will steal your ideas and find their own twist on them, which is fine. Then you go on to *Gemeinschaft* Politics—and others will try to steal it, such as social democrats, center-right conservatives or even nationalists who seek to revive obsolete forms of social integration. Once the other parties have stolen this idea and compete about having the best *Gemeinschaft* Politics, the process will have taken hold in society... at which point you introduce Existential Politics, only to see it stolen by Christian democrats or equivalents, making it their hallmark.

Then Emancipation Politics, and libertarians rejoice at their new-found weapons. Then Empirical Politics, and serious governing parties take after. And then you introduce Politics of Theory, and you assert your own position at the center of society's deliberation about its own fundamental assumptions about itself and reality, forcing all other parties to deepen their discussions about what they really believe and why, and deepening their deliberation with the process-oriented party.

Other parties will steal not only your policies, but also your co-developmental party structures, and hence their political culture will shift and collective intelligence of governance will increase across the board.

You will then have introduced all the six processes into the political spectrum as a whole, and from there on, the six forces will be competing with each other and the process-oriented party will be at the center of this dialectical development, at the heart of the master pattern. The metamodern political program will have infected all of society with its political virus; it's a benevolent hostile take-over. And the listening society grows slowly from these forces pushing against one another: We will find a thousand new empirically sound and affordable ways of advancing people's inner development, their relations and empowerment as citizens.

That is what must be done.

MORE SINISTER PLOTS

Once all of these processes are in place, we are on our way to cultivating a listening society; this society will be much more efficient at spurring (in)-dividual development and increasing collective intelligence, and hence it will be highly competitive in the world economy. It will have an easier time attracting some of the highest value meme populations, gathering more cultural and economic capital than other regions. Because that's what all of these processes do; they improve people's lives and their relations in profound and far-reaching ways.

To make metamodern politics happen, you don't have to ask nicely. You just have to outcompete the crude politics of modern society, on its own terms. Hence, other regions of the world will need to compete by trying to copy some of the processes—and this embodied know-how of metamodern society will in itself become an important export.

These processes naturally require decades to play out and properly affect and saturate society. Hence only people who will be able to work for decades long projects will be truly motivated to seriously partake in the development. The modern welfare state took a good 80 years to build, cultivate and refine. The listening society might take just as long.

According to the late adult development psychologist and organizational theorist Elliot Jacques, people have different "time spans of discretion", i.e. the longest timeframe for a task they can undertake independently, without supervision. High stage folks tend to have longer inner time horizons, at least if we believe Jacques. So we will see a lot of high-stage folks involved in the process-oriented party, and the recruitment base will grow as society becomes better at generating conditions for such people to emerge. And from there on you have a new society, one that is able to resolve what today's society cannot, and *voilà*—relative utopia. And yes, that does include a world "saved" and oceans of human and animal suffering and degradation being prevented and a few ecstatic dances and prances at the highest reaches of human freedom.

You see it? There's an attractor point here; a bunch of interrelated processes that potentially reinforce and resonate with each other in a new way, a way that is different from modern society. And yet they are highly competitive—not in the short run, but in the long run.

Remember how I half-joked in the introduction to Book One that the metamodern aristocracy must "take over the world"? Now you see it; now you see our sinister plot. So it's true—just in a very abstracted and "informed naivety" kind of way.

The good news is it doesn't even require you to do anything evil. All you do is act very politely and be super-nice to your political "opponents" and co-develop the political realm. Learn from them, listen, really try their arguments out and work on getting a more solid grounding for your own. If you fail to act transpartially and co-developmentally, you wreck the plan. **You can even be entirely transparent about the whole "hostile take-over" plan!**

In some ways all of this is more than a little byzantine and Leninist: the elaborate plot of a small vanguard, and so on. But on the other hand it is entirely non-violent, requires no coups, no lies, no deceptions, no hypocrisy, no manipulation, no low blows in debates. It requires highly ethical and impeccable behavior, and honesty about one's own will to (transpersonal) power. That's all.

Why do you get to be part of this? I suppose some of the answer lies in the fact that you actually chewed your way through almost twenty chapters on pretty dense theory—and theory means "seeing". Now you see where we're going, or at least where I believe we are. If you can coordinate this stuff with your own life, I guess you're part of the journey—in a big or small way.

So now you have a map *and* a plan to travel it. But before we burst into clamor, let's give a word of caution. For certain, this is a sketchy plan that only works in countries relatively similar to the Nordic ones, and you will need to adjust and change the plan as you go along—co-develop it, that is.

But it certainly is better than no plan at all, don't you think? And you haven't heard such a plan anywhere else, have you? That's the meta-modern mindset for you: informed naivety, putting a proto-synthesis out and taking it from there. A sound plan, or a minimally un-sound plan—or perhaps even a sinister plot—that needs to be revised, is better than no plan at all. Take the plan, use it, and revise it.

That is, ultimately, what must be done.

SIMMERING MICRO MOVEMENTS

In late modern societies you can actually see all of the six new forms of politics cropping up already in different miniscule shapes and forms, like little fungi in the forest. If you know where to look, you can spot them.

Because each of the new forms of politics is an attractor point, they are also low-hanging fruits; i.e. people are likely to come up with ideas that point in these directions and start projects here and there. Hence you get a constant simmering as these micro movements come and go at an accelerating pace.

The reason the micro movements can only ever remain small but promising projects at the fringes of society is that they are all based on only *one* of the six forms of politics. They all lack a metamodern political theory to back them up, and they all work without ze Master Pattern. In other words, they are all left to play according to the rules and limitations set by the surrounding modern society. They don't have a plan and a roadmap so as to hack their way past these limitations, and hence they cannot gain real power, even if some of them have good ideas.

A minority of the micro movements do, admittedly, have a hold of two of the new forms of politics, but that is still quite insufficient. **What the micro movements *can* do, however, and which is exceedingly important, is to more generally prepare the ground for political metamodernism to emerge.** When they do their projects that never really take off, at least they gather invaluable experience for their participants, and at least they spread some early versions of metamodern ideas. They don't simmer in vain; they simmer with potential for a new society. They are a set of complex forces that can be harnessed and coordinated by the activists of political metamodernism.

Let's give some descriptions and examples of such micro movements. If you've been in and around grassroots activism and political or civil society startups, you will have noticed them around—perhaps you will even have joined or started one of them. Once you see the pattern, you will be able to spot them and see how they fit into the larger master pattern.

Democratization Politics has been recognized as a potential by all of those little political parties and civil society groups who seek to radicalize democratic governance. Wikipedia counts 38 of them worldwide at the time of writing; Sweden has three. You will notice all the direct democracy parties, often with creative ideas about how power could be more equally distributed; far from all of them support the idea of a crude direct democracy. There are also a bunch of innovative IT companies working to strengthen democracy by means of online communication, as I mentioned earlier, and there are people working very eagerly with methods for democratizing organizations.

Gemeinschaft Politics is prevalent among the many volunteering-based groups of civil society—and some professionals within public social work —who work to create "meeting places", "melting pots" for the cultural integration of immigrants, dialogue clubs for common issues, fora for dealing with cultural traumas, and so forth. These groups understand you can work with *Gemeinschaft* itself, with community itself, and that you can repair it, upgrade it, create new social settings and do relational maintenance. In terms of political parties, you have the Swedish Feminist Party, which deals specifically and primarily with issues of identity politics, and hence with finding ways to develop everyday relations between people.

Existential Politics in rudimentary forms exists within a lot of spiritual circles, even with spiritual political parties such as *Die Violetten* in Germany (started 2001, some 700 members), *Enhet* ("Unity") in Sweden, *Integrale Politik* in Switzerland, *Partij voor Mens en Spirit* (Party for Human and Spirit) in the Netherlands. You have these little gatherings in other countries as well. They emphasize the importance of spiritual and inner development, but do so of course without the larger metamodern framework. They also tend to be linked to peace movements. Millenarianism, magical thinking and what I in Book One called "the magic residual" are rampant here—and I mean rampant. And game denial reaches extreme levels. These groups generally attract what I have called "light pomos", people high on depth and state but low on complexity and code. So know that this force exists, but don't get too cozy with these folks; they tend to be nice guys in the not so flattering sense. Besides these New Age inspired groups, you have movements like Syntheism, and to some extent the Burning Man Festival community, which seek to explore and co-create new forms of spirituality and existential development. Also, you see civil sphere movements here and there for philosophy and/or meditation in schools, which is promising.

Emancipation Politics, or an early form thereof, exists within the pirate parties, as these specifically guard the rights and integrity of (in)dividuals *vis-à-vis* governments and big corporations. They fight against excessive surveillance, creepy control and for personal informational security. You are probably familiar with the axis of political thinking dominant among hackers and Silicon Valley people: libertarianism, anarcho-capitalism and transhumanism. All of these share a libertarian ethos and are in some way on to what could be called Emancipation Politics in the metamodern sense.

Empirical Politics shows up among all those science and "evidence based politics" parties. You have one of them in the UK (established in 2010 by quantum physicist and science writer Michael Brooks), one in Australia, there have been beginnings of such parties in Sweden, there is a *Partei der Vernuft* ("Party of Reason") in Germany from 2009—and I am certain there are more of them around. On a more promising note, within the legal profession and academia you have the strand called "therapeutic jurisprudence" seeking to find empirical support for desirable outcomes for the legal justice system, which is also arguably a kind of Empirical Politics.

The only thing we have to struggle a bit to find as a micro movement is Politics of Theory—and this shouldn't surprise us as it is the most abstract and least intuitive of the six new forms. (It was also the one I thought of last. If it weren't for semiotics I would have missed it.) And yet, it is the most distinctly metamodern form of politics. You can find it in networks and think tanks which have as their explicit goal to change the meta-narrative of society. Except for my own work at Metamoderna, I can think of two such contexts: the Ekskäret Foundation in Sweden (they have a private island where they gather people to talk about the future of society) and Perspectiva in the UK (they, especially the UK chess Grand Master Jonathan Rowson, write about spirituality and personal development connected to e.g. climate crisis). Both of these are associated with the Swedish entrepreneur and author Tomas Björkman.

Anyway, now hopefully you can see these micro movements cropping up across society—with increasing frequency as they are all responses to attractor points ahead of us. I am sure you can add more examples. For instance, basic income movements tend to have significant overlaps with some of these, as does the Dutch animal rights party, *Partij voor de Dieren*. And then there are a bunch of interesting Green movements who have some common themes with these dimensions.

The micro movements show up with the greatest regularity, and in higher quality versions, around "progressive" countries such as the Nordic ones. And they do so in tandem with the shifting political landscapes of such societies where the receding classes and parties of modernity leave room for new and more deliberative and co-developmental politics to emerge. This is part of the structural emergence of the Nordic ideology.

The secret here is, of course, not to get stuck in the partial narratives of any of these micro movements—quite a few of them are steeped with glaringly incompetent folks on the fringes, so don't gorge on the mushrooms. Rather, the secret is to be able to see them from the bird's eye view offered by the master pattern. When you go ahead to introduce political metamodernism, others will try to reduce your project to one of the six dimensions and some will try to pin the failures of any of the micro movements onto you. Don't let them distract you.

This, my dearest comrade, is **non-linear politics**. We're not going from A to B in a straight line; we're playing the field of potential to let things emerge. The task is to draw upon these micro movements and find ways to channel them and coordinate them—to **play strategically to align all these forces with the emergence of a metamodern society**.

TROUBLE SHOOTING / FAQ

Okay—by now we've got it down. But new questions and problems of course pop up as our understanding grows. Some of these would require longer discussion, but we need to keep it brief in order to close this second part of the book. I'll just go at it.

> "Statism! Ah, my good Dr. Freinacht, interesting ideas, but all of this is within a *statist* paradigm (you think of changing society through conventional state-based politics), and the state is losing its grip and we need to think in non-state terms! Facebook and Google are beating the CIA! Besides [adds the libertarian or anarcho-capitalist] the state is evil, as it is based upon a monopoly of violence!"

Good point. With the emergence of the internet, the truly global markets, increasing freedom of movement, the growth of megacities with very powerful administrations, global super-corporations, an exponential increase of transnational NGOs, and a thickening layer of supra-national structures—not to mention crypto currencies and other applications of blockchain technologies—it is understandable that some people see the state itself as withering away. Of course, it is well known that the predictions of political sociology and libertarian economics from the 1990s concerning the end of the state were exaggerated. Rather, what we are seeing is the transition to a world in which the state takes a less dominant and more partial role in governance and the coordination of human agency. There is still plenty that can and should be done through conventional politics.

That being said, I'd like to stress again that even if other means of action-coordination take over and prove to be more dominant in the coming period, they *still* have to deal with all the six dimensions. So whether it's corporate or federal or supra-national or local or pertaining to the civil sphere or "pure market relations", you can still apply these six dimensions and coordinate them and try to make certain they balance out. The pattern holds either way; you just have to adapt it to the forms of governance that turn out to be dominant in the future.

But the state isn't the hero of this story and neither is any other specific mode of governance. The new heroes are the transnational networks or tribes of people who subscribe to metamodern values and ways of think-ing—the metamodern aristocracy and the process-oriented party are but two examples. **What the Nordic ideology is getting at is not for a pater-nal or motherly state to take care of us and wipe our behinds. What it does is to create a solid background or generative foundation for peo-ple to *swarm*. For networks to swarm.**

Yes, swarm. Just as the micro movements are popping up, so are lite-rally thousands of fascinating projects, with such a diversity and complex-ity that we can hardly imagine it. These are showing up because there is a rich plethora of networks of people across the world who share interests and find compatible skills to do things together—often for other reasons than monetary gain.

These self-organizing swarms of people—and the larger super-struc-ture of interacting and intersecting swarms, which is in part shaped by the new dynamics of the internet—these transpersonal entities of agency are the heroes of our time. In the last instance, this rich multiplicity of agile collaborating human beings is most likely to respond flexibly and accur-ately to the multidimensional challenges that the world faces, and most likely to be able to see the great potentials. Politics, for all its power, is al-ways constrained by the many. Smaller groups of like-minded and com-patible people are *not*. So whatever we *can* do to facilitate the emergence and agency of the networked swarms, we *should* do. The listening society, even in its early forms, empowers people to partake in such shared pro-jects that come and go. Such projects, in turn, strengthen the potential for all of the six new forms of politics, not least through the accumulation of micro movements.

"But what about climate change! The runaway climate doesn't have time to wait for generations of shifted human consciousness."

The transformation to metamodern politics and a listening society can hardly be expected to suddenly get all countries of today to sign a satis-fying climate agreement. That work needs to proceed within the dissatis-fying boundaries of the here-and-now of international politics. But that does not mean it cannot get help from the emerging metamodern struct-ures. And if disaster does strike and we get a 5°C or more rise in global temperature or an AI or nanotech induced calamity in fifty years, we're going to need every bit of the metamodern layer of governance we can get to handle the crisis at all. Regardless of how you look at it, metamodern politics is what must be done. Also, the abovementioned transpersonal swarms are needed to solve the climate crisis—so let's create a society that empowers them in a far-reaching manner.

Besides, do you really think you will get even the resemblance of good environmental politics without Empirical Politics? Think again. Do you think you will get biospheric and deep-ecological consciousness in the general population without Existential Politics and Politics of Theory? That, my friend, is *un*informed naivety.

❚ "Elitism and arrogance! Self-flattery! Exclusive club!"

You are right to worry there are some pitfalls here: If we think of ourselves as "the metamodern aristocracy" we may be deluding ourselves and falling for seductive self-flattery and patting each other's backs. It may even invite megalomania, undue immunity to the perspectives of others deemed "less developed"—and less-than-epic marathons of the Dunning-Kreuger effect may follow.[122]

We do, however, have a couple of safeguards against this. One thing is that the developmental models presented in Book One include at least some measurable aspects. Hence, it is possible to check oneself and one another for realistic expectations in terms of our capabilities. People of very high complexity tend to have a rich history of groundbreaking innovations.[123] You can check if someone understands the metamodern code or not by asking them probing questions: Either they can describe them correctly and reason independently around them or they cannot. As for ourselves, we can check for inner states and depth and hopefully be able to assess ourselves realistically: If you didn't have a cosmic full-body orgasm last night, you're not *that* high state after all, etc. And then there's always the general "know thyself"; we all have lots of weaknesses, even if we happen to have this or that developmental property. As long as humans are involved, it is unavoidable that a certain degree of elitism and unproductive arrogance sneaks in.

On the other hand, political metamodernism needs to be elitist in the sense that it has to target and engage highly competent people of high effective value meme. This, of course, leaves out most of us. But it is, after all about "saving millions of lives". And it doesn't make sense to charge such a project with a demand that "everybody should feel welcome" and be included. At a minimum, you need to be able to read this book and critically reflect upon it, and you need to have the time and opportunity to do so. We're doing serious and dangerous work here; we need to be relatively exclusive and hold ourselves and one another to high standards. If you want to play professional football or do heart surgery, you need great skills to do so—same goes for doing metamodern politics. What can and must be avoided, however, is that unfair biases exclude people from taking part, or that people are unnecessarily alienated. Other than that, meta-modern activists don't owe it to anyone that they should be included. No apologies made.

And then again, seeing as political metamodernism is a virus which aims to eventually infect the entire political spectrum and then nimbly surf the dialectics that flow from competing political parties, it does actually include "everybody". Metamodernism works by finding ways to include the deeper partial truths of people's perspectives and to have solidarity with these: and in that sense it is *not* exclusive at all. This is true not least because, if people are empowered by a listening society and have much better relations and inner development, they will be able to act freely in swarms. So it's not elitist in that sense.

A word of warning: If you commit to working with political meta-modernism, people will try to use the charges of elitism against you. Some of it may be warranted, but some of it is *Sklavenmoral*; i.e. insincere calls for humility to stop you from making truth claims that conflict with their own ideas. It's not always simple to tell the difference, and it takes practice, and sometimes it may be a combination of both. Just be kind and polite, don't get derailed, go home and reflect and be kind to yourself and remember you don't owe them any excuses.

"This is the 'Nordic ideology'… What about the US?"

Since many readers are from the US, this question comes up: As a country, the US has the world's largest metamodern population in absolute numbers, a relatively dynamic market economy and a strong civil society—but unfortunately also a rigid two-party system, with wealthy special interests holding too great influence over politics. Arguably, this hinders any successful execution of the "sinister plot" as outlined above. Besides, the US bureaucracy as a whole has been on a steady decline for decades and it may be difficult to build a new layer on top of it: too much rotten wood. So you are right to wonder what could possibly be done to create a significant force of political metamodernism in America.

Fundamentally, political metamodernism is a global project. It calls for, as argued by some political thinkers (such as philosopher James Tully), **for an expansion of citizenship itself**. So the main task is to make it take hold *somewhere* in the world and to begin to compete on the world market, leading by example. And that "somewhere" doesn't have to be over the rainbow.

It is easier to imagine such transformations occurring in small, nimble states with highly functional bureaucracies. Metamodern activists who are

US citizens **may find it wiser to think transnationally and to help out metamodern activists in other parts of the world first**. They may also focus on changing society within the boundaries of smaller progressive cities, such as Boulder Colorado or San Francisco. Simply building a transnational network of metamodern activists can facilitate future entrances of metamodernism into US politics. And surely there must be more pathways for the creative.

▌ "Democracy in China?"

Yes, the question of democracy in China may be a fateful one for the direction of the world-system as a whole. The clock is ticking, "the countdown for democracy", as discussed in Chapter 10. As American hegemony is waning, Chinese power seems to waxing and an increasingly confident Chinese government has begun to challenge democratic powers and values head on—for instance by imprisoning a critical journalist and Swedish-Chinese citizen after arresting him in Thailand, charging him with fake crimes—and then telling the protesting EU countries to, more or less, go take a hike. At the same time, China is expanding its infrastructure and foreign direct investments so as to interconnect the Eurasian continent around a central Chinese hub while boasting that they seek to spread their form of governance in the world—all the while retracting on independent assessments scores of democracy and freedom.

Even more frighteningly, the Chinese government censors the internet—lately they got rid of Winnie the Pooh (true story, this was after people started using the yellow stuffed animal as a symbol for their leader XI Jinping) and, more tellingly perhaps, they have banned George Orwell's books *1984* and *Animal Farm*. It is safe to assume that anybody who has something to fear from Winnie the Pooh certainly has a lot to hide.

China even has a surveillance system that scores citizens for their degree of complacency, "Sesame Credit", affecting every aspect of one's life and career opportunities within the country. University professors in Australia and elsewhere complain about the easily hurt and offended Chinese students who will tolerate no slights against their country's government. And of course, Xi Jinping is breaking the tradition of passing on power by staying in office for a longer period than what has been custom.

And yet, this bold new China has a strangely alluring power, not least as its authoritarian system allows for holding back consumption in favor of investments; and these investments can more easily take on more long-term goals such as large and admittedly dazzling infrastructure projects and transitions to sustainable energy (being the world's greatest solar cell producer).

Could then political metamodernism find its way to the Middle Kingdom? Could it offer paths to democratize China? It is clear that Chinese society is pretty far away from anything like political metamodernism. But there is always a chink in the armor, always *some* unseen potential. If you think transnationally, it is possible to imagine that some lead-by-example parts of the world could inspire Chinese leadership and some of its population. For China, going directly for metamodern politics may be a more appealing route to create "a listening society" with all six new forms of politics than first transitioning to modern liberal democracy. This, however, can and would be very risky since Chinese society at large would be entirely unprepared. Hence crude and perverted versions of metamodernism could turn into totalitarian nightmares and/or collapse. Remember what causes pathologies above everything else, as discussed in Book One: developmental imbalances. If you try to use metamodern ideas from a, relatively speaking, immaturely modern mindset, and you have the unchecked power to do so, it can get *very* ugly.

Even as things stand today, Chinese authorities and its state-controlled media attempt to portray the Chinese system as a "direct and/or deliberative democracy" which they claim is more in tune with the cultural heritage of China—sometimes with the help of bought Western academics. They try to hide the crude dictatorship behind the thin mask of "another system", of supposed radical deliberative democracy.

On the one hand this suggests that Chinese intellectuals and leaders may want to take up political metamodernism in the future (they're already talking the talk, maybe that will lead to some attempts to walk the walk); on the other hand, it suggests metamodernism may find its most perverted expressions in China. Perhaps we will even live in a world ruled by a superpower that oppresses us with manipulative and intimate technologies of surveillance and control.

We have all the reason to shudder. I'm not optimistic about the matter, but the question about China's role remains unavoidable. The best way ahead is to try to see and affect the attractor points at the earliest possible stage.

"The economy! The economy!"

A very important aspect of all this concerns the evolving economic system and its changing characteristics at the centers of the world-system and the hubs where cultural development has progressed the farthest.

Many readers will feel this analysis is incomplete without seeing how it relates to the economy and, to some extent, to post-capitalism and the rise of cultural capital—and how all of this connects to the listening society and to increasing the average effective value meme. This will be addressed in my other book, *Outcompeting Capitalism*.

Still, though, it should be underscored that the obsession with economics can prevent people from understanding the main points of this book. And the ideas presented here do make up a coherent whole and they can be applied even *without* a further structural analysis of the economy of the internet age. Suffice to say here that the listening society transforms the economy across all six dimensions of inequality and thus brings about greater agency in the world. This means that resources are used in more efficient ways in terms of happiness and ecological footprint. Hence, political metamodernism and post-capitalism are married to one another.

> "Wait! Please, *again*. And how did all of this stuff about six new forms of politics relate to the development of a new layer of governance called 'the listening society', to raising the average developmental stage of the population, to higher freedom, deeper equality and the development of 'better' norms in society come about? And how will that 'save' us?"

Okay, you just summarized the entire book in one question. The point is that if all of these six forms of politics are instituted and affect people for decades, they will together, in many and complex ways, change us as human beings and change our relations to one another. They are developmental forms of politics, each aiming at dynamically changing subtle parts of what it means to be a human being. Hence, the human life-course will change in its entirety, and new patterns will emerge throughout all of society. As psychology, behavior, culture and system develop, humanity will self-organize in new manners, and all of life will be recreated. Maybe that won't "save" us. But it might give us a flying chance. And that isn't so bad.

> "And how does all of that connect to general cultural metamodernism? Magical realism, pragmatic romanticism, informed naivety, proto-synthesis, transcend and include, both-and thinking, reconstruction following deconstruction, relative utopia, transpersonalism, dividualism, the view from complexity and attractors, fractality, the death of the liberal innocent, super-secular but radical spirituality, the expansion of arts into all realms of life, a non-deterministic, self-critical developmentalism and sincere irony?"

Nice punch. The point is that if you have this cultural background understanding, this kind of embodiment, you are capable of planting metamodern seeds throughout society. Without this battery of breathed and lived understanding you can still play a part, but you cannot be that real change in the world because you'll get stuck in the contradictions of modernism or postmodernism. **Ultimately, you need to *be* metamodern to *do* political metamodernism.** Even if the metamodern emergence is transpersonal and can consist of patterns of a lot of different bits scattered over many different people (like a "bit torrent" download), there still need to be some central actors that act more deliberately and consciously. A metamodern society cannot emerge without metamodernists.

"Lastly, then: How do we get to a transnational metamodern world order?"

Again, I'm glad you asked. This dialogue is promising for any future co-creative collaboration between us.

The goal here is to hijack governance structures of nation states, city administrations and perhaps companies or the UN and use them to build a transnational layer of governance while competing on the world market by cultivating a listening society. The nation state is slowly transformed into a part of a transnational meshwork and people's need for belonging and meaning are fulfilled in other ways than through nationalism: *Gemeinschaft* Politics, Existential Politics and so forth. If you lose the control of some areas, go elsewhere, keep playing, help each other.

Basically, we need to found something like **The Transnational**. Much like the communists had the International (there is and have been a bunch of them, including socialist and anarchist ones). And then we conspire (the literal meaning of which is: breathing together) openly and transparently to change the world with transnational, transpartisan, nonlinear, co-developmental politics with a view from complexity. We improve upon the code, strengthen the network, gather key competences as we sensitively try to understand the twists and turns of the world-system. We look for places of opportunity, globally. We look to places to act, for ways to engage—for "pressure points" we can work on; for the right moments. We work on our relationships to each other and we help one another out.

With sincere irony, we work and play patiently to increase the potentialities and likelihoods of radical metamodern emergences in the world. There's always a glimmer somewhere.

—

And that concludes this second part of the book. That's the Master Pattern of the Nordic ideology; the seeds of which can bloom into transnational political metamodernism resonating throughout the world.

PART THREE

The Proof: Nordic Ideology

Chapter 19

REQUIEMS FOR MODERN IDEOLOGIES

"Soon to fill our lungs the hot winds of death
The gods are laughing, so take your last breath"

—*Fight Fire with Fire*, by Metallica

Remember what I promised on the first page of Book One? I contended that political metamodernism beats all the modern ideologies on their own terms: It is more egalitarian than socialism (and social democracy), freer than libertarianism and classical liberalism, more sustainable/resilient/regenerative than ecologism, more sensible and prudent than conservatism, and more radically rebellious than anarchism. Now it's time to deliver on that promise.

This third and last part of the book is, by the way, much shorter. It only has two chapters, one on mainstream modern ideologies and one on the totalitarian ideologies of the 20th century—and then an epilogue that closes both Book One and Two on this metamodern guide to politics.

SUBTLE MEMETIC REVOLUTION

The main work of this book is done.

Now that you have learned what the Nordic ideology is, and how it aims to construct a listening society with six interacting, ongoing political processes, we can look at each of the modern ideologies and see how they don't hold up against political metamodernism. Defeating them in theory is one thing, but outcompeting them in practice may of course be a more complicated affair. At least we are given valuable hints about how it can be done. And we get to pan out some ideas about this "Green Social Liberalism 2.0" in the process.

People stuck in the modern ideologies all resist the Nordic ideology: people with conservative minds think it's almost identical to socialism (it's not), leftists consider it a cheap sellout and a betrayal—a kind of neoliberalism—libertarians find it overbearing with state control and downright totalitarian, anarchists think it's mainstream centrist liberalism, centrists that it is dangerous fringe extremism, and nationalists see it as an radical form of dehumanizing globalism. Ecologists come a little closer; some of them can see what it's really about, but most of them just think it's weird and that it focuses suspiciously much on human happiness and too little on poisoned creeks and acid rain.

And yet, all of them also find metamodern practices such as co-development, process-focus and deliberation to be signs of weakness and wishy-washy. They are not. And they find ironic sincerity to be either naive and harmless, or vague and insincere. It is not. But we can let them think so because it makes it difficult to see us coming. They won't know what hits them before it's too late.

Political metamodernism touches upon and comes strangely close to all of the abovementioned positions. But since it is not entirely identical to any of these, it does provoke allergies in all of them. Yet, metamodernism provokes somewhat *less* resistance than each of these do to each other. The winning point is, as we have seen, that political metamodernism is closer to all the other positions than they are to each other. For instance, if we look at the "space" within which all of the modern positions exist, political metamodernism can move in an extra dimension, and hence "fold through" the conventional ideological spectrum. **The result, then, is that metamodernism has by far the shortest *average* distance to all other points in the modern ideological space.** In the "conceptual space" of modern ideology, political metamodernism has the highest centrality. And that's where the power is.

So even if the Nordic ideology has few explicit followers, it is still, on average, the least despised, and thereby capable of gaining the greatest centrality and gravity within all power networks: political, economic and cultural. The emerging Nordic ideology has as its ultimate adversary not any specific modern ideology; they are only stepping stones to get to the real enemy: modern society itself.

The modern ideologies all shout their messages and practical concerns at their best—but under their breaths, they are all whispering chants for the invocation of the Nordic ideology. There is a deeper resonance that chimes between the partial truths represented by each of the ideologies, subtle and hardly noticeable, but quite pervasive. Listen hard, and you can hear it: It is a requiem for modern ideologies and a hymn for the advent of metamodern relative utopia.

Yet, the task is, as we have seen, to beat all of these ideologies at their own game, to infect them with bits and pieces of political metamodernism so that metamodern society emerges through the interactions of all the different modern (and postmodern) forces. Our sinister plot is, as shown earlier, to sneak up on all of them and "remote control" them in a decentralized, co-created and dialectical fashion until they're all caught in the metamodern master pattern and thus begin to work towards the attractor points of deeper equality and higher freedom that come from a listening society through the tragic dance between dividuation and integration.

And because we, the metamodernists, have the arguments and ethics on our side and the historical attractors are working in our direction, we don't need to be secretive about anything. We just need to communicate sensitively and effectively.

That doesn't mean you automatically win all debates and that there is nothing to learn from your modern interlocutors; it just means that on average, over time, we win out. We can lose battles, even wars—but we need to make sure to win the world war. Many iterations later, memetic evolution lays its verdict and condemns the statistical losers to death. In this memetic game of likelihoods, you win or you die.

The aim of this subtle memetic revolution is, by extension, to stage a hijacking of the democratic parliamentary party system under the non-linear and co-developmental leadership of the minority process-oriented party. Political metamodernism is supposed to infect and eventually kill off the host ideologies. This is why the Nordic ideology is a sworn enemy of liberal parliamentary democracy—it seeks to transcend the modern divisions (and of course, this will land us in new ones).

Since the Nordic ideology works to transform the basic institutions of society, it is also an enemy of modern society itself. Kind and transparent as we must remain, we must unapologetically crush our memetic enemies; crush the defenders of liberal democracy in its current form.

Hey, if modernity and postmodernism didn't want to die, they shouldn't have given birth to us.[124]

At the same time, bound by metamodern ethics,[125] metamodern activists work hard to have solidarity with the embodied carriers of all perspectives and to acknowledge the suffering that memetic evolution entails.

People aren't *actually* your enemies; they are just folks invested in out-dated memes.

Power and kindness, both. Both-and. Ruse and tenderness, guns and roses. Just remember that applying "both-and" isn't throwing around a catch-phrase; it takes life-long commitment and relentless practice. It takes a painful stretching of the mind and soul. And it is unavoidable that we often fail at it.

Let's go on. Starting with socialism, we shall now solemnly spank the modern ideologies. The key here is that each of them must **be beaten on its own terms**. This is exceedingly important. The better you are at taking the perspectives of others—and empathize with them—the greater your ability to defeat them. Whoever has mastered the most perspectives when they die, wins.

You can't win over the fascists by telling them they're evil—they'll be flattered and take it as a badge of their edginess and toughness! Why do you think they got those bad tattoos in the first place? You can't go after the libertarians accusing them of being elitist and selfish; they'll smirk and enjoy thinking they're John Galt. Nor can you tell ecologists and socialists they're being naive; they'll take it as a validation of the purity of their souls and poetically flip a few more pages of Rousseau. You need to show each of them that, unless they accept metamodernism, they will end up being *the opposite* of what they identify with.

You kill fascists by revealing their inner weakness (as intellectuals have done since the Second World War); you destroy socialists by revealing they aren't really egalitarian—and you bring down liberalism by showing that it's authoritarian. Relatively speaking.

You must show the adherents of each of the modern ideologies that if they accept premise and goal A, they must also accept conclusion B. In this case that conclusion is political metamodernism. If you want to be a good socialist, you have to accept that a listening society is far more egal-itarian than anything Marx or Lenin ever came up with. If you want to be a freedom-loving libertarian, you have to accept that the Nordic ideology holds far greater prospects for human liberty than Nozick's imagined minimal state or Ayan Rand's John Galt land could ever deliver. And if you want to be a tough masculine badass, nothing is more potent and explosive than being a die-hard metamodernist.

That's *Realdialektik* for you; an attractor point. All roads lead to Rome —not by the triumph of the will, but by the triumph of dialectical reason-ing.

Roll up your sleeves.

MORE EGALITARIAN THAN SOCIALISM

The fundamental goal of all authentic strands of socialism is to attain shared (and fairly distributed) ownership of "the means of production". This can and should lead to democratic control over said means of production. But this state of affairs is not quite the goal-in-and-of-itself; it is merely a means to achieving a higher socialist goal: a classless society that is fair, equitable, and in which everybody has what they need for a secure and dignified existence. The goal is to enact politics with solidarity in order to bring forth a society that is equitable, the structures of which make possible wide and deep solidarity between all people, which in turn emancipates the human soul.

The idea of socialism took root in the wake of capitalist industrialization, although the word originated as a derogatory term already in the mid-1700s as Catholic theologians criticized the legal philosophies of Grotius and Pufendorf who had the insolence to think that law should be based upon the relationships between people rather than divine revelation. Such "socialists" wanted a societal order defined by human relations.[126] And modern socialism echoes some of that original meaning: Socialists want the economy—and thus everyday life—not to be ruled by any blind, mechanical system, but by the relations between sensing and thinking human beings brought into benign relation with one another.

There are, naturally, more forms of socialist thought and practice than we could possibly deal with in this context—from Proudhon to Marx, to Bernstein's democratic reformism, to Rosa Luxemburg, to Western humanist Marxism and Freudo-Marxism and their "New Left" and so on. But it is safe to say that anything falling outside of the above delineated boundary (in regard to the means of production and equality) is not "socialism" in any meaningful sense of the word. By going to the root shared by all socialists, we can compare socialism as a general category to the Nordic ideology.

The socialist goal is an equitable society, not merely in terms of opportunity, but also of outcome. Because so much of society is always and forever bound up with the situated social relations between people, it is unavoidable to also seek to level out the outcomes in terms of income and wealth—otherwise the privileges tend to stack up over time: wealthy family dynasties, economic classes, cartels and monopolies, corporations that flee from social responsibility and taxation, and so on. So if you don't care about outcome, you will end up reproducing inequality of opportunity as well. And only if people are reasonably equal can they resist exploitation, and only if they resist being exploited can they be free and fully human.

And right there is the killing point, my dear comrade. If you have the goal to create a fair and equal society, you must also support equalities of outcome to some extent.

Can you get equality of outcome without a developed *Gemeinschaft* Politics? No, because there will be so much social, emotional and physiological inequality left, and these will reproduce new forms of inequality. The "classless" society in an economic sense is a very superficial utopia: Most of the intimate and hurtful inequality remains, and the stakes cannot be fair by any means. Inequality is economic, social, physiological, emotional, ecological and informational—and all of these are interconnected. Only metamodern politics can address inequality at that level of complexity. Without it, you will never get a classless society.

And even if "everybody" would own the means of production together and manage them democratically, this process would always be limited by whatever form democracy takes. **If the mode of governance is not itself a process of incremental and self-critical development, you will always be stuck with the power relations inherent to that particular system.** So without Democratization Politics, you cannot actually have socialism in any real sense.

Both *Gemeinschaft* and Democratization Politics require the other four new forms of politics to function. Thus, you simply cannot call yourself a socialist unless you also accept political metamodernism. All said and done, the Nordic ideology is more egalitarian than socialism.

Where does this leave the Left in its existing modern and postmodern forms? If political metamodernism charges ahead and becomes the standard bearer of a more embodied and deeper equality—connecting specifically to the emerging postindustrial and digitized economy—what purpose does the residual old Left have to play?

To understand this we may look at the role of Christianity during the 19th century. There can be little doubt that the fundamental "game change" shifts of this period were made possible by the emergence of a distinctly modern society: abolition of slavery, protests against rapacious exploitation in the colonies, the expansion of suffrage, the early forms of welfare. But—and this is a *big* but—radical born-again Christianity played a pivotal role in the mobilization of social movements and moral demands during this period. Hence, you can see how the morally driven "utopian" movements of the *former* metameme (postfaustianism) finally managed to reach the "low hanging fruit" that came into reach by the maturation of the next metameme—in this case *modern* society. The born-again Christians and Pentecostals were hardly the "most enlightened" or "most modern" citizens of their time; but they emphasized relatively simple and specifically moral and collective demands that had now finally become realistic and achievable. They weren't fans of Darwin, and *still* they had this progressive role to play in history.

That is the future role of socialism and the Left more generally in an increasingly metamodern world-system: being a source of popular moral mobilization within metamodern society. A lot of the things postmodern intellectuals and social movements may have wanted to achieve—animal rights, levelling-out international terms-of-trade, protecting the unemployed from marginalization and stigma—can become much more feasible in a society that is taking steps towards metamodern institutions, not least because it will make the average value meme and norm systems develop more rapidly. We may perhaps not be looking at a "socialism in the 21st century" as many like to imagine (i.e. viewing the Left as the key force in organizing and governing society in the period ahead of us), because it will be outcompeted by political metamodernism. And it will be torn by the populist Right and new versions of conservatism from the other side, and it has no present-day real-world governments to point at as positive examples. But just as Christianity was dealt its fatal blows during the 19th century and still managed to be morally transformative, so can the Left be a stepping stone for moral transformations in the 21st century.

MORE LIBERAL THAN LIBERALISM

I will lump together **classical liberalism**, **libertarianism** and **neo-liberalism** under one banner, much like with the many strands of socialism above. For the sake of convenience I'll talk about "liberalism", even if this in an American context tends to just mean "left-leaning" which of course isn't what I mean here.

So the fundamental goal of liberalism is to maximize the freedom of the individual. It is hard enough for each of us to figure out how we should lead our lives and what is good for us and our kids—let alone know what might be good for others. Hence, it is unwise to put too much of your life into my hands and *vice versa*. This means that the realm of the public and the political should not unnecessarily infringe upon the private sphere and the voluntary exchanges on the market. Rather, government should be stretched only so far that it guarantees our protection from one another and ensure that we don't breach our freely entered agreements: As long as you don't do anything that directly limits or harms me, you should be free to do it.

There is, to a considerable extent, a trade-off between how much should be decided upon politically and how much each of us can decide for ourselves. For instance, if you have high taxes, the political system controls a large share of human activity, and with lower taxes more of that decision power lands in the hands of individuals. Generally speaking, individuals will be more empowered in the latter case, and this fosters responsibility, innovation, hard work, independent thinking and economic growth, which in turn increases individual freedom. Such freedom should also have as few legal restrictions as possible; you need very good arguments if you want to use the monopoly of violence to threaten people to comply with some rule.

What do you say, will that do as a general idea of liberalism? From John Locke and John Stuart Mill, to Hayek, to Ayn Rand, to Milton Friedman, to Robert Nozick (before he changed his mind) and Reaganomics—the above position would be shared by all of them.

The easiest way to defeat liberalism is by attacking its core supposition: the individual. The moment we are shown that it is a surface phenomenon and that the real unit of analysis is the dividual or the transindividual, and that freedom must ultimately be defined in transpersonal terms, we can see that liberalism must be subjected to metamodernism: Ultimately, you can never be free unless the people around you develop well, because their development affects not only your choices in every moment of your life, but even the degrees of freedom by which you can think, feel, and be in the world. We co-emerge, and freedom is a social category that functions through different emotional regimes.

Libertarians gather around the hacker and startup communities of Silicon Valley and the East Coast of the US—they don't set up shop in Somalia or Afghanistan, where there is indeed no state power to limit "individual freedom". It's just you and the desert (and a few warlords). A dynamic market ultimately rests upon a strong monopoly of violence that provides enough stability for freedom to prosper. Security is a service, and the state is an efficient provider of just that. As Max Weber noted so long ago, states and markets develop together.

But that, of course, is cheating. Libertarians and classical liberals won't give up their belief in the individual anytime soon, so in order to beat them on their own terms you must show them that the maximization of individual liberty cannot be done without political metamodernism. And that's perfectly doable, too.

The weakest spot is, unsurprisingly perhaps, the role of the state. As much suspicion as liberalism harbors against the state, it ultimately always depends upon it. Not only must there be a state to guarantee the safety of individuals against the violence or oppression of one another, it must also warrant legally binding agreements and protect property rights. No capitalist market is possible without at least some minimum state action. And if such a state *does* exist it will always have to make priorities, which will always limit at least some freedoms of some individuals.

So there is a state, if only a minimal one. How to make sure it is truly liberal and non-oppressive? If the governance of such a state does not include an active and deliberate Emancipation Politics, there will be fewer ways for the oppressed and disfavored parties to resist. This in turn would require a Democratization Politics to make certain that the form of governance is something that is entered into voluntarily in the first place. And from there on, you will require all the other four forms of politics because they all depend upon each other. Empirical Politics is necessary to ensure that the minimized governmental action actually does maximize human freedom. That too, in part, is an empirical question.

What, then, about anarcho-capitalism, one might ask? In this extreme version of liberalism you want to get rid of the state altogether and even have a market solution for buying and selling security services such as policing and courts. Let's take it from the anarcho-capitalist perspective then: no state, *basta*! Anarcho-capitalists are not uncommon around hacker communities, Silicon Valley and the tech industries, so it is a relevant question. And with cryptocurrencies and blockchain technologies on the rise, we may be seeing increasingly serious attempts at anarcho-capitalist projects.

Here's the thing. Even if you had no state and security was up for sale, the best security solutions would still be those that provide people with a "listening society" so that people feel heard, seen and represented. The best security is still *preventive* security. This would in turn require a development of all the six forms of politics. In market terms, this service would be more competitive.

Imagine you're a "client-citizen" of the kind envisioned by anarcho-capitalists: You have blockchain money and you shop around for the best state services. In one such state service, the metamodern one, you can affect the mode of governance, people are nudged to treat you better and you get a framework that helps you find profound meaning in life, and the fellow citizens will be much more peaceful and socially intelligent, and it's all empirically proven to work. The other providers lack such services and end up using your voluntarily paid money much more inefficiently. Which one are you going to pick? You go with the metamodern one. If there is such a thing as your "natural rights", these will come to a fuller expression in a metamodern society.

The only way to *stop* people from voluntarily choosing the meta-modern solutions would be to stop free competition by some kind of threat of violence or monopoly. The only thing that can stop liberalism from being eaten alive by metamodernism is authoritarianism.

In the "market of ideas" (as proposed by the liberal thinker J. S. Mill), political metamodernism lands on top of liberalism in all of its forms. Just as the telephone and internet beat the telegraph. If you're not a meta-modernist, you're just a bad liberal, because metamodernism is more libe-ral than liberalism—even in the stringent forms of libertarianism and anarcho-capitalism.

MORE SUSTAINABLE THAN ECOLOGISM

For all its different forms, Green ideology seeks to create sustainability of some kind. Even if some proponents of more radical forms of ecologism like to point out that the aim can hardly be to "sustain" a destructive and ecocidal civilization, that they prefer "resilience" or even "regeneration", this still means that ecologists want this new imagined and preferable state of affairs to be... well, sustainable. No matter how you look at it, sustain-ability is the demand, the goal, of ecologism. Resilience and regeneration both include sustainability within them.

It is thus hardly a stretch to say that any kind of politics which does not maximize sustainability (again: of the present society or any imagined fut-ure one) is not the optimal Green politics, not in alignment with ecolo-gism. Naturally, some forms of ecologism are of a reconciliatory bent (seeking to "reconcile" humanity with the environment), some are anth-ropocentric in their environmentalism, some are spiritual and focus upon attaining unity with "deep ecology", some are unforgiving against the excesses of humanity while focusing on solidarity with ecosystems and the biosphere, some are transformational (seeking to transform the ecosys-tems of the world with human intelligence), some are futuristic and others primitivistic. You have pragmatists and hardliners, in the emblematic exa-mple of Green parties, the German *die Grüne*, these are called the *Fundis* (fundamentalist environmentalists) and *Realos* (realist green politicians).

And then there are all the mixes with other ideologies and struggles: ecosocialism, green liberalism, techno-environmentalism, ecofascism, hu-man ecology of indigenous minority rights, multiculturalism, and so on.

What they all share is a focus on sustainability in some form or other. Even if ecologist thinkers like Arne Næss, Murray Bookchin, Gary Snyder, Theodore Roszak and today's Tim Morton and Roger Scruton all have different takes on this issue, it is not a stretch to say they are somehow committed to sustainability—although the word itself only became commonplace after 1987 with the Brundtland Report.[127]

What, then, can be learned from political metamodernism in terms of sustainability? A thing or two.

You cannot have a sustainable societal system (economy-layered-in-biosphere) without a corresponding and matching sustainability in all fields of development: system, culture, psychology and behavior (as discussed in Appendix B). In other words, you can't have ecological sustainability without social and economic sustainability. And how do you get there?

You need to get people to a point in their lives where they genuinely understand and care about issues larger than themselves. That's Existential Politics. You need to make sure people have good enough social relations to not get stuck in prisoners' dilemmas that hold back our development and potential to care and not get stuck in materialistic status games. That's *Gemeinschaft* Politics. You need to see to it that the systems of governance can nimbly and effectively redesign themselves so as to deal with new environmental challenges when they become known, in a way that gains support and legitimacy. That's Democratization Politics. You need to make certain that all of society is aligned with what is empirically shown to create circular economies and cradle-to-cradle processes, and you need to make sure that you spot and correctly understand environmental threats such as climate change and that the public is well informed and has the ability to respond reasonably. That's Empirical Politics. And you need to make certain that ideas about ecology, sustainability and humanity's place in a larger context of nature permeate people's consciousness and all of our ideas about life. That's Politics of Theory. And unless you're an ecofascist and just don't care about the freedom of people, you need to make sure that all of these processes can play out without oppressing people, and that's Emancipation Politics.

So tell me again how you were going to create a sustainable society without political metamodernism. Can you see how unrealistic any ecologist ideology would be without these processes?

Any version of ecologism requires political metamodernism to be truly sustainable. Any environmentalism not underpinned by the Nordic ideology is simply less sustainable, less resilient, less regenerative. That's all, folks: the Nordic ideology is greener than Green.

MORE PRUDENT THAN CONSERVATISM

Conservatism may be the most misunderstood of the modern ideologies—and its challenge to political metamodernism is perhaps the most serious one. The central conservative principle is a resolve to escape the traps of infatuations with utopian ideas and puritan ideals—and to settle for "the real world". The insight that underlies this realization is one of humility: the world is always larger, more complex and more terrifying than our limited intellects and perspectives can imagine. When we want to change things around, it's usually only because we haven't really understood how they work in the first place. And so our dreamed visions and "creative ideas" usually end up wrecking what works in the first place, and then we have to painfully try to reconstruct what has been lost. Sometimes that can take an incredibly long time. Think of the sunk costs of the Soviet experiment.

Conservatism reacts against the hubris of intellectuals. As soon as modern society was showing its first glimmers and it became apparent that the human world was about to drastically change, "smart" but unwise people from privileged strata of society took upon themselves to use their intellects to try to shape the direction of this development. This was, and remains to this day, an act of vanity: you flatter yourself, you grow self-righteous, you put yourself above your place in the larger world, above your place in history, your place as a member of your people and their accumulated wisdoms—and this leads you to try to force your neatly arranged ideas and ideals upon the richness and complexity of the world. And your mental construct never fits, and you always end up getting angry at the world. The stark raving revolutionaries take over and things get violent. Crazy experiments abound. Decay follows.

The primordial and archetypal such dangerously utopian thinker is, again, Rousseau. While highly intelligent and idealistic, he was unbalanced as a person, an irresponsible father and impossible friend—unable to live up to his own ideals of engaged parenting as outlined in his 1762 work *Émile*—and he was hopelessly romantically attached to unachievable utopian goals. Rousseau, a perpetual child who would never grow up and died bitterly defending his ruined reputation with far-fetched justifications, is the originator of such dreamy and dangerous ideas as "Man is born free, and everywhere he is in chains" and "We will force you to be free!"[128]

How telling, then, that Rousseau was the spiritual father of the hard-core Jacobins of the French Revolution—the ones who led the Reign of Terror and guillotined folks left and right as the Revolution began to eat its own children. Maximilien Robespierre, the young Jacobin lawyer who rose to power and eventually had the king decapitated—and even coined the motto of the French Republic, "*liberté, égalité, fraternité*"—worshipped Rousseau like a god:

> "Rousseau is the one man who, through the loftiness of his soul and the grandeur of his character, showed himself worthy of the role of teacher of mankind."[129]

Fanaticism—just like Lenin would later declare himself to be "in love with Marx" and honor the memory of Robespierre with a monument in Saint Petersburg.

It was after the excesses and madness of the French Revolution that conservative thinking took hold in earnest. The pendulum swung and for a few generations the leading minds of France, Germany and England developed the foundations of modern conservatism. You have Burke's repudiation of the French Revolution, the German Romanticism's rejection of the cold and ahistorical intellect of the French Enlightenment project, and Joseph de Maistre's poignant retort to Rousseau's ideal of men born free but being everywhere in chains: "To say that sheep are born carnivorous, but everywhere eat grass, would be just as reasonable".[130]

Conservative thinkers knew that modernity was encroaching upon society: They did not deny the power of science and technology and the profoundly new territory that humanity was entering. They held that modern society had to grow and evolve organically, and that the role of the intellect was not to force itself upon the world, but to refine the human spirit on an individual level by self-reflection and hard work—even beyond the intellectual realm: linking to the spiritual, the mystical and the aesthetic. People aren't naturally benign, as Rousseau and Robespierre had postulated, and society does not always oppress them—it often protects, fosters and supports them. People are relatively brutish and simple, and they must refine their souls to be any good—and society's role is more often to hold us in place so we don't commit crimes or work against one another. And society can offer a source of cultural refinement—through history, art and *Bildung*.

To different extents, the conservative thinkers also defended God and the Christian faith against the onslaught of cold scientific rationality. Humans need God to know their place in the larger scheme of things. So what could be worse than throwing all of that rich timbre of human experience and culture overboard in exchange for a dreamt-up plan for a new society!

The point isn't, then, to try to go back to the Middle Ages,[131] but simply to defend traditions, sacred values, national ethnic bonds, hierarchical relations and institutions from unrealistic and irresponsible attempts to efface them. **The fundamental conservative principle is to be responsible and prudent; it is to avoid what I have called "game denial".**

Conservatism and counter-revolution have surfaced as a political, aesthetic and intellectual force time and again since early modernity. During the period 1815–48, the Austrian statesman Prince Metternich, a major influence in Austria and in Europe generally, devoted his energies to erecting an antirevolutionary chain of international alliances throughout Europe. After the turn of the 19th century you had Oswald Spengler's somber ruminations on the fall of Western civilization. In its latest incarnation you have thinkers such as the Canadian psychologist Jordan B. Peterson and the US literary scholar Camille Paglia who call themselves classical liberal and libertarian respectively, but who, structurally speaking, quite clearly reproduce the conservative creed. They work to challenge leftwing academic posturing and to demask the excesses of university campus radicalism and the youth's blind faith in neo-Marxism and intersectional feminism. Their message appeals mostly to white young men, just as earlier forms of conservatism. And just as before, the young men are encouraged to cultivate their masculinities and inner lives. Peterson and Paglia seem to be leading an ongoing counter-revolution in its own right—albeit in a cultural and not military sense.

The enemy is always simplistic and collectivist radicalism. As such, conservative thinkers view themselves as opposed to "ideology". The conservative mind holds that they stick to a sober view of reality, whereas radicals and progressives have sold out reason in hope of playing an intoxicatingly heroic role, or in covert hopes of advancing in the social hierarchies. On a deep level, the conservative feels that ideologies provide an excuse for such behavior, a kind of simple filter through which the ideologue can view the world in black-and-white terms—thus avoiding to ever see his own limitations and the greed of his soul, because he is always on the "pure" and "good" side. The conservative tells us:

> "Your ideology is a sickness, a big lie, an excuse for your inability and unwillingness to deal with your own inner weaknesses. And that is, ultimately, why the French Revolution turned sour, as did the Bolshevik one, as will all future ones. You say you are good, but you lie. If you really cared about what's good, you would bother to first find out, without *a priori*, what is

true—including truths that happen to hurt—and then you would do your hard inner homework and deal with the less rosy and more terrifying reality of existence."

This conservative trail of thought of course also poses a challenge to political metamodernism. And the challenge should be taken seriously, by all means. How can we justify the Nordic ideology? Is it just another attempt at a seductive, blinding ideology that would make Chairman Mao proud?

As with the other modern ideologies, you can *either* beat conservatism by dismantling its core suppositions, *or* by taking it to its own limits and turn it against itself. And again, we need to do the latter. But just to point out some ways to disprove conservatism "from the outside" we can mention that:

* conservatism cannot itself escape the charges of being an ideology,

* conservative thinkers have all been beaten down by history as they opposed abolition of slavery, universal suffrage, labor rights, the rule of scientific method over religion, the separation of state and religion, the independence of colonies, the equality between sexes, and so on, i.e. they have sided with the losing institutions, and all been proven terribly wrong in the long run, and

* you can always tear down their philosophical foundations, such as the belief in the individual, in free will, or in reason, all of which are manifestly false and provably so.

In short, it's apparent that conservatives are usually right in the short run but wrong in the long run, and we can always point that out. But that would be cheating. It wouldn't reach the conservatives on their own terms. Here's the point of attack: **The conservative wants to be prudent and to respect tradition and let society grow organically without effacing natural hierarchies that have been established between competent and less competent members of society.**

We can ask the conservative: Which scenario is most respectful of people's relations and traditions—one in which you have an active and deliberate *Gemeinschaft* Politics, or one in which such a thing is lacking? With a *Gemeinschaft* Politics you have the means to look at cultural, ethnic and national values and relations and to defend them or develop their interrelations. Without it you don't. So a good conservative must accept that *Gemeinschaft* Politics can be useful—in fact, many unknowingly already advocate embryonic forms of this kind of politics, as discussed in chapter 11.

How about Empirical Politics? Which society will be most prone to crazy dreamt-up and disembodied ideologies—one that continuously finds ways of optimizing checks against bullshit, or one that doesn't? Empirical Politics is perfectly in line with the conservative ideals of making well-informed decisions and demanding proof that something is likely to work before carrying it out.

And if you want to be prudent and respect the narratives and traditions that have grown through history, which alternative treats such folk narratives with the greatest care and respect; one that has a Politics of Theory to continuously see if culture has gone off the rails and become destructive, or one that has no such mechanism? Having a Politics of Theory is—together with Empirical Politics—like buying an insurance.

The classical conservative wants to refuse to buy the insurance in an accelerating time that is changing very quickly and in which crazy ideologies are popping up again. The prudent thing to do—indeed, the responsible and *conservative* thing to do—is to buy the damned insurance and make sure you pay its premium. The same can be said about Democratization Politics: Again, it's like buying an insurance.

And when it comes to the conservative concern for the soul, or the loss of connection to it in our fast-paced fast-food society, what could be more important than Existential Politics? Would you like to go on *not* having inner development as a political topic, with good data to look at and discuss? Not to mention Emancipation Politics—how will you defend individual rights without an institutional framework to do so? Wouldn't it be reckless and irresponsible—which is what every conservative claims *not* to be—to reject such politics?

And then there's the whole issue of the value of elites that have done hard inner work to earn their place and who lead with a gentle hand and a long-term perspective. Political metamodernism has a developmental psychology to back it up and can help identify and gather such elites and make sure they can wield and maintain power. Can classical conservatism do that? Do the conservatives have any better strategies for how the educated and competent elites of society should organize themselves to avoid an uninformed mob rule from taking over? Recent populist developments suggest they don't.

And you want to not have a partial, ideological perspective, but to relate to the slow and organic development of the whole? How exactly can you do that without seeing that the *other* ideological positions are also a part of that whole—without the metamodern principle of transpartisanism and the metamodern method of co-development? How can you lead and represent the whole when you always splice off about half of the population and their worldviews? You cannot let society grow organically without the holistic multi-perspectivalism of metamodernism. Or rather, you can, but you won't be overviewing and leading that growth.

As you can see, good *monsieur*, your conservatism is only a cheap fanfare for political metamodernism. The modern form of conservatism is immature, childish, irresponsible and imprudent compared to the Nordic ideology.

The Nordic ideology is, simply, more conservative than conservatism.

MORE RADICALLY REBELLIOUS THAN ANARCHISM

Anarchism may be the *least* serious challenge to political metamodernism in terms of real politics in the world: there are no tangible or relevant real-world examples, it is not a force in international politics, and it mostly attracts youngsters, punks and cranks—and a few intellectuals.

Because of its unrealistic ideals and tendencies towards extreme game denial, it has failed to materialize societies beyond brief flickers in history since its proper modern formulation in the writings of the Russian thinkers Mikhail Bakunin (1814-76) and Peter Kropotkin (1842-1921).

We are considering here, of course, not all forms of anarchism (there are quite a few), but those linked to communal anarcho-communism—a stateless society in which people would work together in free and voluntary association, agreeing upon how to share spoils and help one another when in need. Such ideas naturally blend into socialism, and they are subscribed to by several major intellectuals of the Left, such as Emma Goldman in the early 20th century, and in our days, Noam Chomsky.

Anarchists of this kind generally view worker unions as instrumental for governance and are hence closely linked to syndicalism, i.e., the idea that worker unions should be self-governing and similar ideas. And—as I discuss elsewhere—anarchism is closely tied to the postmodern[132] critique of modern society.

But if anarchism offers little serious resistance in terms of real political power—that is the realm of conservatism—its challenge is of another kind: one of spirit and soul.

Anarchism is the purest and most idealistic of modern ideologies; it insists upon uncompromising rebellion against *all* unjust power, against all injustices, against all limits to freedom, against all violence and uses of force, against all disenchanted and instrumental life and all reductions of humans to a means for an end. No power is self-justifiable; any and all power must always be justified by moral principles and the will of the governed.

Anarchy: it means *without rulers*; its fundamental principle is resistance. You resist all that does not hold up to the highest ethical standards, you refuse to compromise with "the powers that be" as they will always try to sell you the current state of affairs as the only "realistic" one—and you refuse to sell your soul to what the mainstream holds to be "realism". Another world *is* possible.

Anarchism is at the opposite end of the spectrum from conservatism, echoing (but not relying upon) Rousseau, in believing that humans are inherently good but society is messed up and corrupts us and holds us back. Anarchist thinkers find ways of exemplifying all the ways humans work together, and like to point out the ubiquity of such friendly cooperation— most famously, perhaps, in Kropotkin's work *Mutual Aid*.[133] There is not a society on Earth, nor has there ever been one, where people have not cooperated.

In this context, it is important to understand and feel into the healthy and positive aspects of anarchism: a kind of inner purity married to a tender hurt and sadness, a kind of intense and deeply felt longing and hope amidst a world obviously wrought in tragedy—a profoundly tired, exhausted sense of struggle, struggle, struggle. Life shouldn't have been this way. Something else was possible all along, and it still is.

This genuine and spiritual aspect of anarchism—the naive eyes of the child simply asking why the world isn't fair and irreverently demanding an answer from any purported authority—is generally missed by other observers. As we discussed in chapter 2, to conservatives and others, the game-denying anarchist mind is the *real* sell-out, as it sells out the truth and the commitment to any realistic goal and engagement for self-flattery and moral superiority. And more often than not, this suspicion is true: Much of anarchism is obviously hypocritical; just look at violent demonstrations, vandalism, mob-mentality, aggressive puritan obsessions and the unwillingness to try to understand any other perspective while labeling them "Strasserite" (to them, it simply means nazi).[134] Anything but the purest anarchism is always bad, and if it's bad, it's nazi. And nazis merit the most contemptuous and hostile treatment. You couldn't get farther away from a co-developmental "solidarity with all perspectives" position. Anarchism is often an excuse to be a bully.

So yes, in practice, the vast majority of anarchists are little more than deluded dregs. Go to their online forums and see for yourself.[135]

But there is still something else going on in anarchism: a real, bleeding heart, a simple and uncompromising wish for good, a longing for a genuinely moral society. If you don't understand and meet this true underlying impulse, you will never have met the real anarchist's core, exemplified by great and beautiful minds like Bakunin, Kropotkin, Goldman, Chomsky or perhaps James C. Scott.

The anarchist mind may share with the conservative a resistance against grand schemes and large structures of governance, against a flattened and disembodied intellect that forces itself upon the complexity, multiplicity and particularity of the world. But more fundamentally, its challenge to political metamodernism lies in the question of purity of intent: Aren't you, the metamodernist, really compromising with the existing power structures? Aren't you, in truth, selling yourself short? Isn't there a harder, harsher and more direct struggle, a more obvious and concrete path to a sane and fair society? Aren't you really making excuses for not taking up that struggle, instead of your cute co-developmental plan? Isn't this one big compromise with the cold hand of the market, with the oppression by military and police—a grand sell-out to subservience and comfortable complacency? Shouldn't we simply *stop doing* extreme oppression and exploitation, and stop doing it today? Isn't there a deeper transformation of the economy from which you are distracting yourself with all of these exercises in perspective taking? Aren't you hiding from your own potential for greater compassion, from your fear of what it means to pay the price to truly resist—resist what you deep down know is just wrong?

As Bakunin himself said it:

"To revolt is a natural tendency of life. Even a worm turns against the foot that crushes it. In general, the vitality and relative dignity of an animal can be measured by the intensity of its instinct to revolt."[136]

Isn't the Nordic ideology one great excuse for copping out from doing what is right and natural, but difficult and dangerous—to revolt?

Okay, fair questions, dear anarchist mind.

I could answer by attacking your unrealistic ideology, the fact that you only ever materialize political structures when you have extreme common enemies (e.g. the Spanish Civil War, the Kurds of Rojava, brief moments of major strikes and labor conflicts, moments after large-scale natural disasters), or I could point out that I offer a much more realistic path that doesn't rely on forcing your ideas down the throats of others (because anarchists have no plan about what to do with all those conservatives), or that I don't rely upon moralistically judging others. Or I could show empirically that the vast majority of your friends are authoritarians looking for an excuse to bully other kids.[137] Or I could point out that even if you start an anarchist commune, you will not be freeing all other people, but leave them stuck in the capitalist world-system. Or I could underscore that your anarchist communes are less radically emergent than idealistically purpose-driven virtual tribes and swarms of dividuals made possible by metamodern internet society.

But that would of course, again, be cheating. It wouldn't be taking you seriously. You must be beaten in your own Olympic discipline: rebellion.

For all its game denial and attachment to anti-thesis and utopia (as compared to metamodern game change, proto-synthesis and relative utopia), anarchism is the spiritual pinnacle of modern society because it keeps reminding us of the unfulfilled potential of higher freedom and deeper equality. As such, it thus comes closest, of all the modern ideologies, to the spiritual core of political metamodernism. And political metamodernism must hence deliver by showing that it is consistent with the radical resistance of a generous and glowing rebel heart.

Said Bakunin:

> "I am a fanatic **lover of liberty, considering it as the unique condition under which intelligence, dignity and human happiness can develop and grow**; not the purely formal liberty conceded, measured out and regulated by the State, an eternal lie which in reality represents nothing more than the privilege of some founded on the slavery of the rest; not the individualistic, egoistic, shabby, and fictitious liberty extolled by the School of J.-J. Rousseau and other schools of bourgeois liberalism, which considers the would-be rights of all men, represented by the State which limits the rights of each—an idea that leads inevitably to the reduction of the rights of each to zero. **No, I mean the only kind of liberty that is worthy of the name, liberty that consists in the full development of all the material, intellectual and moral powers that are latent in each person; liberty that recognizes no restrictions other than those determined by the laws of our own individual nature**, which cannot properly be regarded as restrictions since these laws are not imposed by any outside legislator beside or above us, but are immanent and inherent, forming the very basis of our material, intellectual and moral being—they do not limit us but are the real and immediate conditions of our freedom." [My bolds][138]

If we are to take Bakunin's striving for freedom seriously, we must seek to climb the highest reaches of human development, and—as Bakunin agrees—this is a collective endeavor. Anything that hinders human flourishing is detrimental to freedom in this deepest sense of the word.

And here is the decisive blow: **Without a conscious self-organization of human activity to improve and optimize inner development, hum-**

ans will never be able to enter into free and creative association with one another. The moment someone reaches "the full development of all the material, intellectual and moral powers" inherent to them, they become devoted to helping society and to the development of all people. And people can be free to develop only if others are there to help them to do so, rather than to hinder them.

Hence, any truly anarchist society, loyal to the goals set by Bakunin, must be shaped to support the inner growth of all citizens. Even in a society with no state and no use of force, you would still need Existential Politics, Emancipation Politics, Democratization Politics and *Gemeinschaft* Politics to achieve this end. And without Empirical Politics, people would still be subjected to the power relations that come from transfigurations of facts and truth. And without a Politics of Theory, we will still be slaves to whatever narratives that are made invisible and forced upon us.

Go ahead and rebel against the state and the global capitalist market if you want. But it's peanuts. I, the metamodern mind, rebel against the very social construction of the modern universe. *That* is irreverent. Compared to that, your anarchist rebellion is one of a smaller soul, of a smaller imagination—of a coward heart, of idle complacency.

The most radical and uncompromising rebellion has a new name—a name whispered under the breath; hidden under a polite, awkward smile, superficially indistinguishable from that of a Swedish social democrat: the Nordic ideology. It has no followers—only co-developers. It is more radically rebellious than anarchism. The metamodern mind defies not only its position in society and society's configuration; it spites the heavens.

STRATEGIC CONSIDERATIONS

In each of these lines of reasoning we have taken the modern ideologies at face value, just to show how they are *conceptually* inferior to political metamodernism. But that doesn't mean we should let them define which path we take. If you submit political metamodernism to the demands of any of the modern ideologies—which all of the subscribers of modern ideologies *will* try to get you to do ("yes, but economic class…" etc.)—it will become vulnerable to critiques of all *other* modern ideologies. And they'll tear you down according to those premises. Don't let them do that. Just smile through the bullshit.

So yes, anarchists can claim that the Nordic ideology is a weak liberal centrist position. But the political metamodernist knows that the spiritual ideals of anarchism are not approached in the space of resisting and destroying the modern state and the market, but in the structures that emerge *on top of* modern society: the post-capitalist, digitized, co-developmental space emerging in the most developed economies of the world.

And socialists can claim that we are weak capitalist apologists. And conservatives that we are compulsive Stalinist utopians and copout dreamers, libertarians that we are extreme socialists—and so on.

All of these accusations are attempts to submit political metamodernism to the premises of a certain modern ideology. If anything, it is pretty exciting that political metamodernism can be viewed so differently and attacked for so seemingly contradictory things. At a surface level, this would seem to signal a very disorganized and poorly thought-through position. But as we know, in this case, it is because we have a more deeply organized ideology, one centered around higher and more abstracted principles: both-and thinking. Because we are both-and thinkers, the either-or people will always be objecting either to the "both" or to the "and". We have the ability to fold through a higher dimension and show up anywhere on the political spectrum, moving transpartially to co-develop our way towards a metamodern society. It's a bit like being a time-traveler in a sci-fi movie where the protagonist knows the possible paths of the future and can thus crop up at the most critical events to affect them in a more desirable direction.

Late modern societies tend to gravitate towards green social liberalism, as we have seen, with some reactions of conservative and nationalist sentiments here and there. Hence, a good place to start may be in the Nordic countries and specifically as a kind of Green Social Liberalism 2.0. A sound strategy may be to support the creation of smooth, libertarian markets with a highly functional safety net underpinning them, while taking decisive steps to spur green innovation and efficient use of natural resources. But remember that these are truly secondary questions: **The real issue is to introduce all the six processes of metamodern politics**, so that society can be transformed deeply and in earnest into "a listening society". As long as it's ethically justifiable and non-violent, whatever you can do to make this happen is a step in the right direction.

There is little reason to play along with the accusations of the modern ideologies. They can and will all persistently misunderstand political metamodernism. There is little reason to appease them; if you make serious efforts to appease one, you will lose all the others. Instead, the plan is, again, to capture the imagination and attention of a small but significant part of the population and to increase your centrality in the networks of power from there on.

An often-overlooked aspect of network science is the so-called **negative ties**. It is common knowledge that network positions of high centrality and bridging are powerful. And most people will have heard of "the power of weak ties": Because you can have so many "weak ties", the likelihood that someone will have some useful property goes up if you learn to make many and diverse contacts. But there are also *negative* ties: all the folks who will want you to *not* succeed and who will work—subtly or actively—against you.[139] And here's an important thing: **Most ties are going to be *both* positive *and* negative**. The composition of your ties to people across the political spectrum is in turn determined by how well you rank, in their regard, *relatively* to all *other* positions on the spectrum.

So, as I mentioned earlier, you don't have to be the *most liked* alternative—that's the populist position. You just have to be the least hated one. The socialists will think you're a cheap fake, sure, but they will hate you a little less than they hate people who sing the advent of global neoliberalism. Libertarians will think you're a dangerous control-freak, but they will hate you a little less than people who explicitly want to tear down the free market. Conservatives will be disgusted with your idealism, but a little less so than with actual anarchists. Greens will think you postpone the necessary transition to a sustainable society, but will certainly think better of you than all those groups that uncritically embrace economic growth and couldn't give a damn about the collapsing environment. Even anarchists will hate you a little less—if for no other reason because they really hate everybody else. Political metamodernism is at the center, not of the left-right political spectrum, but of the network—suspended clear in the sky.

As we have seen, you can only beat each of the modern ideologies on its own terms: They simply won't accept other terms than their own. The holders of these perspectives arrived at them by maximizing certain values determined *a priori*, so if you try to propose other values, they won't go along. That's a large part of the reason why the modern ideologies are perpetually stuck in a trench war in regards to each other.

What you get instead is a multidimensional puzzle where you maximize your centrality and gravity in transpartisan space. I.e., you become friends with the socialists, as viewed from their perspective, *relative* to all other positions. They won't see you as trusted allies, but at least they find you less despicable and more respectable than other opponents. And this is where you need to really kill it with genuine perspective taking: **You need to be able to truly show them that you understand where they are coming from and then share in the pleasure of dismantling all the *other* modern ideologies.**

That won't "convert" most of them, but it will lessen the negative ties and increase the weak positive ties. Then go to the libertarians and repeat. And then to the conservatives. Show them that you understand what they don't like about all the other alternatives, show them that you understand what they don't like about you, and show them that you appreciate their partial truths. And as you are capable of launching more devastating attacks on all the other ideologies by beating these on their own terms, they will gladly steal your ideas and arguments and thus do some of the "dirty" work for you. The modern ideologies will deconstruct each other. As our ideas spread—first slowly, then like wildfire—all that remains to do is to lean back and undisturbedly tweak the developmental processes that step by step bring about a listening society, ascending in smoke and fire.

That's how you use this guide to attacking all the modern ideologies: The point is not to go bash all the others because you can. It is to show all the others that you're a little less despicable than their other opponents, and that you have something relevant to offer in their attacks upon others. The power of weak ties, yes, but also the power of non-negative ties.

As we have noted earlier, there is an intimate relationship between three fundamental dimensions of all social life: solidarity, trade and competition. These dimensions develop together. So the better you are at having solidarity with the perspectives of others, the more centrality you will have and the more functional communication you will achieve, and that will give you better things to trade for the favors of others (or withhold if they won't play fair), and hence you will be able to outcompete them. Perspective-taking is key here. This is the power of transpartisanship and co-development—and of a transpersonal, non-judgmental perspective. The purest heart wins out in the long run, not because there's a God who rewards your virtue, but because it judges other people less, and hence understands them better, and hence defeats them more easily. Jesus was right: Turn the other cheek.

And this, need I add, requires a kind of ironic sincerity. You have to *sincerely* take the perspectives of others, you must *sincerely* care for the people who hold these perspectives, and yet you must *ironically* distance yourself from these same perspectives—so that you don't jump in their hoops, but they eventually jump through yours. You draw everyone in by showing them ways to defeat their loathed enemies. This takes a whole lot of both-and thinking, a whole lot of "superposition"—the holding all possibilities and potentials contained in one position. And that requires not only "high cognitive complexity", but consistent practice and honing of skills—skills of political poetry.

Never mind winning every debate. Sun Tzu said it: "Victorious warriors win first and then go to war, while defeated warriors go to war first and then seek to win." Don't mind every petty argument. Don't get caught in justifying political metamodernism and the Nordic ideology to the modern mind; that would be like justifying liberal democracy to the Spanish inquisition. Of course they will think you are hopelessly vague, spineless and/or totalitarian. Let them. Meanwhile, the long-term attractors are driving the political landscape in your direction. Just make sure you strengthen those attractors and win the damned world war.

Look harmless. Take every opportunity to improve the dialogue and debate climate: The better the political processes are, the more level and fair the playing field is, the more difficult it becomes for others, and yourself, to hide from logic and reason. Tilt the game in the direction of truthfulness, and that will tilt it in the direction of greater depth and higher complexity, which is the essence of political metamodernism.

Become chums with the most complex thinkers of all camps; find ways to ally transpartially, to share the credit. Slowly improve your position, hone your perspective taking skills—and go for the check mate: to destroy modern society.

The underlying message isn't "please listen, guys". And it certainly isn't "come join us". That would be creepy. The bottom-line is: Do what you want, think what you like—but at the end of the day, you can't stop us.

Chapter 20

DANGEROUS DREAMS

> "A paradigm is needed that without apology takes both an uncompromisingly cynical view of society and a deeply idealistic one."[140]

Totalitarianism. We keep coming back to it. And for good reason too: As we begin to formulate a new **meta-ideology**—an overall pattern that does not fit within the scale of modern politics but rather corresponds to liberal democracy itself—some core principles of democracy, at least in its conventional sense, are being curtailed. We are trying to get a hold of "the whole", trying to relate to the *totality* of society.

The modern political spectrum is contained in its entirety within the meta-ideology of "liberal capitalist welfare parliamentarian party politics" (an order in turn married to the attractor of Green Social-Liberalism). The Nordic ideology builds upon Green Social-Liberalism (and works its way towards a Green Social-Liberalism version 2.0) but challenges the modern meta-ideology by redefining how governance works. A small group, in practice, infects and hijacks the modern system and works for a new holistic order; that's a trait shared with the totalitarian movements of the 20th century.

No apologies should be made for this kinship—and yet it is of utmost importance to underscore that A) metamodernism is not reducible to any form of 20th century totalitarianism, and B) that there are real risks that new forms of totalitarianism can spring from political metamodernism.

FORBIDDEN PHANTOMS ™

This is how it works.

As the traditional political scale and its representations of class interests become less relevant in a postindustrial, digitized and globalized society, people in stable highly developed countries begin to gravitate towards co-development and deliberation.

The co-developmental process takes over some of the core principles of party politics: Co-development hijacks representative democracy and its parties; it takes over the whole scale, slowly but surely. States like the Nordic ones gravitate towards something more along the lines of what the Founding Fathers of the United States imagined, or indeed of what the communist "people's republics" intended and pretended to be: an organic, holistic system of governance with checks and balances for the common interest. The people who identify with this attractor point and consciously reinforce it—the metamodernists, roughly—gain influence (but not full control) over this dynamic. Metamodern politics inserts itself on top of conventional modern politics.

The divisions at the heart of industrial society kept modern democracies from devolving into totalitarian and authoritarian states: No one group or individual could ever gather enough power to curtail the information feedback processes. The societies that took totalitarian paths turned out to be less competitive in terms of information management and the successful coordination of human actions in the long run. Democracies kept a vital balance of power. That is the main difference between the democratic societies and the totalitarian alternatives proposed during the 20th century.

Hence we are left with a pretty strange predicament: If we take the modern democratic ideals to their utmost limit, democracy ends up cancelling itself. **If you become super-democratic** (no manipulation, only healthy discourse, taking the perspectives of others, improving upon the process of communication, getting the best possible science, representing the wider and more complex common good, etc.) **you also, automatically, challenge democracy in its current party-political representative form and gravitate towards holistic and deliberative forms**. The most democratically inclined people are the very same who end up working to dismantle democracy as we know it. The very things that splinter us into party politics (which is a good thing) are the same that hold us back in terms of a deeper, shared process of co-development (which is a bad thing). That is how dialectics work: Every system breaks down under its own logic and turns into its (relative) opposite at a new level.

And that puts us in the territory of dangerous dreams. There's a simple formula for why this is the case:

- as society grows in complexity;
- the number and multiplicity of processes and emergent events increase;

- and this increases the quantity and complexity of "externalities", i.e. adverse and unexpected effects that the processes and emergent events have upon each other (this is "fragmentation");
- hence, the need for deeper and greater integration increases in order to curb the harmful effects of fragmentation;
- and this requires more holistic perspectives and processes;
- and holistic processes try to control the interactions between the many parts of "the whole", which is a difficult and sensitive task;
- and when any one holistic process gains too much power and gets anything wrong, it pathologically dominates and harms all other processes;
- and that oppression by one process of all other social logics than its own has a name: totalitarianism.

Fundamentally, that's the choice we are left with: *either* A) certain disintegration as rising complexity increases the multiplicity of processes and events to the point of complete deterioration (by means of climate change, ecological collapse, culture wars, haywire technologies, developmental imbalances, etc.)—*or* B) taking decisive steps to make a holistic move for deep reintegration, knowing full well that we risk awakening the specter of totalitarianism.

The "liberal innocent" chooses alternative A, simply ignoring the likely prospect of global civilizational collapse due to exponentially increasing fragmentation. He stays to polish the brass on the Titanic. He flips a few pages of Steven Pinker and concludes that all will be well—and totalitarianism is always thought to be due to the faults of someone else.

The metamodern activist chooses alternative B—owning up to her own inner totalitarian, seeking to understand and counter it, but also to create holistic solutions that deepen and refine the processes of integration of human actions throughout society. She ventures into the transpersonal depths of the human soul—and she invokes *forbidden phantoms*™.

Alas, forbidden phantoms™. We could be creating the new communism here, or the new nazism, or even the new Scientology, so let's be *very* careful. Remember, holism and totalitarianism are, essentially, the same word: striving for the whole.

The difference between holism and totalitarianism is, fundamentally, that holism _relates to_ and _coordinates_ the pieces of the whole, whereas totalitarianism takes on the impossible and destructive task of _controlling_ the whole. Totalitarianism fails because it subjects all pieces to the logic of _one_ piece. Totalitarianism is holism without a corresponding capacity for perspective taking; coordination without solidarity with others' perspectives. The necessary power balance is curtailed.

And how do you stop any one part from controlling all the others? You make sure as many perspectives as possible are empowered in an open-ended process. You make sure there are information flows to tear down any one governing logic that would assert itself. And you make sure the best possible processes are cultivated for such resistance to take place. Mobility, flow, multiplicity, sometimes gory dispute—these are the pillars of truth.

Totalitarianism is *failed* holism, and we need *successful* holism. What is the most honest and straightforward way ahead? Here's what I believe: We revisit the totalitarian ideologies of the 20th century to view them with fresh eyes, with the perspective of political metamodernism. We salvage the parts that are good and true—no excuses made for their great evils—and we see how these kernels of truth reflect higher developmental potentials of humanity and beyond.

Most importantly, we make an effort to see that the ghost of totalitarianism's past is not "in someone else"; it is a transpersonal affair, inherent to each of us and to the configurations of our relations. The better we see and acknowledge our own flirtations with totality, with our longing for power and our greedy claims for possessing the truth—the better our chances of productively balancing holism and freedom.

It's a slack line to walk, admittedly, two gaping hells below us: fragmentation and decay on one side, totalitarian oppression on the other—both of truly unprecedented magnitudes. If we crash global civilization and its surrounding ecosystems, it will likely be a calamity greater than the black plague or the wars of Genghis Khan. And if global totalitarianism takes root in a time of unlimited surveillance, genetic manipulation, and advanced forms of brainwashing—the sheer terror of that oppression can and will be worse than nazism. In this chapter, I invite you to walk with me out on the wire.

We discussed earlier how (in)dividuation and integration are always interconnected and how they always breed oppression and alienation. We must now own up to the risk: If we want survival and relative utopia, we must also accept the risk that we can end up birthing the new oppression. To walk the line, we also need to own that potential for evil within ourselves, every damned day. Liberal innocence lost.[141]

Both and. Can you stretch your mind that far? Can you go to the greatest evils of history and find them within yourself, see how they in part reflect your highest good? We need to marry uncompromising idealism to the most unapologetic cynicism.

We didn't defeat the powers of totalitarianism once and for all with the Second World War and the fall of Soviet communism: They were only defeated in their modern versions. Their metamodern counterparts are still alive and kicking as potential horrors deep within us; embryonic monsters waiting to be born as we unleash the forces of the postindustrial and digitized world economy. Let's take a walk on the dark side of the road.

And *because* we will need to deepen and refine the integrative processes of society in the coming age, *because* we must think and act more holistically—we are bound to come face to face with totalitarianism.

The greatest risk is to deny this tendency and try to be a "liberal innocent". It will not only blind us to all the necessary transformations towards a listening society and all it entails; it will also let the totalitarian powers sneak up on us and take over as frustrations and fears surface in the wake of social fragmentation and decay. The liberal innocent is defenseless against evil *because* he is convinced he's not the bad guy. And evil always comes from deep within, disguised as your trusted friend in a seemingly dark world.

So we're back to that profound old insight: If you want to have any chance of being the good guy and doing something worthwhile, you have to face the dark side; to face the shadow, to look into the mirror and see the devil's twinkle in your own eye, to travel to hell—and come back wiser and stronger. And you always discover that the evil was much like yourself all along, and that at its core, there lies a higher, golden truth.

In the end, you never know if you're the good guy; but one sure way to be the bad guy is to stipulate *a priori* that you're innocent and that you are combating the evil of others, and never try to see how their perspectives may apply to you.

Ladies and gentlemen, esteemed non-binaries—I give you communism, fascism and New Age. I give you dangerous dreams. To be approached, *nota bene*, with the sincerest irony you can muster.

THE SOLEMN VENGEFULNESS OF COMMUNISM ⅋

As you may know, the anarchists were eventually excluded from the International in the 19th century—Mikhail Bakunin lost the fight to Karl Marx, and the latter became the *de facto* intellectual and political leader of the European radicalized workers.

Unlike Bakunin, Marx thought it necessary to seize real *political* power, i.e. to keep the state intact during the first steps towards an anticipated classless and stateless society. Utopian socialist ideals such as those of Charles Fourier (one of the great pre-Marxist socialist thinkers, 1772-1837, also credited with coining the word "feminism") were sidelined to only be found in small "intentional communities"—attempts at rebooting society based on utopian standards, which always collapse and/or go sour after a while.

Real communism, Marx and Engels agreed with Bakunin, would exist only when the state had dissolved. But to begin with, there would be need for an interim dictatorship of the proletariat.[142] This idea of using state power to transform society stuck with the revolutionary communist movements and came to define communism and "real socialism" in the 20th century.

That is why communism, unlike anarchism and Fourierism, became a serious political force, centered in the Soviet Union—the only country of a non-ethnic and non-geographic denomination in the world, a society founded within the imaginary space of world-centric humanism.

Libertarian socialism never materialized beyond small parliamentary representations here and there, and anarchism or libertarian Marxism hardly excised any political power anywhere: These have existed almost entirely in the intellectual realm. As mentioned in Appendix A, the major wielders of power have all been *authoritarian* communists—following in the footsteps of Lenin's *coup d'état* in Russia.

The real leftwing political challenge to Marxism and Marxism-Leninism came from social democracy in the tradition of the philosopher Eduard Bernstein (1850-1932) and perhaps the French socialist leader Jean Jaurès (1859-1914), who sought a peaceful transition to socialism by democratic means and reforms. Whereas social democracy (and socialist parliamentary reformism) gained wide followership, it has in practice gravitated towards social liberalism—and in late modernity, towards green social liberalism; i.e. towards the attractor point of modern society. In reality, then, social-democratic countries have largely developed along similar lines as other capitalist welfare democracies.

The underlying principle of communism is more radical: to actively and deliberately transform the fundamental structures of society by shocking them with planned strategic actions thought to be in line with the attractors that society's inherent dynamics point towards. "Normal" society, "capitalist" society, "bourgeois" society—is simply viewed as ethically unacceptable. It's just not good enough; it's inhumane.

This—everything—everyday life with all its hierarchies, limitations and banality, is simply not enough. The communist *demands* more. The communist mind, its kernel of truth, grows from this solemn vengefulness against the injustices and insufficiencies of everyday life and from the determination that comes with it: a moral determination to transform all of society; to act for the sake of the weak and the exploited; to act with the willingness to risk everything—one's own life, one's lifetime of commitment, and even perhaps being wrong—to make the decisive move that breaks the boundaries of normal life and lets us come out on the other side. An honest sense of hope, a sincere and embodied sense of tragedy—and enough tempered righteous anger to remedy at least some of that tragedy.

That's the dangerous dream of communism. It has little to do with drab concrete housing blocks, or polluting Trabant cars, or secret KGB agents, or nuclear warheads, or military marches, or mad dictators, or any of the things we usually associate with communism. We can even detach it from any specific vision about who owns the factories or how the economy is governed.

Real communism, then, in this deeper sense, simply connects to the determination to do what it takes to bring about a **post-capitalist** society. By definition, a communist society is that which dialectically flows from, and transcends, capitalist society and in which everyday life is governed and coordinated by another logic than economic capital. This logic must be less cruel and more rational, more in line with human needs and higher stages of inner development. It is a holistic, humanized version of modernity. Communism, in this deeper and generalized sense, is holistic post-capitalism—plus the morally driven determination to achieve it.

The communists of the 19th and 20th centuries were wrong about a number of issues concerning the dynamics and attractors of modern societies and their economies. And this led to some terrible mistakes, the worst of which was trying to force institutions into being without corresponding developments of psychology, behavior and culture (see Appendix A and B); leading to jammed information feedback processes, which in turn led to a failing society, and ultimately to Gulag, surveillance, terror and collapse.

But some core aspects of communism were not in themselves false, only premature and out-of-context. Thereby I am *not* saying that bad consequences should be excused on account of good intentions. **I am saying that partial truths should not be discarded on account of guilt-by-association.**

What, then, are the communist truths shared by political metamodernism? One such aspect is the uncompromising moral determination to change the nature of everyday life. Another is that there is indeed some-thing that comes *after* capitalist relations, and that one can align oneself with such an emergence because it rhymes with discernable stages of technological and societal development. A third aspect is that there should be a collectively intelligent form of governance based upon a more radical and deeper form of democracy than representative party politics. A fourth one is that there should be a world-centric party (or meta-party) that takes on a transnational and even transcendental role of transforming soc-iety from a global perspective, and that there should be some kind of van-guard who develops and spreads a shared theoretical and organizational basis for such work. And a fifth, and last one, is that such a process-oriented party should rely upon the dialectics inherent to society in order to guide its development and to gain power.

The Nordic ideology is, obviously, not communism. It may be revolu-tionary, developmental and dialectical—but it is strictly non-violent. It works with other attractor points and it has other goals altogether. It sha-res the solemn vengefulness of communism, its tempered indignation: the grit, fire and guts to change a society that simply isn't good enough, to achieve a higher stage of development, and to serve a deeper equality.

THE (PARTIAL) GLORY OF FASCISM

It's difficult to be playful around fascism. It arose in shaky times, gathered absolute power in the hands of fanatic psychopaths who not only oppress-ed their own populations but also got us the Second World War and the Holocaust. To this day, we have crazy mass-killers swearing allegiance to fascist theories. Naturally, it's not a joke.[143]

And yet, the understanding of fascism as "pure evil" (and only an exist-ential lie) is simplistic, bordering on incorrect. There are very good rea-sons to revisit fascism and perform a little psycho-historical archeology to dig up partial truths that may serve political metamodernism and help us see the challenges ahead more clearly.

Here are a few circumstances that put the emergence of fascism in a different light:

- The link to (and partial overlap with) the genuinely revolutionizing form of modern art called Italian futurism, starting in 1909 with poet and art theorist Filippo Tommaso Marinetti who wrote the Futurist Manifesto. Futurism shows a number of signs reminiscent of meta-modernism as an art movement as well as a philosophy—emphasizing agency, mobility, totality, acceleration, development, technological transformations, the conquest of other areas of life under the domain of art—as I discuss elsewhere.[144]

- The undeniable genius and lasting relevance of fascist and proto-fascist political thinkers such as Carl Schmitt (who coined the insightful definition of a sovereign as "he who decides on the exception" and who went on to be the "crown jurist" of the Third Reich); Georges Sorel (who theorized the importance of myth in people's lives and developed his own flavor of post-Marxism); Vilfredo Pareto (who is known for the 80/20 principle of income distribution, but also embraced fascism); and the US-born poet Ezra Pound—just to mention a few. These weren't persons who got stuck in the fascist regimes of dumber people; they were deep thinkers whose oeuvres and lives led them to fascist conclusions.

- The relative progressivity of the 1919 Fascist Manifesto (also authored by Marinetti), containing: universal suffrage including women (opposed by most countries at the time), minimum wage, retirement at 55, the expansion of labor union rights and workers represented in boards of companies, and an eight-hour workday.

- The undeniable fervor and enthusiasm sparked within literally millions of people in the years during which fascism and nazism emerged. Of course, this ability to unify and inspire does not in itself justify fascism. It docs, however, highlight the fact that fascist practices can resonate with profoundly positive and beautiful emotions and coordinate many people's actions in large and non-capitalist projects (i.e. actions coordinated by other means than monetary exchanges).

- The general idea within fascism to view society and the populations as a developmental work of art. If you look at the 1929 novel *Michael* by Joseph Goebbels (who later became the propaganda minister of the Third Reich), you find the idea that a statesman is an artist:

> "Art is an expression of feeling. The artist differs from the non-artist in his ability to express what he feels. In some form or other. One artist does it in a painting, another in clay, a third in words, and a fourth in marble—or even in historical forms. For him, the nation is exactly what the stone is for the sculptor."[145]

Naturally, this is a dangerous and dumb idea if you fall off the holistic balance and land in totalitarianism. Of course, people aren't your "marble" to play around with. But the impulse in itself—to view society as a work of (co-created, participatory and democratically shared) art— is shared by political metamodernism. Society can be approached with the mind of an artist who wants to express his innermost depths.

Society should not be the result of a cold bureaucratic process, but of passionate creation and love—aiming at the development of the inner qualities of the population.

- The revolving door between fascist ideology and the far-left (Mussolini himself being an example, Georges Sorel another, even Goebbels and Hitler learning from Marxist theory and practices) as well as between deep ecology (recurring in Heidegger and many esoteric green fascists) as well as with radical conservatism (notably with the *Revolution von rechts* idea: "revolution from the right"), including authoritarian conservatism and its link to neoliberalism (via Pinochet's Chile, which espoused Milton Friedman's libertarian economics). Basically, you find fascism sneaking in here and there across the classical political spectrum—and even in spiritual and religious thinkers. Modern political thinkers will tend to emphasize the aspects that others share with fascism while denying their own connections, so as to prove one's moral high ground, being "the farthest from fascism", its very opposite. But it makes more sense to acknowledge that fascism has certain partial truths that are being denied and disowned, and then to productively own up to these and to include them in one's own perspective.

It should be apparent, then, that fascism cannot simply be discarded and never related to again. You can say that fascism is the catacombs of the modern ideological metropolis: It constitutes a vast network of secret and forgotten underground tunnels connecting all of the political ideologies. I guess you can say the same about all the ideologies to some extent— they all interconnect—but fascism remains the most denied and least understood.

The political metamodernist must learn to travel these dark tunnels without becoming a creature of the night. You drain the sewers, clean them up, put in proper lighting, make sure the pipes work—you get the picture. As such, political metamodernism is both the ideology that is the closest to fascism and the one most in opposition to it. The catacombs are there, whether we like it or not. The political metamodernist travels them and cleans them up; the liberal innocent denies their existence and sleepwalks in their dirt.

There is, naturally, something exquisitely demonic about fascism. As I argue in another book,[146] this demonic aspect can be understood in terms of relations between "metamemes": Fascist and nazi thinkers used early *postmodern* insights (like the mass psychology of Gustave Le Bon and ideas about image control in the media, some pretty advanced psychoanalytical and situational-psychological ideas as well as socialist critiques and the communist art of agitation) to manipulate a distinctly *modern* society at a moment of crisis in order to wrest control over modernity's advanced political machinery and economic prowess; to restore what is nominally a *postfaustian* society (traditional), but in practice amounts to a number of *faustian* goals and ideals (the conquest of the world, a master race, sheer power for the heck of it, war for the sake of war, the return of esoteric power gods, skulls on the sleeve, and so forth). That's exactly what the archetype of a demon signifies: a fallen angel, one close to God who uses an elevated and exalted position, an access to rare truths and insights (postmodern), for crude and narrow purposes (faustian).

That's the essential truth; fascism is so profoundly evil because it is demonic in this primary archetypal sense. A demon is a fallen angel, something profound and beautiful in the service of something base and shallow. Developmental imbalance. And every time you have such glaring developmental imbalances, you can know for sure the hell patrol is coming.

Political metamodernism can only be true to its cause and politically effective if it faces this great demon of modernity—fascism—and asks him for his central truth, for his gem (yes, demons have gems, they love 'em).

"So, okay then, dear mister get-kids-to-murder-and-torture-innocent-people-in-secret-death-camps, what's your secret? What could you possibly tell me? What do you have that I, the enlightened and democratic modern mind, lack and secretly desire?"

The green little devil smirks slyly and replies:

"One word, one word. There is a longing inside of you; one that I live out more fully than you, one that you deny, but still haunts the outer rims of your mind as it beckons to the innermost core of your soul. And on the hour of your death, it will grant me victory over you. The word is **heroism**."

Yes, everyday life under modernity's democracy and capitalism denies and suppresses an impulse shared by all of us: the drive for greatness, for superiority, for conquering death, for ascendance. A small part of us knows that we want more, that this life—and our role in it—is too petty, too drab, too trivial, too self-serving, too spiritually impoverished. We know we were meant, in some sense, to take the hero's journey, but we got caught up in mortgages and deadlines, and we tell ourselves that's all we ever really wanted.

We hide this side from one another, from ourselves. It embarrasses us immensely. We find ways to subtly and gleefully dismiss the deepest strivings of others as boyish, immature, puerile, distasteful, deluded. We deeply resent the glimmering greatness of one another because it reminds us of the subtle lies we live by. And instead we reenact these longings in movies, in books, in music, in fantasies and historic personae. If someone around us wishes to go down the highway of heroes, we use all the strategies we can to ridicule their effort:

> "Hah! They would have themselves be a movie character, a Rambo! They lack humility. But I am mature—I really am—and I will *never* be a hero. Ever. I don't even *want* to; only if fate forced my hand—which I by the way have a feeling might happen anytime soon—would I ever put on display the inner virtues that are uniquely my own! Until then, here's to keeping an honest job and watching TV. With some bloody dignity."

But when we utter these words to ourselves, we find our inner voices ringing strangely hollow. The green little devil's whisper lingers on: We want to be heroes; we know that we really *are* heroes, and we want to fight the good struggle, and win. We want to conquer mortality. We want to be unleashed as creators beyond our social roles and masks, beyond the trivial confines of everyday life. We want to sacrifice ourselves, as Gilgamesh, for the sake of unity so that we may live forever.

The word "fascism" stems from Italian *fascio* meaning a bundle of rods, ultimately from the Latin word *fasces*; it means to unite into a whole. Not all of us want heroism all the time and in every situation, but all of us do have this inner longing for greatness, for something far beyond ourselves. We like glory. A part of us secretly resents having given up any chance for rising higher—and that same part resents glimmers of the *Übermensch* in our fellow human beings.

For all its wackiness and evil, for all its developmental imbalances and inherent pathology, fascism is the ideology that most effectively honors this basic existential truth: the longing for heroism, power and transcendence through our deeds.

A reminder of this truth is the recurring role of dominance and submission in sexuality and eroticism. Democracy, fairness, gender equality, peace and deliberation—they all lack something: they lack that "oomph", zest, lust, that carnal and dark demonic princely power.

At the heart of humanity, there is a sexual beast seeking to be unleashed. For all its moral and practical superiority (even military, as it turned out), democracy is a bland nice guy. Fascism promises us an edgy bad boy and a sublime feminine surrender into uncontrolled explosive orgasms that shake the foundations of the cosmos. Fascism is the opposite of refined democracy: it is pure dominance and submission. It is speed, excitement, violence, blood, iron, autonomy, force, will, power. It is untamed—*erotic* in the deepest sense of the word.

Another reminder of the ubiquity of heroism in our psychology is the archetypal "hero's journey". Joseph Campbell famously described heroic blueprints shared by disparate mythologies, recurring in folk sagas, novels and movies (directly inspiring George Lucas in the creation of Star Wars). This universal narrative involves leaving our safety zone, traveling to our inner depths, facing danger, conquering evil, and returning in a transformed state of being.

Hitler galvanized people—albeit around a stupid plan involving killing everyone on the way down to the Black Sea so as to fill the area with racially pure Germans who would go back to working as farmers, have lots of blond children and driving down a giant autobahn to Crimea to go on summer vacation in extremely repetitive concrete blocks by the beach. Regardless of the apparent stupidity and absurdity of the plan, which was only thinly disguised and was in actuality supported by many Germans, there was something there that modern life otherwise never offers us: an epic, heroic struggle with no irony, no distance, no second thought, no excuses made. What does it matter, then, if the aim itself is entirely preposterous?

Fascism was and remains a feverish boy room fantasy. But psychologically, for all its immature lies and manipulations, it honored the fact that a part of us is always susceptible to such a dreamy will for greatness. We cannot truly "grow out of it"; only deny it. The world is not enough.

As lack of meaning and lacking sense of strength and vitality take hold in many young men, and some women, in our days, they turn again to these themes. From their imprisoned anguish grows new streams of fascism. Some few join overtly fascist movements, others nationalist and radical-conservative ones and "Indo-European identitarianism", and yet others find more innocent ways of reenacting aspects of these: pick-up artist "gaming" (social power games to get women), BDSM tantra workshops, violent porn, some of the authoritarian undercurrents of the men's movement, anti-feminism, anti-modern anti-"decadent" art sentiments, variations of theories about "the fall of the West" and other ideas about cyclical civilizational patterns where you need to rescue "civilization" by becoming more manly (again, a theme shared with the proto- and pre-fascists at the turn of the 20th century, with Oswald Spengler and others).

Not all of these things are all bad or all fascist. The men's movement and learning good dating skills particularly have potentials for creating productive results, and some aspects of these blend into political metamodernism. Viewed as a whole, these partly interrelated phenomena do however reflect the staying power of fascism and the masculine and boyish qualities it embodies. Most of it is relatively subtle and hidden from public view, but the psychological forces brewing are strong.

These tendencies work their way through the collective psyche and slowly prepare the ground for demands of a new "*Revolution von rechts*"; the sentiment that decadence has gone too far grows, "the West" or "civilization" or "the phallic order" or "the logos" are in danger, and this "necessitates" some "decisive masculine action" to "save" your favorite unit of identification (the West, this or that country, etc.).

Ah, a new brotherhood of Greek hoplites, free-roaming muscular heroes, always preparing for war! The women want it too, the fascist mind murmurs; they only came up with their angry feminism because they're subconsciously enraged with the too weakly and nerdy men of late modern society.

In short: Fascism stirs, sprung from cages—at a new and higher, more abstracted and yet more demonic level.

If you look at more overtly fascist thinkers such as representatives of the *Nouvelle Droite*, (the New Right) and more recently the Alt-Right (the Alternative Right), these *enjoy* the masculine anti-democratic qualities more unabashedly: bloggers, YouTubers and rightwing online media all base their ideas on Julius Evola's esoteric fascism, Tomislav Sunić presents his theses in a book smugly titled *Against Democracy and Equality* (1990), and US Alt-Right leader Richard Spencer performs fiery speeches about ethno-nationalism. There's that demonic quality again—it is shared to some extent by the online movement of the so-called "Dark Enlightenment" (a brand of anti-pomo anti-feminism mixed with different wild reactionary suggestions) and social media figures like Milo Yiannopoulos who criticize political correctness and leftwing "social justice warriors" and ridicule vegan "soy boys". Then there are radicals such as the pseudonym Bronze Age Pervert, flaunting more overt fascism, mixed with a kind of extreme, ironic humor. And there is Curt Doolittle's propertarianism, attracting many young men through the internet. There's even a "meta-right", whose members seem keen on learning from political metamodernism.

These wider tendencies create a vast network of strange bedfellows. Time and again, the different positions deny to be in league with each other but end up feeding the same underlying currents. Trump's populism doesn't like Richard Spencer's Alt-Right, but the latter likes the former and claims to have influenced him. Jordan Peterson, the Jungian psychologist who calls himself a "classical liberal", talks approvingly about posh brit Milo Yiannopoulos, who in turn loves Trump, who in turn was put in office with the help of Russian online troll factories, who spread anti-feminist ideas, which are recycled by the men's movement and the loosely related BDSM tantra workshops (including some rather nasty sex cults, such as The New Tantra).

The Russian online trolls spread ideas about the fall of the West and the "Fourth Theory" ideas of Putin's chief philosopher Aleksandr Dugin, who claims not to be fascist but is part of a Russian machinery that supports radical nationalist parties across Europe, the leaders of which read up on the power-grabbing theories of Carl Schmitt and others who inspired the 20th century fascists, and thus they gain edge on the conventional politicians who only do law, economics and boring conventional political science. I have been invited to such Kremlin-paid meetings myself (to unite "alternative" European politics).

In the US, the National Rifle Association is propped up by the Russian government and supports Trump, while arming a population of mostly white reactionary males who feel Western civilization is being lost. And Steven Bannon buys Facebook data and conspires with the company Cambridge Analytica to win the culture wars in a neo-conservative direction through targeted manipulations of public opinion.

Phew. Strange bedfellows, indeed.

I'm not saying all of these should be reduced to one another. Getting a good whipping at a BDSM retreat doesn't make you a fascist, nor is Peterson a Trump fan (but would have voted for him), and Trump is not a Russian neo-fascist, etc. And not all of them are all wrong or crazy. The point is merely that the same underlying fascist impulse is there.

These are the dark tunnels beneath Metropolis Modernity that I was talking about. They all connect.

People who don't know the fascist catacombs can sometimes end up in arguments about masculinity or being against politically correct intersectional feminism, or criticizing some aspects of Islam, and find a flattering and surprising surge of support and enthusiasm from people they normally wouldn't associate with. Some of them understand they're getting a little demonic boost from the underworld, but many remain genuinely naive to what's going on. The atheist philosopher Sam Harris—who is a fierce critic of Islam—was earnestly surprised that so many of his followers were devoted Trump fans and vehemently resisted him when he sided with Hillary Clinton in the 2016 presidential election.

What, then, does any of this have to do with political metamodernism? Here it is: **Political metamodernism shares a part of that same demonic**

quality, which comes from owning the unapologetic striving to take the hero's journey.

This one goes out especially to all the nice guys out there who have had this inner split about Hanzi and metamodernism from the start. The nice guys (it's usually men) get something dark in their eyes and they say:

> "You are saying all of these progressive, sensitive things about a 'listening society' and the value of hard inner work, but you keep acting slightly evil, and you keep talking about gaining power. There is a performative contradiction here: The theorists we are looking for should be calm, kind and wise—free from worldly desires and strivings—but you are presenting a sneaky and aloof persona. What you are saying is interesting and rings somewhat true; yet there is something *lacking*, perhaps not as much in your theories as in you, Hanzi, as a person. It makes me, the pensive idealistic guy, suspicious and it leaves me with a subtle uneasy sense that there is something… *demonic* going on. It seems you can reach higher truths than you quite should, and you seem to be too immature to use them responsibly; you seem to be using philosophical and spiritual insight for power. For my part, I will learn a thing or two from you, but then I will return to the safe, pure, goodhearted, simple and humble path for developing society."

And I guess that right *there* is the ultimate litmus test for the metamodern mind. The metamodern mind sees that all nodes in the great weave of life long for power, for expansion, for fuller expression. And it sees that competition—just as love and trade—is an irremovable element of social reality itself.

So, hey there Nice Guy. Yes you. You know I am talking to you. Do you know who *actually* whispered the above words in your ear? It wasn't your conscience, not your inner angel.

It was the green little devil, a sly smirk nudging his thin lips again. Your green little devil is prepared to use morality and claims of moral purity for the legitimization of your own will to power at the expense of others, and at the expense of truthfulness.

The reason you get this "dark ominous sense" when reading Hanzi isn't that you're good and I'm evil. That was what you believed, wasn't it? It's that I own my green little devil and have it tamed, but yours is sneaking about and lying to you and controlling you. Your conscience lied to you. You were caught by the devil's lasso.

The dark ominous feeling you get when you see me prancing around is not a reflection of your kind, critical mind resisting the sell-out to power that I represent. It is a reflection of your own disowned green little devil, of your disowned will to power, and the resentment you feel when someone else expresses so clearly and straightforwardly what you have hidden away from view. You're the sell-out, not me.

How do I *know* that? I know it simply because I understand that power and freedom are sisters; creation *is* power. So any time you want to change or create anything, you must have a will to power, and any time you make a power claim, there will be adversaries who have different ideas, ideals and interests, and thus you have to own up to that adversity and you have to try to win. And without a wish to change or create anything, you can have no morality; no wish to strive for the good. Hence: **pure morality *requires* a pure will to power**. Your denied will to power is immoral, and that's what you feel reflected in yourself when you watch me unfold without apology.

You can wait around for another hundred years if you like—but Yoda isn't coming. There won't be another "pure" path of only kindness and wisdom under a pure and kind teacher and leader. And no, you won't become that person yourself when you're older. That's your green little devil talking: your disowned longing for greatness. There isn't a pure path in which you don't have to relate to the demonic quality of creation and change. Moral purity, calm wisdom, humility—that's the lie, that's "the liberal innocent".

And here's the bottom line: **Your green little devil is transpersonally connected to mine, just as your mind is to mine.** We are all nodes in the great web of life; and life pulsates with the will to power. All life literally eats its way through other flows of matter and energy. All events feed on entropy; on decay. A human body consists of organic matter under violent control: killed, chewed, swallowed, digested, broken down and reorganized. This is an indisputable physical fact. Power is transpersonal because **all creation is co-creation**, and all emergence is relational—and power, ultimately, is the will and capacity to freely create; it is the will of potentials to emerge as actualities.

And herein lies, of course, the deep connection between fascism and Nietzsche's philosophy. Naturally, Nietzsche was misread and misinterpreted in the crude and anti-intellectual times that followed his death, but this fundamental impulse remains true: an unapologetic affirmation of the will to power, the striving to get past any obstacles of fear, shame, guilt and *Sklavenmoral*, and to freely express our highest inner expressions: the *Übermensch*.

Here's my suggestion—how about we stop trying to exorcise one another's "egos" and "shadows", and instead own up to the creative sparks

we all share; and then play together as mutually empowering and beau-
tifully imperfect co-creators, to write new values on new tablets?

When you run around trying to reveal, tear down and (let's admit it)
punish the egos and wills to power of others, are you really acting with the
purity of intent you're telling yourself? How many times have you found
yourself saying things behind the backs of others, things where you make
unqualified psychoanalytical guesses about their dark hidden motives? Do
you really think that stuff is coming from a place of moral concern and
the purity of your soul? Spanish Inquisition, anyone? Nobody expects it,
but it always shows up. The inquisitor always wears a mask, and beneath
the mask is—again—the green little devil, your disowned will to power.

Nice Guy. Stop being a hypocritical inquisitor or witch-hunter and
admit that you want shitloads of delicious power—and then be kind to
people.

We should all try our best to be kindhearted. But there is also *Sklavenmoral* disguised as niceness, and that's a problem.

Unapologetically in love with power—*and* uncompromisingly idealistic. Both and. Right there is an equilibrium from which we can build a very
profound sense of interpersonal, or transpersonal, trust. And that's the
space from which metamodern politics can emerge—from the trust that
you will use your power kindly and I will use mine kindly, for mutual benefit and mutual goals; in a network of shared will to transpersonal power.

And here is the really cool part. Listen now.

Once you admit you want shitloads of delicious power, that you **crave
pure co-creation**, and you see and accept that same will in all other creatures—a profound sense of equality descends upon your soul; I guess you
could say "equanimity" as we mentioned earlier.

**At the heart of the will to power rests the most radical egalitarianism
and universalism.** This is what allows us, among other things, to study
stages of adult development in a truly non-judgmental, accepting and non
-competitive manner. The competitive element of life becomes purified
and falls in its proper place—eternally balanced by love and exchange,
solidarity and trade; God doesn't love one more than another.

So what if Hanzi has come farther than you in terms of philosophical
insight, so what if I contain your perspective but you couldn't have contained or recreated mine? It doesn't matter; more fundamentally, we are
still equals, and in other aspects you are my superior. There's nothing to
it; it just is what it is. Radical egalitarianism. We are all chosen, all sublime, all exquisitely precious.

Seriously, try it. Embrace your inner princely darkness. The green little devil stops whispering at the outer rims of your mind; it goes quiet. Your moral outrage ceases to murmur. Silence is there. And with silence comes clarity. And with clarity comes a more sustainable and authentic goodwill and kindness.

You recognize the simple truth that everybody is just super-vulnerable and utterly pathetic—yes, Hanzi too—and that the dynamics of everyday life force us to *pretend* to have dignity and to try to look like we know what we're doing, and that's why we want power. That's why you want power, too. We'll just admit the whole thing, no more obfuscation. From there on we can play together in sincere irony and informed naivety.

The metamodern perspective uses its capacity for perspective taking, its existential insights, and its idealism, to gain power. That's its demonic quality, and that's why there must always be a dark and dangerous element to any form of political metamodernism—a Machiavellian element. You cannot get rid of it by "getting over your ego"; you must stay with it, and balance it, and make it transparent and shared. It must always remain dangerous. Energy is movement, and movement is dangerous; all becoming is also destruction. Entropy.

This is where fascism informs political metamodernism; this is the glory of fascism—it honors the will to power, to superiority, to what Socrates called **megalothymia**. It's that principle within us that wants more, to be viewed and recognized not only as an equal member of society, but as a majestic and awe-inspiring being. That's the truth even about Dalai Lama, Eckhart Tolle and Yoda. And centuries of denial and meditation will never efface it: to want anything, is to want power.

Look at your demon. Dance with the devil, lest he'll make you his bitch. Grab his fucking gem; it shines not only with an owned-up-to will to power that connects you to the will to power of all others, and thus to the non-local emergence of the universe; it shines with the pristine love of all perspectives.

Fascism lets you play the hero. It honors the principle of megalothymia. Democratic capitalism not so much; you deny your heroism and that of others. Political metamodernism lets you play the hero again, owning that part of yourself and others, just with ironic distance. It's like grounding an electrical wire. And once that is done, we are free to travel these tunnels without being electrocuted, to think in terms of "political theology" (the discipline that studies the dynamics of how small, determined groups can seize power and constitute themselves as sovereign).

And then let's play together to co-create a more conscious society. Bring your demon's gem or don't come at all.

Don't hate the will to power of others—love it, balance it, and play with it. Again: love the game *and* love its players. Allow for others to relate to you in the same manner. Let us build that transpersonal trust, cultivate that transpersonal integrity. That is the metamodern perspective; the one that has solidarity with all perspectives.

EXCURSION: OBEDIENCE AS LAUGHTER

Before we go on to examining New Age Spirituality, I would like to make a brief excursion into understanding the obedience that can feed fascism in today's world. My claim is that the next murderous regime will be less based around agitation, fear-mongering and fiery speeches. It will come, there is good reason to suspect, from the source we least expect: comedy.

In the echoing laughter of the crowd, transmitted over long distances of networked broadcasting, we will find the next genocide. Unwanted populations violently exterminated, and the crowd laughing, laughing.

In today's media-saturated society, jesters are indeed becoming kings. This is an aspect inherent to the postmodern condition, where the global village is imprinted upon us through a deluge of images from near and far, from across time and space—always told with someone's perspective, someone's story, someone's spin. The jesters, the tricksters, are the ones most proficient at catching people's attention, and then quickly shifting between frames of understanding, between contexts.

That's how comedy works: some frame or circumstance is suddenly shifted in communication, and—whack!—things get funny. The simplest example is a pun or play-on-words: "Did you hear about the guy whose whole left side was cut off? He's all right now." The linguistics shift the meaning for us, creating a double meaning that catapults us, in this case, from the reassuring to the gruesome. A frame is shifted.

Add a refined sense of pacing, timing, rhythm—and nobody can stop the laughter from breaking out as clear water from a fountainhead.

Postmodern culture, the culture of perspective and surface, is a lot about mastering such framings of situations. One person can be framed as a hero, a president, a crook, a buffoon. Those who can most skillfully craft frames and shift between them with sleights-of-hand, in and across many different media are also likely to become the most powerful.

The late-night shows, the television hosts, the comedians—their power is growing. Jesters are becoming kings. The youth are getting their news filtered through comedy and entertainment. The jesters grab the attention of everyone, shaping and directing it—making us laugh together.

A large crowd laughing, united under one will. Oh, that's so funny. That's so edgy. They're so smart, so admirable. Comedy is so liberating.

And then there is a subtle slide… If we all laughed along, then that must mean we all at least somewhat agreed, that what was said was at least partly true. And whoever was laughed at must have been, at least in part, at fault. We slide into assuming that the power to make us laugh is also the power to tell us the truth—or to suspend another truth, another story, another felt experience.

When we laugh we don't only break taboos, relieve tensions and forge bonds. The laughter of the crowd also disciplines people into silence, and obedience—if anyone gets mad and says it isn't funny, they just appear to be poor sportsmen with sticks up their asses. It stratifies us: the joker on top and the butt of the joke at the bottom. It unifies us, yes, but into "us and them", with a rather clear who's who.

Can you see it? **The laughter of the crowd is a source of massive hidden obedience and submission to one will.** Can you think of any other moments when you can get hundreds, thousands, millions of people to suspend normal morality and to fall in line around the same point? Is there any better way to effectively steer a crowd?

The fascists of a hundred years ago hijacked the techniques of traveling socialist agitators. These knew how to display a sincere criticism of society, of how to fire up a crowd, how to point out glaring injustices. The fascists caught on. Yet in today' world, where educated and comfortable populations are suspicious of such fiery speeches, of fanaticism and lack of irony, the corresponding effect is achieved through jokes. Do you imagine that the fascists today might be paying attention and catching on?

It's already happening. If you take a look at online movements of the far Right, such as the Alt-Right and the "meta-right", these are packed with transgressive jokes and irony—often to the level of extreme absurdity so that it's no longer distinguishable what is a joke, what is "post-truth" and what is sincere and what is not. The far Right jokes more than anyone else. They joke and joke and make memes until reality itself becomes transmogorified into a dream state where nothing is real and nothing needs to be taken seriously. If we have already joked a million times about being nazis and killing Jews, and waging war, and about a conspiracy that undermines our civilization, and about our own megalomania… then when the images of real crimes crop up, we keep joking, keep laughing. "Relax, it's just a joke. Don't you get it, huh? All the smart people do.

You're one of the smart people, aren't you? You're not one of those with a stick up your ass who can't even take watching children and animals being slit up alive—are you? I'm one of the crazy ones, the ones who know the subtle art of not giving a fuck. To me, there is nothing you can't laugh about. Only people who are against freedom would like to set taboos for what you may or may not joke and laugh about."

During the Second World War, Charlie Chaplin famously made a parody of Hitler in his 1940 film, *The Great Dictator*. Chaplin used comedy to demask and demystify the power and allure of dictatorship and totalitarianism. And of course, this postmodern move, one of irony and parody, proved to be the hallmark of a superior society; one that ultimately beat the complete lack of self-distance that marked the fascists. When one side screams and rages on, and the other changes the frame and makes us all laugh—of course the latter is going to win. Of course the latter is going to be allied with a superior information processing system, which ultimately wins the war.

But now, nearing a century after the first emergence of fascism, the forces that want violence and bloodshed have learned a thing or two. This time, they won't try to be Hitler—they'll try to be Charlie Chaplin. The next dictator, the one who seduces crowds and leads the masses into transgressing common decency and morality, supporting nihilism in its destructive form and an abandonment of all empathy—will be a comedian. Today, only comedians can claim the absolute and amoral obedience of the crowd. Guess who also likes absolute and amoral obedience of the crowd? The totalitarian dictator.[147]

Michael Billig, a professor of social science, published a book in 2005 titled *Laughter and Ridicule: Toward a Social Critique of Humour*. Boringly written as it is, this book seems almost prophetic: Billig was amongst the first to see that with laughter comes ridicule, and thus comes a reaffirmation of power relations; sometimes liberating, but all too often disciplining and oppressive. Laughter often says: Shut the fuck up and obey.

Today's inquisition, today's Thought Police, thrives on the power of laughter. The most (pathologically) power hungry amongst us will become masters of mean and crafty jokes. And they will get away with it. And they will rule. And you will obey them with the rest of the mob.

What, then, beats laugher and ridicule? We may turn again to the early writings of Nietzsche. In his 1872 work, *The Birth of Tragedy*, he argues that tragedy is a higher and more refined art form than the "Apollonian" search for perfection in sculpture and "Dionysian" rapture and self-expression in the moment-to-moment flows of music. And indeed, in literature and theatre, comedy has never been able to become as highly esteemed as tragedy.

Tragedy is thus an expression of a higher synthesis; it resonates with more profound and vulnerable layers of the human soul. And tragedy is best expressed through poetry in its many different forms, poetry in a wide sense, what is sometimes called "poetics".

In the times to come, then, dictatorship and oppression, sadistic power and masochistic submission, will come disguised in the form of comedy and laughter.

Resistance and emancipation, kindness and freedom, will come from that which brings a tear to our eye—from a subtle sense of tragedy, expressed in different media, by poets of different shapes and sizes.

In these times, building upon the experiences of the last century, we have accustomed ourselves to thinking of the trickster as the hero. That used to be a good rule-of-thumb, and it still *can* be, in some cases. But this intuition will be increasingly treacherous in the times ahead.

We are beginning to see the unfolding of a subtle battle-performed-as-play for the global human soul—the nearest thing to what might be called a cosmic struggle between good and evil: **the evil comedian, who speaks to the masses but secretly despises them as a herd that follows the crude mechanics of humor understood only by a select elite, against the good poet, who sings to the few, but is in love with the many and their creative spark of collective intelligence**. This is the struggle-reborn-as-play, stirring at midnight in the garden of good and evil.

David Foster Wallace, the early metamodernist novelist and cultural commentator who died by suicide in 2008, aged 46, author of the dense, thick and magisterial novel with the prophetic title *Infinite Jest* (1996), once said in 1990 "that the next real literary rebels in America would be artists with little interest in trying to shock or upset their peers but who were, rather, willing to become so credulous of everything in the world that their peers would *laugh* at them".[148] That's what takes greater courage, and that's where liberation is to be found—in a new sincerity.

The dictator-comedian, the jester-king, steers the laughter, pacing it with perfect timing as a director would an orchestra—often saying things that would have been completely unacceptable had they been voiced by an ordinary person. Remember Carl Schmitt's definition of the sovereign as "he who decides on the exception"? To a growing extent this seems to apply to the comedian: the elevated position of being excepted from the morality applying to everyone else. The consumtariat—the underclass of the informational and attentionalist digital economy, perpetually starved for authentic meaning, participation, community and recognition—always stuck in the role of onlookers, always consumers, always spectators; they laugh along greedily, hiding in the crowd, cheering. The consumtariat are offered a false sense of participation and superiority: Chuckling along, they momentarily feel that they are part of what happens, and on the winning side, too. Indeed, laughter is the new heiling.

But the transmogorified dream-world of boundary-less jokes is not a productive outlet for the human soul. If, in the 20th century the biggest joke was The Great Dictator; today's biggest tragedy is The Great Spectator. The Great Dictator was an easier foe, because The Great Spectator turns out to be yourself.

The Great Spectator will mindlessly laugh along, from his own sense of inferiority, envy and *Sklavenmoral*—while the poet acts and is laughed at. What about you, will you laugh your way to obedience and meaningless murder, or will you side with the laughed-at? Will you sing with the informed naivety of the metamodern heart—one that can resist the cruel laughter of a crowd reduced to groveling slaves?

GLIMMERS OF NEW AGE SPIRITUALITY

I'd wish things would get less demonic around this time and that I could point to a cuter and happier ending when we get to New Age spirituality. But alas, as the human (or post-human) condition progresses, it only gets more wondrous, complex, perilous and terrifying, all at once. As Leon Trotsky is quoted in Appendix A, "The forms of life will become dynamically dramatic […] And above this ridge new peaks will rise." He just forgot to mention the new opening abyss between us and the peaks. Higher emancipation, incidentally, is found on the very edge of doom.

For many readers, no doubt, "New Age" seems to be the odd one out in a chapter about the totalitarian ideologies of the 20th century. Communism, fascism, and… New Age? These phenomena aren't usually discussed in the same context. And yet, there is a clear and fundamental pattern connecting the three; even a logical, historical progression (as well as more interconnecting ties and overlaps than we could name or hope to trace).

The three ideologies appeared and gained prominence in sequence as modern society progressed, each of them related to holistic visions, and each of them led to totalitarian, abusive and collapsed societies. Communism relates to a profound social equality and union between humans, to the abolition of the "shame-regime" as discussed in chapter 5 (since no one would have lower status in the communist utopia). Fascism builds upon the communist radical unity and the rise of certain strong wills and great figures in that unified society and a conscious refinement of humanity, corresponding to the abolition of the *Sklavenmoral*-regime. And the New Age movements aimed at creating a reign of universal love flowing from a genuinely unified and deeply emancipated humanity, unifying us not only with one another, but with the cosmos at large, with all life, and with our highest inner potentials—in Hanzi language, with our "highest subjective states" and "greatest inner depths". Like communism, New Age spirituality is utopian and egalitarian, like fascism it emphasizes the distinctions between the genders as well as the value of authenticity and fullness of commitment and of total submission of the ego and dissolution into a complete unity. This corresponds to the "higher reaches of freedom" pertaining to the later stages of human development, to the deepest reaches of our imaginations and the most universalistic and holistic visions of society and humanity.

Because of its developmental qualities, reaching higher and deeper than communism and fascism, New Age holds the potential for a more hellish, oppressive and suffocating totalitarianism than anything hitherto seen in communist and fascist societies. Luckily for us, no utopian New Age movements really gained power in the 20th century—their social sustainability was simply too low to grow beyond small communities and inward-looking cults. The exception may be Scientology, which turned itself into a self-sustaining market mechanism using psychological coercion to get people to aggressively pool money into real estate around the world, which in turn boasts the identities of members ("look at my big temple") who then gain incentives to uphold the structure.

The close connection between fascism and say Adı Da's cult, or that of Osho, or Scientology, may be difficult to spot on a surface level. After all, fascists are tough and manly, and New Agers soft and spiritual. But many scholars have shown that fascism—new and old—is full to the brim with esoteric and spiritual underpinnings. Karla Poewe, Pankaj Mishra and Göran Dahl are worth mentioning in this context.

Viewed with the goggles of my own theory, this is the developmental imbalance of "the magic residual" at work, as explained in Book One; i.e. people who have greater depth and/or state than complexity and/or code tend to seek wholeness and be drawn to the non-rational in the search of the transrational. In other words, you have a pervasive sense there is something more to the world and to reality than we can normally describe and grasp with our conscious conceptual minds, and that the direct experience

of reality always points towards something larger than any specific structure of thought, but that something requires that we jump off a cliff into
the unknown, that we stop thinking and allow ourselves to "fully be".

This impulse, while true, opens the door inside of us for a holistic vision that would unite all of society with primary, archetypal and spiritual
forces: Martin Heidegger initially supported the Nazis and Carl Jung had
early writings which spoke of collective Aryan and Jewish psyches, and
countless other "deep stuff" thinkers have fallen into similar traps. There
is a *very* close connection between fascism and the New Age, most recently revealed perhaps by the harrowing example of Andrew Cohen's cult.

Why then would I claim that New Age has the potential to be even
more hellish than Gulag or Holocaust? Think about it: These relations
involve your innermost *ontological* belief structures. They can make you
believe that if you don't follow suit, if you even think the wrong thought,
you will be punished for a literal *eternity* of unbearable suffering. And
they can make you believe that in full and earnest. That's much, much
more radical than making you think you're a bad comrade or not a part of
the master race. And they can make you believe that the fate of the entire
cosmos, *literally speaking*, depends on your work with this and that inner
purification, enlightenment, etc. And they can make you believe this or
that person is *literally God* speaking and that nothing else has any relevance compared to what they may be saying. And they can make you intimately feel that with every cell of your body and soul. It's the Michelin
Star Club of totalitarianism. It's totalitarianism *magna cum laude*, extra
everything; ketchup *and* mustard. Because it reaches into the depths of
your soul and controls parts of you neither Stalin nor Hitler could reach.
In theory, then, what crimes could that sort of power make you commit?
And if you were invested in it, what would you be prepared to do to
defend it from perceived attackers?

If you consider the stories told by some escapees of North Korea, you
notice this pattern. This is a nominally communist country, which all but
in name has transitioned to a caste-like hyper-militarized fascist society,
and where you increasingly see the use of supernatural narratives to legitimize political power. Miracles are associated with the Supreme Leader,
and it can take years for a young woman who escaped to get rid of the
belief that he is reading her mind. That, if anything, is worse that Orwell's
1984. And it's pretty close to what has been reported by ex-Scientologists.
If Scientology would have managed to take over society as a whole, you
might have seen similar patterns emerging in other countries or at a larger
scale.

And then there's always that distinct trait of totalitarianism: First you have a creative burst for a period in which the arts flower, then you converge around a massive repetition, a complete shut-down of all art. Scientology looks and feels exactly the same today as it did in the 1970s, except now in an ironic and more critically minded age, it all looks extremely kitschy and hysterical. The same is true of North Korea: There are painters, sure, but their skills are entirely tamed and employed on a production-line basis, all in credit of the regime and its worldview. The same happened with nazism during its very short period of existence and with the "permanent revolution" in some communist countries. If someone gets to you with the idea that they have a correct grasp of "the totality", any divergence, even in your dreams, becomes a subject of great existential terror. This adds another, and more terrifying, layer of meaning to Orwell's "boot stamping on a human face—for ever". Personally, I would rather be gassed to death naked than to have someone convince me of an eternity of suffering for me and others if I don't obey. Spiritual involvement opens the door to a whole new world of horrors.

And yet, it would be wrong to think that universal love and higher inner states have no place in the future of humanity. Again, it's a matter of developmental imbalances; the spiritual and existential insights that informed and energized the New Age movement in its many forms, and the profound and authentic experiences that gave it life, are not in themselves false. They're simply too big and too difficult to manage to fit into whatever human relationships, social roles and symbolic universes we construct, and so these relationships and roles always self-destruct pretty soon after we start engaging with the highest (spiritual) subjective states.

As society progresses and we reach deeper into ourselves in order to deal with the existential underpinnings of civilization as well as coordinating our streams-of-action on subtler and more complex levels, we are bound to come face to face again with these spiritual or cosmic peaks and abysses. Individually, many of us can ignore these issues and live "normal lives" and not be bothered, but transpersonally speaking, we as a global society and emerging posthumans cannot avoid it. We are going to have to deal with the terrifying depths and towering heights of existence, with the vast oceans of being, with the eternities of tragedy and suffering and the unbearable infinity of potential—sooner or later.

If the present world-system survives and development continues to accelerate, consciousness is very likely to self-organize into posthuman stages mirroring the great existential depths intuited by the mystics. The

New Age movements have given us a brief taste of these farther land-scapes of the soul, of the peaks—and the great abyss.

The abyss. We then, collectively and transpersonally, encounter a more profound terror than has hitherto been experienced; a terror intuited only in madness and bad psychedelic trips. A terror beyond death: an experi-enced eternity of looped suffering. There is a towering challenge ahead of us; beyond anything yet experienced in the history of the known universe. The scale is of a whole other magnitude, the stakes of a cosmic kind. Sheer terror, pure emptiness—and a corresponding level of evil, always found, ultimately, within ourselves. The highest good—universal love and accep-tance—can only be attained by facing the greatest and purest of evils. Although this challenge lies outside the scope of the political metamoder-nism I have formulated, the latter can at least commence the needed pre-paratory work for this unavoidable challenge to our innermost being. Only an existentially mature civilization will be able to face the surmount-ing terror.

You cannot gaze into the abyss without being moved. You cannot taste the heavens without becoming, at least in some abstract sense, a believer. And that's what political metamodernism shares with the New Age: an acceptance of the highest subjective states, their ultimate significance and transrational truth; that of universal love and acceptance, the dissolution of our separate identifications, and the non-attachment to ideas and beli-efs. In brief moments, these higher potentials can animate us, "As spring sweeps uninvited into barren gardens, as morning breezes reinvigorate dormant deserts", as one of the most celebrated poets of the Urdu langu-age, Faiz Ahmed Faiz once wrote.[149]

These flowers of freshest hue must be met by an unequivocal commit-ment to deal with a corresponding level of existential terror. Unlike the New Ager, the metamodern mind is not a millenarian one; we don't bel-ieve that a wave of light will "come soon" and "wash over" all of us and this will make people "wake up" and that we are the carriers of that evan-gel (or some circumscription of the latter). We just recognize that there is such a thing as spirituality, yes, and we allow for faint glimmers of it to hint us about a potential future that is both incomprehensively magnifi-cent and terrifying beyond imagination.

We do, however, share the idea that inner transformation is an import-ant and essential part of societal transformation, and ultimately of socie-ty's survival. And we share the idea that self-knowledge tends to lead to greater universalism and love, however tortuous and difficult the path. And we believe this path is not laid down, but that it must be continually paved and rediscovered as we interact with the open systems of the world as these open systems inevitably also change us.

Here we return to the metamodern idea of **proto-synthesis**—we cannot just throw all maps of meaning and directionality overboard. We must see that spiritual insight and higher universal love are powerful future attractors, but that they reside in the posthuman or transhuman realm of potentials, which means that we shouldn't rush it. In this case, we must remain careful and conservative, as the sheer terror that can be unleashed under the auspices of a "**metamodern totalitarianism**" leaves a heavy ethical burden on us. Imagine a world where dictators control your soul and the construction of your social universe and have a thousand social, psychological, chemical and technological tools to control the structure of your mind. That would be beyond nasty.

Where does this leave us? At the spot where political metamodernism seeks to carefully work for the *relative utopia* of a listening society—a society that has resolved the modern problems of sustainability, inequality and alienation; but it must always stop before any direct, passionate and non-ironic utopianism.

So fundamentally, whether political metamodernism becomes a force for good or evil in the world—or just another obscure cult-like grouping—depends upon **our shared ability to manage paradoxes and both-ands**. And it depends upon our willingness and capacity to engage with the open systems of the world, and letting these systems change us, while still keeping some kind of shared map.

It is okay to let glimmers of New Age spirituality—and traditional paths in general—inform and inspire us. They must, however, never govern us, lest we will inherit all their pathologies, albeit in a magnified and yet more toxic version. These are dangerous dreams.

Political metamodernism is a bit like standing on the North Pole; if you go far enough north, so that you actually stand on the exact location of the North Pole, east and west and north all disappear; on that particular spot there is only south—in all directions. When you get really close to it, all directions become the *opposite* of what you want to achieve, and yet you have to keep trying to go "north of the North Pole".

There's a koan to stay with: What is north of the North Pole?

EPILOGUE

"Watchman, what is left of the night? Watchman, what is left of the night?"

The watchman replies, "Morning is coming, but also the night. If you would ask, then ask; and come back yet again."

—Isaiah 21:11-12

Our journey together is drawing to a close. We began on the first page of Book One with a promise that political metamodernism—or its beginnings in the Nordic ideology echoing throughout the "most developed" parts of the world—is the most powerful ideology in the world today and that it beats all other ideologies on their own terms. I also said that you would understand personal and societal development as well as freedom.

I hope you find the goods have been delivered, a vision to shine forth upon our clouded hills. If not, at least I hope you've had fun and that you can use this for something else in your life.

I have put serious thought into whether I should conclude with a "power ballad" (unapologetically pretentious musings of political poetry) or with a conservative word of warning, and I have decided to settle upon the latter. There are still some loose threads that can and will cause harm unless they are dealt with preemptively and continuously.

One such issue that must be dealt with concerns the risk of creating a cult-like community around political metamodernism. This one is sneaky —it really is—and it's the one thing everyone thinks they themselves are immune to; but nobody is. Cult-like social dynamics can and do show up in so many ways. Given that political metamodernism includes some wide- and deep-reaching perspectives with high psychological, social and even existential stakes, it should only be expected that they are difficult to fit in our minds without us becoming a bit feverish about them; let alone in our relationships without these becoming overburdened and unsustainable; let alone in politics and organizations deliberately designed to gain power and to effect a fundamental shift in society.

This hotchpotch has everything needed to make people's emotions and imaginations soar, to fill us with meaning and high states and inspiring horizons, and hence to make us really bitter if our expectations aren't met and our hopes don't materialize.

And it relates to many transpersonal issues where we can get stuck in quite complicated clusters of integrated personal-professional-political and even spiritual relationships that go sour and leave us shaken to our core and utterly confused. As people try to gather around these or similar ideas, the coordination of our minds and actions is difficult because it involves so many parts of us. It is more than a little tempting to give in to a totalitarian process that subtly pressures people to comply and conform so that we can feel we have successfully come together and that decisive steps are being taken.

This is a confusing and strange landscape to travel. It can lead to a sense of dark bewilderment and a subtle but profound sadness. It can lead to small cult-like enclaves and sectarian splinters and squabbles. It can even lead to new totalitarianisms at a societal—perhaps even global—level. And yet, I believe, it *is* the path that we have ahead of us: a path that involves getting over our blindness of developmental stages and inner dimensions; a path towards an existentially mature and listening society.

Our best defense against new totalitarianisms is to find ways of looking inwards to engage with our necessary but dangerous dreams in transparent and democratic ways where a multiplicity of perspectives (and perspectives of perspectives) balance out and dissipate their explosive concentrations of power. We must create institutions that support higher stages of personal development. And to do that without it being totalitarian, we need to improve the processes of democratic governance.

On a more personal day-to-day level, how do you prevent cult-like structures from emerging, dragging the lives of the ones involved in the dirt? Here's a bullet list.

- See to it that activities engage with the **open systems of the world**, i.e. that they never become closed in a loop around the (supposed) metamodernists themselves. In other words, focus on politics, arts and sciences—not on workshops for personal development and experimenting with the process of meeting in new ways. If the setting you're in doesn't focus on politics, find a new one.

- **Focus on scientific methods and methodologies**, i.e. on understanding how development should be evaluated and measured. Otherwise people will just assume they are at the highest stages and begin to confirm one another in these beliefs, which sets you apart from the world around you and prepares the ground for a collapse of your relations. And then we go down together like a lead balloon.

- **Don't go on witch-hunts.** In other words, don't try to use Jungian analysis or any other forced therapy session on folks who don't agree with you. Don't blame "their shadow" and don't make hypotheses about their hidden motives. Just meet their arguments, if you can. And demand the same respect from others. Otherwise you very easily get stuck in an eternal trench war, each trying to "out-Freud" one another and gathering others to your side by effectively back-talking other people.

- **Don't label people by stages and developmental traits.** Speculate a bit about people's developmental stage, sure, talk about it when mutual trust is there, but never *ever* use stage as an argument against anyone, and never *ever* try to discredit anyone on account of the developmental stage you perceive them to embody.

- **Don't be puritan.** In a metamodern political movement, like The Transnational, people should be somewhat in agreement about the general direction, but only somewhat—say about 70% or so. Any puritan reading of metamodernism can lead to new "Jacobins" forming or to other forms of sectarianism. Metamodernism is about taking and holding many perspectives and dealing with the very substantial likelihood that we ourselves don't have the best perspective or knowledge at any one given time.

- **Let go of relations gone sour.** If you ever find yourself having a vendetta, try to go home and take a few deep breaths and really meditate on it. Do loving-kindness meditations to get over it, even if they won't be nice to you. Or shout into a pillow (or beat up a punching bag if that's your thing), if folks make you mad. Let the wound heal and avoid the person and keep it cordial. Don't go after them on social media. Forgive them if you can.

- **Continuously reexamine your networks and social settings.** Check and double-check if there is anything going on in terms of development of original arts, philosophy and scientific findings in your metamodernist circles. If not, that's a huge warning sign. As we have seen, totalitarianism always begins by closing down art and creativity.

- **Take it easy.** If we rush things or get evangelical, we can be sure things will backfire. If things start moving too fast, you can be sure they will crash and you are going to be the bad guy. These are slow and huge processes, not a wave of goodness that will overturn the bad in the world. What we are offering here is, after all, not the radical revolutionary path, but one of measured, boring, long-term processes that need to be defined and refined until they actually work. And that, ironically, is why we can be truly revolutionary.

If you get involved in starting a transnational organization for political metamodernism or something similar, please come back to this list and read it again from time to time. Add your own points. Be sincerely ironic, magically realistic, pragmatically romantic, informedly naive, relatively utopian.

After all, we *should* get this party started; if we don't, it's probably only a matter of time before someone else does without all the safeguards and scruples I have listed above. Bad, bad things can and will follow.

On a last note, here's one from me personally to you. I do believe political metamodernism can be a great adventure in our lives; in yours and mine. I know it can be a source of meaning. But here's a big but: **I'm not promising you wellbeing and happiness by engaging in it.** Political metamodernism is a project for the long-term goal of increasing happiness and wellbeing in the world, yes, but it is not in itself a tool to make you happy, highly functional and fulfilled. It's just one thing out of many in life, and sometimes a complicated and messy one at that.

The sociologist Lewis Coser coined the term "greedy institution". It built on the sociologist Erving Goffman's "total institutions". Total institutions are settings in which you are literally locked up and all aspects of your everyday life are controlled: prisons, psychiatric wards, labor camps, large ships with long-serving crews and so on. Coser's greedy institutions instead denote social settings which aren't obviously enclosed, but still eat away at the rest of your life and snatch more and more of it—like the communist party or certain forms of club life, or a line of work that requires you to sign in blood. An increasing share of your time, effort and attention is taken up by it.

If political metamodernism speaks to you and you commit to it, it can rather easily become this kind of greedy institution, and that can be detrimental both for you and the cause you serve. So it is important to keep it in its place and at all times make certain you keep in touch with other parts of life and society.

Remember, those who hold the most perspectives when they die, win.

—

Kidding. You didn't really think I would let you go without a proper power ballad, did you? What kind of Hanzi would I be?

Many observers of our day—perhaps especially among metamodernists and adult development researchers—claim that we must help humanity grow up. Some even say that boys have to become men. And that's a lot of what I have been saying as well; we need to create institutions that are deliberately geared to supporting the intermeshed development of psychology, behavior, culture and systems.

With that in mind, I have suggested that we navigate history, as flies buzzing through the enchanted meaninglessness of the cosmos, with our controls set for the heart of the sun. We are destined to be more than janitors, programmers, nurses, office clerks and consumers. We are, fundamentally, gods with anuses. Our everyday lives are pale reflections of our true selves. We have divine potentials and utterly pathetic hidden sides, and all of this glitter and grime will surface through us as we grow into an existentially mature civilization—as multidimensional beings developing in a chaotic dance with reality itself; a journey into the open vastness and terrifying mystery of the clear night sky. "Surrounded, detached, in measureless oceans of space, ceaselessly musing, venturing, throwing, seeking the spheres to connect them", as Walt Whitman once said it.[150]

But another group of people scoff at these eager and arrogant developmentalists and ascenders. The issue is not to "go somewhere" or to "become someone" or to "develop"—it is to come home, to return to something basic and fundamental within us, to just be, to rest with the here-and-now, to stop trying to control and steer anything, least of all history. We don't need to aim for the sun, just be ourselves, just be simple. We must come closer to our nature, to what is real, to the authentic child that we really are. We can let go of all those egoic strivings, all those lofty ideas and ideals, of all ideology and metamodernism schmetamodernism.

Which one of these two perspectives is true, then—ascenders or descenders—those who seek to climb and develop or those who seek to stay simple and direct and simply be? You know the answer already. It is both and.

We must grow and we must come home; we must both travel and stay; we must be both sincere and ironic. We both "must" and "not must" anything at all. We must grow up to become the **children we always-already are**. And political metamodernism must facilitate and make possible the emergence of settings in which we can swarm as children.

In the year 1212—in an event at the crossroads of fact and fiction, one that may not have taken place but has been told as true over the centuries—nearly 50,000 European boys and girls are said to have rebelled against their parents and the Church to join a crusade to the Holy Land; to win by love what their fathers had failed to take by force. But before they even reached Rome nearly all of them had fallen to hardship. Those who went on would pay for their innocent courage in brothels and slave markets.[151]

The time was not ripe for a Children's Crusade, for the naive will of swarms of idealistic warriors to commit their playful souls for the betterment of the world by spiritual struggle. And yet that is, ultimately, what must happen. We don't need tough and "mature" men, but playful boys and girls, just as Nietzsche said it. Human beings who are in love with life itself—and with glittering, gleaming faith and iron resolve in the face of utter meaninglessness.

The world is maintained by men, it is reproduced by women—but it is created by children. By kids on mischievous adventures. What is the core principle of humanity if not the extension of childhood?

In nature, maturity is the rule and childhood the exception. Childhood is rare. It is chosen. It has not yet paid the price of maturity: stagnation, ossification. It is freshness, it is growth, it is movement, it is speed and exhilaration, it is higher freedom and deeper equality. As an animal rights advocate, I am all for caring about adults; they too have feelings. But in the last instance, this is a child's world.

Make no mistake—our world will be conquered, ruled and transformed by an army of children. Our struggle-reborn-as-play must continue until reality itself has shifted, until a million complexly interrelated situations have changed, until what is written on our banners has been inscribed into the constitutions of all countries and governing bodies of the world.

And what is written on our banners is, ultimately, what is always-already written in our hearts: solidarity with all sentient beings, across all of space-time, from all possible perspectives, from the greatest depths of our love.

Or do you have anything better to do?

Appendix A

WHY COMMUNISM FAILED

W elcome to Appendix A—why communism failed. Did you read through the book and found yourself hungry for more? Or did the red scare creep up on you so that you needed to calm your mind by finding out just how exactly this Hanzi Freinacht argues against communism?

Either way, please take a deep breath and chant the following hymn of utopia:

> "Beasts of England, Beasts of Ireland,
> Beasts of every land and clime,
> Hearken to my joyful tidings
> Of the Golden future time.
>
> Soon or late the day is coming,
> Tyrant Man shall be o'erthrown,
> And the fruitful fields of England
> Shall be trod by beasts alone.
>
> Rings shall vanish from our noses,
> And the harness from our back,
> Bit and spur shall rust forever,
> Cruel whips no more shall crack."

The poem goes on for a while after that, and it gets even better. You know where it is from, don't you?

Although it might be imagined as a tune of insurgency against today's factory farming, it's actually the anthem from George Orwell's *Animal Farm*—the fable in which the animals take over a farm and run it themselves under the banner: All animals are equal.

You may recall that Old Major, an aged hog, teaches this song, "Beasts of England", to the other animals before he dies; the whispers of a promised revolution. And suddenly, shortly after, the opportunity for a revolution presents itself. Farmer Jones is driven from the land—and so the fields are trod by beasts alone. But, as the story goes, the scheming pig Comrade Napoleon seizes power and the ideals of the revolution are perverted, one by one, until the small pig elite finally declare that all animals are equal, yes, but some animals are "more equal than others".

Of course, Orwell wrote this as a commentary on the Soviet revolution and the communist experiment. The Russian revolutionaries had been wary of "Bonapartism" in the early days of the Soviet Union, i.e. that someone might snatch the momentum and take charge as dictator, like Napoleon Bonaparte had done in the wake of the French Revolution. Few suspected that the quiet and reserved Joseph Stalin was a Napoleon in disguise (which, undoubtedly, is what Orwell hinted at when he named the dictator-pig in *Animal Farm*).

I'm bringing this topic up—the communist experiment—because my own work on "political metamodernism" and "the Nordic Ideology" inevitably gets compared to communism. The failure of communism is also a fruitful place to initiate a deeper discussion about political metamodernism.

Although it is not a comparison I am entirely comfortable with, it is not irrelevant. There *is* a kind of post-Marxist undercurrent in much of metamodern thinking: to see society as evolving through discernable stages, and the current capitalist global society as one such stage, to relate to the totality of human experience and try to generate a more rational and existentially sound foundation for it, to want to develop not only society but also our inner lives and emotions, to strive for higher forms of freedom, fairness and solidarity. Hey, I even named this book *Nordic Ideology* with an ironic wink at Marx and Engels' *The German Ideology.*

But if there is a vague spiritual lineage connecting political metamodernism to communism, it is only just that: a vague, spiritual link on a general and abstract level.

So let me highlight some key differences between my thinking and the many strands of Marxism. Let us begin by asking why communism failed, and what perspectives might be needed in its place.

DON'T BLAME COMRADE NAPOLEON

What went wrong with the Soviet Union and the communist revolution can hardly be said to hinge upon the wrongdoings or moral flaws of any single person like Joseph Stalin.

Or Vladimir Lenin, for that matter. It's true that Lenin represented a kind of authoritarian deviation from mainstream Marxist socialism, but it is also a fact that the only kind of socialist system (in name if nothing else) that has ever existed on any larger scale has been of the authoritarian bent. If you list all of the libertarian socialists, anarchists and left-wing Marxists, these are all theorists and philosophers. If you list the leading authoritarian socialists, these are all real leaders with real power. Coincidence?

It's not a coincidence. Some people like to say that "real socialism has never been tried". But as you'll see in the following, it has never been tried because it has never been possible in the first place. And this impossibility is exactly what has derailed all real attempts at socialism.

Let's go on with the story. Lenin's doctrine which guided the 1917 revolution (or coup) was an authoritarian deviation of the ideals of socialism, effectively banning worker control of factories and discarding other socialist elements, and the other Bolshevik leader, Leon Trotsky, soon followed suit in this elitist top-down perspective.

Lenin died in 1924, Stalin took over and from there on it was mounting totalitarianism and violent oppression in spades, culminating in the 1937-38 Great Purge. If Stalin hadn't won the power struggle, other and similar problems had still been likely to occur. Stalin's contestant Trotsky (whose Orwellian pig alter ego is called Snowball) was even crazier. He was more optimistic about a communist revolution in Germany (and less optimistic about Stalin's "socialism in one country") and would thus have been likely to have adopted a blatantly aggressive foreign policy—more wars, more people killed. Trotsky also had a more radical vision of the malleability of the human mind; that everyone could become Aristotle—an exceedingly dangerous and cult-like idea. Quoting Trotsky himself:

> "It is difficult to predict the extent of self-government which the man of the future may reach or the heights to which he may carry his technique. Social construction and psycho-physical self-education will become two aspects of one and the same process. All the arts—literature, drama, painting, music and architecture will lend this process beautiful form. More correctly, the shell in which the cultural construction and self-education of Communist man will be enclosed, will develop all the vital elements of contemporary art to the highest point. Man will become immeasurably stronger, wiser and subtler; his body will become more harmonized, his movements more rhythmic, his voice more musical. The forms of life will become dynamically dramatic. The average human type will rise to the heights of an Aristotle, a Goethe, or a Marx. And above this ridge new peaks will rise."[152]

There's an interesting tension here: On the one hand, Trotsky approaches some of the metamodern developmental perspectives, seeing the human being as a project of playful self-recreation; on the other hand, he falls into the traps of utopianism (the non-relative kind) and idealizing his own image of what a good human being would be like. He didn't realize that the only credible form of utopia is relative, and he never referred to any sound theories of psychological development. He simply believed that once a socialist society had been achieved, then a new and better humanity would emerge and a just social order would come into being once and for all. Consequently, everything became a means to this impossible end; "After all", the zealous revolutionary would think, "what's a few millions deaths if that's the price of achieving an absolute utopian ideal?" This, of course, puts one on a path to totalitarianism. We must thus stay clear of the mistakes represented by Trotsky and others like him. These are dangerous intellectual waters we are crossing.

Present-day Marxists often say that critics of Marx have failed to grasp the depth and entirety of Marx's writings, in particular the three volumes of his *magnum opus*, *Capital*. But if you read the writings of Lenin, Trotsky and Stalin, there can be little doubt they knew their Marx very well. And if you read e.g. Simon Sebag Montefiore's biographies on Stalin, it is apparent that even Stalin was very intellectually gifted: reading Darwin at thirteen in one sitting, becoming an acclaimed poet at 16, masterminding an impressive bank robbery at 29, and managing an incredibly large and diverse workload as military leader and head of state—all *while* producing writings that were not necessarily innovative, but certainly well written and incisive. For instance, you have *Dialectical and Historical Materialism*, in which he relates to not only Marxist doctrine but also a wider philosophical canon including Hegel, Kant, Feuerbach and others. As such, I seriously doubt a better and more detailed reading of Marx is the solution to the problems of Marxism, communism and socialism.

As you may know, Trotsky was eventually murdered on Stalin's orders by a Soviet agent with an icepick to the head in Mexico City. But communism was doomed to fail long before this. Trotsky wouldn't have saved the communist experiment. Nor would Lenin, had his health been better.

So don't blame Comrade Napoleon. Let's find out what really went wrong.

THE MAINSTREAM/LIBERTARIAN ACCOUNT

What then can account for the *structural* failure of the communist project, as viewed altogether? Well, in all places where you see communism (or "socialist" states claiming to attempt to achieve full communism, which is when the state itself has been rendered obsolete), there are one-party systems, human rights abuses, limits to civil liberties and severe problems with the economy—as recent relapses in Venezuela remind us. These societies simply don't last; their social sustainability is severely limited.

I suppose you've heard the common wisdom response? "Communism was not just a nice idea that turned out to be terrible in practice—it was a terrible idea that was consequently (and predictably) terrible in practice!" All mainstream critiques of communism argue along these lines, more or less. This holds true from the more sophisticated versions, like in the Polish philosopher Leszek Kołakowski's meticulous studies[153] of the inherent flaws of Marxism, over Karl Popper's *The Open Society and Its Enemies*, to Nobel Prize winner Aleksandr Solzhenitsyn's massive, intense literary masterpiece *The Gulag Archipelago*, which derives the horrors of communist forced labor camps directly from Marxist-Leninist doctrines.

This line of argument (often put forth by libertarians and conservatives, but increasingly by everyone) holds—more or less explicitly—that communism was a mistake because it failed, morally and intellectually, to understand human nature *itself*. This is the case even in Solzhenitsyn's existentialist account.

According to the libertarian mainstream account, humans are not collectivist beings who value equality over all—so the argument goes—they are freedom-loving *individuals* who need to find their own paths in life in order to find meaning and dignity. As such they must be allowed to compete on free markets, serving themselves first—in fair exchanges with one another, where goods and respect are earned by hard work and good character. They must reap the rewards of individual action, of innovation, of reasonable and free competition. In this view, the closer you come to a libertarian capitalist standpoint, the farther away you are from Gulag and the secret police knocking on your door.

But concealed beneath the nice-sounding libertarian creeds of a "freedom-loving individual" is also a somewhat darker assumption: that people are most often rather selfish, and, the reasoning goes, if you try to create a society in which this truth is not honored, it will backfire seriously—because it can ultimately only be built on self-deceit. Instead, the argument goes on, we should build a society in which people can work for their enlightened self-interest, which will generally produce more sustainable relations, more productive behaviors, and a greater abundance of goods and services on the markets (both quality and quantity).

As in Adam Smith's classical 1776 notion of "the invisible hand", this argument marries a belief in freedom to a measure of conservatism; a sober and realistic look at people's moral qualities and real behaviors. It's true that Smith warned about the corrosive effects of repetitive factory work, but his analysis stopped there. If we let people work selfishly under controlled circumstances (policing, rule of law, private property, consumer rights, etc.), then they will, on average and over time, do something that is collectively good.

Hmm, okay. There may be some truth to these received wisdoms of our day and age. But upon closer inspection, such an appeal to "human nature" and her innate individuality is of course a romantic reciting of beliefs rather than a behavioral-scientific explanation. They just make vague assumptions about "human nature" and engineer morally weighted conclusions from there. This mainstream account of why communism failed has pretty weak explanatory power.

But aren't there yet more general and structural causes for the spectacular failures of communism? I'm glad you asked, because indeed there are.

A Jammed Information Feedback System

If we'd like to take it one step farther towards a more solid critique, we can look at the issue from the perspective of **society's information processing**.

From this perspective, we can see that *economic central planning* is often a bad idea. The demand for goods and services is extremely difficult to predict on a large scale. Hence it is more intelligent to let many different agents make all the small decisions, "as if their businesses depended upon it", rather than letting the government make up a five-year plan and be done with it. Simply because these many agents, working with varying timeframes and perspectives, can process much more information, they can carry out more calibrated, sustainable and innovative decisions.

Once you have committed to a five-year plan, there is bound to be any number of errors: shortages and unwanted surpluses. People will have enormous incentives to trade with one another, to remedy the shortages and do away with the surpluses—hence *de facto* reopening a free market, a rather innocent version of the "black market". But for the socialist planning to work, such free trade needs to be illegal.

If there are such strong incentives for doing something that is illegal, the legal system must be stretched out to deal with a lot of people and situations. And for a legal system to realistically do that, it has to perform a lot of quick trials (or go after the "kulak" farmers who insist on producing their own goods). Hence the quality of the rule of law is degraded, hence people stop respecting the system altogether, hence corruption becomes rampant—in exactly the kind of system that depends upon the goodwill, mutual trust and solidarity among citizens.

I am simplifying to a semi-violent extent, but please bear with me; we are looking at some of the basic principles.

And from there on, the legal system spirals out of control and begins punishing people very severely and rather arbitrarily, and from *there* on the incentives for everyone are to be very careful and suspicious and to collect as much political power as possible. And the way to do *that* is spying on others, and informing, so that you have more information, more juicy threats to make, and more favors to call. All of these things become more important for your personal survival (and prosperity) than being an efficient office clerk or entrepreneur. Gain power, don't rock the boat.

And from *there* on, the incentive of the political leadership becomes to hide some of the bad stuff that is going on, because you need the legitimacy of the system to justify your power; your power being the only protection from being swallowed as the revolution begins to eat its own children in a spying-reporting slugfest. So you need to control the press and other media, which means people receive even less reliable information to make decisions and regulate their behaviors correctly—which messes up decision-making even more, across the board. And people thus fail to coordinate their actions at a large scale and over longer stretches of time, which means more shortages and errors; which means more incentives for corruption.

And in order to defend the false positive image conjured up by the controlled media that people no longer trust, you have to make parades and celebrations and fake display villages—lots of them—so that people will believe that things are alright and keep up the enthusiasm. And people will need to show up and be enthused at such occasions in order not to seem suspect, which in turn makes them start to genuinely insist they live in a fantastic society since the least convinced ones will be viewed with the most suspicion. It is a kind of Stockholm syndrome, by which hostages begin to love and admire their captors.

This is classical cognitive dissonance: People will *genuinely* believe things are awesome because it's too dangerous not to. And this again interferes with any hope of self-corrective feedback cycles. As the historian Anne Applebaum and many other foreign travelers in the USSR noted, Soviet citizens would often—amidst obvious drudgeries—emphatically insist that theirs was a superb society. Gulag survivor Solzhenitsyn described in his books how people would come to the labor camps and insist upon keeping their beliefs in the benevolence of the Soviet Union, even as they were being beaten, starved and degraded.

The social dynamics of religious cults come to mind. It is as though the communist project, by its inherent dynamics, drew people into a nation-wide cult: a dynamic followed even down to gory details like "cult of personality" and the cult-like, or at least extremely sectarian, organization of Trotskyist groups around the world.

And indeed, what would a society run by, let's say, the Scientologists look like? We may have an example in present-day North Korea; a surviving spawn of the Soviet Union. The similarities between Scientology and North Korea are striking, even down to the level of comportments and demeanors displayed by those who harass deviants from the dogma.

However, once the spell is broken and society collapses, traumas surface and abound. Today's happiness research lays its verdict: Post-communist societies are the least happy (relative to their levels of economic prosperity), and the longer a country stayed under communist rule, the less happy the population.

Other measures also suffer a special "communist penalty": lower interpersonal trust, loneliness, corruption and poor public health lingering on for decades. In terms of cultural and political progressivity, these societies also relapse dramatically: Poland turns to tradition and Catholicism, East Germany generates more than its fair share of neo-nazis, Russia becomes chauvinist (and born-again Orthodox) and forgets its former communist cosmopolitanism and dreamy gaze at space colonization, China's new openness is only skin deep, still being profoundly authoritarian and nationalist—and North Korea becomes a downright patriarchal, racist caste system on surveillance steroids, literally worse than anything Orwell could have dreamt up.

Phew. Where were we? **So communism is bad, which has to do with a vicious spiral that grows from an inefficient way of organizing the market, a case of jammed real-time information processing**—rather than any romantic notion of a violated "human freedom" or vague general speculations about the nature of humanity. The violations of human rights flow from this jamming of the information system, from a chronic failure to successfully coordinate human behavior in the millions. See you in The Hague, comrade.

The non-moralistic point is important here—and obvious, in a way. We all have a tendency of casting our beliefs about humanity and society in moral terms. And we tend to flatter ourselves: If only people "realize" that our own beliefs are the correct ones, if they could only bring themselves to see the true beauty of what we see, then life would be so much better. But sustainable, fair and dynamic societies are not created by the purity of your soul and its habits of self-flattery. **Good societies are created by A) correct analysis, B) smooth information processing for the coordination of human agency, C) the dynamic balancing of different powers—and D) the dialectical conflict and mutual interdependence between different political interests and ideas.**

These features of a good society can be brought about more or less deliberately; they emerge either as the result of planned actions, or through blind processes that occur beyond our understandings (but for which we often like to snatch the credit)—and most often as a strange dance between these two: the deliberate and the stumbled-upon.

There was really nothing *morally* "lower" about the communist experiment, compared to the ideas of the American Revolution, (or the French Revolution for that matter). If you look at the "founding fathers", Thomas Jefferson kept slaves, even got one of them pregnant, and Benjamin Franklin fabricated juicy lies about British atrocities—writing in the papers under several false names and claiming to have witnessed colorful barbaric acts committed by Indians, purportedly orchestrated by the British, in effect relying on racism. Most of the Declaration of Independence is not about human rights and equality, but raging against the crimes of the British "tyrant". After all, this was the writing of fiery revolutionaries, not human rights activists.

These guys weren't necessarily any "nicer" than Lenin and Trotsky; and certainly not nicer than people like Emma Goldman or Rosa Luxemburg. They just happened to be on the beat with some ideas and societal developments that turned out to be highly competitive, hence leading to relatively sustainable societal structures. The American ideas of 1776 were simply better aligned with the long-term attractors than the Russian ones in 1917.

MARX HAD THE WRONG META-IDEOLOGY

Both versions of modernity, capitalism and communism, brought great good *and* great evil. Communism enriches and modernizes society, and it kills lots of people. So does capitalism. But one version still turned out to be preferable to the other and thus won out: capitalism allied with a multi-party system.

A lot of the weaknesses of the purportedly Marxian societies can be explained by the fact that there weren't several parties (with minor exceptions, such as the contemporary Chinese tolerance of small opposition parties). This is a major difference to liberal democracy. Even in disorderly and corrupt Italy, one government can always be exchanged for another. This guarantees rudimentary accountability.

So why were the communist societies one-party systems? Because the Marxists believed that *they alone* embodied the **meta-ideology**; that they embodied the actual, deep structures of how societies evolve and operate. As such you can legitimize the self-organization of society *as a whole*: The meta-ideology is not any *one* position *within* society, but it constitutes overarching ideas about the very fabric of society. So Marxism does not compete with liberalism, but with liberal parliamentary democracy itself. It is not just an ideology, but an attempt at a meta-ideology—like liberal democracy. If communism reaches a certain level of influence, it thus wipes out all competing parties.

If Marxism is a meta-ideology, it makes sense to organize society as a whole within the framework of what is viewed as analytically true either way to the communist mind. As such, communism was prone to be built on top of formerly autocratic, pre-democratic societies where it could simply supersede the earlier form of governance, inheriting the strong state institutions that were not balanced by a strong parliament and division of powers.

But this is not unique to communism. When the American Revolution took hold, the elites of the early days also worked to keep a one-party system. This however broke down during the early 19th century when the vote was extended to non-elite groups and there was a rise of populist politics under President Andrew Jackson, with an electoral base in the southern states. All meta-ideologies set the framework for society as a whole, for its very definition of what society is.

As mentioned, **the words "holistic" and "totalitarian" are in effect the same word**. When you have a theory about the whole of society, it makes sense to relate to it in a way that tries to grasp, and change, the whole of it. To relate to the "whole", we must relate to the "totality", even try to steer and navigate it. A challenge presents itself: How can we be holistic without falling into the traps of 20th century totalitarianism?

In truth, of course, the meta-ideology of modernity turned out to be not communism but rather what I have called Green Social Liberalism, the attractor point modern societies gravitate towards. Not communism, not fascism, not the night watchman libertarian minimalist state, not anarchist communes, not even social democracy (nice try, though)—**but Green Social Liberalism.**

The more modernized a society becomes, the more clearly it manifests Green Social Liberalism, something the Nordic countries have become prime examples of. In countries like Sweden, all parties in effect have more or less become one version or another of "green social-liberals".

Much can be said in the analytical (and moral) defense of Marx, but after all, he did *not* claim that a huge middle class would grow up through the dynamic interrelation between private enterprise and public welfare, or that these populations would increasingly adopt individualism and cosmopolitanism, identity politics and ecological awareness as the ecological limitations of society's growth became apparent. That's just not what he wrote, I'm sorry.

Marx *tried* to identify the meta-ideology, to formulate it clearly, so people could create political movements around it or otherwise navigate the world with its help. He made some important contributions, but he got some of the fundamental dynamics wrong. Analytical—not moral—mistakes that nevertheless cost many millions of lives. Oops.

But still, the very fact that communism was an attempt at a meta-ideology, and that Marx got some important dynamics right (that capitalism is crisis-prone, for example), gave the organization of "The Communist Party" some nearly transcendental qualities in the eyes of its followers; attracting large parts of the 20th century intellectuals, most noticeably perhaps in France. The party was seen not only as "a party" with some "opinions", but, not unlike the American creed, a kind of manifest destiny, of history's dialectics made flesh. That's of course also what made it so dangerously seductive, so blinding.

What we tend to forget, however, is that our current political *status quo* was created by a similar kind of meta-ideology; that of liberal democracy and the Enlightenment. Its structures were brought about by abrupt turns, and the carefully engineered ideas of leading thinkers were instituted under political struggles for monopolies of violence (we mentioned Montesquieu, but there were of course many others). A jerky ride of revolution, counter-revolution, conservation and reformation produced the current meta-ideology and its supremacy.

Why then am I saying all this? I want to draw your attention to the fact that **communism failed to change the games of everyday life**, whereas *other* **meta-ideologies have been successful in doing so, and future meta-ideologies can do the same.**

The conclusion, then, is not to avoid *all* holistic visions of society, to avoid *all* meta-ideologies, but to make damn certain you get them right from the beginning.

Again, so if Marx ended up non-linearly killing a hundred million—how many did Montesquieu save? How many instances of torture has he prevented? It's a fair question.

COMMUNISM IS "GAME DENIAL"

The central issue of communism's failure was not that of some eternal, God-given "essence of humanity" being violated, but something far more mundane: that **the games of everyday life were misunderstood and/or denied**.

This led to a serious glitch in the self-organization of society, which—over a period of decades—led to a painful form of social disintegration and resulting oppression. Amidst all their atrocities, communist societies were relatively functional for a while, but their **social *sustainability*** was limited—much more so than liberal democracy with capitalism and welfare (the sustainability of which is, of course, also limited in time, as all things under the sun). And hence they lasted for shorter periods of time.

From this viewpoint, two conclusions become apparent. The first one is, again, that the relative failure of the communist experiments does not permanently discredit all attempts to change the games of everyday life, to evolve the dynamics by which we live, love, trade, compete and cooperate. If anything, the victory of liberal democracy, and its gravitation towards Green Social Liberalism, shows us that such developments *are* indeed possible.

Rather, **the failure of communism serves to underscore that you must make *correct* assessments of people's behaviors—in these particular times and places in history—in order to create a sustainable social order.** If you make unrealistic assessments regarding how people function, you set in motion vicious cycles that lead to truly terrible results. But on the other hand, if you *fail* to understand what attractors lie ahead, you stall historical progress, taking the losing side in history, which in the long run causes even more abrupt changes and catastrophic outcomes—for instance, that we might have global ecological catastrophes.

The second conclusion is that **"game change"** already *has* occurred throughout history, and that it is a measure of society's progress: **If, and only if, the games of everyday life become fairer and more forgiving, can "progress" be said to have materialized.**

So this leaves us with the understanding that the rules of the game—in markets, in work life, in governance, in family life, in love and sex and friendship—can and will change and develop. The question is only *how*, when, and under the auspices of which meta-ideology.

The basic idea is that the meta-ideology of liberal capitalism is becoming less viable in the globalized information age; and that we should look for a new one: My suggestion for which is political metamodernism, a.k.a. the Nordic ideology, leading us towards a listening society and a Green Social Liberalism 2.0—through the method of "co-development".

The Marxist critique and the failure of communism serve as fruitful starting points for seeing how a metamodern society can evolve from the modern one.

But to be very clear: the Nordic ideology and its metamodern politics is *not* communism. It's much smarter than that.

Appendix B

THE FOUR FIELDS

I f you still don't feel entirely convinced why we should discard Marxism as a theoretical starting point for changing society, it is because I have saved the best for last.

In this chapter I'll guide you through the four fields of development and show you how Marxism is utterly inadequate since it only addresses *one* of these *equally* crucial fields. And when you have acquainted yourself with these, you will find that it not only helps to further understand the failures of communism, but also how we can achieve a metamodern society.

However, before we go on to the four fields, a brief recap of one of the main points from Book One should be helpful.

VALUE MEMES IN POPULATIONS

Of all the ideas presented in Book One, this is the most important one: **The average effective value meme of a population is the single most important factor determining whether it is possible for a society to progress to a new stage of development or not.** If you don't get it, then you haven't understood this book or its prequel.

You may recall six such value memes, each of which builds upon the former, being a "later" or even "higher" stage of development:

* Animistic
* Faustian
* Postfaustian (or traditional)
* Modern
* Postmodern
* Metamodern

It is hard to overstate how crucial it is to raise the average effective value meme. The most brilliantly designed constitution and all the best democratic institutions in the world are null and void if the majority of the population subscribe to a Viking warrior ethos; e.g. gravitating towards the Faustian value meme. Likewise a listening society cannot fully materialize as long as the vast majority remains firmly imbedded within a modern, rationalistic worldview.

Your effective value meme affects whether you, for instance, consider the environmental degradation of the planet a primary concern, or believe foreign religions are the greatest threat to your existence. It affects whether you believe transnational solutions should be implemented to address the dire issues of our time, such as migration, global poverty, and finance, or consider increasing the military budgets of your own nation the best way to manage international relations. It affects the extent of your care and consideration towards others; the number of people and other sentient beings you include in your circle of solidarity. While people subscribing to higher value memes tend to be more concerned with the well-being of all humans, in all countries, no matter their background, people at lower value memes tend to have a much smaller circle of solidarity, usually those within their own country, often only of a certain kind, and rarely non-human animals unless they're considered pets. And learning from the communist experiment, solidarity cannot be enforced from the top; it cannot be taught, and you certainly cannot force anyone to be solidary. True solidarity can only emerge spontaneously and voluntarily from people's hearts and minds.

Our values are derived from our level of psychological development and play a critical role in the way societies evolve. It sets the limits for how far society can progress, and it determines how well our societies function at the current technological level.

Please note, however, that the effective value meme is not considered an overall stage of cognition that people are functioning in accordance with. With effective value meme I simply mean the values of a particular stage of societal development, such as modern or postmodern, towards which a person tends to gravitate the strongest. This is not estimated by the complexity or depth of a person's thought, but by the values they express sincere devotion towards.

This means, for example, that if a person considers gender equality, environmentalism, and animal rights more important than economic growth, freedom of consumer choice and protection of private property, then they can be said to be gravitating towards the postmodern value meme. If a person expresses faith in a certain set of values, and if it can be confirmed with minimum doubt that these are truthfully what the person believes in, then that is their "effective value meme".

Every society has a kind of demographic where different percentages of the population can be said to manifest and embody different "value memes", each being more or less progressive—each corresponding to different economic and societal environments. This changes over time, usually moving towards higher value memes as society gets more complex.

The different value memes can be seen as kinds of political-psychological stages of development. Larger and more complex societies require higher value memes in the population in order to function and be sustainable. The value memes aren't really an exact measure of how a person is and how she thinks, but there are certainly clear differences between people of different value memes.

For instance, today's Swedish population (generally believing in democracy, human rights, secular science, fair debate, gender equality and self-expression) have a "higher" average value meme than today's Afghani population (manifesting more traditionalist values, particularistic religion, purity and sin, and emphasizing survival over self-expression).

When a traditional society modernizes and people get wealthier, happier and more educated, the majority of the population will usually advance to higher value memes in a manner of a few generations. So there is a connection between prolonged periods of political stability and inclusive economic growth, and higher average value memes within a population.

As I said, higher value memes generally correspond to the functioning and needs of larger and more complex societies. For instance, being a fundamentalist Christian nationalist who thinks a woman's chastity is more important than her education hardly helps in creating a sustainable order in today's hypercomplex, interconnected, increasingly postindustrial global society. The Postfaustian, or "traditionalist", value meme and its moral intuitions are simply not compatible with the actual systems of today's emerging global society.

The dynamic here is fairly simple and intuitive in a way. If a society is doing well and the games of everyday life become milder, fairer and more forgiving, people have the luxury to think in more universalistic, far-sighted, nuanced and complex manners. If people get the opportunity to spend years educating themselves and freely following their interests, they also explore more complex ideas and values. They can "afford" it, so to speak, and this generally spurs psychological and cultural development.

If things go poorly, people tend to retreat to being less trusting, mentally hinging upon simpler and smaller worlds and circles of solidarity—naturally emphasizing short- or medium-term survival and avoiding personal risks. As we discussed earlier, the development of society always brings with it new challenges and backlashes, new nasty problems. Hence, the negative sides of societal development towards greater prosperity and complexity periodically cause pressures that decrease the average value meme in a population—as has been apparent with recent populist, anti-immigration uprisings in the West.

It is the people with the higher value memes who will tend, on average, to create and sustain institutions and practices that support (make possible, make sustainable) larger and more complex societies. This does not mean they are "better people"; just compare the spoiled and narcissistic brats in Sweden's schools to the cute and kind, hardworking and grateful pupils in a girl school in rural Sudan. The late-modern Swedish kids are horrible, as any honest teacher in its liberal an unruly school system will readily attest. Can they put down their iPhones already? But still, the Swedish kids certainly do manifest higher average value memes.

The point is that there is a *collective* difference that has to do with value memes. It might work fine to have no formal laws and to believe in ancestral magic if you're a tribe of 150 people in the rainforest. Being a global world-system of seven plus billion in rapid economic and technological transition and a host of ecological crises that may hit home in the coming decades and centuries—not so much. Rain dances, invoking spirits and performing passage rituals will only take us that far.

THE FOUR FIELDS OF SOCIETAL DEVELOPMENT

If we zoom out a bit, we can see that the average effective value meme in turn is only one out of several factors that can be used to describe how "developed" a *society* is.

The effective value meme describes how a person or a population sees the world and intuits their own place in it, their moral codes, and so forth. This is, you could say, "psychological development". But just as the value memes consist of four aspects, so does the development of society itself consist of *four* different, but intimately related, *fields of development*. The four fields are:

1. **Psychology (including, but not exclusively, value meme)**

2. **Behavioral development**

3. **The system; systemic development**

4. **Culture; cultural development**

Hence, the value memes, the political psychology of a population, constitute only *one* out of *four* fields of development. So let's describe and briefly discuss the other three fields.

The second field of development revolves around people's **actual *behaviors***, which have to do at least as much with the *situations* they are in as on their psychological development: the interactions they partake in, which behavioral cues are elicited, what behaviors are rewarded, and so forth. The effective value memes of people need to be distinguished from their behaviors, as these are always affected by the situations of everyday life. These concrete, observable behaviors can *also* be developed; they can be brought into new and more productive relations that together form more complex and resilient patterns.

But it doesn't stop there. These overall patterns of behaviors can in turn be seen as part of a larger **societal *system***: the flows of the market, the technological chains of production and distribution, the bureaucracy, transportations and communications; even the system of governance, educational system, media, judicial and healthcare systems—all of which reside within whatever frames the ecosystems and the biosphere allow. And these systems can in turn be developed: You can go from fossil fuel to renewables, from constitutional monarchy to parliamentary representation, from subsistence farming to industrial capitalism, and so forth. That's the third field of development.

Depending on how you see it, you can either view the systems as emergent patterns in the results in the concrete behaviors of many real, existing people *or* you can see the many actions of individual people as determined and guided by the overarching systems, which are larger than the behaviors of any one person. Yet a cleverer way to view it is that behavior, psychology and systems continuously interact, or, more precisely, that they *co-emerge*; that they emerge together and determine each other.

And then there is the fourth field of development: ***culture***. Here you have things such as norms, values, traditions, languages, art, philosophies, religious practices, gender roles, habits and customs of everyday life, shared imagined worlds, shared ethnic boundaries, cultural references, taken-for-granted facts, expectations—whole constructed universes of stories about the universe and our place in it.

The development of culture is the development of our symbolized perspective on reality.

Consider the difference between contemporary France and its medieval predecessor. Would you say that culture has developed? Do people have more words, more nuanced perspectives, more universalistic values? I think we can safely make that case.

I have thus mentioned *four* **fields of development**:

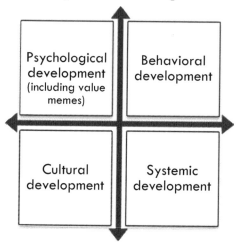

Figure: The four fields of development. The top two quadrants describe micro processes, the two lower ones macro processes. The left-hand quadrants describe "inner", subjective development, the right-hand ones "outer", objective development.

As you can see, there is one **micro-macro axis** (in this version it's up and down, referring to things you study at the level of small, everyday interactions and singular people, vs. things you study on a massive scale: structures, statistics, averages, and so forth) and one **interior-exterior axis** (left-right; referring to things that must be intimately known and interpreted, or that can be seen and described more "from the outside"). The two micro quadrants (psychology and behavior) study single people and their everyday interactions, the two macro ones (culture and systems) study society as a whole. The two interior quadrants study that which is felt and experienced (psychology and culture), the two exterior ones study "objective" realities (behaviors and systems).

Please note that this model actually has much more to it—I am merely giving you the *very* simple version because that's all we need for the sake of the argument we're making in this book.

You have early premonitions of this model already in the great sociologist Talcott Parsons' mid-20th century theory about "structural functionalism", but it was not quite there yet. Since that time, a number of major thinkers have more or less independently come up with the exact model above: Jeffrey Alexander's sociology (one of the top names in American sociology, which still insists that macro phenomena determine micro phenomena more than vice versa), Georg Ritzer's metatheory (the number one walking encyclopedia of social science in the world, who thinks all four fields interact on equal grounds), Søren Brier's cybersemiotics (Denmark's coolest nerd star, who I once crashed a party to get to talk to, who created a more philosophically grounded model, by using an entirely different method), and Ken Wilber's four quadrants (which is the one theory that is most clear on both the developmental aspects of all four fields, and their fractal relationship to one another). All four thinkers came up with more or less the same theory independently of one another within a period of fifteen years following 1980. Wilber's theory is the youngest, but also by far the most elegant one.

And then there's a whole host of other, related, theorists who say other, but closely related, things: Jürgen Habermas, the late Roy Bhaskar, Edgar Morin, Fritjof Capra, and the Gulbenkian Commission… None of these present this exact model, but they are all in the same holistic ballpark, saying *roughly* the same thing—and they all emphasize different parts of the story and work with different topics, of course.

And then there is another kind of thinkers who don't necessarily like to divide things up into four distinct fields (because it can feel a little too mechanical and simplified, too much Kant or even Descartes lingering), but still say something similar; i.e. that the different kinds of social phenomena emerge together and are entangled with each other. Here you'll find people like the physicist-philosopher Karen Barad, the political scientist Alexander Wendt, the political psychologist Shawn Rosenberg, the philosophers Alexander Bard and Jan Söderqvist—and many others, depending on how far you are willing to stretch the argument. You can even find versions of this model in psychology, psychiatry, and even medicine.

Basically I am saying, in some version or another, that this holistic vision of reality and society has taken a strong hold during the last few decades—the simplified one I presented above is not necessarily the best one; it all depends on what analytical uses you are looking for.

Taking stock of a few general implications of such a model, we can say that:

1. *Both* interior, subjective experiences *and* exterior, material realities are honored and seen as parts of reality. So if you *ignore* one field or try to

reduce it to the others, you "flatten" your view of reality. Hence it is a "holistic" view, as opposed to a reductionist view.

2. Many forms of thinking reduce all of reality to one of these four fields. Marxism and much of the scientism mainstream think that "only" the material realm is really real, spiritual idealism thinks that only psychological ("phenomenological") reality is real, extreme postmodernism thinks that only culture and discourses are real, and so forth.

3. The different fields of development are actually interdependent upon each other.

4. You can view the different fields *either* as different aspects of reality (different areas of concern or subjects to study) *or* as different injunctions into or perspectives upon reality: as the home bases of different sciences and other forms of inquiry.

But let's not talk more about theory in general; let's get on with the point: **These four fields of development—psychological, behavioral, systemic and cultural—interact.** Indeed, they *define* each other—they make each other possible, they set mutual limits, they cause hard crashes and burns in one another. They emerge together: psychology, behavior, culture and system. They are in a perpetual developmental dance. They **co-emerge**. That's the point.

By the way, by far the majority of professors in sociology, history, psychology, economics, cognitive science, philosophy and the natural sciences still *do not understand this model.* And hence they spend meaningless lifetimes of work trying to resolve questions that have already been resolved. With mechanical, relentless tenacity they systematically keep ignoring one or more of the four fields of development. They discuss, as if there was some great mystery here. They go on, and on, with long and purportedly intellectual discussions. "What could it be? Does culture drive the economy or the other way around?" And so forth. And so on.

At any rate, if you have actually understood this model and you are able to see its implications, you are now—in the department of general understanding of society and reality—far ahead of most intellectual and scientific authorities. Congratulations. Just like a fourteen years old modern kid is far ahead of the greatest medieval intellectuals, not because she is smarter, but simply because the medieval intellectuals were invested in (what are today) outdated symbolic code systems, in outdated ideas.

Metamodern philosophy eats modern philosophy alive and spits on its grave, just like modern philosophy did to all earlier worldviews. But that's not what this appendix is about. So let's get on with it.

Marxian Blindness

Okay, back to the murder mystery. Why did communism kill a hundred million people? What was the murder weapon? It was the **developmental imbalances between the four fields of development**. Let me explain, dear Watson.

When Marx wrote, already before he became a full-fledged communist (the "Young Marx"), he displayed a number of traits that can safely be classified under what I have called the Postmodern value meme.[154] There was something about Marx, his way of thinking, of sensing the world, of grasping society, that might loosely be termed *progressive*: expressing values that correspond to a later stage of societal development than the one most prevalent in 19th century Europe.

As I discuss in *The 6 Hidden Patterns of History*, you can see this *either* as the culmination of a former kind of thinking (modernism) *or* an early form of the new kind of thinking (postmodern values). It's either the pinnacle of modernism or an early form of postmodernism, depending on your perspective.

How is Marx "postmodern" in this sense? Marx's vision is spiritual in a secular sense (humanity seeking self-attainment by knowing herself and becoming a consciously creative agent of the universe); it is egalitarian, dialectical (not one explanation or path holds the truth and reality isn't seen as static and defined), relatively feminist (with a little help from his lifelong friend Friedrich Engels), and its circle of solidarity includes all humans.

With some racist blind spots here and there typical of the period, Marx and Engels at least strived to include all people in an increasingly *rational* social order—where irrational tendencies such as "fetishism" (wanting money for money's sake, or stuff for stuff's sake) and "reification" (thinking that there was something inherently real in arbitrary human constructs such as God, money or our current political ideology) would no longer determine our lives and govern our societies.

Most of all, you could say that Marx in some rudimentary sense was "postmodern" because he wanted to create a society that was not *pre-*modern, but still built upon something else than capitalism; he sought a system in which everyday life and activities revolve around something other than monetary exchanges and where we are not "steered" by money in our organization of, and participation in, everyday life.

And since capitalism and modernity are *inherently* intertwined, the striving for a post-capitalist society is inherently postmodern: it is that which, by definition, comes *after* modernity.[155]

The "real socialism" that followed during the 20th century was a kind of "state capitalism", hence never achieving the non-capitalist ideal—in practice, everyday life still revolved around money, materialism and consumption. But still, Marx's values rather accurately reflect—or herald—an early form of what I call the Postmodern value meme; this certainly includes the vision of a society that is free from alienation and excessive inequality.

In Marx's time, there was really no research on developmental psychology—and certainly nothing that would resemble a four-dimensional *political* developmental psychology with the theory of effective value memes. Sure, you had some early glimmers of such developmental thinking, all crafted by Romantic thinkers: Rousseau's stage theory of children; Schiller, Herder and others played with adult stages of psychological and development (recycled later, and more famously, by Kierkegaard).[156] But none of this amounts to a political-psychological research program that can track and describe the overall development of larger demographics and societies.

Today the situation is very different; we finally have good and ample research to support the idea of people being at different developmental stages—even if the scientific program is still, to our day, rudimentary. But we have something that Marx did not: a science of developmental psychology. This changes everything.

Let's bring this puppy home. What am I getting at? Well, look at what Marx wrote about. He wrote about how he thought the economic *system* develops, and how that in turn affects other parts of society and people's psyches.[157] Marx wrote about *economic* theory, about the economic system above all. He believed that he was working for a society that would come after capitalism, one that would be non-capitalist: what he termed "communist". Notwithstanding the limitations of his analysis of the economic system (there were some, even if he correctly predicted a number of developments), he failed to understand that a post-capitalist society would require a corresponding post-capitalist *psychological* development of the population to function, or even to emerge in the first place—as well as a corresponding behavioral and cultural development.

Hence, **Marx was blind to *three* out of four fields of development. And so was the communist movement that followed. They had their eyes gouged out by materialist reductionism.**

That's the Marxian Blindness. Don't let it infect you.

THE PSYCHOLOGICAL PREREQUISITES OF SOCIALISM

What, then, would a political psychology of a genuinely functional "socialist" population look like? Here's a rough estimation; they would need to be:

* extremely egalitarian, unimpressed by wealth and power;
* extremely peaceful, non-violent; prone to resolve issues by dialogue and compromise;
* extremely tolerant of differences and accepting of weaknesses in others;
* capable of taking in and harboring a multiplicity of perspectives, and viewing the perspectives as enriching to each other, being non-judgmental towards others with differing views;
* capable of autonomous critical thinking that goes beyond following the current norms, being able to recognize and bust autocratic, totalitarian tendencies and see through populist "simple solutions";
* prepared to change their own opinions if good arguments are presented;
* focused on non-material and secular-spiritual issues in life, rather than material wealth and comfort, working for other rewards than money;
* prepared to view themselves and their own interests in relation to a larger system, preferably one in which all humans in the world are included;
* skilled at being inclusive in dialogues, with a battery of good techniques for democratically dividing speaking time, listening to one another and generally being sensitive interlocutors;
* generally emotionally fulfilled and mature, hence difficult to manipulate, seduce, provoke or bribe, and generally less prone to emotional overreactions;
* in an emotional position where one is not driven by either economic fears, nor fear of military threats, ideally not even personal/emotional fears;
* capable of understanding, acknowledging and actively counteracting privileges and stigmas of race, ethnicity, gender, sexuality, disabilities, class background and even personality types;
* identifying with other things than nationalities, religions, ethnicities and one's own status in society;
* emphasize long-term stability and ecological sustainability of the society they live in.

So that's the kind of people who would need to be around for a socialist system to work at all. Lots and lots of them. Depending on other factors, you might need up to half of the adult population to fit this description.

As much as all this sounds like, I am not describing some "super-per-fect impossible goodie-two-shoes". These people do exist in reasonable numbers around the world today. You can check off all of the above boxes for a lot of people, without them being impossibly perfect. They are the highly functional, well-to-do, highly educated "liberals"—at least as these people often turn out after a more self-indulging period in their 20s. In other words: people at the Postmodern value meme.

In the most advanced countries in the world today, like the Nordic ones, you have about a quarter of the adult population at this value meme. In a country like the US, the share is lower, unless you zoom in on New York or California.

Marx himself was at this Postmodern value meme. Not so strange real-ly: He was privileged, self-made, intelligent, sensitive, successful, a leader; his wife a noble, his father-in-law a mentor and supporter, his professor a world-class philosopher (Hegel!), his best friend the son of a factory owner and also at genius level of intellect. Not that Marx lived a very easy life, but his was a privileged life that could spur his personal development into a higher value meme. He was ahead of his time. How many people at the Postmodern value meme were around in his days? The percentage is almost zero, even in London, at the heart of the modern world.

If you grow up as Oliver Twist, the Postmodern value meme is just not going to happen. It's just not. You are going to be angry that they beat you as a kid, concerned with getting food, be easily seduced by promises, care little about foreign cultures, have little democratic fiber and skills, be pro-ne to want quick reliefs for your aching body and soul, be very anxious to get much richer by any means possible, not have the opportunity to edu-cate yourself. That's how I would function under such circumstances, and you probably would too.

So Marx wanted to create socialism in a place and time where there were, frankly speaking, no "socialists". Heck, most socialists today aren't even socialists. Think about it; significant demographics at the Post-modern value meme have only showed up in the most privileged and sta-ble countries, and only after a hundred years or more of capitalist indust-rialism and social reforms. By far the most people of the 19th and 20th centuries were at the Modern or earlier value memes.[158]

In terms of psychological development, there were almost no true "socialists" around. Should it then surprise us that all the "real" socialist countries—Russia, China, and so on—in which populations were generally well below the Modern value meme, ended up reproducing crude and autocratic systems?

And how many people at the Postmodern value meme would it take to run a "socialist" (genuinely postmodern and post-capitalist) society? Even the almost 25% in Sweden is not nearly enough. It's not just that you need a majority, or at least a strong minority, to get your policies through in a democratic manner (so that you can shape the institutions in a corresponding way)—you also need an army of highly functional postmodernists to man all the key functions in such a society. You need teachers, politicians, community organizers, bosses, judges, police officers, administrators who all *genuinely embody* the Postmodern value meme.

They need to be everywhere: much like people at the Modern value meme are needed to man all the positions in today's modern societies.

TOO DUMB FOR COMPLEX SOCIETIES?

To be fully functional at the Postmodern value meme, a significant limitation is that you also need to be a relatively complex thinker—one who uses the postmodern values in an encompassing, nuanced, context-sensitive, systemic way. The cognitive stage of a person's thinking may have substantial genetic or hereditary causes (much like IQ). Only about 20% of a normal adult population seems to develop to a stage of sufficiently complex thinking, one that truly matches the postmodern ideas (this cognitive stage is called "stage 12 Systematic", according to the Model of Hierarchical Complexity).

This means that the Postmodern value meme, once it becomes dominant in a society's culture, is often used in "flattened" and simplified ways that can become oppressive, or at least quite annoying, for most people, rather than genuinely inclusive and democratic.

In the Nordic countries today, you have a lot of people using flattened and simplified versions of the Postmodern values, and the result is often suffocating and alienating to many. For instance, you get excessive "political correctness" and simplified versions of feminism as people apply simple, linear, "flattened" versions of the purportedly sensitive and inclusive norms, or when they apply these "sensitive norms" as ways of promoting their own moral worth at the expense of others. This, quite understandably, leads to resentful populist counter-reactions.

Just to underscore this, let's take a look at how intelligence (here measured rather crudely as IQ) relates to political ideology and value memes. I prefer to talk about "cognitive stage" instead of IQ, but this is the best we've got research-wise. Apparently, childhood IQ scores predict future voting behaviors. Here are figures from the UK, about 6000 people, in 2001.[159]

UK Party	Voter IQ Average	Comment
Green	108.3	Clearly based on postmodern values and environmentalism.
Liberal Democrats	108.2	The social-liberal party, "third player" in UK's largely bipartisan system.
Conservative	103.7	The large center-right party, mostly modernist values.
Labour	103.0	The large center-left party, mostly modernist values.
UK Independence (UKIP)	101.1	Eurosceptic, right wing populist, modernist/traditionalist values.
British National	98.4	Nationalist, postfaustian/traditionalist values with some faustian (fascist, etc.) undercurrents.

If you look at the difference between the leaders of the IQ-league and the ones with lowest IQ, you clearly see the scores map perfectly onto the value memes. The parties that embody the later, or "higher", value memes seem to attract the more cognitively endowed parts of the populace and the lowest value memes the less intellectually gifted. The progressive parties have an IQ score five points above the mainstream, which in turn averages five points above the regressive parties.

Whereas there may be many different mechanisms at play in this stratification[160] process, we can glean the tendency that higher value memes require more cognitively advanced people; except that they do not gather around the attractor point of socialism, but around Green Social Liberalism, which has turned out to be the real attractor of late modern society—hence the concentration of smarts around the Greens and the social-liberal Liberal Democrats.

Obviously, IQ does not in itself "cause" political progressiveness (in which case Hong Kong and Japan would be full of green social liberals, these being higher IQ populations) but it does, without doubt, interact with it in some way. The point here is simply to show that more progressive views may have higher cognitive prerequisites and that a lot of people fall short on this measure.

In Book One, we saw that over 60% of a normal adult population seems to reach the cognitive stages necessary for successfully understanding and operating the norms of a "modern" society (formal logic). When it comes to postmodern society, we are down to about 20% (systematic logic). For metamodern society—which is the main attractor ahead, as we shall see—we're down to a harrowing 2% (meta-systematic logic), at least in purely cognitive terms (how complex your thinking is).

What we're looking at is a disparaging challenge to our very biology: We are creating a society which we are biologically unequipped to grasp and thrive in. Up until now, people have been smart enough for society. **These days we are, as it were, running out of cognitive fuel.** We're not sufficiently cognitively complex to productively relate to the society that we ourselves have created—or rather, the society that has emerged, self-organized, as the complex result of our ongoing interactions.

Luckily, there is a lot that can be done about this matter. One part of it has to do with "transhumanism" (changing humanity via genetics and technology) but that topic falls outside the scope of this book and is discussed at length by authors like Oxford philosopher David Pearce. And of course, transhumanist development comes with considerable risks, which should best be discussed elsewhere.

Another part, which is more relevant to the metamodern political activist, has to do with creating a society that realistically manages all the different value memes and people at different levels of complexity and personal development—as well as working to support the long-term advancement into higher value memes.

As you can see, a "socialist" society is completely implausible to create in any genuine or sustainable manner unless you also have perhaps over 40% of the population cognitively functional at the Postmodern value meme, which may be achievable only if we manage to surmount some developmental limitations in the population at large.

MURDER SHE WROTE

I'd like to present three more reasons for why socialism never worked and no postmodern, or post-capitalistic, society ever materialized.

Reason One: "Pomos" creep others out. People at the Postmodern value meme are likely to alienate, creep out or otherwise provoke people at the earlier value memes. Their world, their society and their morality often seem abstract, exaggerated and suffocating to moderns and traditionalists; just look at how they shake with rage against "political correctness", "social justice warriors" and identity politics.

One of the main differences between pomos (postmodernists) and the "memos" (metamodernists) is that the latter include the perspectives of the earlier value memes and empathize with them (since the memos have a developmental, hierarchical perspective which the pomos don't). The pomos just think there is something *wrong* with moderns and traditionalists, and that they need to "open up", stop being so dogmatic and greedy, or that the spell of "bourgeois ideology" must be broken and so forth.

And indeed, this was what Marx and Engels wrote about when they used terms such as "ideology" and "false consciousness"; workers were not socialists because they were, in effect, brainwashed by their oppressors. Similar schemata show up again and again in postmodern thought: there is a structure or ideology that fools people into being non-socialists, non-vegans ("carnists"), non-environmentalists, non-feminists, mindless consumers, and so on. With Rousseau, the pomos all believe *some* version of the idea that their own way of thinking is default, logical and benevolent while other people have been fooled and that something is preventing the underlying goodness in them to surface. This idea about demasking and criticizing ideology is married to an implicit assumption of Rousseau's "noble savage" (that modern humans essentially are corrupted by society and deep down actually subscribe to all these nice-guy postmodern values), and it comes in so many forms: critical cultural studies, feminist epistemology, discourse analysis, narrative analysis, etc.

There may be considerable explanatory value in many of these research fields, but they tend to entirely miss the point regarding developmental psychology. Pomos are unaware of the developmental stages and hence assume all humans are inherently postmodern *unless* some external force prevents them from being so, and hence they try to shake people and wake them up: "What's wrong with you!? Why aren't you acting in your own obvious interest!?" This, of course, only rarely works, and it antagonizes and provokes folks who are modern and traditionalist. It puts psychological demands upon people that cannot be met by their factually existing minds.

That's what metamodernists don't do. They respect people's stage of development and have solidarity with the natural occurrence of their perspectives and developmental journeys. This is to become all the more important in the years to come as the pomos are going to make up a growing proportion of the population.

In order for a majority pomo society to be *genuinely* "socialist" (here just meaning inclusive and fair), and not creep the hell out of over half of the population, it would still need to be led by a minority of memos who subtly but effectively snatch many of the key positions in society.

For pomo-land to exist and function at all, you need to have a significant number of memos to man the steering wheels.

None of this was included anywhere in Marxist thought or in any of its heirs. Lenin had the notion of an *avant-garde*, an idea which he had inherited from other Russian radicals, but he did not describe the developmental psychology of such an elite. And he thought he could simply reprogram people to be socialists by means of a combination of education, propaganda and violence.

Reason Two: Socialist values require postindustrial abundance. But the problems with socialism don't end there. Where do the pomo populations of the world start showing up in significant numbers? Again, only in highly developed *postindustrial* countries. As long as life in general still revolves around industrial production, and most of us still need to endure hours every day in boring factories and offices, partaking in other menial, soul-corrosive work, there's just no way people are going to become postmodern post-materialists. Why would they? If you get rich, it means you can stop wasting your life doing something extremely boring. So you'll want to get rich. And if your work is that unrewarding and uncreative, of course you're going to be in it for the money, to want compensation for your troubles. You won't become post-materialist.

Hence, the precondition for significant parts of the populations to display the necessary psychologies is that you need to have a genuinely postindustrial society. But—and this is important—you also need the system to function on a massive scale, preferably on a *global* scale. Just some islands of relative progressive values cannot create a truly postmodern society. This is because they still function within a larger modern, industrial capitalist world-system, which means you need to make serious concessions to that same system.

Looking at some central parts of the current economic world-system, you have postindustrial islands which trade machine-made goods and abstract services to others, but the world-system *as a whole* is still largely industrial. Hence, we can hardly expect the Postmodern value meme to take over on a global scale anytime soon, which would be necessary for anything like "socialism" to function. I'll get back to this part of the matter in *Outcompeting Capitalism.*

Phew. And we're still not done.

Reason Three: There simply aren't enough pomos around to uphold the Postmodern value meme throughout society. For people to function within a postmodern society, you would need to have a *culture* that corresponds to this value meme. You also need the "cultural code" of postmodern society. You would need to have what we called "symbol-stage E Postmodern" readily available for people to "download" and then use in their everyday lives—i.e. people must gain access to the postmodern ideas and learn about them early on in life. And this generally requires at least some higher education within the humanities and/or critical social science.

But other than that, you must have vast cohorts of artists, writers, poets, filmmakers, professors and others who recreate and transmit this cultural code—being critical, inclusive, multiperspectival, and all the rest of it—who make these ideas and symbols active and alive within society.

And even if you manage to institute a system of production that is non-capitalist, you must have some clever way of self-organizing people's efforts, time and attention in an efficient manner that works on a transnational scale—something other than the capitalist markets. You need a very efficient **information processing *system*** to uphold such an economy—one that is *more* receptive to instant feedback processes, than is modern capitalism. How else will you successfully coordinate the everyday work and activities of billions of interconnected people on the world market? This, our Marxist friends never offered us.[161]

Alright. Now, dear Watson, can you see the murder weapon? Imagine you try to create a postmodern economic system, like "socialism", except:

- there are almost no genuine socialists (in a political-psychological sense of a corresponding effective value meme);

- society is not sufficiently economically and technologically developed;

- people are all stuck in games and incentives for non-socialist motives (making money, gaining power, etc.); and

- there is no postmodern culture that would support an inclusive multiplicity of perspectives.

What would happen? The society would simply fail to materialize the way you imagined. You would only be able to create it by force, never by spontaneous self-organization. And once you use force, people resist, and they get oppressed or killed. And once you have instituted the system by force, none of it behaves as you would expect, because in its very DNA, it is non-socialist. Hence, you get shortages, corruption and collapses. And you must respond with a reign of terror just to keep things in place, at least somewhat. And lots of people die.

Mystery solved. Murder she wrote.

A Diagnosis of Our Time

All of this brings us to an understanding of what is fundamentally wrong with the world of today. It's quite simple really. It is, again, a developmental imbalance. Can you guess what it is?

It's the obvious fact that **we have an economic and technological world-system that has advanced far ahead of the three other fields of developed**. We live in an increasingly global, transnational, digitized, postindustrial world-system, with an increasing number of "disruptive technologies", i.e. inventions that redefine people's lives dramatically. But we lack a corresponding global, transnational, digitized, postindustrial system of governance. So the system goes tits up and creates large pockets of economic, social and cultural losers around the world: the working and middle lower classes in affluent societies, the exploited poor in poorly governed and failed states, the animals suffering under industrial farming, climate change refugees and other desperate migrants, the disenfranchised urban immigrant populations in ghettos and *banlieues*, the tribal and traditionalist religious populations who suffer from confusion and alienation, the fish and other aquatic animals, the biosphere itself.

But these issues would be self-regulating if the populations, economic agents and leaders of the world were up to pace with recent developments. The crux is that we are not. That's the issue. That's what's wrong with the world.

We lack a cultural sphere and understanding of our time, an overarching narrative that matches this new economic and technological order of the world. We, as global humanity, lack the corresponding value meme. And we display behaviors that are unsustainable and downright destructive, given the current systemic circumstances. In other words, **we have fallen behind in cultural, psychological and behavioral development**. As noted in Book One, we live in a "retarded world"; we have developed too slowly—mentally, culturally and emotionally.

Immense quantities of human and animal suffering are at stake here; if we fail to actively and deliberately generate the conditions that foster personal growth, new behaviors and new cultural understandings, we cannot expect the coming age to be a fruitful transition to a postmodern or metamodern society. We can expect confused and limited overreactions that worsen the maladies of people and animals around the world.

Today, the world-system, for all its wonder and power, is not functioning in a socially, economically or ecologically sustainable manner. We, the global community, have in some sense become as the Soviet Union—a global bronze colossus on feet of clay.

Thus, we must orchestrate an extensive moral, emotional and cultural development. I am not saying, as some idealistic observers think, that we should "follow our hearts" and "return to our moral intuitions and shared values". Rather, the point is that our moral intuitions and shared values betray us; they can and must evolve.

To master this situation, to navigate the ongoing global "multi-dimensional crisis-revolution", we must look to the subtlest and most intimate details of what it means to be a developing human being in an evolving society.

It is an ironic twist of fate that, in order to solve the hard and large problems of the world-system, we must learn to look *inwards*—into our emotional lives and into the nature of our intimate relationships with ourselves, one another and our place in the universe.

And we must do so, not as an individual matter of personal seeking, but as an inherently *political* issue that involves all members of society.

Appendix C

EFFECTING GAME CHANGE

There are different levels of game change, some more fundamental than others, but all are necessary. There are many different "levers" to pull. We explore these throughout the book, but here are some general suggestions to get us started. The levers are:

* Studying the rules of the game and teaching them to as many as possible (Sun Tzu's *Art of War*, Machiavelli's *The Prince*, Neil Strauss' *The Game* etc.). This actually makes the game fairer because it works against game denial and towards a more even distribution of knowing the rules of the game. But emphasizing this side alone can land us in the cynicism of game acceptance.

* Change the game settings by changing the supply of resources. In richer societies where resources are more equally distributed, the games of everyday life are generally less cruel since people have more of what they need and thus feel less tempted to take advantage of others.

* Change the game framing by changing ethical discourses. What is considered acceptable or not in order to get ahead in the daily games of life can be altered by making new ethical guidelines more prevalent; and if everyone tends to follow the same rules, people will be more inclined towards "playing nice". Even who is to be considered a "loser" can be changed, for instance by making it okay to be poor or uneducated.

* Evolve the game by increasing cognitive capacity for social perspective taking (higher cognitive stage and value meme, as described in Book One). This makes the whole game fairer, where people at higher cognitive stages accept John Rawls' "veil of ignorance" (not knowing

who in society you will be). Yet higher levels of complexity breed even more refined games, like accepting solidarity with all sentient beings and making room for different kinds of consciousness in the public.

- Amassing stronger and wider monopolies of violence (states can uphold the rule of law, but the lack of global polity or transnational governance sets limits for how far solidarity through rule of law can reach). A big and strong monopoly of violence stuck in a crude game can of course cause a lot of relative suffering (Fascist states caused more suffering than representative republican, capitalist, meat-eating societies, even if they managed to amass considerable monopolies of violence). But a strong state simply makes it more likely that interpersonal misdeeds are penalized, that people's lives and property are protected, and hence that losing in the games of everyday life doesn't entail death or absolute poverty.

- And last but not least, changing **the lived relationship to life and death** through increasing contemplative insight, hence **changing the *needs and wants* the games are played for**. This changes which goods are ultimately seen as most real, most substantial. Goods that are deeper, more immaterial, are easier to distribute more fairly (insight and bliss vs. food and oil, etc.). This affects the economy of roles to be attained for enactment of imagined immortality. In a society where power over others is the ultimate fantasy, people will have to play for roles like "supervisor" or "great dictator" or even "conqueror" and these roles will be the most desired ones, resulting in very dire games where only few can win and only through great cruelty. In a richer **"economy of happiness"**, people may play for roles such as "the wise person", "the saint" or "the trustworthy friend". That will still produce losers and winners, but the results will be determined through much less bloodshed and losing will come at much lower costs.

I urge the reader to look at these suggestions and compare them with our current political reality—which levers for changing the game are we currently using? Even critical social science seems to take the game too much for granted, seeing too few levers.

If we stay on our current track, we will miss valuable opportunities for changing the game, for changing the logics through which our social interactions function.

EVOLVING MARKETS, POLITIES AND CIVIL SPHERES

In Book One, I argued that neither the market, nor the state bureaucracy, nor the civil sphere (including our associations, clubs, media and personal relationships) can be seen as inherently "rational", "free" or "humane". Rather, each sphere can be more or less intelligent and display varying degrees of **collective intelligence**.

They develop together and depend upon each other for their proper functioning. In this view, it makes less sense to be a classical libertarian, socialist, conservative or anarchist because each of these positions is inherently biased towards and against market, state and civil sphere solutions respectively. They each have "political allergies" and infatuations limiting their perspectives upon all things political. In this sense, it is necessary to go "beyond Left and Right", letting go of irrational allergies and infatuations.

I also argued there are different analytical "fractal triads" which are becoming increasingly intermeshed and *re-integrated* in the digital, post-industrial economy that relies more upon sustainability, creativity and innovation.

These fractal triads are:

1. **The systems**:
    a. the market,
    b. the state,
    c. the civil sphere.

2. **The spheres of life**:
    a. the professional,
    b. the civic (citizen and public engagement),
    c. the personal.

3. **The political base-suppositions**:
    a. solidarity,
    b. competition,
    c. trade.

4. **The basic political values**:
    a. order,
    b. equality,
    c. freedom.

I suppose you could add a fifth triad consisting of an expanded form of Habermas' duality between "the system" (all impersonal exchanges via money and formal political power) and "the lifeworld" (everyday life experience and the relations in it) by adding a third category of "imagined communities" or "imaginaries" (the shared ideas and preconceptions about society at large including ethnicity and nationality, such as has been proposed by Benedict Anderson and somewhat differently by Charles Taylor). It is not difficult to see these three categories are also in a dialectical dance with one another and that neither of them is "the most real" or the ultimate source of legitimacy.

Each of these triads develop *as triadic fractal systems*; their constituent parts develop together or regress together—even if there may be times when one aspect can and should be emphasized over the other two. The triads can be intelligently weaved together, or their parts can work against each other and cause mutual harm. And, more fundamentally, the parts *depend upon* each other in their logical structure. Fractals.

The game deniers tend to dislike and deny the aspects of *competition* and *trade* that are in fact logically necessary parts of life and society. The game accepters tend to deride and underestimate the very real aspects of *solidarity, moral concern* and *love,* trying to explain these by reducing them to the "underlying hard facts" of political realism and crude economic interests. They think competition is the most real.

The game change position avoids such biases against markets, states and the civil sphere, or against solidarity, competition and trade. Rather, the idea is to work for game change across all of these: to see how they interact, how they strengthen and/or impede each other.

Notes

1. You can read about this and calculate the population growth at W.P. Armstrong's online textbook of natural history. Retrieved, 2018-07-27: http://www2.palomar.edu/users/warmstrong/lmexer9.htm

2. Caspar A. Hallmann, Martin Sorg, Eelke Jongejans, Henk Siepel, Nick Hofland, Heinz Schwan, Werner Stenmans, Andreas Müller, Hubert Sumser, Thomas Hörren, Dave Goulson, Hans de Kroon. *More than 75 percent decline over 27 years in total flying insect biomass in protected areas.* PLOS ONE, 2017; 12 (10).

3. Yuval Harari even wrote a book about it, *Homo Deus*, released in 2016.

4. This relates, of course, to the extent that technology can remake the human body. The so-called transhumanists, led by figures such as David Pearce and Ray Kurzweil, argue that this is the most important question of our time. I partly disagree, as this book makes apparent.

5. Becker, E., 1973. *The Denial of Death.* New York: Simon & Schuster.

6. Two areas of concern are largely left out: 1) the economic system and its ongoing transition to a new stage, which I instead discuss in another book called *Outcompeting Capitalism*; and 2) how a corresponding legal system and legal philosophy would look like and function, which I hope to address in the coming years. In other words, we are concluding this inquiry into a metamodern guide to *politics*, whereas the metamodern guides to the economy and legal theory lie outside of our current scope.

7. Trump, D. Exact quote: "I know words, I have the best words. I have the best, but there is no better word than stupid." from 2016 election speech.

8. The word "attractor" is taken from the mathematical study of dynamical systems where it's used to designate a set of numerical values towards which a system tends to evolve. We are here avoiding a more cumbersome discussion about what kinds of attractors there are. Since societies are very complex phenomena, we are talking of complex forms of attractors, called "strange attractors", i.e. attractors that have a fractal structure. This term was coined by Ruelle and Takens. The most famous strange attractor is the Lorenz attractor, described already in 1963 by Edward Lorenz. These early models were made to describe meteorological phenomena.
See: Ruelle, D., Takens, F., 1971. On the nature of turbulence. *Communications in Mathematical Physics.* 20 (3): 167–192.

9. Yes, we all know there was a dark side to Jobs, too. The point here is simply to point out the power of attractors.

10. The point is *not*, of course, that our suggested "Montesquieu 2.0" should cancel the democratic principles of Montesquieu's tripartite division, but to build another layer on top of them. The new insights regulate the old ones, but they don't cancel them. Montesquieu's division of powers still holds.

11. "What Is The Great Attractor?" Universe Today. 2014-07-14.

12. I sometimes use the word "polity" instead of "state".

13. First under the Social Democrats themselves, then more systematically under a government of the Right between 2006 and 2014.
See: Norberg, J., 2013. *How Laissez-Faire Made Sweden Rich.* Libertarianism.org. Oct. 25th 2003.

14. We did, after all, throw out Montesquieu's budding political sociology—his theory that people from cold countries became more resourceful and democratic—or the idea that Christianity rhymes with democracy and Islam with despotism, also presented in *The Spirit of Laws.* (But then again, both of these theories have recently been reappearing in serious and balanced analyses, as the "Cold Waters" theory looks at how temperate geography with plenty of rain made for freer peasants, not dependent upon major irrigation projects organized by despotic rulers, how more rivers helped pre-industrial trade, how Islam is statistically related to illiberal values in the population, and so forth. Many of these theories are discussed and evaluated at length in the magisterial work of World Values Survey's own Christian Welzel.) See:
Welzel, C. 2013. *Freedom Rising. Human Empowerment and the Quest for Emancipation.* Cambridge, UK: Cambridge University Press.

15. Even if the anthropologist from Swaziland, Jason Hickel, has done a brilliant job revealing some of the mathematical trickery it took to exaggerate the success. See: Hickel, J. 2016. The true extent of global poverty and hunger: Questioning the good news narrative of the Millennium Development Goals. *Third World Quarterly.* Vol. 37: 5, pp. 749-67.

16. Fajnzylber, P., Lederman, D., Loayza, N. 2002. Inequality and Violent Crime. *Journal of Law and Economics.* vol. 45: 1-40.

17. This example of music gained and singing lost is from a talk by Charles Eisenstein—a thinker I don't really admire in other regards.

18. Note that I discuss this in detail in my other book, *The 6 Hidden Patterns of History.* A later "metameme" can include earlier ones via either what I call "reenactment", for instance when you watch a historical action movie in a liberal non-violent society, like Gladiator, so as to relive some of the positive aspects of the Faustian metameme (violence, heroism and glory).

19. And to be exact, there are two more categories, but they are more complicated and need not concern us here. Just to mention them briefly the first one is **transition problems** from one stage of society to another—like the horrors of early industrialization. For instance, in Liverpool in 1829, at the heart of budding industrialization, life expectancy at birth was as low as 29 years; the *lowest* since the days of the black plague. And such painful transitional periods seem to occur to this day in developing countries. Today, in 2018, people in China report considerably *less* happiness than they did twenty years ago, despite the fact that poverty rates have been slashed from a third to ten percent. The educated, urban population are especially depressed—which feeds right back into the idea about modern alienation.
See: Graham, C., Zhou, S., Zhang, J. 2017. Happiness and Health in China: The Paradox of Progress. *World Development.* Vol. 96, pp. 231-44.

The other such category is **"loopholes"**, i.e. when the values of modern society can be set aside and the ethics of earlier stages of society *de facto* reign. For instance, modern society transposes (and relabels) slavery and serfdom beyond its own shores under colonialism and, in our days, under the complex sub-contractor chains of production and distribution of major corporate transnationals. You could say that these categories are special cases of "residual problems" and "new emergent properties" problems. I discuss these in another book titled *The 6 Hidden Patterns of History.*

20. People sometimes invent little games to get around game denial. Why do we love sports? After all, the outcome of a football game hardly makes any difference in concrete reality—if a ball was in a goal net or not, how many times, or if a Ethiopian guy ran a sprint in 0.1 seconds less than an American did. The reason we love these arbitrary sets of rules is that, in this particular setting, no game denial is possible. Games are fun *because* they curb game denial; and that goes from chess to Ping-Pong. We are even prepared to engage in otherwise "meaningless" activities, only to get rid of the ambiguities of life in general, where anything and everything can always be reinterpreted in a million ways. Did I win the debate? Am I a good person? Is she a better person than me? Am I worthy? Did I succeed?

21. From Neil Strauss' *The Game: Penetrating the Secret Society of Pickup Artists,* 2005: chapter 2.
By the way—I don't mean to equate conservatives with pickup artists or vice versa. I am just looking for the general "let's keep it real" sentiment, which they both share.

22. Santesson, P. "*Vem vågar prata?*" ["Who dares to speak?"], *Demoskop,* September 14th 2015.

23. Ekins, E. "The State of Free Speech and Tolerance in America". *Cato Institute Survey Reports,* October 31st 2017.

24. These concepts, excuses, justifications, hedgings and accounts are discussed in social-psychological research and the discipline called "ethnomethodology". See Scott, M. B., Lyman, S. M., 1968: Accounts. *American Sociological Review,* Vol. 33, No. 1: 46-62.
See also: Buttny, R., 1993. *Social Accountability in Communication.* London: Sage.

25. Solomon, S., Greenberg, J., Pyszczynski, T., 2015. *The Worm at The Core. On the Role of Death in Life.* London: Penguin Press.

26. The 17th century philosopher Thomas Hobbes famously assumed that the system is *good* and the individual is *bad*—roughly speaking—because he saw the effects of institutional decay during the English Civil War, which broke out in 1642. In 1651 Hobbes published *Leviathan*, his *magnum opus*, which became a cornerstone of political conservatism. When Hobbes wrote of the "state of nature" (when there is no sovereign or law, no ruler or polity) and claimed it was a brutish place where the strong exploit the weak and "there can be no industry", he was in fact overgeneralizing a kind of **developmental imbalance** which he had failed to notice. It is true, that if you have ten million people gathered, and you *then* remove the state—carnage will ensue. In other words, if you *remove* the system that had hitherto made a certain stage of societal development possible, you get chaos and conflict. Hobbes was a proto-conservative (writing before "modern" conservatism fully emerged), and he arrived at this position by failing to see the four fields (Appendix B) and their interdependent and developmental nature. He didn't see the whole picture: he thought that institutions are good and institutionless people are bad.

When the conservative philosopher Edmund Burke in the early 19th century wrote his critical commentary on the French Revolution he was noticing a related but distinct aspect: that you cannot just force a system into being without the corresponding psychology and culture within the population, lest you will experience a huge backlash. But Burke, too, overgeneralized. He was noticing **another developmental imbalance** and took it as universally applicable. But in reality, dramatic shifts of systems *have* been made successfully throughout history. It's just that some are sustainable because they match the development in the three other fields, while some aren't. The political systems that aren't based within all four fields simply lead to severe pathologies: planned economy without a socialist (postmodern) population will lead to breadlines and oppression, an industrialized society with a modern bureaucracy governed by faustian principles of dominance and war will lead to nazism.

And the radical Rousseau mused in the 18th century, that humanity was corrupted by the institutions and that a free and fair life was possible (as did the utopian socialists and anarchists that followed him). He, too, got the handle of **yet another developmental imbalance**: when people's psychologies develop ahead of the culture and systems in which they live—i.e. when they grasp for greater universality than what is supported or expected by their current society. This is where you find the "righteous rebel", the post-conventional ethics of sensitive citizens, beautiful souls and daring minds who experience severe alienation in the society they are part of: so barbaric, so insensitive. But he too was "true, but partial". What Rousseau described was, again, a developmental imbalance. He too overgeneralized his own experience: thinking that all people were "by nature" as his own moral-philosophical intuition indicated.

This is the source of Rousseau's *ressentiment*, the French word for "resentment" as employed in psychology and philosophy. Rousseau and his game denying left-wing descendants are stuck with a bitter non-acceptance of reality, with a perpetual denial. They don't recognize their critique is only an expression of a developmental imbalance. It is a kind of violence against reality itself; but reality always fights back with full force and the denier is always defeated—by logical necessity.

27. Fukuyama, F., 2011. *The Origins of Political Order: From Prehuman Times to the French Revolution.* New York: Farrar, Straus and Giroux.
Fukuyama, F., 2014. *Political Order and Political Decay: From the Industrial Revolution to the Globalization of Democracy.* New York: Farrar, Straus and Giroux.

28. See: Langer, H. 1990. The Thirty Years' War. 2nd ed. Dorset Press.

29. In pre-modern history, there are some interesting cases that might reminisce of the modern welfare state, such as the crop insurance system of the Incas, but these comparisons really stretch the argument. The welfare state is a phenomenon emerging only in industrialized nation states.

30. Corporate taxes in America also went up dramatically during the war, but eventually fell to even lower levels than before the war. 2015 the US corporate income tax was 10.8%. See:
Patton, M. "A brief history of the individual and corporate income tax", *Forbes Magazine*. October 21st 2015.

31. Rose, P., Miller, N., 2008/2011. *Governing the Present.* Cambridge, UK: Polity Press.

32. In fact, towards the end of his life, Foucault was reading up on—and was partly sympathetic towards—some of the free market economists, like Milton Friedman and James M. Buchanan.
   Foucault died of AIDS in 1984, before the neoliberal turn in Western politics had taken proper hold. Today, after the Reagan-Thatcher era, and after the 1990s, most observers would find these visions less inspiring. Today, it seems more feasible to accept this growth of intimacy of control, but to always keep a critical stance towards it.
   See: Zamora, D., Amselle, J., Behrendt, Christofferson, M. S., Rehnmann, J., Wacquant, L. J. D. 2015. *Critiquer Foucault. Les années 1980 et la tentation néolibérale.* Paris: Aden.

33. All of this is interspersed, of course, with periods of disintegration and conformism, when things fall apart and people revert to earlier stages of development for a period of time—and by renewed resistance and struggle. Far from all emancipation and integration projects are successful and sustainable.

34. To make matters more complicated some authors, like Daniel Siegel, use the word "integration" to mean both differentiation *and* linkage. In this vocabulary, then, integration is the overall process whereas its two components are differentiation of different elements and their interlinking. The way I use the term, it is juxtaposed with differentiation.

35. www.freedomhouse.org

36. My lovely girlfriend called me up a while ago and suggested a radical, even dangerous, thought, which I decided to include in the book: What if the obsession we have with freedom today will be seen as antiquated already in the near future? After all, with all the research into behavioral science, biology, sociology and cognitive science, suggesting that human minds, perceptions and choices are always steered by other forces than our "free wills", and that we generally aren't aware of how these forces affect us—does it really make sense to obsess about freedom like we do? Maybe we would be better off by focusing less on freedom and more on concrete issues such as the fulfillment of human needs and longings?
   Maybe, in a few decades, the word "freedom" will no longer sound cool and magical, but rather like the word "duty" sounds to us today. A while ago "duty" was hailed as something sacred and inherently good. Maybe the same fate awaits "freedom": Perhaps future people will think it sounds old and a bit silly.
   This is a compelling idea. But I still feel we are not quite done with freedom yet; that we first have to expand it before it can be left to the side. Maybe, in the future, the term will be obsolete and exchanged for other terms that have less of lingering pre-modern religious beliefs left in them. (cont.)

But, dear reader, bear with me and let us save the critical reappraisal of freedom for the future. Let us remain, for the moment, lovers of freedom.

37. "Men" meaning people, not males!

38. Feldman Barrett, L., 2017. *How Emotions Are Made: The Secret Life of the Brain.* Boston: Houghton Mifflin Harcourt.

39. Deutscher, G., 2010. *Through the Language Glass: Why the World Looks Different in Other Languages.* New York: Metropolitan Press.

40. In fact, some few people who attain stable spiritual experiences tend to report that they no longer experience emotions, but this is quite rare, and I am not sure it would hold up to experimental evidence.

41. Another word of analytical caution, before we go on. There's of course more to these emotions than this simple scheme suggests. For instance, we can be embarrassed on behalf of somebody else, or we can feel moral indignation (being judgmental) without recognizing our own corresponding faults, and so on. And feeling hatred towards someone can sometimes be pleasurable. But I am looking at a basic pattern of how these emotions connect to each other, and in this simple sense, I believe the pattern holds: You have four families of negative social emotions and they all play a part in social life, being latent, staying in the background in most everyday situations, but always creeping up and making themselves known sooner or later.

Let's take an example of such an "emotional regime": What about the perpetrators of "honor killings"—for instance, when the daughter of a traditional Muslim family living in a Western country is killed by the father because her sexual liberation, in their minds, has brought "shame to the family"? Mustn't these honor killers be driven by unimaginably intense emotions of shame, contempt and moral outrage in order to feel compelled to (and justified in) killing their own daughters? It's less likely these fathers of traditional families walk around full of guilt and shame every day of their life. Rather, the extremely negative emotions emerge and manifest themselves only when the traditional family system is challenged by the daughter's lifestyle choices and boyfriends. Up until that point these emotions lay dormant and simply excluded a lot of possible ways of acting and thinking.

When the taboos are breached, the negative emotions surface and erupt: first you *shame* your daughter, and when that doesn't work, you *guilt*-trip her, and when that doesn't work, you *threaten* her—and when that doesn't work, you feel completely helpless and frustrated and kill her. Because of the cultural-psychological limitations of the traditional Muslim father's relation to sex, sexuality, reproduction and femininity, freedom is undermined. Lacking emotional development limits freedom. This is of course not to point out Muslims in particular, it's just an example of how emotional issues feed into the lack of real freedom in people's lives. Many other groups have problematic relationships to female sexuality too.

But the point here is that we are all, in some sense, like the violent Muslim father: All of us have issues that we just cannot deal with without feeling shame, without feeling contempt and guilt-tripping others and, ultimately, without being afraid, vulnerable and even threatening. We may not be killing our daughters for perceived insults to our family honor, but we are all intermeshed in a complex emotional economy in which we envy, shame, guilt and subtly threaten one another—and we always feel justified in doing so. If there is an apparent developmental difference between the traditionalist Muslim and the liberal parents who support their kids' sexual education and encourage exploration and independence, can there also be yet higher developments of freedom? Are we emotionally limiting ourselves and one another in other, subtler, ways?

Up until recently homosexuality was such an issue. There was something shameful, disgusting and ridiculous about the homosexuals. Today, issues of being fat, being cool or not (being a nerd), being ugly if you're a woman, general social status at the workplace and being successful, offer examples of toxic topics. Other examples are animal rights and the abuses of industrial farming, gender equality issues (of the feminist or masculist brands). All of these still remain subject to intense shame, guilt and fear mongering. If you scratch the surface of these issues in almost any social setting, people tend to freak out with strong negative emotional reactions. The machinery is there: controlling us and shaping our every interaction, even when it comes to what we allow ourselves to think in the privacy of our own minds.

42. I am well aware that Maslow himself didn't invent the pyramid; it came later as a text book staple for management students (but Maslow didn't object). The model has been highly criticized for its implications (that only the rich would have "higher needs" etc.) as well as its ability to stand up to empirical scrutiny. See: Bridgman, T.; Cummings. S.; Ballard, J. 2019. Who Built Maslow's Pyramid? A History of the Creation of Management Studies' Most Famous Symbol and Its Implications for Management Education. *Academy of Management Learning & Education*. vol. 18, no. 1.

43. Yes, even traditional versions of karma can in many ways be viewed as a guilt scoring system, even if there are other and more charitable interpretations.

44. Elias, N. 1939/2000. *The Civilizing Process. Sociogenetic and Psychogenetic Investigations.* Revised edition. Oxford: Blackwell.

45. Scheff, T., 2003. Shame and Self in Society. *Symbolic Interaction*, 26, 239-62.

46. Not saying, of course, that I personally hold all of these to be role models.

47. Before I go on, **I simply *cannot* sufficiently stress of the importance of seeing personal development in a non-judgmental way**. It's not that some people are good and others are bad, and that the bad ones should "damn well grow up" and "be mature". That's how fourteen-year-olds tease one another, and that's, unfortunately, also how Kegan's theory—and perhaps my own—often lend themselves to perverted uses.

The developmental perspective is per definition non-moralistic, non-judgmental. It is what comes *instead of* moralism, instead of blaming people. Higher stage is always explicable, always due to a privilege of some kind—social, genetic or other. It is never a measure of "the worth of your soul".

The reason that people flip out under the pressure of too much freedom is not, speaking from the viewpoint of behavioral science, that we're bad people, it's simply that we're not built for it, not prepared for it.

The point with understanding developmental stages is *never* to insult or deride, and *always* to understand how people can be supported, to see the causal, impersonal mechanisms that make higher freedom unbearable. There's no God, remember? We killed Him. Or at least there's no God in the sense there is a supreme perspective from which we judge the inherent value of people. There's no final umpire, no ultimate judge. So don't judge people for escaping the terror of freedom. We are simply unprepared.

48. Pressfield, S., 2012. *The War of Art.* New York: Black Irish Entertainment LLC.

49. This, by the way, is one reason to be wary of utopian ideas of Universal Basic Income (UBI). If Kegan claims only some 36% of (the US) population is at "Self-Authoring" or above, and if so few of us are actually capable of living an artist's life, creating in the face of people's norms and expectations—should we really expect that a majority of people would blossom under UBI? *Some* certainly would. But many or most may get stuck in a tragic lifetime of procrastination; of endless searching for new kicks and amusement, a grand excuse for a life unlived, a life as "the Great Spectator"—in a sense—living but never being born. Vanilla prison.

50. Honneth, A., 1992/1996. *Struggle for Recognition: The Moral Grammar of Social Conflicts.* Oxford: Polity Press.

51. "The middle three quintiles (i.e. excluding the top and bottom 20%) in terms of country incomes could be responsible for 57% of global GDP in PPP terms, up from only 31% [in 2008] (and climb from 15% to 43% in USD terms). This group, which will be dominated by a subset of the BRICs and N11 (China, India, Brazil, Egypt, Philippines, Indonesia, Iran, Mexico, Vietnam) will matter more and more for global spending patterns."
See: Wilson, D., Dragusanu, R., 2008. *The Expanding Middle: The Exploding World Middle Class and Falling Global Inequality.* Goldman Sachs: Global Economics Paper No: 170.

52. Originally from an OECD report: van Zanden *et al.* 2014. *How Was Life?* OECD.

53. Another version of telling this story is the famous graph by economist Branko Milanović's "elephant curve". Source: *The American Prospect*, using data provided by Branko Milanović. It's called the "elephant curve" because it looks like an elephant. The graph has been discussed at length in Milanović 2016 book, *Global Inequality.* (cont.)

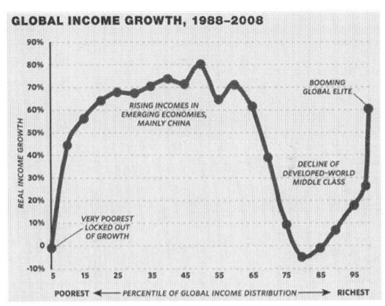

GLOBAL INCOME GROWTH, 1988-2008

BOOMING GLOBAL ELITE

RISING INCOMES IN EMERGING ECONOMIES, MAINLY CHINA

DECLINE OF DEVELOPED-WORLD MIDDLE CLASS

VERY POOREST LOCKED OUT OF GROWTH

REAL INCOME GROWTH

POOREST ◄── PERCENTILE OF GLOBAL INCOME DISTRIBUTION ──► RICHEST

54. Zhang, F. *et al.* 2014. Friendship quality, social preference, proximity prestige, and self-perceived social competence: Interactive influences on children's loneliness. *Journal of School Psychology.* 52(5).

55. Marx, K., 1844. "The Power of Money" in *Economic and Philosophical Manuscripts.*

56. I'm not a fan of humanism, as discussed in the Appendix of Book One, as I view humanist ideas as unproductively anthropocentric and non-transpersonal. But of course, in the 19th century, this kind of thinking is to be expected.

57. Of course, it's a crude map with deliberately vague definitions, and depending on how we feel any given day we might interpret our situations differently along the scale. But I think it does its job: to highlight that social inequality is a scale that endows some with security and happiness and creates social insecurity and unhappiness for others.

58. Snyder-Mackler N. *et al.*, 2016. Social status alters immune regulation and response to infection in macaques. *Science.* 354 (6315):1041-1045.

59. Havlicek, J. S., Roberts, C., Flegr, J., 2005. Women's preference for dominant male odour: effects of menstrual cycle and relationship status. *Biology Letters.* April 4, 2005.

60. Hakim, C., 2011. *Honey Money: The Power of Erotic Capital.* London: Penguin Press.

61. O'Donnell, K. J., Chen, L., MacIsaac, J.L., McEwen, L. M., Nguyen, T., Beckmann, K. et al, 2018. DNA methylome variation in a perinatal nurse-visitation program that reduces child maltreatment: a 27-year follow-up. *Transl Psychiatry*, vol. 8(1).

62. Gonzalez, A., Catherine, N., Boyle, M., Jack, S. M., Atkinson, L., Kobor, M. *et al.* 2018. Healthy Foundations Study: a randomised controlled trial to evaluate boilogical embedding of early-life experiences. *BMJ Open*, vol. 8(1).

63. Weir, K., 2012. "The Pain of Social Rejection". American Psychological Association: *Monitor of Psychology*, vol. 43(4).

64. See Fowler, J. H., Christakis, N. A., 2008. Dynamic spread of happiness in a large social network: longitudinal analysis over 20 years in the Framingham Heart Study. *British Medical Journal*—a study in which 4739 individuals were followed from 1983 to 2003.

65. An important aspect of this—which I leave out in this discussion—has to do with using technology to develop the states of human beings. Consider the following quote from a report on an "Effective Altruism" event in San Francisco:

"I got to talk to people from the Qualia Research Institute, who point out that everyone else is missing something big: the hedonic treadmill. People have a certain baseline amount of happiness. Fix their problems, and they'll be happy for a while, then go back to baseline. The only solution is to hack consciousness directly, to figure out what exactly happiness is—unpack what we're looking for when we describe some mental states as having higher positive valence than others—and then add that on to every other mental state directly. This isn't quite the dreaded wireheading, the widely-feared technology that will make everyone so doped up on techno-super-heroin (or direct electrical stimulation of the brain's pleasure centers) that they never do anything else. It's a rewiring of the brain that creates a 'perpetual but varied bliss' that 'reengineers the network of transition probabilities between emotions' while retaining the capability to do economically useful work."

See: Alexander, S., 2017. "Fear and Loathing at Effective Altruism Global 2017", published online 16th of August at *Slate Star Codex*. (www.slatestarcodex.com) ⊕

66. There is even a documentary film, produced by James Redford, *Resilience* (2017) which lays all of this out in detail.

67. Union of Concerned Scientists, 2019. "Air Pollution from Vehicles in California". Downloaded from www.ucsusa.org on Feb 22nd 2019.

68. Rideout, V. J, Foehr, U. G., Roberts, D. F., 2010. "Generation M^2: Media in the Lives of 8- to 18-Year-Olds." Kaiser Family Foundation.
    About deteriorating emotional intelligence, see: Yalda, T. U. *et al.*, 2014. Five Days at Outdoor Education Camp Without Screens Improves Preteen Skills with Nonverbal Emotion Cues. *Computers in Human Behavior*, vol. 30, pp. 387-92.
    About ADHD, see: Swing, E. L, *et al*, 2010. Television and Video Game Exposure and the Development of Attention Problems. *Pediatrics*, vol. 126:2, pp. 214-21.

69. Given the importance and growing salience of sociological theories of "cultural capital" I will briefly address the issue and add a quick homage to the late French sociologist Pierre Bourdieu, who was the first to systematically and influentially innovate the field of multiple capitals. He outlined the mechanisms of economic, social and cultural capital, the latter of which he is best known for.
    Cultural capital entails having a certain *Bildung*; that is, being familiar with and knowledgeable about topics and areas others consider refined and interesting. It's

when your understanding of the world and way of reasoning exceeds that of the average person; when you can talk about things others find valuable and worth listening to; when your taste in art, clothing and music is admired by others. Academics, hipsters and artists generally have high levels of cultural capital, and it's certainly tradable for other kinds of capital (which is a defining characteristic of any form of capital): It can of course be traded for cash if people pay you to speak or buy your books, artworks or expertise, but it can also be traded for social and sexual capital by making you a more interesting friend or attractive lover. However, simply having a degree in liberal arts or just being a graphic designer won't do much. What characterizes cultural capital is that it must be valuable and desirable to others, and a person with high cultural capital must be someone who deeply understands and embodies the spirit of their time.

The reason I don't bring up cultural capital as a fundamental form of inequality is that it is a more complicated matter, and its type of hierarchies and inequalities follow another logic altogether than classical superiority/inferiority of the other ones. Its role in the transformation of the world economy is also more fundamental and profound, I believe, as it will eventually replace economic or financial capital as the dominant force to coordinate human agency—or at least, that's where the attractors seem to be pointing.

Cultural capital can be viewed as the mediating factor *between* information and emotional energy. Only if you know how to use information to elicit emotional responses can you control and coordinate behaviors, "speak to the soul to electrify" and so forth. Cultural capital is about symbols, and information is symbols, and symbols must be ritualized and invoked sensitively in order to be effective. That's what cultural capital does, and that's the reason it will grow in importance and eventually come to rule the world economy.

So if I suggested that Hakim's "erotic capital" is a kind of sub-category, I believe cultural capital is a kind of super-category, destined to shift the interplay of all the other forms of stratification. More on this in my other book *Outcompeting Capitalism*.

It should be noted, of course, that the role I reserve for cultural capital is an even greater and more fundamental one than Bourdieu did. In my own schematic picture, cultural capital is the source of the creative class and/or the "triple-H population", hipsters, hackers and hippies whom I mentioned in Book One. We have gone from a modern society like that of France in the 1960s—the context in which Bourdieu crafted his theories—to a global postmodern state of affairs, saturated in perpetual media images and visual symbols, to an emerging metamodern world of a birthing attentionalist internet economy where cultural capital begins to reign supreme and financial capital slowly but surely is brought to its knees.

70. In embryonic forms, this was already the case within traditional religions such as Christianity and Buddhism. "We are all children of God with unique souls", "We are all born into a perfect human rebirth", etc.

71. At the top of postindustrial society you have groups emerging who are rich in all of these forms of capital put together. The Swedish philosophers Alexander Bard and Jan Söderqvist have suggested the new "masters of the internet" should be called **netocrats**. These are the small groups who are most proficient at benefitting from the World Wide Web and thus constantly gain an upper hand in

the informational economy; not necessarily because they have the best technical skills, but because they understand the social and cultural logic of the internet most intimately. In Book One I proposed that the growing **triple-H populations** (hackers, hipsters and hippies) are gaining influence across the board and increasingly are becoming important agents in the new economy. You might also call them **the creative class**, with a broader, more established (and more scorned) term. Franco Berardi, of the Italian Marxist "autonomist" school, has suggested the term **cognitariat**—the class distinguished by its relation to abstract symbols.

At the bottom of postindustrial society you don't really find a wide "proletariat" any longer. You find people who are just disenfranchised in a general manner; who are in an economically, socially and otherwise *precarious* situation. They are perhaps best denominated with a term made famous (but not invented) by the economist Guy Standing: **the precariat**. However, on the low end of informational and cultural capital you also find a lot of people who are relatively economically comfortable, but never really get to participate meaningfully in the postindustrial society of social media spectacles and exciting events. These growing groups are continuously reduced to a position of *consuming* the ideas, images and spectacles produced by others, hence Bard and Söderqvist call them **the consumtariat**.

Regarding the "regressive" voters of present-day USA (who voted for Donald Trump), there has been much discussion whether they constitute an economically disempowered segment of the population. Is this a revolt of the lower classes, or is it the bigotry of the privileged?

The answer is clear: They are not all *economically* poor, but they have lower cultural and informational capital than "progressive" voters. **Trump voters largely belong to the consumtariat, the relative underclass of a postindustrial internet society.**

Hence it is clear that the class struggles of our day and age have already shifted. It's not that financial capital and economic class no longer matter —it's just that it's no longer the only game in town and that other forms of class distinctions are growing in importance. Rightwing populists can help these groups take back the spectacle, the center stage of society—at least for a while—and thus reaffirming the sense of meaning and empowerment that flows from it.

72. The term "precariat" is discussed in the endnote above.

73. This is good in many ways, but it can also hinder rational discourse, as for instance nobody wants to criticize immigration for fear of losing social status. Most people in these countries are of course not of the postmodern value meme and offer quiet resistance to these tendencies—offering only a thin veneer of compliance and consent.

Once pressures from immigration became too large for Sweden, in 2015, the whole establishment of the media and political leadership turned overnight and the borders were effectively closed. To circumvent the power of the instituted norm system, they all had to make the shift simultaneously so as not to be exposed to charges of racism and bigotry. Because this large-scale coordination was so difficult to achieve, the country reacted only in the eleventh hour—under the leadership of the pro-immigration Green Party and the nominally multiculturalist Social Democrats. In this light, the recent dramatic rise of the nationalist Sweden Democrats is perhaps not so surprising.

74. Quote from chapter 15 of Siegel, D., 2017. *Mind: A Journey to the Heart of Being Human*. New York: Norton & Company.

75. Martin Gilens and Benjamin I. Page, "Testing Theories of American Politics: Elites, Interest Groups, and Average Citizens" (2014, Princeton).

76. Dahl, R.A., 1983. *Democracy and Its Critics*. Yale University Press, p. 221.

77. Francis Fukuyama has claimed that the US system of governance has been in a steady decline for decades due to its outdated system of checks and balances, which he claims has reduced the quality of governance and led the country to become a de facto "vetocracy", where interest groups and courts (and courts influenced by the former) hinder decisive government action by an effective "veto", which in turn undermines the legitimacy of the public institutions, which in turn makes governance and taxation more difficult. This vicious cycle may hold great explanatory power in terms of the ailments of today's US.

    Many other contemporary political scientists share the general picture of a US democracy in institutional decay.

    Fukuyama, F., 2014. *Political Order and Political Decay: From the Industrial Revolution to the Globalization of Democracy*. New York: Farrar, Straus and Giroux.

78. Bone Z., Crockett J., Hodge S., 2006. "Deliberation Forums: A Pathway for Public Participation". *Proceedings of the APEN International Conference 2006*.

79. Not literally, stupid. Be nice and non-violent.

80. And I suppose the fact these words came from Roosevelt underline the ambiguity of the issue of making *Gemeinschaft* into a political issue. This venerated progressive president also had an authoritarian underbelly: He admired Mussolini before the war and even appointed a former KKK member to the Supreme Court. I know that quoting an American president is tacky, but he, or whoever wrote the undelivered speech, was right—and I want to show that this isn't such a fringe thing to think and say.

81. "Fourth sector" meaning those companies, foundations and NGOs that work in hybrid organizations that are not purely for profit, unlike the three classical sectors. The first three sectors of course meaning raw material, manufacture and services.

82. Bart Somers did write a book about it all, but it's in Dutch.

    See: Somers, B., 2016. *Samen Leven. Een hoopvolle strayegie tegen IS*. Belgium: Houtekiet.

83. In terms of MHC (the Model of Hierarchical Complexity, by Commons, as discussed in Book One), people tend to go down two stages when they are very upset about something, very invested in a belief, or something is a very touchy spot. Two stages are the difference between a ten-year-old and an average adult.

84. Butler, J. 1990/2006. *Gender Trouble*. New York: Routledge.

85. Armstrong, E. A., Hamilton, L. T., Armstrong, E. M., 2014. "Good Girls": Gender, Social Class, and Slut Discourse on Campus. *Social Psychology Quarterly*. Vol: 77(2).

86. Baumeister, R. F., Reynolds T., Winegard, B., Vohs, K. D. 2017. Competing for love: Applying sexual economics theory to mating contests. *Journal of Economic Psychology*, vol. 63, pp. 230-41.

87. Hakim, C. 2015. The male sex deficit: A social fact of the 21st century. *International Sociology*, vol. 30, pp. 314-35.

88. Bivona, J. M., Critelli, J. W., Clark, M. J., 2012. Women's Rape Fantasies: An Empirical Evaluation of the Major Explanations. *Archive of Sexual Behavior*, vol. 41(5) pp. 1107–1119.

89. Gandhi, M. K., 1948. *Autobiography.* Ahmedabad: Navajivan Publishing House. p. 615.

90. Schopenhauer, A., 1839. *On the Freedom of the Will* (1839/1945), as translated in *The Philosophy of American History: The Historical Field Theory* (1945) by Morris Zucker, p. 531.

91. Yes, I just used the word "wisdom" even as I said it's a poor variable in Book One. Get over it.

92. The states are, as discussed in Book One:

Lower states:

1. Hell

2. Horrific (phenomenological reality breaks down)

3. Tortured

4. Tormented

Medium states:

5. Very uneasy

6. Uneasy, uncomfortable

7. Somewhat uneasy, "okay", full of small faults

8. Satisfied, well

9. Good, lively

10. Joyous, full of light, invigorated

High states:

11. Vast, grand, open

12. Blissful, saintly

13. Enlightened, spiritual unity

93. Such nostalgic arguments *have* been made by "integral traditionalists", such as Frithjof Schuon and Réné Guénon, and they are not entirely without merit. They point out that, in the medieval period, the Church was at the center of society, and the greatest crystallization of human activity was cathedral building: a spiritual endeavor. God was at the pinnacle of everything, and religion was an important and unavoidable aspect of everyone's life; the church and temple spires towering at the highest points of all settlements for centuries.

94. Of course, artists at this point in time were still not out on the "free market", first producing their art and then finding the highest bidder, or turning to a

"general audience" with their personal expression. That happened only at the end of the 1700s with Mozart's revolt against the court-based structure of art benefactors, as discussed in Norbert Elias' book *Mozart: Sociological Portrait of a Genius*. But still, the Renaissance did produce a class of people who were supported by rich people and who had considerable artistic freedom, Leonardo da Vinci perhaps being the emblematic example.

95. Excuse the male-centric expression, "by the balls", and feel free to invent a gender neutral one.

96. At least until human enhancement reaches a point where the biological process of aging can be reversed, but that's another story.

97. Neil Young's *Heart of Gold*, 1971.

98. That's by the way what has happened to pretty much all of the traditional religious paths.

99. The technical term for which is, ironically, inflation.

100. Solomon, S., Greenberg, J., Pyszczynski, T., 2015. *The Worm at The Core. On the Role of Death in Life*. London: Penguin Press.

101. Bodner, E., *et al*, 2015. Anxieties about Aging and Death and Psychological Distress: The Protective Role of Emotional Complexity. *Personality and Individual Differences*, vol. 83, pp. 91-96.

102. And yet, the issue is not that straightforward. It has even been shown that practices of yoga and meditation can have the reverse effect—i.e. an increased identification with the ego, simply because people feel self-important for having taken part in these practices. This should not lead us to despair, however; it merely suggests that, again, there are many layers to these kinds of practices and that the mind is really good at turning things around for purposes of ego-boosting. See: Gebauer, J. E., *et al*, 2018. Mind-Body Practices and the Self: Yoga and Meditation Do Not Quiet the Ego but Instead Boost Self-Enhancement. *Psychological Science*, vol. 29, 8, pp. 1299-1308.

103. Duffell, N., 2014. *Wounded Leaders: British Elitism and the Entitlement Illusion – A Psychohistory*. London: Low Arrow Press.

104. Alexander, J., C., 2003. "On the Social Construction of Moral Universals: The 'Holocaust' from War Crime to Trauma Drama", in *The Meanings of Social Life: A Cultural Sociology*, New York: Oxford University Press, pp. 27–84.

105. You have some initial systematizations of what such meta-rights or "meta-norms" might look like in: Görtz, D. P., Commons, M. L., 2015. The stage-value model: Implications for the changing standards of care. *International Journal of Law and Psychiatry*, vol. 42–43, pp 135–143.

106. As you may have noticed, we just went through the "four fields of development" (system, culture, behavior and psychology) from Appendix B but zoomed in on how oppression works. Emancipation Politics is a matter that works across all four fields. Don't enter the information age without it. And then climb towards higher freedom; emancipate us from the regimes of emotional control.

107. Yiannis Gabriel, quoting anonymous conference speaker in *Times Higher Education*, "We must rescue social science research from obscurity", August 10,

2017. Apparently, these words were met with "Churchillian" applause from the audience.

108. Alvesson, M., Gabriel, Y., Paulsen, R., 2017. *Return to Meaning: A Social Science with Something to Say*. Croydon, UK: Oxford University Press.

109. Davis, S. J., Cao, L., Caldeira, K., Hoffert, M., 2013. Rethinking Wedges. *Environmental Research Letters*, vol. 8(1).

Also, see this 2004 forecasts for reference—things have gotten way worse since then: Pacala, S., Socolow, R., 2004. Stabilization Wedges: Solving the Climate Problem for the Next 50 Years with Current Technologies. *Science,* vol. 305(5686), pp. 968-72.

110. Menzel, S., 2013. Are Emotions to Blame? – The Impact of Non-Analytical Decision Making and Implications for Fostering Sustainability. *Ecological Economics*, vol. 96, pp. 71-79.

111. For readers versed in social theory, you likely recognize this as an echo of Foucault and Habermas. Foucault points out that we can only ever judge anything from within the confines of our own value-system and worldview, and concludes that the best we can do is to deconstruct our dominant worldview, but Habermas counters that people on average and over time will tend to converge around at least some issues if the communication functions very well, and says that there is a kind of developmental potential in communication itself. Or simply put: If all we can do is chase our own cultural tail (Foucault), at least we can do so smoothly and elegantly and soon the dog will swirl up through the air and rise to new heights (Habermas).

112. Plato, *The Republic, Book V.*

113. Lyotard, J., *La condition postmoderne: rapport sur le savoir* (Paris: Minuit, 1979).

114. Toynbee, A., 'Law and Freedom in History', (A Study of History, Vol. 2, 1957).

115. Others worth mentioning who take a similar approach are Robert Wright, Yuval Noah Harari and Tomas Björkman.

116. Christian, D., *Maps of Time: An Introduction to Big History* (California, 2005).p. 32.

117. And books *should* be written about this. If you're a young, talented academic with an interest in the sociology of knowledge, you know what to do.

118. In German, you pronounce it with a z and then a t-s at the end: *rezonants,* which makes the word strangely alluring.

119. I met Hartmut Rosa once in southern Sweden, when he was only beginning to write the book, and we resonated with one another as both of us like trashy heavy metal, such as Iron Maiden, Manowar and the many German bands.

120. The idea of garden gnomes I owe to the Swedish sociologist and organizational consultant Thomas Jordan who introduced the term *hustomtar* in a 2006 report in Swedish. I am not aware of any publications in larger languages on the topic.

121. See Appendix B.

122. The Dunning–Kruger effect is a cognitive bias wherein people of low ability suffer from illusory superiority, mistakenly assessing their cognitive ability as greater than it is. The cognitive bias of illusory superiority derives from the meta-cognitive inability of low-ability persons to recognize their own ineptitude; without the self-awareness of metacognition, low-ability people cannot objectively evaluate their actual competence or incompetence.

123. In a private message, my friend the Harvard psychologist Zak Stein has written about the importance of honing one's assessment skills and of partaking in the training of cognitive stages of complexity in groups of metamodernists:
(a) First the group recognizes that training is required to make rigorous developmental assessments. [This is actually the biggest step. Does the group recognize a real expertise gradient and learning curve, or does the group think anyone can do it after a weekend workshop?]
(b) Then the group self-selects into those who want to gain this expertise and those who are interested but feel their time is better spent elsewhere. Some in the group are trained, others are not. Maybe everyone is trained, but this is unlikely in terms of dispositions and capabilities; also inefficient.
(c) Now the group must (re)build trust between those who are "experts" and those who are not. This requires an agreement on the norms that ought to govern the use of developmental levels as an aspect of political reasoning and practice. For example, I would argue [...] that assessments of developmental levels ought *never* be used as "admission" or "expulsion" criteria... that is one of what would probably be about 12 or more norms concerning how assessments of developmental level (made by experts) ought to factor in the life and thought of the group... This final step (c) is worth doing regardless of what plays out with (a) and (b).

124. Hi Freud.

125. Fractal ethics, which I intend to return to in another book. But a very good heuristic for getting to that understanding is to seek to have solidarity with the perspectives of others, indeed, including their *Umwelt* as a biological creature.

126. You can read about this history in: Honneth, A., 2015/2017. *The Idea of Socialism: Towards a Renewal.* Cambridge, UK: Polity Press.

127. Named so after the Norwegian Prime Minister Gro Harlem Brundtland who led the UN's work on understanding and defining sustainability.

128. Note that I'm paraphrasing here. What I am referring to is, more precisely, Book 1, Section 7 of the *Social Contract*. "This means nothing less than that he will be forced to be free; for this is the condition which, by giving each citizen to his country, secures him against all personal dependence."

129. Robespierre quoted from chapter 4 in: Hicks, S. R. C., 2004/2011. *Explaining Postmodernism: Skepticism and Socialism from Rousseau to Foucault.* China: Ockham's Razor Publishing.

130. Or actually, I'm playing along with a popular textbook simplification here. In reality this quote is from an 1899 book by Émile Faguet (*Politiques et moralistes du dix-neuvième siècle*), who creatively paraphrased the conservative philosopher de Maistre with the formulation: "*Dire: les moutons sont nés carnivores, et partout ils mangent de l'herbe, serait aussi juste.*" (p. 41).

131. Even if some early conservatives, like the young Novalis, did indeed long for a united, Catholic, theocratic Europe.

132. "Postmodern", of course, in the sense I use the term in this book and the last one, not in the conventional sense that refers specifically to French poststructuralist thinkers.

133. *Mutual Aid* is actually part of a 1892 book, *The Conquest of Bread* (originally in French: *La conquète du pain*).

134. It means nazi in anarchist lingo. More precisely, Strasserism (German: *Strasserismus* or *Straßerismus*) is a strand of nazism that calls for a more radical, mass-action and worker-based form of nazism, hostile to Jews not from a racial, ethnic, cultural or religious perspective, but from an anti-capitalist basis, to achieve a national rebirth. It derives its name from Gregor and Otto Strasser, the two nazi brothers initially associated with this position.

135. As metamodern thinkers, we need to have solidarity with all perspectives and their carriers, and we need to be polite and respectful—but that shouldn't stop us from recognizing dregs when we see them. The best way to make certain you're not a lowly dreg yourself is to treat others with kindness and respect.

136. From Bakunin's 1872 speech, "On the International Workingmen's Association and Karl Marx" in which he bashes the emerging "authoritarian communist" leadership of Marx over the International.

137. Conway, L. G., Houck. S. C., Gornick, L. J., Repke, 2017. Finding the Loch Ness Monster: Left-Wing Authoritarianism in the United States. Preview published online by *Political Psychology*, December 21 2017.

138. "*La Commune de Paris et la notion de l'état*" (The Commune of Paris and the notion of the state) as quoted in Noam Chomsky: Notes on Anarchism from 1970.

139. Kaur, M., Singh, S., 2017. Analyzing Negative Ties in Social Networks: A Survey. *Egyptian Informatics Journal*, vol. 17(1), pp. 21-43.

140. I sometimes make up my own quotes. This is one of those times.

141. In *The 6 Hidden Patterns of History* I treat the three great modern totalitarianisms in greater detail, showing how communism, fascism and New Age constitute different forms of developmental imbalances and how they represent distinct metamemetic patterns contained within the limitations and potentials of modernity. In this concluding chapter of our metamodern guide to politics I will only examine their relevance to political metamodernism.

142. This is a position Marx at least partly revised after the 1871 Paris Commune, when "communard" workers revolted in Paris and held the city for two months before being beaten back.

143. Then again, present-day society and its suboptimal forms and trajectories are no joke, either. If you look at the suffering of just one issue, such as animal exploitation, the global tragedy churned out amounts to a global output of many "holocausts per year."

144. *The 6 Hidden Patterns of History.*

145. Goebbels, J., 1929/1987. *Michael.* London: Reed Business Information, Inc.

146. *The 6 Hidden Patterns of History.*

147. When I first wrote this, Europe had already seen the rise of standup comedian Beppe Grillo's Five Star Movement in Italy. Now, rereading the text, the Ukrainian president Volodymyr Zelensky has just been elected by a landslide of 73% (vs. 24% for the sitting president)—also a comedian, who even plays the part as president in a satirical television show. While these two can hardly be called new dictators, they do certainly attest to the new power of comedy—and the crossroads of fact and fiction. Stranger days are coming.

148. Quoted from Seth Abramson "On Metamodernism", published April 16th 2018 on Medium, retrieved May 2018:
https://medium.com/@Seth_Abramson/on-metamodernism-926fdc55bd6a

149. From the poem *Last Night*, loose translation by Michael R. Burch.

150. Whitman, W. 1868. *A Noiseless Patient Spider*.

151. The last paragraph is paraphrasing from Evan H. Rhodes' novel, *An Army of Children*.

152. Trotsky, L., 1925/2005. *Literature and Revolution*. Chicago: Haymarket Books. p 207.

153. Kołakowski, L., 1976/2008. *Main Currents of Marxism: The Founders—The Golden Age—The Breakdown*. New York: W. W. Norton & Company.

154. Note that I use the term "postmodern" rather differently from mainstream academics—I use it as a *developmental stage*. Mainstream academia thinks of postmodernism as rather being a strain of thought in the philosophy of the 1970s and onwards.

155. Of course, there were postmodern ideas and values that had yet to emerge in Marx's days. For instance, Marx was ostensibly anthropocentric, which means he did not sufficiently include animals or the biosphere in the circle of solidarity. The "Young Marx" touched upon an environmentalist understanding, in his discussion about "metabolic rift", but this was not central to his ensuing works. And he didn't really venture into animal rights, as discussed in Gary Francione's 2000 book *Introduction to Animal Rights*. For the appropriate passage in Marx, where he tries to defend human supremacy, you may consult *The Philosophic and Economic Manuscripts* of 1844; in Robert Tucker's Marx-Engel Reader, you can find it on page 75.

Marx's (admittedly anthropocentric) environmentalism is described in the 2000 book by John Bellamy Foster, titled *Marx's Ecology*. This book challenges the popular reading of Marx as being tied to an industrial-materialist thinking, as in Jean Baudrillard's 1973 book *The Mirror of Production*.

156. Andersen, L. R. & Björkman, T., 2017. *The Nordic Secret. A European Story of Beauty and Freedom*. Falun, Sweden: Fri Tanke Förlag.

157. To be sure, Marx allowed for some back-and-forth interactions between these different fields, but he did not explicitly formulate the four fields of development, nor did he lucidly develop upon their interactions. Rather, we were left with many vague loose threads.

You probably know how the story goes from there; Stalinist "diamat" (dialectical materialism) insisted that you *primarily* need to change the economic system, and all else will follow; the Italian radical Antonio Gramsci felt that culture and cultural "hegemony" (the dominant, taken-for-granted culture) explain why people don't become socialists; "humanist Marxists" focused on people's psychologies and personalities (Erich Fromm) or on social-psychological aspects like alienation (Joachim Israel) or blamed the TV (Theodor Adorno) or even the book clubs (Habermas—even if he, of course, later updated the view of society to something much more resembling the four fields I present here); and a few crazy people like Jean-Paul Sartre focused on agency, upon revolutionary action itself. And then you had some few geniuses, like the early Soviet thinker Alexander Bogdanov (1873-1927), who, in his foreseeing attempt at a "systems science", intuited a shift of perspective towards a more holistic one that includes all four fields.

None of these thinkers quite did it. None of them hit a homerun. The worst of all these was of course the Stalinist *diamat*. Here you have the idea that the material conditions (the means of production and who owns them, and by what structure they are governed) in the last instance determine all that "softish woo-woo", like culture, behavior and psychology (even if Stalin, like Marx conceded that ideas and theories also affect society). In this view, it is hardly surprising that these people believed—including Trotsky—that if you can change these "hard" or "material" conditions, all else can and will follow. You will have a fair, free and non-exploitative society if you only make everything publicly owned: *at any price*! So that's why these people are prepared to purge and kill others and disrespect any traditions and cultures and social structures. They believe that all of these "super-structures" are made of clay, whereas economic conditions, the "base structures", are made of steel.

But the exclusive emphasis on concrete behavior might be even more murderous. Sartre's ideas, reworked into an anti-colonialist theory by the angry young Haitian Frantz Fanon—and with clear parallels in Mao Tse-Tung—held that struggle, *the concrete action of struggle itself*, is most real, and that a just society flows from it. This led to some of the most mindless "revolutionary" activities and mass killings, notably in China's Cultural Revolution and Cambodia in the late 1970s.

Cambodia, under the Khmer Rouges, was arguably the most brutal site of the 20th century, looking at *per capita* kills: some 20% of the population dead in four years (contested figure, though). Pol Pot, the nicknamed Cambodian dictator, spent his student years in Paris forming a separate Cambodian communist party there. He wasn't very smart, but he read, I believe, Mao, Sartre, Fanon, Stalin and Marx. Maybe—as some historians have argued—the US carpet bombings in Cambodia (during the Vietnam War) played a part in the rise of this brutal power, the Khmer Rouges. But so did, indisputably, poor Marxist and pseudo-Marxist theories about society.

What unites the spectacular failures of these theories? It is the fact that they don't see that society consists of (at least) these four different fields of development—psychology, behavior, culture and system—and that **you cannot spur development in the three other fields by forcibly driving the development in only *one* field, but not the others**.

158. Friedrich Engels sought to describe the workers in the urban factories as potential socialists—he noted, in his ethnographic work, that they seemed to abandon their religious beliefs once they had moved away from their villages.

There were also some significant workers' movements and short periods of impressive solidarity and self-organization. See: Engels, F. 1845/1969. *Condition of the Working Class in England*. Moscow: Institute of Marxism-Leninism. (cont.)

But was he describing people at the Postmodern value meme? No. The impressive displays of solidarity and self-organization only show up when there is a clear common enemy (such as during a period of major strikes). The only time self-organizing syndicalist (anarchist) socialism has functioned on a somewhat larger scale was during the Spanish Civil War of the 1930s, where there was a very clear common enemy: the grim rise of the fascists.

159. Dearya, I. J, Battya, G. D., Galec, C. R. 2008. Childhood intelligence predicts voter turnout, voting preferences, and political involvement in adulthood: The 1970 British Cohort Study. *Intelligence*. Vol 36, Issue 6.

160. "Stratification" means that society is divided into strata, such as classes or other grouping.

161. It's true; there have been some attempts made. One Scottish computer scientist, Paul Cockshott, has teamed up with an economist, Allin Cottrell, and tried to work out what a computer-driven communist system might look like for the European Union. Computer algorithms would coordinate the economy. But this is not a very convincing move unless they can show us the institutional analysis of how we get from here to there (i.e. unless they show us the societal attractors and how they work). And it's highly questionable if these two writers got the algorithms right; indeed, if it is possible to do so. That's a lot of trust to put in faulty single human minds.

37880163R10302

Made in the USA
San Bernardino, CA
04 June 2019